QUANTITATIVE ANALYSES
OF BEHAVIOR

Volumes in the **QUANTITATIVE ANALYSES OF BEHAVIOR** series:

- Volume I: DISCRIMINATIVE PROPERTIES OF REINFORCEMENT SCHEDULES. Edited by Michael L. Commons, *Harvard University* and John A. Nevin, *University of New Hampshire*

- Volume II: MATCHING AND MAXIMIZING ACCOUNTS. Edited by Michael L. Commons, *Harvard University*, Richard J. Herrnstein, *Harvard University*, and Howard Rachlin, *State University of New York, Stony Brook*

- Volume III: ACQUISITION. Edited by Michael L. Commons, *Harvard University*, Richard J. Herrnstein, *Harvard University*, and Allan R. Wagner, *Yale University*

- Volume IV: ACQUISITION PROCESSES. Edited by Michael L. Commons, *Harvard University*, Richard J. Herrnstein, *Harvard University*, and Allan R. Wagner, *Yale University*

HARPER & ROW, PUBLISHERS

NEW YORK

Cambridge London
Hagerstown Mexico City
Philadelphia Sao Paolo
San Francisco *1817* Sydney

QUANTITATIVE ANALYSES OF BEHAVIOR

Discriminative Properties of Reinforcement Schedules

**Volume I
of
Quantitative Analyses of Behavior
A Four-Volume Series**

Edited by
MICHAEL L. COMMONS
Harvard University

JOHN A. NEVIN
University of New Hampshire

BALLINGER PUBLISHING COMPANY
Cambridge, Massachusetts
A Subsidiary of Harper & Row, Publishers, Inc.

International Standard Book Number: 0–88410–377–3 (v. 1)

Library of Congress Catalog Card Number: 81–2654

Printed in the United States of America

Library of Congress Cataloging in Publication Data

Main entry under title:

Quantitative analyses of behavior.

  Based on the annual Harvard Symposium on Quantitative Analyses
of Behavior, held in April 1978.
  Includes index.
  Contents: v. 1.   Discriminative properties of reinforcement
schedules / Michael L. Commons, editor, John A. Nevin, editor—
  1. Conditioned response—Congresses.   I. Commons, Michael L.
II. Nevin, John A.   III. Harvard Symposium on Quantitative
Analyses of Behavior.   [DNLM: 1. Behavior—Congresses.
2. Reinforcement schedule—Congresses.   BF 319.5.R4 D611
1978]
BF319.Q36   150.19′43   81–2654
ISBN 0–88410–377–3 (v. 1)   AACR2

CONTENTS

List of Figures   ix

List of Tables   xv

Preface—*Michael L. Commons*   xvii

Introduction—*John A. Nevin*   xxi

PART I   *AN INTEGRATIVE APPROACH TO STIMULUS
           AND REINFORCEMENT CONTROL*

Chapter 1
Psychophysics and Reinforcement Schedules:
An Integration—*John A. Nevin*   3

PART II   *RATES OF REINFORCEMENT AS DISCRIMINATIVE
           PROPERTIES OF REINFORCEMENT SCHEDULES*

Chapter 2
A Psychophysical Analysis of Time-Based
Schedules of Reinforcement
—*Charlotte Mandell*   31

Chapter 3
How Reinforcement Density is Discriminated
and Scaled—*Michael L. Commons*   51

PART III   *RESPONSE REINFORCER RELATIONS
AS DISCRIMINATIVE PROPERTIES OF
REINFORCEMENT SCHEDULES*

Chapter 4
Learning as Causal Inference
—*Peter R. Killeen*   89

Chapter 5
Reinforcement Contingencies as Discriminative
Stimuli: Implications for Schedule Performance
—*Kennon A. Lattal*   113

PART IV   *TEMPORAL FACTORS AS DISCRIMINATIVE
PROPERTIES OF REINFORCEMENT SCHEDULES*

Chapter 6
Temporal Discrimination: From Psychophysics
to Reinforcement Schedules
—*D. Alan Stubbs and Leon R. Dreyfus*   137

Chapter 7
Two Kinds of Ambiguity in the Study
of Psychological Time—*John Gibbon*   157

PART V   *RESPONSE-BASED CUES AS DISCRIMINATIVE
PROPERTIES OF REINFORCEMENT SCHEDULES*

Chapter 8
Fixed-Ratio-Counting Schedules: Response and Time
Measures Considered
—*Sally L. Hobson and Frederic Newman*   193

Chapter 9
A Signal Detection Analysis of Counting Behavior
—*Paul K. Brandon*   225

PART VI   *DISCRIMINATIVE FACTORS AFFECTING*
            PERFORMANCE ON COMPLEX SCHEDULES

Chapter 10
Discrimination of Correlation
—*William M. Baum*   247

Chapter 11
Reinforcement as Input: Temporal
Tracking on Cyclic Interval Schedules
—*Nancy K. Innis*   257

PART VII   *DISCRIMINATIVE EFFECTS OF RESPONDING*
            AND REINFORCEMENT IN STUDIES OF
            STIMULUS CONTROL

Chapter 12
The Analysis of Memory for Signals and Food
in a Successive Discrimination
—*Mark Rilling and R.C. Howard*   289

Chapter 13
Behavioral Dynamics of the Psychometric
Function—*Michael Terman*   321

Chapter 14
The Role of Differential Responding in
Matching-to-Sample and Delayed
Matching Performance—*Leila R. Cohen,*
John Brady, and Michael Lowry   345

Chapter 15
Local Contrast, Local Dimensional Effects,
and Dimensional Contrast
—*John C. Malone, Jr., and David W. Row*   365

PART VIII   A QUANTITATIVE INTEGRATION OF
             REINFORCEMENT AND DISCRIMINATION

Chapter 16
Matching and Signal Detection
—*Dianne McCarthy and Michael Davison*   393

Afterword—*John A. Nevin and Michael L. Commons*   419

Name Index   423

Subject Index   429

About the Editors

List of Contributors

LIST OF FIGURES

1-1 Some continuous relations between procedures that involve variations in rate of stimulus presentation and rate of reinforcement in two successive experimental conditions 5

1-2 Isosensitivity curves for two rats when the relative probabilities of reinforcement for correct detections and correct rejections were varied and isobias curves for the same rats when relative reinforcement probability was kept constant while stimulus difference was varied 9

1-3 Schematic representation of the signal-detection model 10

1-4 Theoretical isosensitivity and isobias curves derived from a behavioral model of signal detection 13

1-5 A measure of response bias plotted as a function of obtained reinforcement ratios for individual human, pigeon, and rat subjects, and a measure of discrimination plotted as a function of obtained reinforcement ratios for the same subjects 16

1-6 Probability of responding to a key (R_2) that led to reinforcement in the presence of an 86 DB noise (S_B) as a function of noise intensity and the data for each noise level plotted against each other to give a curve for sensitivity to reinforcement ratios 20

1 – 7   An isoreinforcement curve for a study of multiple and concurrent schedules, and an isoreinforcement curve for a study of multiple and concurrent schedules   22

1 – 8   Theoretical isoreinforcement curves derived from the behavioral model of signal detection   25

2 – 2   Schematic diagram of procedure   34

2 – 2   The proportion of hits and false alarms over the course of training   37

2 – 3   The effect of the ratio of reinforcement rates on d' 38

2 – 4   The proportion of hits and false alarms as a function of the duration of a schedule sample   39

2 – 5   The proportion of hits and false alarms as a function of the duration of the interreinforcement interval immediately preceding the choice response   40

2 – 6   The proportion of hits and false alarms as a function of the total duration of the two intervals immediately preceding choice   42

2 – 7   The proportion of hits and false alarms as a function of the duration of the initial interval of the schedule sample   43

2 – 8   Sample cumulative records   45

2 – 9   Proportion of $R1$ ($P(R1)$) as a function of average schedule value during generalization testing   48

3 – 1   Stimulus sample diagram and contingencies during an entire trial   55

3 – 2   The distribution of reinforcement for the first center-key peck for four- and six-cycle substimuli   57

3 – 3   Isosensitivity curves for four birds   60

3 – 4   Perceived density plotted against cycle length in log seconds   64

3 – 5   Perceived density shown as a function of actual density   66

3 – 6   Perceived density shown as a function of the ratio of the number of cycles before choice   71

4 – 1   Receiver-operating-characteristic curves for three pigeons discriminating between peck-generated and computer-generated stimulus changes   98

4 – 2   Receiver-operating-characteristic curves for four pigeons discriminating between peck-generated and computer-generated stimulus changes   99

4-3   Bias as a function of relative value   100
4-4   Hypothetical discriminal dispersions underlying signals
      and noise at various lags   101
4-5   The probability of saying "I" as a function of the
      delay between a key peck and the ensuing stimulus
      change   102

5-1   Schematic diagram of a trial in which different con-
      tingencies served as stimuli for choice responses   120
5-2   Percent correct choice responses for two birds in the
      matching procedure   121
5-3   Isosensitivity curves for each subject   123
5-4   The indexes d', A', and B'' as a function of the proba-
      bility of a DRL contingency during the sample compo-
      nent for each bird   125
5-5   Percent of total session time spent pausing   127
5-6   Probability of a peck on the DRL choice key   129

6-1   Probability of a green key response   144
6-2   Probability of time spent in the presence of green   145
6-3   Comparison of response and time probability data for
      Pigeon 32   147
6-4   Response rate data in the different time classes across
      different experimental conditions   148
6-5   Summary measures of performance across conditions   149

7-1   Schematic presentation of index response distributions   159
7-2   Subjective remembered time as a function of real time   161
7-3   Subjective time as a function of real time   163
7-4   Short response probability as a function of stimulus
      value   169
7-5   Indifference as a function of the geometric mean of the
      short and long duration values   170
7-6   Short report probability as a function of the log of the
      probe duration normalized by the geometric mean   171
7-7   Three alternative subjective time scales   173
7-8   Similarity–dissimilarity measures at intermediate sub-
      jective times   176
7-9   Bisection data fit with the log timing and scalar timing
      psychometric functions   181

8–1   Typical examples of relative frequency distributions
      obtained using ratio-counting schedules   206
8–2   Typical examples of relative frequency distributions
      from the basic FI timing schedule   208
8–3   Mean run length as a function of ratio size   210
8–4   Weber functions for ratio-counting schedules   214
8–5   Weber functions from several timing studies   216

9–1   An ROC graph   231
9–2   The hypothetical relative frequency distributions of
      run lengths for the ROC points plotted in Figure 9–1   232
9–3   ROC points derived from several data sources   234
9–4   ROC points, indexes of sensitivity and bias, and run
      length distributions for four rats on an RC–3 schedule
      and for one rat on an RC–3+ schedule   236
9–5   ROC curves derived from latency distributions   240

10–1 Discrimination as a function of programmed rate of
      reinforcement   252
10–2 Cumulative records of sessions with VT 10 seconds   253

11–1 Mean postreinforcement pause during each interval of
      the experimental sessions for two seven-valued cyclic
      interval schedules   264
11–2 Mean postreinforcement pause during each interval of
      test sessions for groups of birds exposed to schedules
      in which interval durations changed according to a
      logarithmic or a geometric progression   266
11–3 Mean postreinforcement pauses across the forty-five
      intervals of the session for Experiment 2a, and an
      average pause cycle for all five intervals of each dura-
      tion in the series   270
11–4 Mean postreinforcement pause cycles for groups of
      birds exposed to various cyclic interval schedules   272
11–5 Mean postreinforcement pauses over the last five
      sessions of Condition 1 and Condition 2 of Experi-
      ment 3 for two birds   274
11–6 Histograms of mean postreinforcement pauses for
      subjects in Experiments 3 and 4   276

12–1 Mean rates of responding for nine test stimuli   298
12–2 Mean rates of responding for nine test sequences   302

12-3   Retention curves for food and a key light   306
12-4   Diagram of the procedure used during Experiment 4   308
12-5   Retention curves for a discriminative stimulus, a conditioned stimulus presented alone, and a conditioning trial in which the CS always paired with food   310
12-6   Retention curves for the rate of responding during the white choice period   313

13-1   The unit square of signal detection theory   327
13-2   Cumulative latency distributions for hits and false alarms across loud and soft signal conditions   330
13-3   Theoretical normal distributions of sensory effect for signal and noise   332
13-4   Psychometric functions, cumulative latency distributions, and isobias functions   334
13-5   SI cycles averaged across fifteen successive testing days   340

14-1   Delayed matching-to-sample performance for Bird 42   361

15-1   Illustration of the main features of local contrast and of local dimensional effects   372
15-2   Maintained gradients during two stages of training   378
15-3   Log response rate in all stimuli as a function of log response rate in the preceding stimulus   380
15-4   Maintained gradients for individual birds shown as five-day averages during five stages of training   382
15-5   Data from the same period as those in Figure 15-4   384

16-1   Matrix of events in a standard yes–no signal detection procedure   395
16-2   Log response ratios as a function of the logarithm of the obtained reinforcement rate at the two levels of difficulty   402
16-3   Discriminability as a function of the arranged probability of reinforcement for errors   412

LIST OF TABLES

1-1 Schematic Representation of the Yes–No Signal
Detection Paradigm 7

1-2 Outcome Matrix for the Pliskoff, Shull, and Gollub
(1968) Study 21

1-3 Outcome Matrix for the Nevin (1974) Study 23

3-1 Decision Rules at the Molar Level 68

3-2 A Comparison of Obtained Sensitivity to Maximally
Possible Sensitivity 76

4-1 Experimental Conditions 97

5-1 Examples of Combinations of Schedules Arranging
Different Response Reinforcer Relationships 116

6-1 Summary of Experimental Conditions in Order of
Presentation and Number of Sessions Under Each 142

8-1 Summary of Procedures Used to Study Response-
based and Time-Based Reinforcement Schedules 196

8-2 Summary of Ratio-Counting Procedures for Individual
Subjects 203

8-3 Weber Fractions for Individual Subjects Under Several
Counting and Timing Schedules 212

9-1   Schematic Representation of the Signal Detection
       Paradigm Applied to Response Counting   229

10-1   Order and Number of Sessions and Conditions   251

11-1   Procedural Details for Six Experiments   262
11-2   Average Postreinforcement Pauses for Individual
       Subjects   280

14-1   Experiment I Procedure   351
14-2   Results for Differential and Nondifferential Schedules
       in Experiment I   352
14-3   Experiment II Procedure   355
14-4   Results for Experiment II   356
14-5   Results for Differential and Nondifferential Sample
       Schedules in Experiment III   359

16-1   Analysis of Data from Three Reinforcement for Errors
       Experiments   409

PREFACE

The study of behavior has consisted of a number of somewhat separate traditions. One tradition, starting with Thorndike and then Skinner, has experimentally analyzed the control of behavior by events subsequent to it. A second tradition, starting with Bechterev and Pavlov and coming down to the present through Watson, Spence, and others, analyzed the control and transfer of control by events antecedent to behavior.

Starting in the 1930s, both traditions have become more quantitative. In the experimental analysis of behavior, quantifiable variables, such as the rate of responding, were used to represent the behavioral outcomes. At the same time, more elaborate quantitative studies were carried out in the Hullian tradition. Quantifiable measures such as response probability and latency were introduced. In that period, and extending through the 1950s, mathematical models were developed by Hull, Spence, Estes, Bush, and Mosteller and Logan, among others. Both groups carried out some parametric studies in the tradition of psychophysics. By the early 1960s, a whole tradition of mathematical psychology had developed to deal with problems from a number of domains. In each domain, explicit mathematical models were proposed for the processes by which performances were acquired and maintained within that domain. While the models generated a number of experiments, the models were of limited generality.

"Quantitative analysis" now generally refers to the fact that theoretical issues are represented in quantitative form. An analysis is not a matter of fitting arbitrary functions to data points. Rather, each parameter and variable represents part of a process that has both a theoretical and an empirical interpretation. The matching law, a model of maintained performance, is one example from the analysis of behavior tradition. The Rescorla–Wagner model of acquisition processes is a second example. These models represent effects of interactions of environmental and behavioral events. Since neither model requires otherwise, there is the possibility that both the organism and the environment modify each other. A quantitative analysis has forced an explicit representation of a number of variables within the phenomenon and formulation of the relations between those variables. The models also have explicit representational notions and economical rules about parameter estimation, ratio of number of data points to number of parameters, and cross-situation parameter invariance. The rules of interaction may be represented by an arithmetic that accounts for the results of a large class of studies. The models are designed to account for the maximum amount of variance found in a number of experimental situations to which the processes described by the model apply. The adequacy of quantitative models is tested by comparing obtained data to theoretically predicted data. This is to be contrasted with the testing of relatively simply hypotheses. As in other areas of science, looking for the generality of a formulation has made the models more testable. Independent routes of verification are possible because of the increased scope of the models.

Each volume of series examines a particular topic that has been discussed at the annual Harvard Symposium on Quantitative Analyses of Behavior. The topic for this first volume is the discrimination of schedules of reinforcement. It was chosen because it represents an area that has been highly quantified through the application of psychophysical methods and analyses to maintained performances. The second volume explores matching and maximizing accounts of the allocation of behavior, another area that has been highly quantified. The generality of such formulations and how they apply to the behavior of animals in both the field and the laboratory and to humans in choice situations in economics are explored. In the third volume, models of acquisition processes are considered; and in the fourth volume, transfer of training and schedule interaction will be dealt with.

The symposium out of which this first volume grew was co-organized by Michael L. Commons and James E. Mazur. The authors wish to thank James Mazur for helping to coordinate the symposium leading to Volume I and the entire program committee, consisting of Richard J. Herrnstein and Howard Rachlin in addition to the editors of the present volume, for organizing the second, third, and fourth symposia. For the third and fourth symposia, Allan Wagner also served on the program committee. The symposia were supported in part by the Department of Psychology and Social Relations at Harvard University and by the Dare Association. Local arrangements were provided by Patrice M. Miller and Julie Bisbee, with assistance from John R. Ducheny and Stuart L. Mattson. Patrice M. Miller informally served as an associate editor, improving the style and organization of many of the chapters. It was a pleasure working with Carol Franco (editor) and Michael Connolly (president), Steven Cramer (assistant editor), Arks Smith (copy editor), and Gerry Galvin and Leslie Anderson on the production staff. We would like to thank them for their help in producing the book.

Michael L. Commons
Harvard University

DISCRIMINATIVE EFFECTS OF REINFORCEMENT SCHEDULES
An Introduction

John A. Nevin

Skinner (1938) introduced an experimental method for the study of operant behavior that has since become standard. An unrestrained food-deprived rat was allowed to press a continuously available lever, and each lever press produced a pellet of food. Skinner observed that lever pressing was rapidly acquired and well maintained under these conditions. He referred to lever pressing as operant behavior, because it operated on the environment to produce food and because there were no obvious environmental stimuli that elicited lever pressing in the sense that, for example, foot shock would elicit leg flexion in a dog. The consequence of lever pressing—food—was termed a reinforcing stimulus because the rate of lever pressing increased when food was presented after each press and decreased when food was discontinued (extinction). If food was presented after lever presses only when a light was on, so that the absence of light signaled extinction, the rat would come to press the lever only when the light was on. Skinner referred to the light as a discriminative stimulus that came to control responding because it set the occasion for reinforcement.

Skinner's distinction between reinforcing stimuli (e.g., food) and discriminative stimuli (e.g., light) initiated two major themes in the study of operant behavior during the years since 1938. One has concentrated on schedules of reinforcement—the control of behavior by its consequences and the rules by which those consequences are presented. Characteristic performances generated and maintained various rules for presenting reinforcers have been identified and codified in introductory text books, and various ways of accounting for schedule performance have been explored and tested. Reviews, theoretical articles, and book chapters by Baum (1973), de Villiers (1977), Herrnstein (1970), Morse (1966), Nevin (1973b), Rachlin (1978), Shimp (1969), Staddon (1979), and Zeiler (1977), among others, attest to the vitality and diversity of current approaches to the interpretation of behavior on schedules of reinforcement.

The second theme, developed with equal vigor, has concentrated on the control of operant behavior by environmental stimuli that precede or accompany responding and how that control depends on the conditions of reinforcement signaled by the stimuli. The basic properties of stimulus control in operant discrimination, generalization, and related procedures have been established, and a number of integrative formulations have been advanced. Reviews and theoretical articles by Blough (1975), Gilbert and Sutherland (1971), Heinemann and Chase (1975), Mackintosh (1977), Nevin (1973a), Rilling (1977), and Terrace (1966), among others, provide examples of current issues and theories in the stimulus control of operant behavior.

The control of behavior by reinforcing stimuli that follow responses and discriminative stimuli that precede responses need not be treated separately. After all, reinforcers such as food pellets presented in a tray are sources of stimulation, and their occurrence usually signals the availability of additional reinforcers for continued responding. For example, in simple continuous reinforcement procedures (CRF), responses are reinforced in the presence of cues arising from preceding reinforcers. The removal of reinforcers in extinction (EXT) has two effects—termination of the strengthening and maintaining effects of response-contingent reinforcement and elimination of stimuli that previously were correlated with continued reinforcement. The discriminative function of reinforcers during extinction has been demonstrated by Reid (1958), who showed that presenting a reinforcer independently of the response would occasion a burst of responding. The discriminative effects of the transition from reinforcement to extinction were studied by Bullock and Smith (1953), who alternated periods of reinforcement and extinction and observed increasingly rapid cessation of responding during extinction across successive alternations. In related work, Dufort, Guttman, and Kimble (1954) showed that the nonoccurrence of reinforcement in a discrimination reversal procedure was sufficient to cue rapid reversals after extended training. Finally, Harlow (1949) observed near perfect asymptotic performance on the second trial of a series of learning set problems, suggesting discriminative control by the consequences of responding: If the subject obtained a reinforcer on the first trial of a new problem, it repeated the reinforced choice, while nonreinforcement cued responding to the object not previously chosen.

These studies of the discriminative effects of reinforcers used continuous reinforcement versus extinction and were concerned with the acquisition of discriminative control by the reinforcer. By contrast, research on reinforcement schedules has explored an enormous number of conditions that are intermediate between continuous reinforcement and extinction and has emphasized the properties of performance maintained in a steady state after extended training. Among the variations that have been explored in the study of intermittent reinforcement are schedules that arrange reinforcement for a designated response depending on the number of prior responses, either fixed (FR) or variable (VR), or upon the passage of some period of time, either fixed (FI) or variable (VI), since the preceding reinforcer. Response-dependent schedules are termed ratio schedules, while time-dependent schedules are termed interval schedules.

Ratio and interval schedules differ in the contingencies they imply. For example, ratio schedules arrange for a positive linear relation between average response rate and average reinforcement rate over long periods, whereas interval schedules limit the maximum rate of reinforcement and typically maintain that rate as long as average response rates are fairly high. Molar contingencies of this sort may be contrasted with relatively molecular contingencies that operate at the level of individual sequences of responses. For example, a reinforcer is relatively likely to follow a high rate burst of responding in ratio schedules, whereas it is relatively likely to follow a long time between successive responses in interval schedules.

In all intermittent reinforcement procedures, there is a delay between unreinforced responses and the eventual delivery of the reinforcer. Reinforcers may depend directly on such responses—for example, the initial responses in a fixed ratio schedule—even though those responses are temporally remote from reinforcement, while in other schedules, such as fixed interval, the scheduling of reinforcers is independent of unreinforced responses. Some schedules, termed fixed (FT) or variable time (VT), present reinforcers that are independent of any responses. Ratio contingencies, interval contingencies, and response-independent reinforcers have been combined in various complex schedule arrangements to illuminate their interaction.

The foregoing is not intended to be a complete catalogue of the possible contingencies between responses and reinforcers in intermittent reinforcement procedures, but merely to suggest some contingencies that may be dissected out for analysis. In addition, there may be contingencies between one reinforcer and the next. For example, on fixed interval schedules, each reinforcer precedes a period during which no further reinforcers are available, with the result that subjects do not begin to respond until a roughly constant fraction of the fixed interval has elapsed.

Parametric analysis of steady-state performances maintained by intermittent reinforcement has generated a wealth of orderly, quantitative data, such as the relation between pause duration and fixed interval length cited above. These relationships have considerable generality across species, responses, and reinforcers. Thus, although schedules may be artificial contrivances of the laboratory, their effects must be based on some fundamental behavioral processes. To isolate and explore these basic processes, it is essential to identify the dimensions of schedules that control behavior and to determine how their effects interact. At the least, this enterprise requires the discovery of discriminable dimensions—that is, those aspects of reinforcement schedules that can be differentiated by the organism. For example, if one can show that a pigeon can discriminate the relationship between its own key pecking and the food reinforcers it receives, it becomes plausible to interpret various schedule performances in terms of the contingencies between responding and reinforcement implied by those schedules.

Now, the fact that an organism can discriminate a dimension of a schedule does not imply that the dimension will control responding under all circumstances. Consider an analogy employing familiar exteroceptive cues. The fact that a pigeon can discriminate the orientation of a line projected on a response key does not mean that line orientation will always serve as an effective dimension, because it may be overshadowed by other, more salient cues in the environment or by other cues that are more closely correlated with food availability. A continuing concern of research on stimulus control is the delineation of the conditions that determine whether a given physical stimulus will in fact control behavior. In like fashion, the study of discriminative effects of reinforcers must move beyond the basic demonstrations that reinforcers can serve discriminative functions, to determine which dimensions of reinforcer scheduling can be discriminated and what may be the boundary conditions within which the dimension is effective.

The contributors to this volume were drawn together by a common interest in how the dimensions of reinforcement schedules that determine steady-state performance may also operate as discriminable dimensions of the environment. More concretely, we were concerned with such questions as whether the rate of presentation of reinforcers, the contingency between responses and reinforcers, the temporal intervals between events in reinforcement schedules, and the cues emanating from schedule-controlled responding would serve the same sort of function as the lights and sounds typically used as stimuli in studies of discrimination and generalization. Modern psychophysics, which is concerned with the quantitative analysis of sensory discriminations, may provide methods and theoretical approaches for the study of schedule discriminations as well. Nevin (Chapter 1) proposes an integrative, molar approach to stimulus control and reinforcement schedules that derives from the procedures and results of signal detection research.

Other contributors address some specific dimensions of reinforcement schedules from a psychophysical perspective. Mandell (Chapter 2) and Commons (Chapter 3) demonstrate that the rate of reinforcement or its reciprocal—the average time between reinforcers—can function as a discriminative cue for choice responding. In like fashion, Killeen (Chapter 4) and Lattal (Chapter 5) demonstrate discriminative control by the dependency between responding and reinforcement. Hobson and Newman (Chapter 6) and Brandon (Chapter 7) demonstrate that the behavior engendered by ratio schedules of reinforcement can function as a discriminative stimulus, while Gibbon (Chapter 8) and Stubbs and Dreyfus (Chapter 9) explore the discriminative functions of time since a preceding event, which must inevitably enter into the stimulus aspects of schedules of reinforcement arranged in time.

Baum (Chapter 10) reports a procedure in which positive or negative correlations between response rate and reinforcement rate serve as cues for free operant responding, and Innis (Chapter 11) analyzes conditions in which periodic variations in the time between reinforcers serve to signal cyclic changes in response rate. Innis also reports transfer from one periodic series to others, a result analogous to generalization after training with conventional discriminative stimuli. Rilling and Howard (Chapter 12) analyze the control of responding by prior stimulus-reinforcer sequences in relation to concepts derived from the study of memory in human information processing, and Cohen, Brady, and Lowry (Chapter 14) demonstrate that schedule-controlled performance can be a potent determiner of the accuracy performance in delayed matching procedures. Terman (Chapter 13) reports that prior reinforcement or nonreinforcement affects performance on subsequent trials in psychophysical discrimination task, and Malone and Rowe (Chapter 15) show how responding to a given stimulus in a free operant discrimination and generalization procedure depends on the rate of responding engendered by preceding stimuli. Finally, McCarthy and Davison (Chapter 16) show how stimuli and reinforcers combine to determine performance in signal detection tasks.

Taken all together, these research reports demonstrate the many ways in which schedule-controlled behavior, its consequences, and the temporal factors relating them enter into the determination of further behavior.

REFERENCES

Baum, W.M. 1973. The correlation-based law of effect. *Journal of the Experimental Analysis of Behavior 20*: 137–153.

Blough, D.S. 1975. Steady-state data and a quantitative model of operant generalization. *Journal of Experimental Psychology: Animal Behavior Processes 1*: 3–21.

Bullock, D.H., and W.C. Smith. 1953. An effect of repeated conditioning-extinction upon operant strength. *Journal of Experimental Psychology 46*: 95–98.

De Villiers, P.A. 1977. Choice in concurrent schedules and a quantitative formulation of the law of effect. In W.K. Honig and J.E.R. Staddon, eds., *Handbook of Operant Behavior*. Englewood Cliffs, New Jersey: Prentice–Hall.

Dufort, R.H.; N. Guttman; and G.A. Kimble. 1954. One-trial discrimination reversal in the white rat. *Journal of Comparative and Physiological Psychology 47*: 248–249.

Gilbert, R.M., and N.S. Sutherland, eds. 1971. *Animal Discrimination Learning.* New York: Academic Press.

Harlow, H.F. 1949. The formation of learning sets. *Psychological Review 56:* 51–65.

Heinemann, E.G., and S. Chase. 1975. Stimulus generalization. In W.K. Estes, ed., *Handbook of Learning and Cognitive Processes.* Hillsdale, New Jersey: Erlbaum.

Herrnstein, R.J. 1970. On the law of effect. *Journal of the Experimental Analysis of behavior 13:* 243–266.

Mackintosh, N.J. 1977. Stimulus control: Attentional factors. In W.K. Honig and J.E.R. Staddon, eds., *Handbook of Operant Behavior.* Englewood Cliffs, New Jersey: Prentice–Hall.

Morse, W.H. 1966. Intermittent reinforcement. In W.K. Honig, ed., *Operant Behavior.* New York: Appleton-Century-Crofts.

Nevin, J.A. 1973a. Stimulus control. In J.A. Nevin, ed., *The Study of Behavior.* Glenview, Illinois: Scott, Foresman.

_____. 1973b. The maintenance of behavior. In J.A. Nevin, ed., *The Study of Behavior.* Glenview, Illinois: Scott, Foresman.

Rachlin, H. 1978. A molar theory of reinforcement schedules. *Journal of the Experimental Analysis of Behavior 30:* 345–360.

Reid, R.L. 1958. The role of the reinforcer as a stimulus. *British Journal of Psychology 49:* 202–209.

Rilling, M. 1977. Stimulus control and inhibitory processes. In W.K. Honig and J.E.R. Staddon, eds., *Handbook of Operant Behavior.* Englewood Cliffs, New Jersey: Prentice–Hall.

Shimp, C.P. 1969. Optimum behavior in free-operant experiments. *Psychological Review 76:* 97–112.

Skinner, B,F. 1938. *The Behavior of Organisms.* New York: Appleton-Century-Crofts.

Staddon, J.E.R. 1979. Operant behavior as adaptation to constraint. *Journal of Experimental Psychology: General 109:* 48–67.

Terrace, H.S. 1966. Stimulus control. In W.K. Honig, ed., *Operant Behavior.* New York: Appleton-Century-Crofts.

Zeiler, M.D. 1977. Schedules of reinforcement. In W.K. Honig and J.E.R. Staddon, eds., *Handbook of Operant Behavior.* Englewood Cliffs, New Jersey: Prentice–Hall.

I AN INTEGRATIVE APPROACH TO STIMULUS AND REINFORCEMENT CONTROL

1 PSYCHOPHYSICS AND REINFORCEMENT SCHEDULES
An Integration

John A. Nevin

The introduction noted a distinction between molar and molecular aspects of the relations between responses and reinforcers. At a molecular level, the consequences of brief episodes of responding are explored as potential determiners of behavior, whereas a molar analysis invokes long-term relations between responding and environmental events without regard for the structure and outcomes of brief episodes. In some cases, the control of particular responses by local environmental events may be isolated, and the properties of larger aggregations of responses may be derived from them (e.g., Commons, Chapter 3). In other cases, properties of behavior averaged over extended periods are not readily derived from episodic relations (e.g., Baum, Chapter 10). Some issues that divide molar and molecular approaches to the study of behavior are explored (but not resolved) in the second volume of this series. Here, I will argue that the molar orientation permits a systematic integration of stimulus control and schedule effects that may not otherwise be possible.

As noted in the introduction, schedules of reinforcement are ordinarily thought of as rules for assigning reinforcers to responses, where the reinforcing stimulus is contingent upon the response and follows

Preparation of this manuscript was supported in part by grants from the National Science Foundation. I am indebted to Charlotte Mandell, Peter Jenkins, Stephen Whittaker, and Peter Yarensky for many discussions of the ideas presented here.

it in time. By contrast, discriminative stimuli are usually presented before or during responding, to signal the availability of reinforcement. Thus, discriminative and reinforcing stimuli are conventionally distinguished on the basis of their temporal relations to the response.

A molar view of behavior, which emphasizes rates of occurrence of stimuli and responses during extended periods of time rather than discrete episodes, may eliminate this conventional distinction. In a molar analysis, the consequences of responding are frequently specified in terms of rate of reinforcement, and the operant contingency may be described in terms of the correlation between response rate and reinforcement rate (Baum, 1973). This correlation has been termed the feedback function. For example, ratio schedules imply strict proportionality between response rate and obtained reinforcement rate—the higher the average response rate, the more often reinforcers are obtained. When response rate changes, reinforcement rate also changes and feeds back to produce further changes in response rate. The feedback cycle continues until other factors operate to limit its effect (cf. Baum, 1981). The feedback function for interval schedules is less obvious, but recent work has suggested a function form that describes empirical feedback results fairly well (Nevin and Baum, 1980). The crucial point is that according to a molar feedback approach, steady-state performance is the outcome of behavior–environment interactions based on average response and reinforcement rates over relatively long periods, where responses follow as well as precede reinforcers.

The rate of occurrence of a brief "neutral" stimulus has also been shown to control the rate of responding. For example, Reynolds and Limpo (1969) arranged that food would follow responses during extended periods correlated with a flashing light and observed that response rate depended on flash rate even though responses preceded as well as followed the brief flashes. Thus, distinctions between discriminative and reinforcing stimuli based on their temporal relations to responses disappear in a molar analysis. It remains true that the rate of stimuli traditionally called discriminative is determined by the experimenter independently of responding, whereas the rate of stimuli traditionally called reinforcing depends on response rate according to the relevant feedback function. The question of whether this difference implies different behavioral processes is essentially the same as the question of whether classical conditioning, in which stimulus presentation is experimenter controlled, and operant conditioning, in which reinforcer delivery is subject controlled, imply different behavioral processes. The jury has been out on the latter question for nearly fifty years. Nevertheless, it is worth pursuing the possibility that a molar approach to behavior may facilitate a unified account of schedule control and stimulus control.

The possibility of unification is further suggested by some continuous relations that arise in experiments that employ two stimuli and two schedules of reinforcement—the minimal conditions for establishing differential responding. Imagine an experiment in which two stimulus conditions differ along a single dimension—say, rate of a flickering light—while two reinforcement conditions also differ along a single dimension—say, rate of reinforcement. These differences in stimulus and/or reinforcement conditions alternate successively while the subject is responding on a single key. Some possible interrelations are suggested in Figure 1–1, which expresses differences in stimulation in terms of relative flash rate and differences in reinforcement in

Figure 1–1. Some continuous relations between procedures that involve variations in rate of stimulus presentation and rate of reinforcement in two successive experimental conditions. See text for explanation.

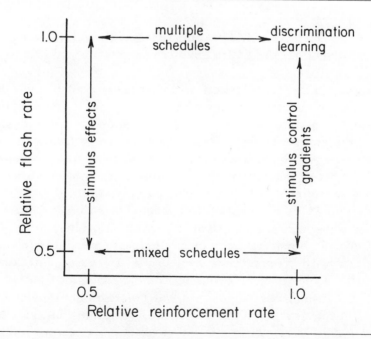

terms of relative reinforcement rate. On both axes, a value of 0.5 signifies no difference, while a value of 1 signifies a maximal difference. Various regions of the graph are designated according to common usage. In the upper right corner, where both flash rate and reinforcement rate differ maximally, the acquisition of differential responding is studied under the rubric of discrimination learning. When reinforcement differences are reduced while stimulus differences remain large, a set of multiple schedules varying in the degree of differential reinforcement is defined along the upper edge. Conversely, if stimulus differences are reduced while differential reinforcement remains maximal (along the right edge of the graph), stimulus control gradients analogous to psychophysical functions are obtained. Variations in reinforcement rate differences when the stimuli are the same (along the bottom edge) define a set of mixed schedules, and finally, variations in flash rate when the reinforcement rates are the same (along the left-hand edge) permit the study of stimulus effects such as dynamism in the absence of differential reinforcement. Interactions are certain: Stimulus effects are more pronounced when differential reinforcement is arranged, and schedule control is more evident when different stimuli signal the two schedules.

SIGNAL DETECTION METHODS: ISOSENSITIVITY AND ISOBIAS CURVES

If it is granted that stimulus control and schedule control are conceptually continuous, the next question is whether behavioral relations are also continuous—that is, is there a class of functional relations that holds throughout the various regions of the domain sketched in Figure 1–1? And if so, what might it be? Clearly, it is not going to involve functional relations of the usual input–output variety, in which a measure of behavior is plotted in relation to a measure of stimulation. There is no reason to expect (for example) that a graph of responding in relation to flash rate with reinforcement conditions constant will resemble a graph of responding in relation to reinforcement rate with flash rate constant unless we rescale our variables arbitrarily. In general, functions relating responding to any parameters of discriminative stimulation will not resemble those relating responding to any parameters of reinforcement without special rescaling in every case. We must look to other sorts of relations for true generality.

A likely candidate for generality is the class of relations between responding in one condition and responding in the alternated condition—an R = R (response–response), rather than an S = R (stimulus–response) relation. Galanter (1970) has emphasized the fundamental importance of such relations in all sciences. The receiver-operating-characteristic (ROC) or isosensitivity curve of signal detection is an example of an R = R relation, and its value in the study of sensory processes and related areas is well known (see Swets [1973] for a discussion of the broad applicability of operating characteristic analyses). Accordingly, I will argue here for the use of the signal detection paradigm and its associated data analyses in the unified study of stimulus and schedule control.

The standard "yes–no" signal detection paradigm arranges that two stimulus conditions are presented successively in discrete trials, with two responses available to the subject, resulting in a 2 × 2 matrix of stimulus–response events (see Table 1–1). The stimuli are either S_A (e.g., a signal superimposed on noise) or S_B (e.g., noise alone). The subject emits response R_1 (yes) or R_2 (no). Reinforcing outcomes are given for correctly detecting the signal (hit) or for correctly reporting its absence (correct rejection), and penalties may be contingent upon falsely reporting the signal in its absence (false alarm) or missing the signal when it was present (miss). For the pur-

Table 1–1. Schematic Representation of the Yes–No Signal Detection Paradigm.

	Responses	
Stimuli	R_1 (yes)	R_2 (no)
S_A (signal plus noise)	Correct detection (Hit) R_{A1}, o_{A1}	Miss R_{A2}, o_{A2}
S_B (noise)	False report (False alarm) R_{B1}, o_{B1}	Correct rejection R_{B2}, o_{B2}

poses of later sections of this chapter, the numbers of responses and outcomes in each cell of the matrix are designated by the appropriate subscripts (R_{A1}, o_{A1}, etc.). Usually, the data take the form of conditional probabilities or proportions of responses in each of the cells of the matrix and are commonly presented by plotting the probability of making a response in the presence of one stimulus as a function of making the same response in the presence of the other stimulus.

With signal strength constant, variation in the relative frequencies or values of the reinforcers and penalties generates a receiver-operating-characteristic (ROC) or isosensitivity curve relating the probability of hits to the probability of false alarms. This curve presumably reflects constant sensitivity to the signal, while reinforcers and penalties are presumed to affect only the bias toward responding yes or no. With the consequences constant, variation in signal strength generates an isobias curve, presumably reflecting the constant differential effects of the reinforcers and penalties. The possibility of estimating stimulus effects and consequence effects independently of each other has accounted for much of the appeal of signal detection analyses.

The application of signal detection analysis is illustrated by some data on luminance discrimination by rats (Nevin et al., 1975). In a two-lever chamber, rats were trained to press one lever (R_1) in the presence of a relatively dim light (S_A) and the other lever (R_2) in the presence of a relatively bright light (S_B). The stimulus terminated as soon as one or the other response occurred, and water reinforcers were delivered with various probabilities for R_1 given S_A and for R_2 given S_B. The physical difference between S_A and S_B was also varied. The upper panel of Figure 1-2 shows the effects of varying the relative probabilities of reinforcement, plotted as isosensitivity curves. The extent of departure from the major diagonal indicates sensitivity to the stimuli. The lower panel shows the effects of varying stimulus differences at two different relative reinforcement probabilities, plotted as isobias curves. The forms of both plots are similar to those obtained with other species, stimuli, and reinforcers, so they are quite general. They are also consistent with the conventional distinction between sensitivity to differences in discriminative stimuli that precede responses and bias by differential consequences that follow responses. Alternative analyses will be considered later.

Figure 1−2. Upper panel: Isosensitivity curves for two rats when the relative probabilities of reinforcement for correct detections and correct rejections were varied. The smooth curves were derived from the theory of signal detectability, assuming constant discriminability of the stimuli. Lower panel: Isobias curves for the same rats when relative reinforcement probability was kept constant while stimulus difference was varied. Dashed lines connect the data for a relative reinforcement probability of 0.35 for correct detections, and solid lines connect the data for a relative reinforcement probability of 0.65 for correct detections. Redrawn from Nevin et al. (1975).

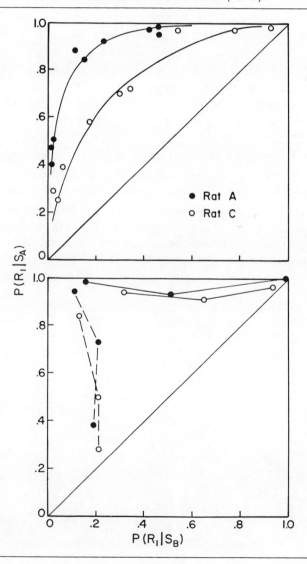

MODELS OF SIGNAL DETECTION PERFORMANCE

A widely accepted model of signal detection (Green and Swets, 1966) represents the sensory effects of the stimuli, S_A and S_B, by overlapping normal distributions. Thus, a given effect may arise from either S_A or S_B. The subject is said to establish a response criterion, always emitting R_1 when the observation falls above it. Thus, the probabilities of $R_1|S_A$ (a hit) and of $R_1|S_B$ (false alarm) are given by the areas under the distributions for S_A and S_B on the R_1 side of the criterion line. A strict decision rule of this sort, coupled with adjustment of the location of the criterion according to the relative probabilities or values of the outcomes, leads to the maximization of the expected value of the outcomes.

When the distributions representing stimulus effects are held constant while the criterion is moved along the effect line, an isosensitivity curve of the sort shown in the upper panel of Figure 1-2 results. Its distance from the minor diagonal may be characterized by the theoretical parameter d', which represents the separation between the normal distributions of Figure 1-3, in standard deviation units. Conversely, if the response criterion (characterized by the theoretical parameter β, the ratio of the ordinate heights of the two distributions) is kept constant while the separation between distributions is varied, isobias curves of the sort shown in the lower panel of Figure 1-2 are generated. The model provides an excellent account of sig-

Figure 1-3. Schematic representation of the signal-detection model (Green and Swets, 1966). See text for explanation.

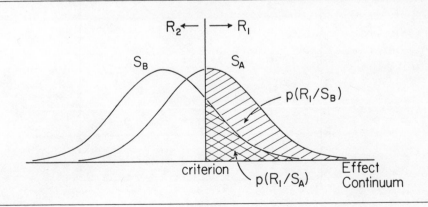

nal detection data and embodies the conventional separation between the effects of the stimuli and other variables that determine performance.

A simpler model, based on known properties of behavior on schedules of reinforcement, may also account for the same data. As noted in a review of Green and Swets' book (Nevin, 1969a), the conventional signal detection paradigm may be construed as a multiple schedule with concurrent schedules as the components. That is, in the presence of S_A, reinforcers are available for R_1 concurrently with extinction for R_2. In the presence of S_B, reinforcers are available for R_2 concurrently with extinction for R_1. Performance on concurrent schedules is well described by the matching law (Herrnstein, 1970): The ratio of responses to the two alternatives equals the ratio of reinforcers obtained by those alternatives. The matching law holds for concurrent schedule performance in several species, with diverse reinforcers, in a wide variety of experimental procedures (cf. De Villiers, 1977), including discrete trial procedures (Nevin, 1969b) and multiple schedules of concurrent schedules (Pliskoff, Shull, and Gollub, 1968), so it may reasonably be expected to apply to performance in signal detection procedures as well.

Strict application of the matching law to the signal detection paradigm leads to a problem. On S_A trials, all reinforcers are arranged for R_1, so the subject should emit R_1 on every S_A trial. Likewise, on S_B trials, all reinforcers are arranged for R_2, so the subject should emit R_2 on every S_B trial. In brief, performance should be perfect. Why, then, do errors occur?

Nevin et al. (1977) advanced a simple model to explain the occurrence of errors. It assumes that the effect of a reinforcer for a response in one stimulus generalizes to strengthen the same response in the presence of the other stimulus. The subject distributes its responses so as to match the ratio of direct and generalized reinforcement. More formally,

$$\frac{R_{A1}}{R_{A2}} = \frac{o_{A1}}{\eta \, o_{B2}} \qquad (1.1a)$$

and

$$\frac{R_{B1}}{R_{B2}} = \frac{\eta \, o_{A1}}{o_{B2}} \qquad (1.1b)$$

where o_{A1} and o_{B2} represent the frequencies of reinforcement obtained by R_{A1} and R_{B2}, respectively. The parameter η designates the similarity of S_A and S_B. It ranges from 0 when the stimuli are perfectly discriminable to 1 when they are indistinguishable. Its reciprocal, $1/\eta$, may be construed as an index of discriminability and is closely related to d', the sensitivity index of signal detection theory (Green and Swets, 1966; Luce, 1963).

If Equation (1.1a) is divided by Equation (1.1b), the reinforcement terms are eliminated, and the result is the isosensitivity curve:

$$\frac{R_{A1}}{R_{A2}} \cdot \frac{R_{B2}}{R_{A1}} = \left(\frac{1}{\eta}\right)^2 \qquad (1.2)$$

If Equations (1.1a) and (1.1b) are multiplied, eliminating η, the result is the isobias curve:

$$\frac{R_{A1}}{R_{A2}} \cdot \frac{R_{B1}}{R_{B2}} = \left(\frac{o_{A1}}{o_{B2}}\right)^2 = b^2 \qquad (1.3)$$

where b designates response bias.

Equations (1.2) and (1.3) are identical to expressions derived by Bush, Luce, and Rose (1964) from a linear learning model and by Luce (1963) from rather abstract considerations of choice theory. They are also identical to expressions derived from other assumptions by Davison and Tustin (1978) and discussed by McCarthy and Davison in Chapter 16. I will return to the Davison–Tustin model shortly.

The isosensitivity and isobias curves derived from the matching model are portrayed in Figure 1–4, left panel, in the conventional unit square of signal detection analysis. Three theoretical isosensitivity curves were constructed, with η taking on values of 0.2, 0.5, and 0.8. The curves are symmetrical about the minor diagonal and have the general form of most curves reported in the literature (e.g., Figure 1–2, upper panel). The curves approach the major diagonal, which represents the absence of discrimination as η approaches 1. Five isobias curves are also shown, with the ratio o_{A1}/o_{B2} set at $7:1$, $3:1$, $1:1$, $1:3$, and $1:7$. The form of these curves is rather unusual, in that they curve inward toward the minor diagonal and intersect the major diagonal at values that exactly match the proportions of reinforcement frequencies. Their form results from the assumption that

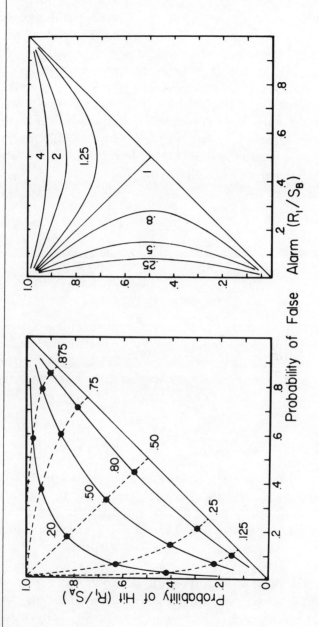

Figure 1–4. Theoretical isosensitivity and isobias curves derived from a behavioral model of signal detection. See text for explanation.

the ratio of obtained frequencies of reinforcement, o_{A1}/o_{B2}, actually remains constant, independent of the distribution of responses.

In the majority of signal detection experiments with animal and human subjects, outcomes are arranged on every trial, so that the obtained frequency of reinforcement is equal to the frequency of responding in the appropriate cell of the signal detection matrix. When intermittent reinforcement is employed, reinforcers are often scheduled probabilistically for each correct response (e.g., Nevin et al., 1975), so that reinforcement frequency is directly proportional to the frequency of correct responding. Such contingencies of reinforcement lead to an interesting implication of Equations (1.1a) and (1.1b), which may be rewritten:

$$\frac{R_{A1}}{R_{A2}} = \frac{p_{A1} \cdot R_{A1}}{\eta \cdot p_{B2} \cdot R_{B2}} \tag{1.4a}$$

and

$$\frac{R_{B1}}{R_{B2}} = \frac{\eta \cdot p_{A1} \cdot R_{A1}}{p_{B2} \cdot R_{B2}} \tag{1.4b}$$

where p_{A1} and p_{B2} represent the probabilities of reinforcement in the appropriate cells. The isosensitivity curve remains unchanged, as may be seen by dividing Equation (1.4a) by Equation (1.4b). However, a different family of isobias curves is generated. Multiplying Equations (1.4a) and (1.4b) and simplifying:

$$\frac{R_{B1}}{R_{A1}} \cdot \frac{R_{B2}}{R_{A2}} = \left(\frac{p_{A1}}{p_{B2}}\right)^2 \tag{1.5}$$

Some theoretical isobias curves derived from Equation (1.5) are plotted in the right panel of Figure 1–4, for values of p_{A1}/p_{B2} of 0.25, 0.5, 0.8, 1.0, 1.25, 2.0, and 4.0. The functions curve outward from the minor diagonal toward the upper right and lower left corners of the plot and are similar to isobias curves derived from the Green and Swets (1966) model on the assumption that the subject chooses a response criterion that maximizes expected payoff. Thus, a simple behavioral model based on the matching law with generalized reinforcement effects and with proper consideration of the reinforcement contingencies leads to predictions that cannot readily be distinguished from those of the elaborate conceptual machinery of classical signal detection theory.

COMPARISON WITH DATA

To show that the matching model gives a plausible account of signal detection performance, I have taken data from individual subjects in several discrete trial, signal detection experiments and reanalyzed them to show how the parameters of the model depend on ratios of obtained reinforcement. The results are shown in Figure 1–5. Green and Swets (1966: 90) reported data for a human observer detecting signals in noise. The subject received one point for each correct detection or correct rejection and was fined for false alarms and misses. For present purposes, only positive outcomes are considered. The probability of signal presentation was varied systematically, and an isosensitivity curve resulted. The data, represented by the filled circles, show that the discriminability index $1/\eta$ remained essentially constant, while bias varied systematically with the ratio of obtained positive outcomes.

Very similar data have been reported by McCarthy (1979; see also McCarthy and Davison, 1980; and Chapter 16) for pigeons trained to peck one key (R_1) after exposure to a short interval (S_A) and another key (R_2) after exposure to a long interval (S_B) with intermittent food reinforcement. McCarthy varied the probability of presenting S_A under two conditions—a large difference between S_A and S_B (unfilled squares) and a small difference (filled squares). The relation between bias and obtained reinforcement ratios is the same for both levels of difficulty, while $1/\eta$ remains essentially constant within each level of difficulty.

Whittaker (1977) performed a related experiment with rats as subjects. Pressing one lever (R_1) was reinforced with water in the presence of a relatively intense light (S_A) and pressing a second lever (R_2) was reinforced in the presence of a relatively weak light (S_B). Unlike McCarthy and Davison, Whittaker held the probability of S_A constant and varied the probabilities of reinforcement for correct responses under conditions with a large (unfilled triangles) and a small (filled triangles) difference in luminance of S_A and S_B. Again, $1/\eta$ was constant within each level of difficulty, and the relation between bias and obtained reinforcement ratios was independent of difficulty.

Finally, Stubbs (1976) trained pigeons on a temporal discrimination procedure similar to McCarthy and Davison's (1980) and varied the number of reinforcers that could be obtained for each class of

Figure 1−5. Upper panel: A measure of response bias is plotted as a function of obtained reinforcement ratios for individual human, pigeon, and rat subjects for several experiments. In two experiments, performance was evaluated with both easy and difficult discriminations. Lower panel: A measure of discrimination is plotted as a function of obtained reinforcement ratios for the same subjects. See text for derivation of measures and details on experiments.

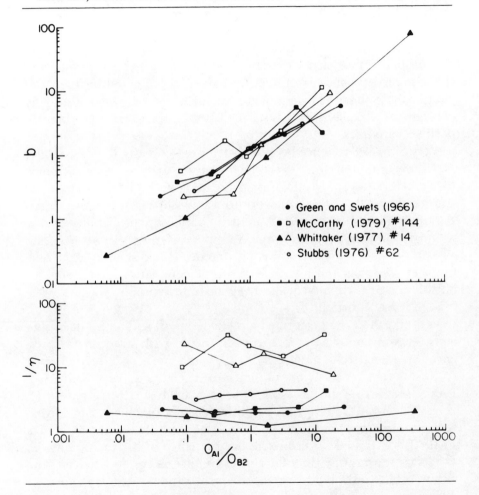

- Green and Swets (1966)
- ■ □ McCarthy (1979) #144
- ▲ △ Whittaker (1977) #14
- ○ Stubbs (1976) #62

correct response, regardless of how responses were distributed. Thus, his study specified the values of o_{A1} and o_{B2} in advance. The value of $1/\eta$ (unfilled circles) remains appropriately constant, and the bias function conforms quite nicely to those generated by procedures in the studies discussed above, in which the subject can determine the obtained ratio of reinforcers. Thus, there is substantial agreement in the data across species, kinds of stimuli, levels of difficulty, and methods for shifting response bias.

How well do the data conform to the model? The constancy of the discriminability parameter $1/\eta$ indicates that the data conform well to the predicted isosensitivity curve when reinforcement is varied, and the separation of functions for different levels of difficulty shows that $1/\eta$ is appropriately sensitive to stimulus variables. The orderly relations between bias and obtained reinforcement ratios conform reasonably well to the isobias curves predicted by Equations (1.3) and (1.5). However, there is a systematic discrepancy. In the double-logarithmic coordinates of Figure 1–5, matching implies a slope of 1. However, the slopes of the bias functions are consistently less than 1, indicating undermatching to obtained reinforcement ratios. This point was made earlier by Davison and Tustin (1978), who also analyzed the Green and Swets (1966) and Stubbs' (1976) data. We turn now to their model.

According to Davison and Tustin (1978), the ratio of responses depends directly on the ratio of reinforcers obtained by these responses according to the generalized matching law (Baum, 1974):

$$\frac{R_1}{R_2} = c \left(\frac{o_{A1}}{o_{B2}} \right)^a \tag{1.6}$$

where c represents inherent bias toward one or the other response, attributable, for example, to constant effects of different force requirements, and a represents the sensitivity of responding to reinforcement, which may depend on a number of variables (cf. Baum, 1979).

Equation (1.6) is silent on the role of the stimuli, S_A and S_B. Clearly, the contingencies of reinforcement dictate that R_1 should predominate in the presence of S_A and R_2 should predominate in the presence of S_B. Davison and Tustin (1978) made the novel suggestion that the stimuli be construed as biasing variables, analogous to different force requirements. Thus, S_A acts to bias responding toward R_1, and S_B acts to bias responding toward R_2. Incorporating stimulus bias in Equation (1.4), they proposed:

$$\frac{R_{A1}}{R_{A2}} = cd \left(\frac{o_{A1}}{o_{B2}} \right)^a \tag{1.7a}$$

and

$$\frac{R_{B1}}{R_{B2}} = c\frac{1}{d} \left(\frac{o_{A1}}{o_{B2}} \right)^a \tag{1.7b}$$

where d is the bias toward R_1 given S_A, and $1/d$ is the bias away from R_1 given S_B. Thus, d is equivalent to $1/\eta$ as defined above (Equations 1.1a and 1.1b). When Equations (1.7a) and (1.7b) are multiplied, the resulting isobias curve includes the parameter a, which neatly captures the consistent undermatching shown in Figure 1–5.

In conventional signal detection theory, there is a rigid separation between the effects of stimuli and reinforcers: Stimuli provide information on which responding is based, whereas reinforcers bias the subject toward one or the other response given the stimulus presentation. A comparable distinction exists in the model proposed by Nevin et al. (1977) and summarized above: Stimuli modulate the allocation of the effects of reinforcement, and responding depends on the resulting allocation. The interpretation advanced by Davison and Tustin (1978) is more radical in that it assigns a biasing role to stimuli as well as to reinforcers. Their approach is consistent with the initial arguments of this chapter to the effect that no distinction between the discriminative and reinforcing functions of stimuli is logically necessary. As such, it is worth pursuing further.

THE DERIVATION OF ISOREINFORCEMENT CURVES

It may be that the traditional separation of sensitivity, which is presumed to depend on stimulus variables, and bias, which is presumed to depend on reinforcement variables, has more to do with our conventional identification of the factors that affect responding than on any fundamental distinction between discriminative stimuli and reinforcers. Consider a recent study by Mandell and Nevin (1977), in which pigeons were trained to peck one side key (R_1) in the presence of one noise intensity (S_A) and the other side key (R_2) in the presence of a different noise intensity (S_B). The reinforcer was not immediate food, but access to a schedule of food reinforcement on the center key. Rates of reinforcement for center-key pecks following correct side-key pecks were varied over the course of the experiment, resulting in biases to one or the other side key. When performance was stable in each reinforcement condition, a maintained generalization test was conducted with nine different noise intensities presented in random order, twenty times each. Figure 1–6 (left panel) shows two functions relating the probability of pecking one side key (R_2) to stimulus intensity. In one case, R_2 given S_B was followed by access to a random interval 25-second schedule of reinforcement, while R_1 given S_A was followed by access to a random interval 100-second schedule of reinforcement, resulting in a 4:1 ratio of reinforcement rates. In the other case, the schedules were reversed, to give a 1:4 ratio of reinforcement rates. The psychometric function relating response probability to stimulus intensity is shifted down and to the left for the latter case relative to the former. This shift would conventionally be construed as reflecting the biasing effect of differential reinforcement.

An alternative analysis is possible, however. These functions may be construed as reflecting control by the reinforcement schedules, with responding biased by the value of the stimulus (cf. Davison and Tustin, 1978): Low intensities bias responding toward R_1, and high intensities bias responding toward R_2, with the control by differential reinforcement constant. Following this line of analysis, we would construct an "isoreinforcement" curve by plotting the probability of R_2 under one set of reinforcement conditions against the probability of R_2 under the other set of reinforcement conditions for each stimulus value. This mode of graphing leads to the plot on the right of Figure 1–6 (see also Nevin, 1965). The general character of the relation is quite similar to the isosensitivity curves of Figure 1–2. This exercise in replotting suggests the essential arbitrariness of identifying the axes of the signal detection graph with responding conditional upon stimuli, where reinforcement schedules generate successive points along a curve. We can just as well turn our thinking around and identify the axes with responding conditional upon schedules, where stimulus values generate successive points.

Once it is accepted that responding conditional upon a schedule may be treated just like responding conditional upon a stimulus, the

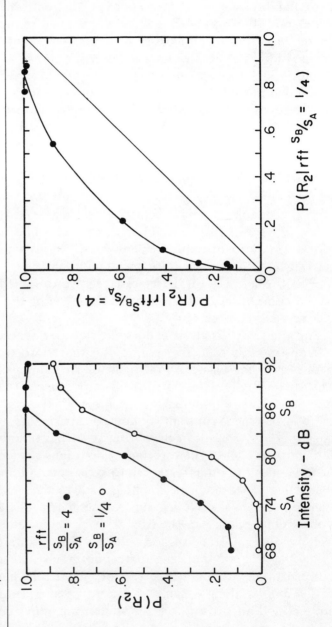

Figure 1–6. Left panel: Probability of responding to a key (R_2) that led to reinforcement in the presence of an 86 dB noise (S_B) as a function of noise intensity. Responding on the other key (R_1) led to reinforcement in the presence of 74 dB (S_A). The filled points are average data for a condition in which reinforcement was four times as frequent in S_B as in S_A, and the unfilled points are average data for a condition in which reinforcement was one-fourth as frequent in S_B as in S_A. Adapted from Mandell (1977). Right panel: The data for each noise level in the left panel are plotted against each other to give a curve for sensitivity to reinforcement ratios.

way is open for a more general analysis of schedule control. The analysis is illustrated by two experiments on free operant multiple and concurrent schedules of reinforcement—one by Pliskoff, Shull, and Gollub (1968) and the other by Nevin (1974).

Pliskoff and his associates arranged a multiple schedule of reinforcement on one key, while a common schedule of reinforcement was available concurrently on a second key, with pigeons as subjects. In one portion of their study, the rates of reinforcement in the two components of the multiple schedule were forty and ten reinforcers per hour respectively, while the common concurrent schedule arranged zero, twenty, or sixty reinforcers per hour. The procedure may be summarized in the signal detection paradigm shown in Table 1–2. Training continued at each combination of schedule values until performance was stable. The left panel of Figure 1–7 presents the proportion of responses on the multiple key (Key 1) in Component 1 as a function of the proportion of responses on Key 1 in Component 2, where successive points are given by the different conditions of concurrent reinforcement on Key 2. The extent to which the data are shifted away from the major diagonal reflects the degree of control by differential rates of reinforcement in the components of the multiple schedule.

Nevin (1974) arranged a multiple schedule with 10-second components on one key, concurrently with a fixed interval (FI) 50-second schedule of reinforcement on the second key. Over the course of the experiment, the reinforcement rates arranged in the components of the multiple schedule varied systematically, while the concurrent FI schedule remained constant. Illustrative data are presented from the first condition, which arranged seventy-five reinforcers per hour in the presence of red and fourteen per hour in the presence of green.

Table 1–2. Outcome Matrix for Pliskoll, Shull, and Gollub (1968) Study.

	Key 1	Key 2
Component 1	40 rft/hr	0, 20, 60 rft/hr
Component 2	10 rft/hr	0, 20, 60 rft/hr

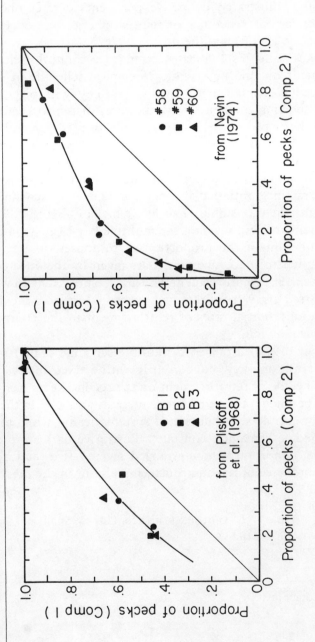

Figure 1-7. Left panel: An isoreinforcement curve for a study of multiple and concurrent schedules by Pliskoff et al. (1968). Right panel: An isoreinforcement curve for a study of multiple and concurrent schedules by Nevin (1974).

As for Pliskoff et al., the procedure may be summarized in signal detection form (Table 1−3):

After extended training, response rate on the FI key increased and response rate on the multiple key decreased systematically across successive 10-second periods within the FI. Thus, graded proportions of responses to the multiple key were generated for both components within the FI over the course of a session. The right panel of Figure 1−7 presents the proportion of responses to the multiple key (Key 1) during Component 1 as a function of the proportion of responses to Key 1 during Component 2, where successive points are given by temporal position within the FI schedule on Key 2. The result is an orderly isoreinforcement curve, where the departure from the major diagonal again reflects the degree of control by differential reinforcement.

These experiments illustrate the feasibility of generating orderly R = R relations in the study of reinforcement schedules. Moreover, the general form of these curves is quite similar to the isosensitivity curves of psychophysics. Therefore, I suggest that they are general throughout the domain schematized in Figure 1−1, and I urge their use to provide a common form of data treatment in the study of stimulus and schedule control.

It is possible that the isoreinforcement curves generated by plotting performance maintained by one schedule against performance maintained by another will yield information comparable to that obtained from other approaches. For example, Mandell (Chapter 2) reports that the discriminability of two variable interval schedules, assessed by a psychophysical method, depends systematically on the ratio of their average values. In like fashion, theoretical isoreinforcement curves for signal detection performance depend on the ratio of obtained reinforcement rates and on the parameter a for sensitivity to differential reinforcement (cf. Equation 1.6). To see this, consider

Table 1−3. Outcome Matrix for Nevin (1974) Study.

	Key 1	Key 2
Component 1	75 rft/hr	FI 50 sec
Component 2	14 rft/hr	FI 50 sec

a pair of schedule conditions, X and Y, which differ in the ratios of reinforcers obtained by responses R_1 and R_2. Let S_i $(i = 1 \ldots n)$ represent one of a set of stimulus conditions that bias responding toward or away from R_1 in varying degrees, as suggested by Davison and Tustin (1978). The basic equations for response allocation are:

$$\text{Given Condition } X: \quad \frac{R_{i1}}{R_{i2}} = cd \left(\frac{o_{1X}}{o_{2X}} \right)^a \qquad (1.8a)$$

$$\text{Given Condition } Y: \quad \frac{R_{i1}}{R_{i2}} = cd \left(\frac{o_{1Y}}{o_{2Y}} \right)^a \qquad (1.8b)$$

The isoreinforcement curve is obtained by dividing Equation (1.8a) by Equation (1.8b) to eliminate inherent bias, c, and stimulus bias, d:

$$\frac{R_{i1_X}}{R_{i2_X}} \cdot \frac{R_{i1_Y}}{R_{i2_Y}} = \left(\frac{o_{1X}}{o_{2X}} \cdot \frac{o_{2Y}}{o_{1Y}} \right)^a \qquad (1.9)$$

Some representative isoreinforcement curves are plotted in the form common to signal detection research in Figure 1–8 for various reinforcement ratios and values of a. They are identical in form to the theoretical isosensitivity curves of Figure 1–4, but here the curves are ordered according to the ratios of reinforcers obtained in Conditions X and Y and the value of the sensitivity parameter a. For a given pair of reinforcement ratios, a plays exactly the same role as the theoretical discriminability parameter $1/\eta$—the greater its value, the more remote are the functions from the major diagonal. Viewing data in this way (cf. Figures 1–6 and 1–7) suggests that a is indeed properly viewed as an index of sensitivity to differential reinforcement.

It is an empirical question as to whether sensitivity to ratios of response-produced reinforcers, indicated by the isoreinforcement curve, is different from sensitivity to ratios of reinforcers that serve as cues for choice responding in psychophysical procedures of the sort described by Commons (Chapter 3) and Mandell (Chapter 2). The same kind of question may be asked about other dimensions of reinforcement schedules, such as response–reinforcer contingencies or delays. To the extent that data from experiments with constant stimulus conditions and varied reinforcement conditions yield data

Figure 1–8. Theoretical isoreinforcement curves derived from the behavioral model of signal detection proposed by Davison and Tustin (1978). The five curves represent different combinations of reinforcement ratios and sensitivities to reinforcement (characterized by the parameter a) as follows: Curve 1, reinforcement ratio 4.0, $a = 1.0$; Curve 2, reinforcement ratio = 4.0, $a = 0.6$; Curve 3, reinforcement ratio = 3.0, $a = 1.0$; Curve 4, reinforcement ratio = 3.0, $a = 0.6$; Curve 5, reinforcement ratio = 2.0, $a = 0.6$. Note that reducing the reinforcement ratio and reducing the sensitivity to reinforcement both shift the curves toward the major diagonal. See text for derivation.

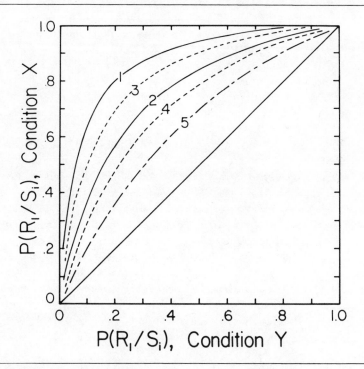

that are consistent with those from experiments with constant reinforcement conditions and varied stimulus conditions, the continuity of the discriminative and reinforcing functions of stimuli is supported.

REFERENCES

Baum, W.M. 1973. The correlation-based law of effect. *Journal of the Experimental Analysis of Behavior 20*: 137–153.

_____. 1974. On two types of deviation from the matching law: Bias and undermatching. *Journal of the Experimental Analysis of Behavior 22*: 231–242.

_____. 1979. Matching, undermatching, and overmatching in studies of choice. *Journal of the Experimental Analysis of Behavior 32*: 269–281.

_____. 1981. Optimization and the matching law as accounts of instrumental behavior. *Journal of the Experimental Analysis of Behavior* (in press).

Bush, R.R.; R.D. Luce; and R.M. Rose. 1964. Learning models for psychophysics. In R.D. Atkinson, ed., *Studies in Mathematical Psychology*. Stanford: Stanford University Press.

Davison, M.C., and R.D. Tustin. 1978. The relation between the generalized matching law and signal-detection theory. *Journal of the Experimental Analysis of Behavior 29*: 331–336.

DeVilliers, P.A. 1977. Choice in concurrent schedules and a quantitative formulation of the law of effect. In W.K. Honig and J.E.R. Staddon, eds., *Handbook of Operant Behavior*. Englewood Cliffs, New Jersey: Prentice-Hall.

Galanter, E. 1970. On the nature of laws in psychology. In J.R. Royce, ed., *Toward Unification in Psychology: The First Banff Conference on Theoretical Psychology*. Toronto: University of Toronto Press.

Green, D.M., and J.A. Swets. 1966. *Signal Detection Theory and Psychophysics*. New York: Wiley.

Herrnstein, R.J. 1970. On the law of effect. *Journal of the Experimental Analysis of Behavior 13*: 243–266.

Luce, R.D. 1963. Detection and recognition. In R.D. Luce, R.R. Bush, and E. Galanter, eds., *Handbook of Mathematical Psychology*, vol. 1. New York: Wiley.

Mandell, C., and J.A. Nevin. 1977. Choice, time allocation, and response rate during stimulus generalization. *Journal of the Experimental Analysis of Behavior 28*: 47–57.

McCarthy, D. 1979. A behavioural analysis of signal-detection performance. Doctoral dissertation, University of Auckland, New Zealand.

McCarthy, D., and M.C. Davison. 1980. Independence of sensitivity to relative reinforcement rate and discriminability in signal detection. *Journal of the Experimental Analysis of Behavior 34*: 273-284.

Nevin, J.A. 1965. Decision theory in studies of discrimination in animals. *Science 150*: 1057.

_____. 1969a. Signal detection theory and operant behavior (review). *Journal of the Experimental Analysis of Behavior 12*: 475-480.

_____. 1969b. Interval reinforcement of choice behavior in discrete trials. *Journal of the Experimental Analysis of Behavior 12*: 875-885.

_____. 1973. Stimulus control. In J.A. Nevin, ed., *The Study of Behavior*. Glenview, Illinois: Scott, Foresman.

_____. 1974. On the form of the relation between response rates in a multiple schedule. *Journal of the Experimental Analysis of Behavior 21*: 237-248.

Nevin, J.A., and W.M. Baum. 1980. Feedback functions for variable-interval reinforcement. *Journal of the Experimental Analysis of Behavior 34*: 207-217.

Nevin, J.A.; P. Jenkins; S.G. Whittaker; and P. Yarensky. 1977. Signal detection and matching. Paper presented at the meetings of the Psychonomic Society, Washington, D.C., November.

Nevin, J.A.; K. Olson; C. Mandell; and P. Yarensky. 1975. Differential reinforcement and signal detection. *Journal of the Experimental Analysis of Behavior 24*: 355-367.

Pliskoff, S.S.; R.L. Shull; and L.R. Gollub. 1968. The relation between response rates and reinforcement rates in a multiple schedule. *Journal of the Experimental Analysis of Behavior 11*: 271-284.

Reynolds, G.S., and A.J. Limpo. 1969. Attention and generalization during a conditional discrimination. *Journal of the Experimental Analysis of Behavior 12*: 911-916.

Stubbs, D.A. 1976. Response bias and the discrimination of stimulus duration. *Journal of the Experimental Analysis of Behavior 25*: 243-250.

Swets, J.A. 1973. The relative operating characteristic in psychology. *Science 182*: 990-1000.

Whittaker, S.G. 1977. Scaling probability of reinforcement with a signal-detection procedure. Doctoral dissertation, University of New Hampshire.

II RATES OF REINFORCEMENT AS DISCRIMINATIVE PROPERTIES OF REINFORCEMENT SCHEDULES

2 A PSYCHOPHYSICAL ANALYSIS OF TIME-BASED SCHEDULES OF REINFORCEMENT

Charlotte Mandell

Much of the research in the experimental analysis of behavior has shown that subjects are extremely sensitive to differences in reinforcement schedules. In choice situations, subjects distribute their responses in ways that vary with both the rate and the distribution of reinforcers. For example, when different schedules are presented concurrently, the relative rate of responding often matches the relative rate of reinforcement in many species. Studies of animals foraging in the wild suggest that the rate at which prey are consumed is a critical factor in determining the allocation of feeding behavior. Such findings pose the problem of how the average rate of discrete food presentations, occurring irregularly in time, can serve as a stimulus controlling the overall allocation of responding. More generally, it poses the question of how any time-related events can come to control behavior. Various approaches have been developed to determine the rule or rules that best describe the manner in which behavior is controlled by the rate and distribution of reinforcers.

One approach to this problem has been to infer the subjective value of different schedules from behavior in a choice situation. This procedure uses the degree of preference for one schedule over another as a measure of schedule value. Preference is generally determined by examining the relative rate of responding in the initial links of concurrent chained schedules. In such a schedule, access to one

31

of two terminal-link reinforcement schedules is dependent on the choice between two concurrently available response alternatives during the initial link of the chain. When both terminal-link schedules are variable interval (VI), subjects generally match their relative initial-link response rates to the relative rate of terminal-link reinforcement (Autor 1969; Herrnstein, 1964). If, however, one of the schedules is fixed (FI) and the other variable, marked preference for the variable interval schedule occurs. This has suggested to a number of workers that the average interreinforcement interval of the variable schedule is not best described as the arithmetic mean of the intervals composing that schedule, but rather by some other rule, such as the harmonic mean.

The application of such a transformation to an arithmetic progression of intervals composing a variable interval schedule results in an average interval smaller than the arithmetic mean. Thus, if a fixed interval schedule is equated to the arithmetic mean of a variable interval schedule, the latter will have a higher effective density of reinforcement, and preference for the variable schedule should result. Unfortunately, this averaging rule does not always describe the integration of sequences of interreinforcement intervals. The degree of preference is found to vary with a number of factors, including the initial-link length, the range of values composing the terminal-link schedules, and others that have not yet been identified. Thus, investigators working in different laboratories have produced results that have not always been quantitatively consistent with one another (Davison, 1969, 1972, 1976; Duncan and Fantino, 1970; Herrnstein, 1964; Hursh and Fantino, 1973; Killeen, 1968).

In order to obtain more consistent information about the manner in which subjects integrate sequences of time intervals, the discriminative properties of both fixed and variable interval schedules differing in reinforcement frequency were examined. In this work, schedules of reinforcement were themselves treated as stimuli to avoid contaminating their discriminative properties with their hedonic value, as is the case in the concurrent chain procedure. Subjects were required to make one response after exposure to a schedule with a low rate of reinforcement and a second response after exposure to a schedule with a high rate of reinforcement. Following training, subjects were exposed to a series of schedule values, with either fixed or variable interreinforcer intervals. The tendency for each subject to respond to the novel schedule in the manner appropriate for the lean or dense training schedule was related to the programmed rate and pattern of reinforcement.

The procedure used to train the subjects was similar to that used in other studies in which schedules of reinforcement have served as discriminative stimuli (cf. Chapters 3, 4, and 5). Subjects were initially exposed to a brief sample of the schedule. They were then required to respond differentially in a two-alternative, forced choice situation according to which schedule immediately preceded the choice response (Commons, 1979; Hobson, 1970, 1975; Pliskoff and Goldiamond, 1966; Rilling and McDiarmid, 1965). These studies have obtained results that are comparable to those obtained with psychophysical procedures in which more traditional stimuli are used.

The method for generalization testing following training was based on a procedure used by Heinemann and his associates (1969) in which psychophysical functions were obtained for stimuli varying along intensive dimensions. In this procedure, nonreinforced generalization trials employing stimuli chosen from a range of values exceeding that used in training are interspersed with occasional training trials. As a consequence, generalization testing can be maintained for fairly extensive periods without producing changes in the form of the generalization function and without significant deterioration in accuracy on the training trials.

METHOD

Using the specific training procedure, diagrammed in Figure 2-1, two pigeons were trained to discriminate between two VI schedules of different reinforcement density in a three-key experimental chamber. Each VI schedule was composed of three reinforcement intervals, a short one (equal to the mean interval × 0.5), a middle one (equal to the mean interval), and a long one (equal to the mean interval × 1.5). Within each trial, the pigeons were exposed to a "schedule sample" during which the subject pecked the center key and obtained 1-second presentations of the food magazine according to the programmed schedule. Each schedule sample began with a reinforcer presentation and consisted of a variable number of "units." A unit, measured from the presentation of a reinforcer, was composed of the three intervals that made up the VI schedule. Thus, the

Figure 2–1. Schematic diagram of procedure.

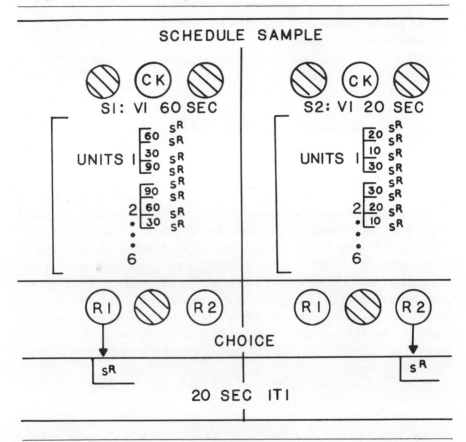

value of each unit was equal to the mean value of the schedule as a whole. For example, a unit for the VI 60-second schedule would be composed of a 30, a 60, and a 90-second interval. For a given schedule sample, the number of units varied between one and six, thus permitting the number of reinforcers per schedule sample to vary between four (initial reinforcer plus one unit) and nineteen (initial reinforcer plus six units). The number of units presented was identical for the dense and lean schedules over the course of a session. Thus, it was not possible for the absolute number of reinforcers per sample to serve as a cue to the schedule value. As a consequence, the total duration of a schedule sample was variable, and there was some overlap between the lean and dense schedules. Thus, sample duration could not serve as a reliable indicator of schedule value. Finally, the order in which the intervals were arranged in each unit was varied, so that no particular interval was more likely to precede a choice response than any other. This was intended to decrease the likelihood that subjects would attend to the presence or absence of one particular interval.

At the start of a trial, the center key was illuminated with a green light, and the schedule sample was presented. The two side keys were then illuminated with white light, and the center key was darkened. Reinforcement for a given side-key peck depended on the value of the preceding schedule. Reinforcers for correct choice pecks were longer than for center key schedule responses. In addition, the two reinforcer types were made more distinctive by correlating the color of the food magazine light with the associated key color (green for the center key schedule sample reinforcers and white for choice reinforcers). A left-key peck (R_1) after the completion of the less dense reinforcement schedule (S_1) was called a "'hit" and produced 6-second access to grain followed by a 14-second intertrial interval (ITI). A right-key peck (R_2) after the completion of the dense schedule (S_2) was called a "correct rejection" and produced identical consequences. Either R_1 after S_2 (a "false alarm") or R_2 after S_1 (a "miss") produced a 20-second ITI. After several months of training on this procedure, performance was characterized by large oscillations in response bias (the probability of choosing a particular key irrespective of the stimulus value). To compensate for shifts in bias, the relative durations of the reinforcers for correct side-key pecks were manipulated until indifference was obtained.

Next, a series of generalization tests was administered. These tests were composed of schedule samples denser, leaner, and intermediate to the training schedules and were interspersed between training trials. In addition, FI schedules of varying length were included among the generalization trials. Each generalization trial consisted of three schedule units. As in the training procedure, a unit was initiated by reinforcement and consisted of three interreinforcement intervals. For the variable schedule, the units were composed of intervals in the same relation to each other as those composing the training units (0.5, 1.0, 1.5). For the fixed schedules, each interval was equal to the average schedule value. The outcome of this procedure was the development of two psychometric functions, one showing the proportion of left-key pecks $[P(R_1)]$ as a function of schedule value for the VI schedules and a similar function for the FI schedules (see Figure 2-9). During testing, reinforcement was available only for appropriate responses following training schedule values. In order to prevent deterioration in performance during testing, at least two days of training intervened between tests. If substantial bias levels were observed during training sessions, testing was postponed until bias returned to approximate indifference.

The schedule values initially used in training were VI 20 and VI 80 seconds. These were discriminated with approximately 100 percent accuracy. Subsequently, the schedule values were changed to VI 20 and VI 40 seconds, resulting in a severe loss of accuracy. Finally, schedule values of VI 20 and VI 60 seconds were selected to produce an intermediate level of accuracy.

RESULTS AND DISCUSSION: TRAINING

Acquisition of this task can be studied by examining the proportion of hits $(R_1|S_1)$ and false alarms $(R_1|S_2)$ that occurred during training. These data are presented in Figure 2-2. Both the subjects, Birds 90 and 91, achieved a fairly high degree of accuracy after only ten days of training. The speed of acquisition was comparable to the rate at which easy visual discriminations are acquired, suggesting that the rate of food presentation is a salient aspect of the environment for the pigeon. This should not be surprising if the rate of predation is in fact a critical variable in foraging.

Accuracy of choice performance is indicated by the degree of separation between the "hit" and "false alarm" functions. A wider separation indicates more accurate performance. Thus, Figure 2-2 indicates that the greater the difference between the schedules in the three training conditions, the greater the accuracy. The effects of schedule similarity on discrimination performance can also be determined by examining d', the bias-free index of sensitivity derived from the Green and Swets (1966) model of signal detection, as a function of the ratio of reinforcement rates. Figure 2-3 demonstrates that d' values are related, at least ordinally, to the ratio of schedule values. Thus, d' is highest for the 20 to 80 second condition and lowest for the 20 to 40 second condition.

In addition to a comparison of overall accuracy levels, a more molecular analysis of behavior during training on the VI 20 to 60 sec-

Figure 2-2. The proportion of hits $(R_1|S_1)$ and false alarms $(R_1|S_2)$ over the course of training.

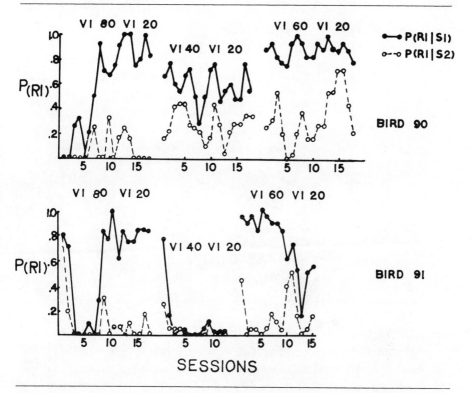

ond condition was performed. Figure 2-4 presents the probability of pecking R_1 (the key associated with the leaner schedule) as a function of the total duration of the schedule sample (determined by both the average value of the schedule and the number of units in a given sample). As noted earlier, the ranges of schedule sample lengths overlapped. For the denser schedules (S_2), the range of sample durations extended from 60 seconds (one unit) to 360 seconds (six units). For the leaner schedule (S_1), the range of sample durations extended from 180 seconds (one unit) to 1080 seconds (six units). The range in which the sample durations overlapped was between three to six units of the denser schedule and one to two units of the leaner schedule. If the total duration of the sample contributed to choice responses, we might expect longer duration samples to be correlated with higher proportions of left-key (R_1) responses because the S_1

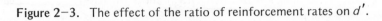

Figure 2–3. The effect of the ratio of reinforcement rates on d'.

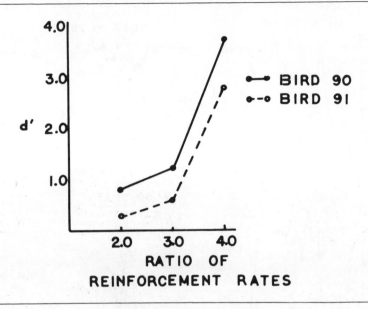

samples tended to be longer. Further, we might expect a loss of accuracy within the range of schedule overlap. Figure 2–4 shows (1) that the tendency to emit R_1 does not increase with increases in sample duration and (2) that there is no loss of accuracy within the range of overlap. These data suggest that the total duration of the schedule sample does not mediate choice response.

A second analysis was done to determine whether subjects might be timing the duration of each interval and ignoring the values of the preceding intervals. If this were the case, we might expect the proportion of R_1 responses to be lowest when the 10-second interval immediately preceded choice, highest when the 90-second interval preceded choice, and intermediate when the 30-second interval (common to both dense and lean schedules) preceded the choice. Figure 2–5, in which the probability of R_1 is shown as a function of the length of the reinforcement interval immediately preceding a choice response (irrespective of the duration of the sample and the order of earlier interreinforcement intervals), suggests that this is not the case. Although there is a very slight trend toward an increase in the probability of R_1 when interval length increases, there is no evi-

Figure 2-4. The proportion of hits $(R_1|S_1)$ and false alarms $(R_1|S_2)$ as a function of the duration of a schedule sample.

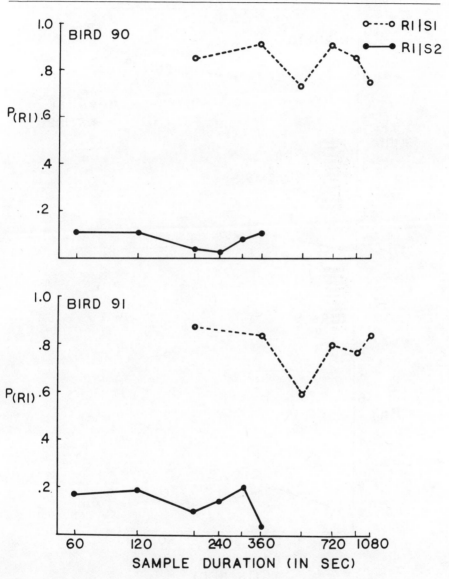

Figure 2–5. The proportion of hits $(R_1|S_1)$ and false alarms $(R_1|S_2)$ as a function of the duration of the interreinforcement interval immediately preceding the choice response.

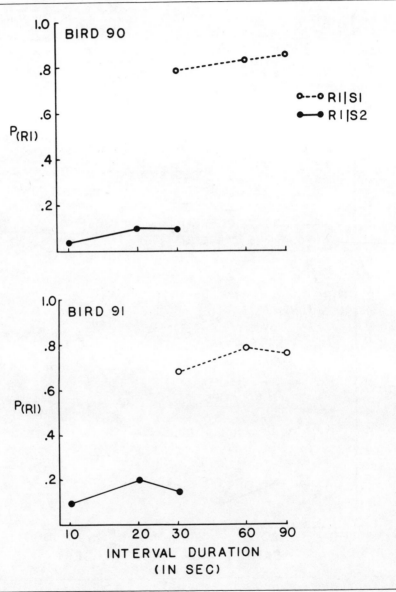

dence of confusion when the common 30-second interval preceded the choice response.

The probability of R_1 as a function of the value of the two intervals that immediately preceded a choice response is shown in Figure 2-6. First, it should be noted that within a given schedule value, the probability of R_1 does not tend to increase as the sum of the two intervals preceding a choice response increases. For example, $P(R_1)$ remains constant whether the choice was preceded by a 10- and a 20-second interval (summing to 30 seconds) or a 20- and a 30-second interval (summing to 50 seconds). Second, it should be noted that if the order of occurrence of the two intervals is taken into account, there was a greater tendency to emit R_1 when the longer of the two intervals immediately preceded choice than when the shorter of the two intervals preceded the choice response. This is true for both subjects in five out of six cases. These data suggest that the value of the most recent interval may be weighted more heavily than earlier intervals in determining choice behavior. This would not be surprising in view of the fact that the training procedure requires that subjects ignore reinforcement intervals experienced on previous trials. However, it is important to remember that the previous analysis indicated that the value of the terminal interval could not in itself account for discrimination performance.

The data were also examined to determine whether the first interval to which the subjects were exposed was a relatively potent determiner of choice responding. Schedule samples contained a number of repeated intervals, creating considerable redundancy within a sample. It would be quite possible, in theory, for the subject to discriminate between schedule classes perfectly after exposure to only the first two intervals of the first unit. If the initial information presented to the subject was weighted more heavily than subsequent information, increases in the probability of R_1 might be expected to covary with the length of the initial interval. Figure 2-7, which shows the probability of R_1 as a function of the duration of the initial interval, reveals no such trends.

It is possible that some properties of the schedule other than overall density of reinforcement might be responsible for the production of differentiated choice responses. For example, the extreme intervals composing a unit (shortest and longest) may be sufficient to determine choice behavior, and these intervals alone may serve as the relevant discriminative stimuli. That is, the subject may respond left

Figure 2–6. The proportion of hits $(R_1|S_1)$ and false alarms $(R_1|S_2)$ as a function of the total duration of the two intervals immediately preceding choice. The order of intervals is indicated above each point.

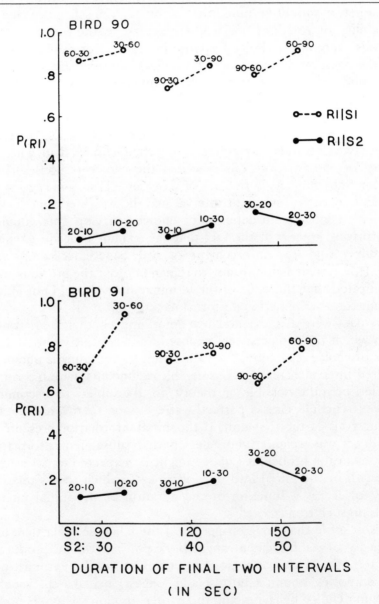

Figure 2-7. The proportion of hits $(R_1|S_1)$ and false alarms $(R_1|S_2)$ as a function of the duration of the initial interval of a schedule sample.

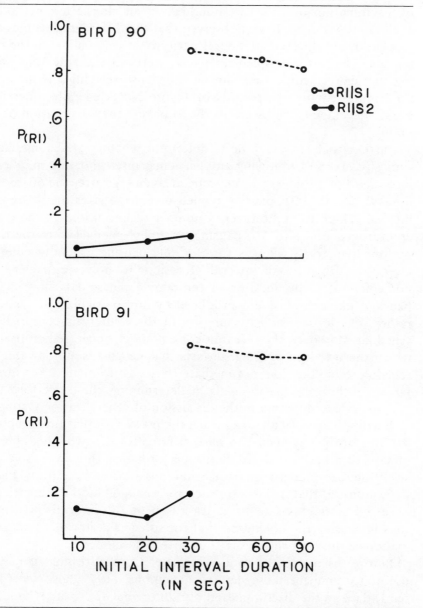

if and only if it experiences the 90-second interval at some point within the previous trial and right if and only if it experiences a 10-second interval. With the present design, this could not be assessed by examination of choice responding, so an alternative method of analysis was sought. It was observed that the different schedule samples produced different temporal patterns of responding on the center key. The postreinforcement pauses were considerably longer during the lean schedule than during the dense schedule, as shown in the sample cumulative records of Figure 2–8. Generally, once long pauses developed, they were likely to persist for the duration of the sample.

Further analysis was done to determine whether these long pauses typically emerged following any particular interval or any number of intervals. For Bird 90, pausing tended to emerge after the 60-second interval; for Bird 91, pausing tended to emerge after the 90-second interval. There were, however, a number of exceptions to these generalizations. For Bird 90, pausing generally emerged after the third or fourth interval, whereas for Bird 91, pausing generally emerged after the fifth or sixth interval. Occasionally, however, pausing did not emerge for the duration of the sample. These data suggest that pausing, like choice, is not produced by any particular interval, but rather, develops after exposure to all three intervals comprising a schedule. Moreover, the fact that correct choices occurred on trials in which there was no pausing suggests that pausing is a by-product of schedule value but does not mediate choice performance. The importance of the extreme intervals in determining choice performance will be evaluated further in the discussion of generalization testing.

Finally, it is difficult to exclude the possibility that topographical features of the key peck may have differed for the two schedules and may in turn have mediated choice performance. However, the analysis of the relation between choice and initial interval duration (Figure 2–7) indicates that if this were the case, topographical differentiation occurred after exposure to at least two of the intervals presented, thus increasing the likelihood that the subjects performed some integration of the intervals before this pattern developed.

Before discussing the results of generalization testing, it may be useful to compare these data to Commons' (1979; also see Chapter 3) data on the discrimination of reinforcement density. Commons used signaled T schedules (Schoenfeld, Cumming, and Hearst, 1956), which varied only in reinforcement density (probability of reinforce-

Figure 2-8. Sample cumulative records obtained from the start of several trials.

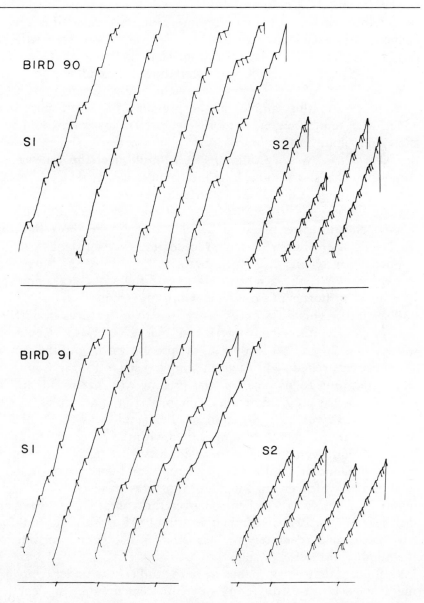

ment equaled 0.25 or 0.75), rather than traditional variable or random interval schedules. As in the present work, Commons reported rapid acquisition of the discrimination task and high accuracy in the final performance. Commons also reported that as the position of the final reinforcer became more remote from a choice, there was a decrease in the tendency to emit the response associated with the denser schedule. This relation is somewhat similar to that shown in Figure 2–5, in which choice behavior showed a tendency to covary with the length of the interreinforcement interval nearest to choice. Because all stimulus samples in the present work both started and ended with reinforcement, a more accurate comparison would be to those substimuli in Commons' work that also began and ended with reinforcement. Two of Commons' substimuli meet this criteria, one composed of a short and a long interreinforcement interval and the other of a long and a short interreinforcement interval. As in the present work, the probability of the response associated with the denser schedules was likely to be higher when the short interreinforcement interval immediately preceded the choice response.

There were several differences between Commons' and the present procedure. First, the average duration of the schedule sample was considerably shorter in Commons' work (12 seconds versus 210 and 630 seconds). This difference was related to differences in both the average interreinforcement interval (4 and 12 seconds in Commons' work versus 20 and 60 seconds in the present work) and the number of reinforcers scheduled in a given sample (zero to four in Commons' work and four to nineteen in the present work). Second, far less redundancy was programmed in Commons' stimulus samples. Finally, in Commons' work the duration of the sample was fixed, and the number of reinforcers per sample varied with the programmed probability of reinforcement. Thus, behavior may have been under control by the number of reinforcers per sample or by the average length of the interreinforcement interval. In the present work, however, the number of reinforcers scheduled over the course of a session was identical for the two discriminative stimuli. Thus, subjects could not have performed accurately if their behavior had been controlled by the number of reinforcers per sample.

It appears that performance in both studies was under control by the average rate or probability of reinforcement, that the length of time needed to acquire the task was similar, and that the value of those intervals nearest to the choice response contributed relatively heavily to the determination of choice. These similarities are impressive when the procedural and parametric disparities in the two studies are considered.

GENERALIZATION TESTING

Figure 2–9 presents the generalization gradients for the two subjects. Average schedule values during generalization testing ranged from 10 to 70 seconds in 10-second steps. Solid lines represent responding on VI schedules, and dashed lines represent responding on FI schedules. These functions are based on twenty-two testing sessions for Bird 90 and sixteen for Bird 91. These gradients should be considered preliminary because the number of exposures to each stimulus is low in comparison to other similar work. Heinemann and his associates (1969) for example, used thirty exposures to each stimulus value. In general, the following observations can be made:

1. The functions are similar in form to those obtained by Heinemann and his associates using the intensity of white light or white noise. The failure of the asymptotes to reach 1 can be related to evidence of strong response bias. Otherwise, these gradients resemble those obtained with traditional stimuli. It is not uncommon to find a dip in the gradient at the extreme end, as in the case of Bird 91. This dip may be attributed to the effects of nonreinforcement at those stimulus values that are most discriminable from the training stimuli.

2. The functions for FI and VI schedules are quite similar to each other. There is no systematic tendency to associate FI schedules with R_1 (the response associated with the leaner VI schedule) more frequently than VI schedules. In other words, VI schedules do not seem to be judged shorter on the whole than equivalent FI schedules. This finding implies that theories that rely on nonlinear averaging rules to account for preference for variable over fixed interval schedules may be somewhat misleading in terms of the psychological representation of schedule density. Moreover, pursuant to the analysis of the determinants of choice during training, the absence of consistent differences between FI and VI schedules at the training values makes it unlikely that the

Figure 2-9. Proportion of R_1 $(P(R_1))$ as a function of average schedule value during generalization testing.

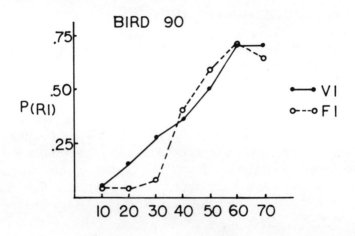

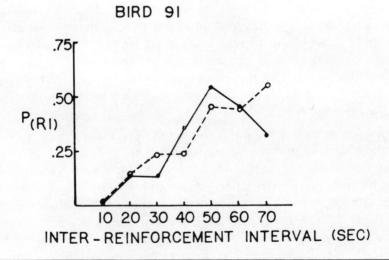

extreme intervals used in VI schedules were responsible for differentiated choice performance during training, as was suggested earlier.

3. The slope of the FI function seems somewhat steeper than that of the VI function. If, as has been suggested, the slope of a psychometric function is related to the difficulty of the discrimination, this implies that it is easier to discriminate between two schedules of reinforcement when the intervals comprising them are fixed rather than variable.

In summary, then, this work indicates strongly that the stimulus properties of reinforcement rate in time-based schedules can be examined in much the same way as other intensive stimulus continua. Further, the data indicate that there is no significant effect of the distribution of intervals in determining stimulus control by the schedule density.

This work is still in its early stages. Currently, it is being repeated using schedule values that are in the same relation to each other as those in the previous study, but whose absolute values differ. It is also being extended to situations in which two schedules are presented concurrently rather than sequentially. Finally, the generality of these findings is being extended to situations in which nonreinforcing discrete events occur irregularly in time and in which the response-reinforcer contingencies are varied. If successful, these analyses will relate the perceptual properties of reinforcement schedules to their effects in controlling behavior.

REFERENCES

Autor, S.M. 1969. The strength of conditioned reinforcers as a function of frequency and probability of reinforcement. In D.P. Hendry, ed., *Conditioned Reinforcement*, pp. 127–162. Homewood, Ill.: The Dorsey Press.

Commons, M.L. 1979. Decision rules and isosensitivity curves for the discrimination of reinforcement density using a choice procedure. *Journal of the Experimental Analysis of Behavior 32*: 101–120.

Davison, M.C. 1969. Preference for mixed-interval versus fixed-interval schedules. *Journal of the Experimental Analysis of Behavior 12*: 247–252.

_____ . 1972. Preference for mixed-interval versus fixed-interval schedules: Number of component intervals. *Journal of the Experimental Analysis of Behavior 17*: 169–176.

_____ . 1976. Preference for fixed interval schedules: Effects of unequal initial links. *Journal of the Experimental Analysis of Behavior 25* : 371–377.

Duncan, B., and E. Fantino. 1970. Choice for periodic schedules of reinforcement. *Journal of the Experimental Analysis of Behavior 14* : 73–86.

Green, D.M., and J.A. Swets. 1966. *Signal Detection Theory and Psychophysics*. New York: Wiley.

Heinemann, E.G.; E. Avin; M.A. Sullivan; and S. Chase. 1969. Analysis of stimulus generalization with a psychophysical method. *Journal of Experimental Psychology 80* : 215–225.

Herrnstein, R.J. 1964. Aperiodicity as a factor in choice. *Journal of the Experimental Analysis of Behavior 7* : 179–182.

Hobson, S.L. 1970. Discrimination of fixed-ratio schedules by pigeons: Sensitivity and bias. Doctoral dissertation, Columbia University.

_____ . 1975. Discriminability of fixed-ratio schedules for pigeons: Effects of absolute ratio size. *Journal of the Experimental Analysis of Behavior 23* : 25–35.

Hursh, S.R., and E. Fantino. 1973. Relative delay of reinforcement and choice. *Journal of the Experimental Analysis of Behavior 19* : 437–450.

Killeen, P. 1968. On the measurement of reinforcement frequency in the study of preference. *Journal of the Experimental Analysis of Behavior 11* : 263–269.

Pliskoff, S.S., and I. Goldiamond. 1966. Some discriminative properties of fixed-ratio performance in the pigeon. *Journal of the Experimental Analysis of Behavior 9* : 1–9.

Rilling, M., and C. McDiarmid. 1965. Signal detection in fixed-ratio schedules. *Science 148* : 526–527.

Schoenfeld, W.N.; W.W. Cumming; and E. Hearst. 1956. On the classification of reinforcement schedules. *Proceedings of the National Academy of Sciences 42* : 563–570.

3 HOW REINFORCEMENT DENSITY IS DISCRIMINATED AND SCALED

Michael L. Commons

Understanding how reinforcement schedules are discriminated and scaled should help explain behavior occurring in two different situations. The first of these is where some property of a schedule sample acts as a cue for future behavior, either in the laboratory or in the field (Kamil, Peters, and Lindstrom, 1981; Williams, 1981). As one important example, the effective value of a series of reinforcers may determine upcoming decisions of the subject—for instance, in a foraging situation where the relative density of reinforcement for foraging in a patch controls the choice to stay in that patch or to shift to another. In the second situation, understanding the perceived or scaled value of schedule samples should be useful in explaining the strengthening effects of reinforcement schedules on operant behavior. This is likely because of the high degree of correlation between

Portions of this chapter were reported at the Midwestern Association for Behavior Analysis, Chicago, 1976, by A.A. Thompson; M.P. Krupa; J.J. Andersen; and M.L. Commons, and at the Eastern Psychological Association, Boston, 1977, by M.P. Krupa; M. Hirvonen; J. Pohl; M. Lamb; and A.A. Thompson. A number of people have contributed to the analysis. They include, in alphabetical order, Michael Cohen, John R. Ducheny, Richard J. Herrnstein, Gene Heyman, Duncan Luce, John A. Nevin, Joel R. Peck, William Vaughn, and Michael Woodford. Rose P. Meegan and John R. Ducheny wrote the computer program for the analysis. Computer facilities at Boston University and Northeastern University were used. The organization of the complex material is the work of Patrice M. Miller, who edited the text. The line of research leading up to the present research was developed under the guidance of John Anthony Nevin. The analysis was carried out with the support of Richard J. Herrnstein. Research support was also provided by the Dare Association, Inc.

51

perceived value and choice, as shown by Commons and Ducheny (1981). For example, in chained schedules of reinforcement, the perceived value of the reinforcers in the terminal link may be predictive of behavior in the initial link, whose only reinforcement is the occurrence of the terminal link.

The primary purpose of the present studies is to explore the processes by which pigeons discriminate and scale reinforcement density. The subjects obtained occasional reinforcers on schedule samples for center-key pecks (R_C). These schedule samples then served as stimuli to be discriminated. After obtaining the sample, a pigeon indicated whether the sample was from a rich or a lean schedule by a peck to either the left or the right key. In previous work using this method, Commons (1979) found that on the average, pigeons matched probability of a choice, indicating which sample had occurred, to the relative expected payoff for making that choice. They did not maximize payoff by exclusively choosing the appropriate response alternative, as an ideal observer would. However, departures from ideal observer performance may depend on the temporal pattern of reinforcers within the sample. Samples could have reinforcement occurring during any of four sequentially presented 3-second cycles. Therefore, a single reinforcer might occur temporally just before choice or temporally remote from choice. A sample with a single reinforcer occurring right before choice produced more left-key peck choices (the peck indicating that the sample came from the rich schedule) than the sample with the single reinforcer 9 seconds earlier. Choices after samples when the time of reinforcement was either just before or remote did not follow the matching law, whereas the average decision across samples did. Similarly, a sample with a single omitted reinforcer (having three rather than four possible reinforcers) placed immediately before choice produced fewer left-key pecks than a sample with the single omitted reinforcer placed 9 seconds before choice. The change was less for the single missing reinforcer, suggesting that the presence of reinforcement was more salient than its absence.

These previous findings suggested that forgetting might account for the measured discriminability and perceived value of the samples from the two schedules, where forgetting is defined as a decrement in control by a prior event over a future choice as a function of time. The question now is, How might one conceive of a detection and scaling mechanism that is reasonably sensitive to average reinforcement density, but is sent awry by changes, due to forgetting, in the temporal distribution of events within a sample?

To analyze the detection and scaling process, the effect of changing the amount of time between reinforcement opportunities in a schedule sample and the length of the sample were studied in order to learn how decision rules and isosensitivity functions (see Nevin, Chapter 1 for definitions of these two terms) depend on forgetting within a sample in a density of reinforcement discrimination situation. Three experimental manipulations were used to answer these questions. In two of these, cycle length in the four-cycle sample was changed. In the third, the number of cycles was changed, while base (standard) cycle length was kept constant. Cycle length was changed in two ways—either to produce a change to a new cycle length for an extended number of sessions (stable) or to produce a momentary change on a small set of trials within a session (probe).

It is proposed that the determination of perceived density is at least a two-step process. First, summative trace decay theory (Wickelgren, 1974) should account for the relative contribution of each reinforcer within a schedule sample. Summative trace decay theory is modified here and is called the relative-time-weighted sum theory, suggesting that the value of each reinforcer is weighted by how it is discounted, how well it is remembered (Wickelgren, 1974), and that the weighted values are summed. It would predict that as cycle length is increased, whether in a stable or a temporary fashion, the perceived value contributed by each reinforcer should decrease. Second, a set of theories, here referred to as base rate or base time theory, suggests that steady versus momentary changes in cycle length have different effects on perceived density of a sample. One version suggests that a time base and time window are established and that perceived density of the sample reinforcement rate is found relative to those bases. For instance, doubling the cycle length on a probe trial halves the actual rate of reinforcement, which may cause the perceived density to be scaled as half its value on standard or base cycle length trials. This also would leave half the possible events occurring outside the base time window, thus lowering the perceived value further. The effects of adding more events by adding more cycles required explicit examination.

By increasing the number of cycles in a sample while keeping maximally obtainable discriminability constant and comparing the results to those obtained with an equivalently long schedule sample, it is possible to examine the relative contribution of these two sources of discounting information within the sample. First, discounting in the form of forgetting occurs because time between reinforcement opportunities increases and the corresponding number of unprogrammed events increases. Second, as the number of cycles presented within the stimuli to be discriminated increases, the information-processing capacity of the organism is taxed, interference results, and forgetting occurs (D'Amato, 1973; Grant and Roberts, 1973). In either case, both signal detection measures of discriminability and sensitivity (d') and measures of bias ($p(L)$) indicating that the rich schedule has been presented, should decrease, but for different reasons. In Experiment I the effect of changing cycle length is explored.

EXPERIMENT I: PROCEDURE

Birds were run in one 256-trial session per day. Trials consisted of a stimulus period followed by a choice period, as shown in Figure 3–1. The present task is similar to one in which the subject identifies whether a randomly chosen urn is the rich one that has three reinforcer balls and one nonreinforcer ball or whether the urn is the lean one that has one reinforcer ball and three nonreinforcer balls. On each trial there are four draws from that trial's urn. After a ball is drawn, it is put back into the urn. After the four draws from the urn presented on that trial, the subject indicates whether the sample came from the rich or the lean urn.

Here, the stimuli to be discriminated were rich, $p(S^{R+}|R_C) = 0.75$, and lean, $p(S^{R+}|R_C) = 0.25$, schedules for center-key pecks, R_C presented as modified T schedules (Commons, 1979; Schoenfeld and Cole, 1972; Schoenfeld, Cumming, and Hearst, 1956; Weissman, 1961). On each trial, a sample from one of the two T schedules was presented during the stimulus period. Each one of these sixteen sub-stimulus samples consisted of four equal duration cycles. On each cycle, a center-key peck was ($v_i = 1$) or was not ($v_i = 0$) reinforced. The cycles, c_i, were numbered so that $C1$ is the cycle at the end of the stimulus period and right before the choice period and $C4$ is at the beginning of the stimulus period and the furthest from the choice. An unlikely example of what might happen during a presentation of a 1110 substimulus sample is shown in the upper portion of Figure 3–1. As is shown, each cycle began with the illumination of

Figure 3−1. The top portion shows a state diagram for a sample from a 3-second cycle schedule. It illustrates what may happen if center-key pecks occur and do not occur when reinforcement has been programmed or not. It is for illustrative purposes only and would be very unusual because there is a cycle without a peck occurring in it. The bottom portion shows the contingencies during an entire trial. The stimulus period contains substimuli of the form shown in the top portion. The choice period immediately follows the stimulus period. There is no intertrial interval.

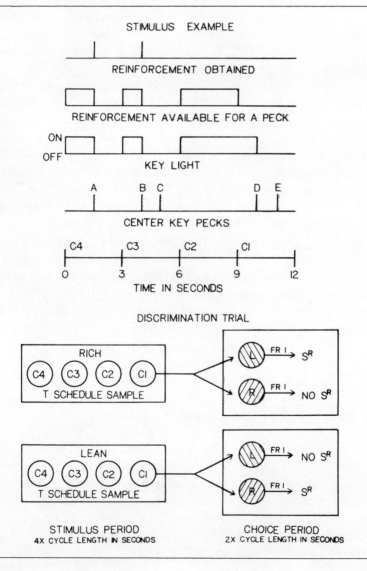

STIMULUS EXAMPLE

REINFORCEMENT OBTAINED

REINFORCEMENT AVAILABLE FOR A PECK

KEY LIGHT

CENTER KEY PECKS

TIME IN SECONDS

DISCRIMINATION TRIAL

STIMULUS PERIOD
4X CYCLE LENGTH IN SECONDS

CHOICE PERIOD
2X CYCLE LENGTH IN SECONDS

the center key. The first center-key peck darkened the key and was reinforced with the same probability as the rest of the cycles on that trial, $p(S^{R+}|R_C)$ being either 0.75 or 0.25. No other center-key pecks during that cycle were reinforced, although they occurred.

At the onset of the choice period the side keys were illuminated and the center key stayed dark or was darkened in those rare cases where no key peck occurred in the last cycle of the substimulus. The choice period duration was always twice the standard or base length cycle, as shown in the lower portion of Figure 3-1. The first side-key peck, whether correct or not, darkened both keys, and no further pecks were counted. If a substimulus sampled from the rich schedule had been presented on the center key, the first left-key peck was reinforced (a hit or left correct); a right was not reinforced (a miss or right error). If a substimulus from the lean schedule had been presented on the center key, the first right-key peck was reinforced (a correct rejection or right correct); a left was not reinforced (a false alarm or left error).

Three different standard cycle lengths were used—2 seconds, 3 seconds, and 4 seconds ($T = 2, 3, 4$). Each was run until the birds stabilized. In daily sessions the standard (base) cycle length was of standard length (i.e., T multiplied by 1) on 224 trials, doubled (T multiplied by 2) on 16 probe trials, or tripled (T multiplied by 3) on another 16 probe trials. The position of the probe trials within a session was randomly distributed. The frequency of the occurrence of the possible substimuli for standard and probe trials is shown in the left panel of Figure 3-2. The modal density of the rich schedule is 3; the modal density of the lean schedule is 1.

Stimulus Description

There are four levels of description of the stimuli.

1. On a "macro" level, each probabilistic reinforcement schedule, either the rich ($p = 0.75$) or the lean ($p = 0.25$), is viewed as a single "substimulus," here called S_{rich} and S_{lean}, respectively; sampling considerations are of no concern. These stimuli are equivalent to cued random interval (RI) or variable interval (VI) schedules with a T–second limited hold and average intervals equal to $4/3\,T$ seconds and $4\,T$ seconds.

Figure 3–2. The distribution of reinforcement for the first center-key peck $(S^{R+}|R_C)$ for four- (the left panel) and six-cycle substimuli (the right panel) are shown. The number of center-key pecks and proportion of trials on which reinforcement occurs in a sample is shown for the rich (positive slope hatching) and lean (negative slope hatching) schedules. The respective $p(S^{R+}|R_C)$ are 0.75 and 0.25 for the four-cycle substimuli and 0.767 and 0.233 for the six-cycle substimuli.

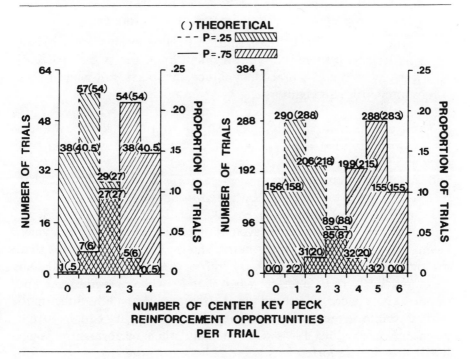

2. At the "molar" level, all substimulus samples with the same number of reinforcements are viewed as the same "stimulus." Each substimulus, S_n, has a reinforcement density, $D(S_n)$, equal to N_d, the number of center-key peck reinforcement opportunities over the four cycles in the substimulus. Density, the defining characteristic of a stimulus at this level of analysis, ranges from zero to four reinforcers per substimulus, giving rise to five such "stimuli," designated S_{N_d}. This level of analysis distinguishes between the number of reinforcements within a sample stimulus but not between the particular T-second cycles within that $4T$-second stimulus period on which those reinforcements are programmed.

3. At the "molecular" level, the definition of a "stimulus" involves the pattern of reinforcement in a substimulus. Each substimulus is represented as a four-digit binary number. A number such as 0001 indicates a sample with three cycles without reinforcement opportunities followed by one cycle with an opportunity. The substimuli, S_n, are numbered from 0000 to 1111. The leftmost digit represents the cycle furthest in time from choice, and the rightmost represents the cycle immediately before choice.

4. At the "micro" level, the definition of a "stimulus" depends on whether or not there is a reinforcement opportunity on a particular cycle, T-seconds preceding choice, irrespective of what is programmed for its neighbors.

There are sixteen possible combinations in a 4-cycle substimulus. The probability that a particular set of four events will occur was obtained by expanding the binomial $(p+q)^4$ with $p = 0.75$ or 0.25 and $q = 1 - p$. Actual presentation frequencies deviated somewhat from the expected frequencies because of sampling.

A molecular substimulus, even 0000 or 1111, could occur with either schedule stimulus. However, the greater the number of cycles having a reinforcement opportunity, the greater the likelihood that the rich schedule was in effect. Therefore the lean (or rich) schedule was more likely to be in effect when 0 or 1 (or 3 or 4) reinforcement opportunities were presented on a trial (respectively). Substimuli with 2 reinforcement opportunities occurred about equally often given either schedule. Birds were run until their performances stabilized. The data reported here were collected in the five sessions following stabilization.

Results

The results of the present study encompass several levels of description along two stimulus dimensions, one reflecting the number and distribution of reinforcers in a sample substimulus and the other, cycle length, which determines the temporal distance of reinforcers to choice. For the reinforcement dimension, at the macro level, the sensitivity of the birds to the difference between two different reinforcement distributions will be described for the nine possible combinations of cycle lengths. At the molar, molecular, and micro levels, the decision rules, which describe the relationships between choice and particular substimulus parameters such as number of reinforcements in a substimulus and their relative distance from the choice point, can be studied in such a way as to explain the birds' sensitivity to and perceived value of the substimulus.

For the second dimension, cycle length, two operations were used to generate the temporal distance of a reinforcer in a given substimulus from choice. Each can be used to examine the effects of cycle length on perceived value. One operation established one of three standard or base cycle lengths over a large number of sessions (stable change). The second operation either doubled or tripled the standard cycle length on probe trials (momentary change). Presentation of results will proceed from most aggregated to least aggregated, along both dimensions. Sensitivity will be discussed before perceived density, although the former may depend on the latter.

First, the effects of lengthening cycles on d' and $p(L)$ are examined at the macro level. The leftmost panels in Figure 3–3 show the p (Hit) and p (False Alarm) coordinates for each value of overall cycle length, irrespective of how the cycle length was obtained (i.e., from a standard or a probe trial). These are superimposed on receiver-operating-characteristic (ROC) curves, which were calculated for a number of levels of sensitivity, according to the continuous binomial method detailed in Commons (1979). There are two values associated with each point. These are d', which reflects sensitivity to the difference between the density of the rich and lean stimuli, and $p(L)$, the probability of a left-key peck, which is the tendency to indicate that the substimulus came from the rich schedule. The value, $p(L)$, is a measure of perceived reinforcement density (bias). From an examination of the position of the points relative to the ROC curves for sensitivity and to the negative diagonal for bias, one can see the effects of increasing cycle length or of the number of cycles on sensitivity and perceived value.

Both d' and $p(L)$ decreased as cycle length increased. The decrease in d' was indicated by the points falling nearer the positive diagonal, the isosensitivity curve that reflects no sensitivity. The decrease in perceived density was indicated by points falling closer to the x axis and farther from the negative diagonal. On probe trials, both sensitivity and perceived density should decrease together, because assigning a lower density to a sample than it has decreases the hit rate (see Nevin, Chapter 1, for a definition) without decreasing the false alarm rate.

Figure 3–3. Column 1.: Isosensitivity curves for four birds (top four panels) discriminating four-cycle samples and three birds discriminating six-cycle samples (bottom panels) are shown. The probability of a hit, p (Hit), is equal to the number of correct left-key pecks divided by the number of possible correct left-key pecks. The probability of a false alarm, p (False Alarm), is equal to the number of incorrect left-key pecks divided by the number of possible correct right-key pecks. The solid lines show isosensitivity curves for eight values of d', a measure of sensitivity. The top curve would be obtained if the subject followed an ideal decision rule derived from the continuous binomial distributions in Figure 3-2. The closer points fall to the 0,0 corner the smaller the perceived density of the substimulus. Throughout the rest of the figures a common symbol code is used. Circles, triangles, and squares represent 2-, 3-, and 4-second base (standard) cycle length. The open, half-filled, and completely filled symbols represent trials with standard cycle length (open) and probe trials obtained by doubling (half-filled) and tripling (completely filled) standard cycle lengths. The second, third, and fourth columns plot d', a sensitivity measure found from the inverse to the normal probability distribution as an approximation to the binominal. Column 2 shows d' versus cycle length irrespective of how obtained; whereas Column 3 shows d' as a function of the base, doubling of base, and tripling of base cycle length on probe trials; and Column 4, as a function of base cycle length. Best fit lines indicate the other parameter.

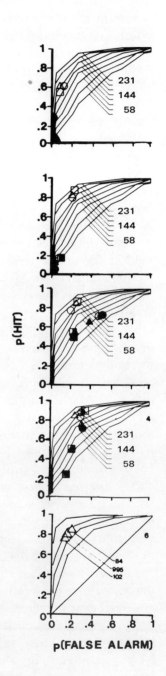

p(FALSE ALARM)

Figure 3-6. continued

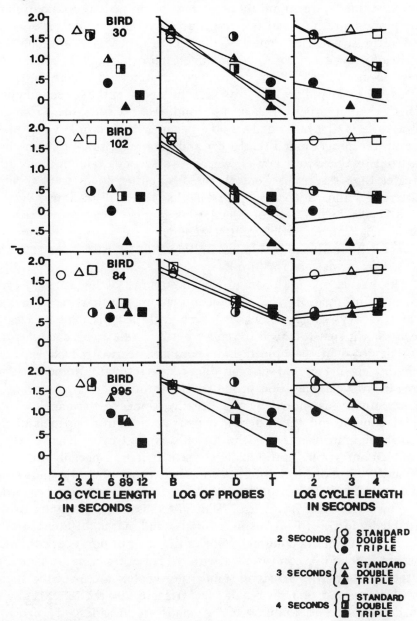

The general decrease in d' as a function of increasing cycle length is more clearly seen in the second column of panels in Figure 3–3. The d' values were found by assuming the normal approximation to the binomial rather than the continuous binomial model reported in the leftmost panel of Figure 3–3. Here, the sensitivity, d', is plotted against log cycle length, the time dimension being logged to make the relation more linear. Bias is examined separately in Figure 3–4. For Birds 30, 102, and 995, d' was slightly higher at the 3-second cycle length than at either the 2- or 4-second base cycle lengths. From our observations, the birds had trouble pecking the center key and picking up the programmed reinforcer and then repositioning themselves in front of the center key all within two seconds. The cycle lengths greater than 4 seconds were obtained by either doubling or tripling different standard (base) cycle lengths. When disregarding how a given cycle length was obtained, this graph clearly shows that as cycle length increased beyond 4 seconds, there were large decreases in d' for Birds 30 and 995, a less uniform but large drop for 102, and no consistent pattern for Bird 84.

The panels in the third and fourth columns of Figure 3–3 segregate the information from the second column so that the effects of the two ways of producing different cycle lengths may be clearly seen. Sensitivity to the differences between the two schedules did not decrease in a simple fashion because the two mechanisms for lengthening cycles did not produce equal effects. Momentary increases in cycle length on probe trials produced the largest decrease in sensitivity, as shown by the negative slopes in the panels of the third column and the different heights of lines in the panels of the fourth column. Generally, the longer standard cycle lengths, when doubled and tripled, produce lower sensitivities, especially for Birds 30 and 995, indicating an interaction between probe ratio and standard cycle length. This can be seen by the generally descending order of sensitivity from the logged standard (base) cycle lengths to the doubled and tripled probes in column 3 and by the difference in the slope of the lines in column 4. One critical pair of points in column 4 occurs for the 6-second cycle length, because it can be obtained by either doubling the 3-second standard or tripling the 2-second standard. The former point is a half-filled triangle, and the latter is a fully shaded circle. The doubling of 3 seconds produces less of a sensitivity loss than the tripling of 2 seconds.

The leftmost panel of Figure 3-4 replots the perceived value (bias) of the stimuli as a function of cycle length. This information was previously shown in the leftmost panel of Figure 3-3, but in Figure 3-4 it is plotted separately from sensitivity. Calling bias, which is produced by a stimulus, perceived density can be justified as follows: If $p(L)$, the tendency to indicate that a sample came from the rich schedule, equals 1, when a sample from the rich schedule has been presented, then the bird has responded correctly and is reinforced. If $p(L)$ equals 0 when a sample from the lean schedule has been presented, again the bird has responded correctly and is reinforced. Hence, the value of $p(L)$ indicates the perceived density of a schedule sample. The tendency to say that the sample came from the rich schedule, $p(L)$, was transformed into the corresponding z value by the probit, or inverse probability, transformation in order to produce more linear functions. The resulting quantity, $z_{p(L)}$, is the perceived density of a schedule sample. The $z_{p(L)}$ was plotted against the log of cycle duration. The first panels show the effect of cycle length at the macro level. The perceived value of a substimulus generally rose or stayed nearly the same as cycle length increased from 2 seconds to 3, either decreased or stayed the same for cycle length from 3 to 4 seconds, and decreased in a not entirely linear fashion for cycle length above 4 seconds.

At the molar level, the perceived value of substimuli with one reinforcer is shown in the middle panels and that of substimuli with three reinforcers in the rightmost panels. While performance characterized at the macro level reflected the birds' scaling of the perceived value of all the substimuli together, the molar level analysis focuses on their responses to substimuli with the same reinforcement densities. The perceived values changed in a reasonable fashion for substimuli with one reinforcer or one missing reinforcer. The panels in the middle and right columns of Figure 3-4 indicate that most of the birds show maximum perceived value at around 4 to 6 seconds. There was no consistent change in perceived value as a function of standard cycle length alone. However, when combined with doubling and tripling on probe trials, there is generally a decrease in perceived value as a function of overall cycle length (i.e., the half-filled and filled points generally fall below the unfilled points). The form of the function is not due to different density substimuli being treated differently, as can be seen from the similarity of patterns in the panels in columns 2 and 3, whereas the height of the function is.

Figure 3−4. Perceived density, $z_{p(L)}$, plotted against cycle length in log seconds. The left-hand column shows the effect of cycle length on the perceived density of all substimuli considered together. This is the macro level relation. At the molar level, Columns 2 and 3 show the relation between perceived density and cycle length for substimuli with one reinforcer and substimuli with three reinforcers (one missing reinforcer).

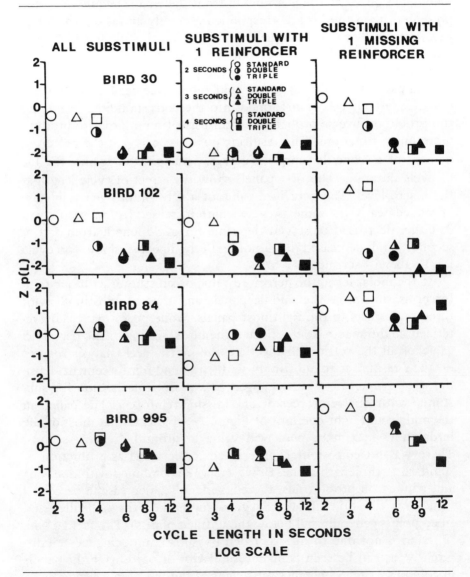

In the following account of the foregoing performance at both the macro and the molar level, it is predicted that perceived density (the inverse probability transform of the probability of a left-key peck) is a linear function of actual density. First, because of the way that substimuli are distributed between the rich and lean schedules (Commons, 1979), the relative expected payoff, Rel $EP(L|S_{N_d})$, was an ogival function of reinforcement density. The relative expected payoff for a left-key peck at a given density substimulus, $D(S_{N_d}) = N_d$, is just the probability of a left-key peck being correct, LC, at that density, N_d, when amount of reinforcement for each correct choice is equal.

$$\text{Rel } EP(L|S_{N_d}) = \frac{p(LC|S_{N_d})}{p(LC|S_{N_d}) + p(RC|S_{N_d})} ,$$

$$\text{but } p(RC|S_{N_d}) = 1 - p(LC|S_{N_d})$$

$$= \frac{p(LC|S_{N_d})}{p(LC|S_{N_d}) + (1 - p(LC|S_{N_d})}$$

$$= p(LC|S_{N_d})$$

The counterpart of Rel $EP(L|S_{N_d})$ or $p(LC|S_{N_d})$ in free operant schedules is programmed reinforcement rate. This fact will be used to suggest that the mechanism that gives rise to the matching result will generalize to the more usual free operant schedules.

Second, applying a probit transformation (the inverse of the standard normal cumulative distribution function) to the function that relates relative expected payoff to density turns it into a straight line with slope 1.084, intercept –2.110, and an $r^2 = .996$; $z_{p(LC|S_{N_d})} =$ –2.1 $(1 - N_d/2)$. This linearity results from the goodness of the normal approximation to the binomial, which was used to generate the stimuli. In Figure 3–5, the independent variable can be expressed in two ways—actual reinforcement density of the substimulus or probability transform of relative expected payoff for indicating that a substimulus had high density. If perceived density is a linear function of actual density, it is also a linear function of relative expected payoff in z form and vice versa. As a consequence, the matching relation

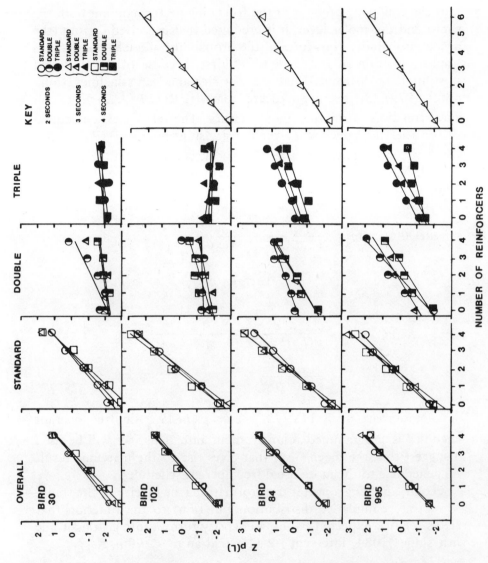

Figure 3–5. Perceived density, $z_{p(L)}$, shown as a function of actual density (the number of reinforcers in a substimulus). This molar relation is shown for all trials together (Column 1), for trials with standard cycle length (Column 2), for probe trials where the standard length was doubled (Column 3) and tripled (Column 4), and for six cycles at standard length (Column 5).

holds (i.e., perceived density is equal to the probit transform of relative expected payoff) if perceived density is found to be a linear function of actual density. Since matching was found to hold for similar substimuli, but without probe trials being included in the sessions (Commons, 1979), it would be predicted to hold here.

Figure 3–5 shows that matching at the molar level holds when the entire session is considered. The relations shown within the figure rejected a number of ways that pigeons might scale reinforcement density in samples, while supporting others. The decision rules for each bird at the molar level are graphed with respect to different parameters. The decision rule examined here is the psychophysical relation between the perceived reinforcement density, $z_{p(L)}$, and the actual reinforcement density—with cycle length, obtained by two different manipulations, being the parameter. The leftmost column of panels in Figure 3–5 shows the molar relation between the perceived density, $z_{\text{average } p(L|S_n, D(S_n) = N_d)}$, and actual substimulus density, N_d, for three different cycle lengths for the combination of probe and standard trials. The parameter is cycle length. The points were well described by the regression lines fit by the median method (Mosteller and Tukey, 1977), with the r^2 values ranging from .98 to .99, as shown in Table 3–1.

That the birds linearly scale reinforcement density in the schedule samples of the duration studied here implies that the matching law holds at the molar level, since linear density scaling implies matching, as discussed above. The matching law and linear density scaling were further supported by a number of related facts. In z form, the mean perceived density was 0 for the mean actual density of 2 (density 2 substimuli), as it should have been: This means that these substimuli were seen as coming equally from either distribution. The perceived values were symmetrically distributed about 0 with perceived density ranging from a value of −2.2 for density 0 substimuli to +2.2 for density 4 substimuli.

For the standard cycle lengths alone in Figure 3–5, functions relating perceived density to number of reinforcers were steeper than those for the combined trials. This suggests if matching is fundamental, then the birds compensate for the inclusion of decrement-producing probe trials by overvaluing substimuli on standard trials. The r^2 values for the best fit lines range from .98 to .99.

One can see how density was scaled by examining the role played by two ways of lengthening cycles in producing the decrement in

Table 3–1. Decision Rules at the Molar Level.

	Slope $Z\,P(L)$/Density ($Z\,EP(L)$/Density)	Intercept $Z\,P(L)$	R^2	Ratio of Slopes of Standard Cycle Length to Given Slopes	Model I Predicted Ratios of Slopes	
Predicted by matching	(1.084)	−2.11	.992			
Overall 2 sec	0.919	−1.941	.984	1.464		
3 sec	0.979	−2.04	.972	1.230		
4 sec	0.953	−1.917	.975	1.282		
Standard 2 sec	1.054	−2.16	.992	1.000	1	
3 sec	1.204	−2.37	.993	1.000	1	
4 sec	1.222	−2.22	.993	1.000	1	
Double 2 sec	0.485	−1.462	.556	2.17	2	standard/ double
3 sec	0.421	−1.735	.457	2.86	2	
4 sec	0.451	−1.741	.659	2.71	2	
Triple 2 sec	0.234	−1.286	.106	4.50	3	standard/ triple
3 sec	0.226	−1.402	.155	5.34	3	
4 sec	0.112	−1.557	.087	10.91	3	
Six cycle standard 3 sec	0.690	−2.21	.976			

sensitivity. Again, the two ways were to change cycle length on selected probe trials by doubling or tripling the standard cycle length or to change the standard cycle length over an extended period of time. Any model that suggests that the birds responded simply on the basis of number of reinforcers, independently of context or time, must predict that momentary changes in cycle length should have no effect on perceived value. Any model that proposes that the birds responded on the basis of the relative time between reinforcers or rate of reinforcement must predict that perceived value should be inversely proportional to momentary cycle length. If the standard cycle is doubled on a series of trials, the perceived value should be halved. Likewise, the ratio of the slopes of functions relating perceived density to actual density should be halved. A third alternative is that the birds perceived something like a weighted average rate or weighted average time between reinforcers. This model should include a term for the interaction between standard cycle length and ratio of probe length to standard.

How well these various models are supported by the data is seen in all the panels in columns 3 and 4 of Figure 3-5. The perceived sub-stimulus density decreased more with the insertion of probes than with increases in standard cycle length, as is shown by the flattening of the slopes for doubles and triples. The probes caused even greater decrements as the standard cycle length increased.

Any model that depends on number of reinforcers alone is rejected by the fact that there were changes in slope with increased cycle lengths, indicating that time was indeed important. The standard cycle slopes were 1.0, 1.2, and 1.2 at 2, 3, and 4 seconds, respectively; doubling slopes were .49, .42, and .41 (clearly lower); and the tripling slopes were lower still—.24, .21, and .15 (as shown in Table 3-1).

Doubling and tripling standard cycle lengths decreased the perceived density more than predicted by time- or rate-averaging models. The ratio of the slopes, double to standard and triple to standard, would be 2:1 and 3:1, respectively, if the weighted average rate or weighted average time model were true in its simplest form. As shown in Table 3-1, the ratios of the slopes for the average of the four birds are 2.0, 2.9, and 2.9 for 2-, 3-, and 4-second cycle lengths for doubling and 4.2, 5.7, and 8.0 for tripling. There may be an interaction between standard cycle length and probe value: At least for Birds 84 and 995, tripling the 4-second standard had a larger dec-

Figure 3–6. Perceived density (or its negative), $z_{p(L)}$ or $-z_{p(L)}$, shown as a function of the log of the ratio of the number of cycles before choice of either the cycle with the single reinforcer or the one missing reinforcers. For substimuli with one reinforcer, the top row shows this as a function of the various cycle lengths. The second row shows this for standard trials and probe trials on which standard cycle lengths were doubled and tripled. The bottom two rows show this relation for substimuli with one missing reinforcer (three reinforcers). The y axis is inverted for the bottom two rows so that a direct comparison may be made between the top two rows and the bottom two rows, with row 1 and 3 corresponding and row 2 and 4 corresponding.

remental effect on the slope than tripling the 2-second standard. While these slope changes are in the right direction, they clearly deviate from ratios predicted by time or rate averaging, especially as standard cycle length increases. This is not surprising. The birds do not compensate for the fact that the probe substimuli start much earlier than the standard. The decrement in perceived density is greater than would be the case if those earlier events in the substimuli were not there.

If average reinforcement rate determined perceived density, reinforcers occurring more cycles away from choice would not be weighted less. However, as weights decrease farther from choice, two versions of weighting have to be considered—one that hypothesizes exponential decay (i.e., relative time alone is important) and a second that hypothesizes a limited event window or short-term working memory (i.e., number of intervening events is important).

To see whether this decrease occurs, the effect of a single reinforcer (or single missing reinforcer) occurring farther from choice is examined at the molecular level. Averages of four birds' perceived density are shown in Figure 3–6 as a function of how far the choice is from either a single reinforcement opportunity or a single missing reinforcement opportunity, both here called critical events. Averages of the four birds' performances were used because, at least for the probes that doubled and tripled standard cycle length for each particular substimulus, the frequencies of those substimuli were small, resulting in noise. The data for substimuli with one reinforcer are shown in the top two rows of panels of Figure 3–6, and those for one missing reinforcer in the bottom two rows. A point in Figure 3–6 at density 1 is the average across birds for density 1 substimuli of the same cycle length. Likewise, a point at density 3 is an average

(Figure 3–6)

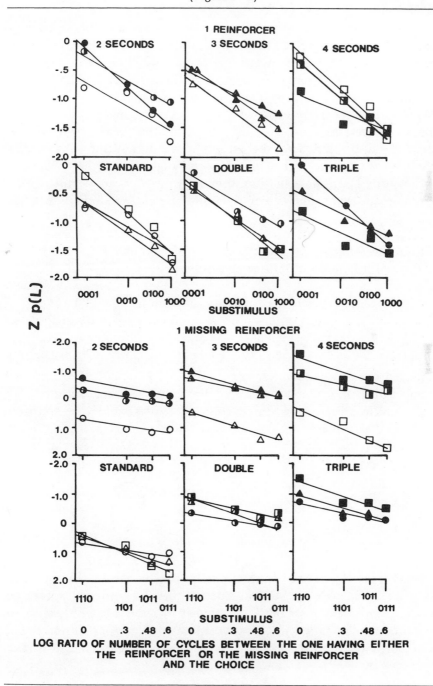

across birds of density 3 (one missing reinforcer) substimuli of the same length.

The data are again graphed in two ways. The standard cycle length parameters are graphed as circle (2 seconds), triangle (3 seconds), and square (4 seconds). How much a particular symbol is filled depends on whether it represents a standard (unfilled), doubled (half-filled), or tripled (completely filled) cycle. Some general properties emerge. There is a larger decrement for one reinforcer than for the one missing reinforcer, as shown by the slopes for the former being greater than for the latter. This suggests that the diminution of control is greater for an event rather than for a missing event. Other effects are not as orderly, perhaps because some of the events are occurring very far from choice in time, and $z_{p(L)}$ values are close to either -2 or $+2$.

A Micro–Molecular Model that Accounts for Perceived Density of a Substimulus

I suggest that perceived density of a substimulus, $D^*(S_n) = z^*_{p(L|S_n)}$, is the sum of the weighted values of reinforcers that occurred in the substimulus. On each cycle, c_i, a reinforcer in a substimulus may occur ($v_i = 1$) or not occur ($v_i = 0$). Cycle number, c_i or i alone, is counted backwards from choice and has values 1, 2, 3, 4, the value 1 being right before choice and at the end of the stimulus period.

A multiple regression was performed to determine the contribution of a reinforcer on a given cycle. Remember that a substimulus has four such cycles, so that there are four coefficients, a_i for v_i, and a constant, a_0, to be estimated for this molecular model.

$$D^*(S_n) = z^*_{p(L|S_n)} = a_0 + a_1 v_1 + a_2 v_2 + a_3 v_3 + a_4 v_4$$

$$= a_0 + \sum_{i=1}^{4} a_i v_i$$

The weights, a_i, represent the contribution of a reinforcer on a respective cycle, c_i. For substimulus, $S_0 = 0000$, all the v_is are 0, so that a_0 represents the perceived density of a substimulus with no reinforcers. The independent variable was v_i, whether or not a reinforcement opportunity occurred on a given cycle number; the perceived value of each of the sixteen substimuli at 2-second standard cycle length was the dependent variable. As shown in the second column of Figure 3-5, the other functions were almost identical, so only the analysis of the 2-second data is reported. This analysis of all four birds together yielded a molecular model with five estimated parameters, a_0 through a_4, -2.16, 1.40, 1.168, 0.900, and 0.7125, and a multiple r of .91. For individual birds the coefficients were slightly different, and r values were slightly higher ranging from .96 to .99, since variability between individuals was eliminated. Since linear regression depends on the predictor variables being additive, the fact that so much of the variance was accounted for suggests that substimulus density is the sum across the i cycles of the contribution of events on each of the ith cycles. This finding is consistent with Wickelgren's (1974) assumption that the contribution of multiple occurrence of the events to be remembered is additive.

The heart of the matter is to see if Wickelgren's (1974) suggested exponential equation, which represents forgetting, accounts in a more specific fashion for the contribution of the programmed events on a given cycle. While the previous multiple regression reduced the number of parameters necessary to describe the data and showed additivity, using an exponential model should allow a more compact description. The coefficients, a_i, for each cycle were previously the parameters to be estimated. Since the micro model suggested that each term was exponential, the parameters, a_i, now become the dependent variables, and the independent variables, c_i, were used in the expression $a_i e^{b_i c_i}$ to predict them. The values of $a = 1.793$ and $b = -0.229$ so found yielded a correlation between cycle number away from choice and log cycle number weight (from the previous regression) of -0.9975, $r^2 = .995$. Hence, the model's coefficients predicted perceived value as well as the multiple regression and yet had only three parameters for sixteen substimuli. To further test this model of what happens on a given cycle (micromodel), the predicted coefficients were entered into the multiple regression as multipliers of v_i. If the micro model worked well, the multiple r value should be the same as the molecular, in which the coefficients were directly obtained as a best fit ($r = .912$), and the coefficients should be very close to 1. The residuals should not be correlated with cycle number. The obtained r for this procedure was .912; the coefficients were 0.98, 1.03, 1.00, and 0.99; the constant was -0.216; and the residuals were uncorrelated. The combined micro–molecular model equation for the perceived density of a substimulus is:

$$D^*(S_n) = z^*_{p(L|S_n)} = -2.16 + \sum_{i=1}^{4} v_{c_i} 1.8e^{-.229c_i}$$

This finding on the form of the decay function is similar to Wickelgren's (1974) in that for the short term, events lose impact as a function of the negative exponential of time, $a_i e^{b_i T_i}$. Some comparisons of the present model for pigeons with his model for adult humans should be made. Here, it was the number of cycles before choice (the relative temporal distance away from choice, c_i) on which each reinforcement and non-reinforcement opportunity fell that accounted for the decay, instead of time away from choice, T_i. The latter had no effect on perceived density, as shown for standard length cycles in column 2 of Figure 3–5. Here, because it was how many cycles before a choice that mattered and not simply time before choice, a pure timing or temporal decay interpretation is unwarranted. Each cycle may act like an event. Knowing how many cycles before choice a given event fell tells us how many intervening events there are. Whether or not the form of the decay function is due to interference of intervening events or simply to the passage of time was not answered by Wickelgren. The fact that number of events to be processed may be the critical variable suggests an examination of the effects of number of cycles on perceived density and sensitivity, the next experiment to be described.

EXPERIMENT II: SIX 3–SECOND CYCLE SAMPLES

Method and Procedure

The subjects and apparatus for this experiment were identical to those described in Experiment I, except that one less subject was used. The discrimination task was similar to that used in Experiment I, except that the number of cycles was increased from four to six. The stimulus on each trial, then was one of 64 substimuli (of six equal duration cycles) randomly selected from one of two T schedules. The two schedules to be discriminated were, again, two

overlapping distributions (stimuli) of reinforcement opportunities—
one with $p(S^{R+}|R_C) = 0.767$ (the rich schedule) and one with
$p(S^{R+}|R_C) = 0.233$ (the lean schedule). These probabilities were
chosen so that the ideal observer's discriminability, d', based upon
the overlap of the discrete binomial distribution, was the same as in
the four-cycle case. The rich and lean binomial frequency distributions are shown in Figure 3-3.

Results

The d' values reported in this section were found by assuming a continuous binomial model and were then compared to the d' values
calculated in the same manner for the same birds in the four-cycle
case. These d' values differed slightly from those obtained with the
normal approximation to the binomial reported everywhere else in
this chapter.

The d' values shown in Table 3-2 were lower for the six 3-second
cycle sample discrimination than for the four 3-second cycle sample
discrimination, whether the values were found by assuming a continuous binomial or a normal approximation to the binomial. The discrimination efficiency, e, was much lower for the six 3-second cycle
sample (18-second long sample) than for the stimuli with four 4-sec-
ond cycles (16-second long sample). Here, e is the ratio of obtained
d' to maximum possible d'. This supports the notion that there is
much more of a problem with processing more programmed events
than with processing extraneous events occurring over time, such as
the house light, which was off, or the hopper light, which was on.

The slopes of the six-cycle decision lines were not as steep as
the four-cycle ones. The addition of two extra events to the four-
cycle samples decreased sensitivity and altered the decision rules
more than might be expected if maximizing one alternative as soon
as it became more favorable held instead of matching. If a maximizing account were closer to the truth, the birds might have treated
both a density 0 and 1 substimulus the same as a density 0 substimulus and a density 5 and 6 substimulus the same as a density 5 one,
thereby maintaining the slope. The fact that they did not shows that
their decision rules are not based on a simple strategy such as counting number of reinforcers or discriminating simple rates of reinforcement. Instead, they showed the same pattern of anchoring the end

Table 3–2. A Comparison of Obtained Sensitivity to Maximally Possible Sensitivity.

Bird	Six 3-second Cycles			Four 3-second Cycles			Four 4-second Cycles		
	Obtained d'	Maximal d'	$(E)^a$	Obtained d'	Maximal d'	(E)	Obtained d'	Maximal d'	(E)
102	1.78	2.99	.60	2.0	2.19	.91	2.17	1.19	.99
84	1.83	2.99	.61	1.8	2.19	.82	1.8	2.19	.82
995	1.70	2.99	.57	1.9	2.19	.87	1.7	2.19	.77

a. (E) = efficiency.

points of the density distribution to the same extreme perceived values—$p(L) = 0$ for density 0 substimuli and $p(L) = 1$ for density 6 substimuli. These are the same as the perceived values found for the four-cycle case. Also, their performance is necessarily limited by the discriminability of the densities since they discriminated the same densities better in the four-cycle case. They seem to scale density in both cases in a linear fashion, matching perceived density to relative expected payoff for indicating that density.

MATCHING AT THE MACRO AND MOLAR LEVEL IS A CONSEQUENCE OF ADDITIVITY AT THE MOLECULAR LEVEL

In this next section, matching will be shown to be derivable from the present micro–molecular model. While the matching law derived here is for the scaling of reinforcement density, Commons and Ducheny (1981) show that a similar model works for a preference situation that reflects response strength. To show how the matching relationship is determined at the micro–molecular level for the scaled density, the terms in the model are put in a form closely akin to traditional matching language. Here a matching relation is between relative response probability (probability and rate are similar measures) and relative payoff for the response indicating the higher density. Relative response probability is just response probability, since $p(L) + p(R) = 1$, making $p(L)/(p(L) + p(R)) = p(L)$. Relative response probability is then just perceived density. The micro–molecular model showed that each reinforcer makes an equal contribution to relative perceived density when it is exponentially weighted by the decrement in control. The aggregated effect of the total number of reinforcers in a substimulus is the simple sum of the effects of each single reinforcer.

The fact that perceived substimulus density was shown to be the sum of the contributions of each reinforcer on the cycle in which it occurred implies that perceived density is matched to the payoff for indicating the higher density. The proof involves two steps— how molar level substimuli are defined and how linearity implies matching. The contribution of a reinforcer was shown to be an exponentially decaying function of how far the cycle precedes choice.

Perceived reinforcement density at the molar level is for an entire set of substimuli with the same number of reinforcement opportunities. Each reinforcer that contributed to the density of the group was equally likely to fall in any one cycle. Since for each individual substimulus, the effects of a reinforcer on perceived density add, the number of reinforcers occurring in the molar level substimulus class would be additive.

In the derivation of matching at the molar level from the molecular model, the perceived density, $D''(S_{N_d})$, of the molar substimulus, S_{N_d}, is defined in a slightly different manner than previously. Here the perceived density is the average of the perceived density of each same density substimulus, $z_{p(L|S_n)}$, already in z form, rather than the z transform of the average $p(L)$s. The matching relation for this perceived value and payoff for the 2-second standard data is just as good; the r^2s were all greater than .98 and equal two places beyond the decimal point.

Some of the properties that make this derivation possible depend on empirical properties embedded in the molecular model—specifically, the symmetrical dispersion of $D^*(0000)$ and $D^*(1111)$ around 0. This allows the value of the Σa_i, the sum of the contributions of each reinforcer, to be found in terms of a_0, the perceived value of (0000).

The following molecular model is assumed to be true:

$$D^*(S_n) = z^*_{p(L|S_n)} = a_0 + \sum_{i=1}^{4} v_i a_i$$

Because the value of the contributions of a reinforcer on a given cycle, Σa_i, will be needed later, it is found next.

$$\text{The value } D^*(0000) = a_0 + \sum_{i=1}^{4} 0 \cdot a_i = a_0 = -2.16$$

$$\text{and the value } D^*(1111) = a_0 + \sum_{i=1}^{4} 1 \cdot a_i = a_0 + \sum_{i=1}^{4} a_i$$

$$= 2.03 \approx 2.16$$

Then, by solving the equations simultaneously:

$$\sum_{i=1}^{4} a_i = -2a_0$$

The next part of the derivation shows how many a_is appear in each molar substimulus, S_{N_d}. It is necessary to know how many substimuli of the same density there are in each molar substimulus. The cardinality of S_{N_d} is just the combinations of 4 cycles taken N_d at a time:

$$CS_{N_d} = C\left\{S_n | D(S_n) = N_d\right\} = \binom{4}{N_d} = \frac{4!}{N_d!\,(4-N_d)!} \quad \text{Then}$$

$$D^*(S_{N_d}) = \frac{1}{\binom{4}{N_d}} \sum_{S_n \in S_{N_d}} D(S_n)$$

$$= \frac{1}{\binom{4}{N_d}} \sum_{S_n \in S_{N_d}} \left(a_0 + \sum_{i=1}^{4} a_i v_i\right)$$

To expand this expression, the appropriate number of 1s and 0s have to be put in for v_i for each of the substimuli of a given density. The number of reinforcers ($v_i = 1$) per substimulus is N_d; the number of distinct substimuli, S_n, in the class of same density substimuli, S_{N_d}, is $\binom{4}{N_d}$. Therefore, a total of $N_d\binom{4}{N_d}$ terms with $v_i = 1$ occur in the sum. Each of the four cycles contains a reinforcer for an equal fraction of the time, so the total number of times each a_i is multiplied by a $v_i = 1$ is $\frac{1}{4}N_d\binom{4}{N_d}$. Hence:

$$D^*(S_{N_d}) = \frac{1}{\binom{4}{N_d}} \sum_{S_n \in S_{N_d}} \left(a_0 + \sum_{i=1}^{4} a_i v_i\right)$$

$$= \frac{1}{\binom{4}{N_d}} \sum_{S_n \in S_{N_d}} a_0 + \frac{1}{\binom{4}{N_d}} \sum_{S_n \in S_{N_d}} \sum_{i=1}^{4} a_i v_i$$

$$= \frac{\binom{4}{N_d}}{\binom{4}{N_d}} a_0 + \frac{N_d}{4} \frac{\binom{4}{N_d}}{\binom{4}{N_d}} \sum_{i=1}^{4} a_i$$

$$= a_0 + \frac{N_d}{4} \sum_{i=1}^{4} a_i$$

$$\text{but } \sum_{i=1}^{4} a_i \approx -2a_0$$

Therefore,

$$= a_0 - \frac{N_d}{2} a_0 = a_0 \left(1 - \frac{N_d}{2}\right) = D^* (S_{N_d})$$

This last expression is the same for the relative payoff probability shown earlier, so the derivation is complete.

WHY HIGHER LEVEL MODELS FAIL

Schedule samples have a number of characteristics. At the macro level, they may differ in overall density. While much may be learned from an examination of the relationship between gross density and response rate or choice, what is controlling about schedules and how that control is exerted may lie at a number of lower levels. First, one would expect the most orderliness at the level that the contingencies constrain the most and at the level where the mechanisms embedded within the contingencies work. Here this took place at the molecular and micro levels. The macro level performance simply reflects the accumulation of all the values from the micro, molecular, and molar levels.

There have been three demonstrations that, in a density discrimination situation, birds match their choices to relative expected payoff for making these choices. In the first (Commons, 1979), relative expected payoff was shown to encompass the effects produced by varying the amount of reinforcement for a correct discrimination of density. Matching was obtained to relative expected payoff for an aggregation of standard and probe trials, with changes in perceived value at the standard lengths compensating for the changes at probe lengths. Matching was also obtained when the number of cycles was increased with the discriminability between schedules held close to constant.

There are a number of implications that follow from matching having been obtained. For the small range investigated here of 0 to 4 and 0 to 6 reinforcers, perceived density was linearly related to actual density, with increments in one producing proportional increments in the other. The perceived value is reflected by probabilities ranging from very close to 0 ($z = -2.2$) to close to one ($z = +2.2$). The $z_{p(L)}$ values representing perceived density are almost perfectly correlated with the actual densities ranging from 0 to 4 and 0 to 6. This suggests that perceived density lies on a ratio scale. However, the fact that perceived density is linearly related to actual density at the molar level indicates very little about the perceptual process for two reasons:

1. The effect of changing cycle length does not produce a simple change in perceived density; and
2. The perceived value of different substimuli with the same average density varies a great deal.

One class of molar model states that perceived density simply reflects the total number of reinforcers obtained on a trial, irrespective of when they occurred or their distribution. That momentary increases in cycle length produce decrements in perceived value leads to a rejection of these models, because birds should have been insensitive to the temporal spacing.

Any molar model that states that perceived density reflects average reinforcement rate or average interreinforcement time was also rejected as an overall model. These models were closer to the truth, especially if an interaction of momentary increases in cycle length with standard cycle length is allowed. One reason they were rejected is summarized in Table 3–1, where it is shown that the ratio of slopes of the standard to the obtained perceived value greatly exceeded the predicted value of 2 and 3 for cycle length doubling and tripling, respectively. A second reason for rejecting these molar models was that the contribution of a reinforcer to perceived density decreased as a function of how far before choice that reinforcer occurred, as was also found by Commons (1979). Here, when the probability measure of perceived value was put in z form and number of cycles away from choice of the critical event was logged, the relation between the two was approximately linear, although there was a good deal of variability for some individual points. A slightly better fit would have been obtained if the exponential transformation used in the micro–molecular model had been used.

To the extent that the micro–molecular model is successful, it suggests the following processes: Perceived density is determined by decremental weighting, with the number of reinforcers weighted by a negative exponential of their number of cycles before choice. Changes in cycle length did not appear to change the exponent. The effects of the number of events or expected number of events or expected duration of a stimulus period may potentially be described by the coefficient multiplying the exponential terms. Narens (1979) has suggested that varying cycle length from cycle to cycle within a trial, while keeping overall substimulus length constant, may clarify some of these interference and timing issues. Herrnstein (1980) has suggested using fractional probes such as one-half the standard cycle length to see the effect of the probe per se. Including probes that change cycle number but not overall substimulus duration should also be tried.

The results here are entirely consistent with those found by Mandell (Chapter 2). Changing standard cycle length produced minimal changes in discriminability, and the relative time between reinforcers within a substimulus was much more important in determining performance than absolute cycle length in degrading performance. One would predict that discrimination of much leaner densities—that is, much greater cycle lengths—would not be terribly difficult.

SUMMARY

The way that reinforcers sampled from a schedule are discriminated and scaled is best explained at the micro and molecular level. Each reinforcer as it is weighted makes an equal additive contribution to both the discriminative choice behavior as measured by d' and the scaled or perceived density as measured by $z_{p(L)}$. The weighted value of a reinforcer was the negative exponential of how many cycles before choice that reinforcer fell. Since cycle length per se did not matter, a decay theory based on number of intervening events was supported. Sensitivity was lower when six 3-second cycle samples were discriminated than when the equivalent number of 4-second cycle samples were discriminated, also supporting a decay theory based on number of intervening events. Furthermore, probes that momentarily increased cycle length (and hence sample length) caused a decrease in perceived density greater than the amount predicted by a model asserting that rate or time between reinforcers was being scaled. This also raises the possibility that, to the bird, the momentarily increased sample length was perceived as an increase in the number of events to be processed, some of which may have fallen outside of the time or number of events window that the bird is prepared for. This supported a notion that number of events embedded in some time base was controlling perceived density and discriminability.

At the molecular level, the perceived substimulus density is simply the sum of the weighted values of the reinforcers occurring within the sample substimulus. This value systematically deviates from matching, with the reinforcers occurring near choice being overscaled and the ones far way being underscaled. However, at the molar level, matching has been shown to be a direct consequence of the micro–molecular level model holding. The scaled density is not only proportional to the actual density but is equal to the probability of reinforcement for indicating that the particular molar substimulus was rich when put into z form. This in turn implies that at the macro level, the scaled value of the overall schedules was the same as the perceived value of the molar components with density 3 and density 1. The rich stimulus had a mean density of 3 and had a corresponding scaled density equal to the molar density 3 substimulus. Likewise, the lean substimulus had a mean density of 1 and a scaled density equal to a density 1 substimulus. The discriminability degradations were also completely accounted for by the micro level performance. The weight of each reinforcer decreased as the reinforcer occurred further and further before choice. This decrement accounted for the decrease in d' from the maximum value of an ideal observer. The details of the latter statement are left to a further exposition.

In Commons and Ducheny (1981), it will be shown that a micro–molecular model in a preference situation (where the substimulus effectiveness rather than scaled value is established) will also explain most of the variance. Since contributions of reinforcers on a cycle will also be additive, the matching law relating the strength of responding to the relative amount of reinforcement will also be demonstrated. What is yet to be done is to show how general the micro–molecular model is, as the length and number of cycles are increased to the values usually found in VI schedules.

REFERENCES

Commons, M.L. 1979. Decision rules and signal detectability in a reinforcement density discrimination. *Journal of the Experimental Analysis of Behavior 32* : 101–120.

Commons, M.L., and J.R. Ducheny. 1981. The relationship between perceived reinforcement density and effective reinforcing power. In M.L. Commons, R.J. Herrnstein, and H. Rachlin, eds., *Quantitative Analyses of Behavior, Volume II: Matching and Maximizing.* Cambridge, Massachusetts: Ballinger (forthcoming).

D'Amato, M.R. 1973. Delayed matching and short-term memory in monkeys. In G.H. Bower, ed., *The Psychology of Learning and Motivation: Advances in Research and Theory.* New York: Academic Press.

Grant, D.S., and W.A. Roberts. 1973. Trace interaction in pigeon short-term memory. *Journal of Experimental Psychology 101* : 21–29.

Herrnstein, R.J. 1970. On the law of effect. *Journal of the Experimental Analysis of Behavior 13* : 243–266.

_____ . 1980. Personal communication.

Kamil, A.C.; J. Peters; and F. Lindstrom. 1981. An ecological study on the allocation of behavior. In M.L. Commons, R.J. Herrnstein, and H. Rachlin, eds., *Quantitative Analyses of Behavior, Volume II: Matching and Maximizing.* Cambridge, Massachusetts: Ballinger (forthcoming).

Krupa, M.P.; M. Hirvonen; J. Pohl; M. Lamb; and A.A. Thompson. 1977. How time between reinforcement opportunities in base cycles and on probes affects the discriminability and perceived value of a reinforcement schedule's reinforcement density. Paper presented at Eastern Psychological Association, Boston.

Mosteller, F., and J.W. Tukey. 1977. *Data Analysis and Regression.* Reading, Massachusetts: Addison–Wesley.

Narens, L. 1979. Personal communication.

Schoenfeld, W.N., and B.K. Cole. 1972. *Stimulus Schedules: the t–T Systems.* New York: Harper and Row.

Schoenfeld, W.N.; W.W. Cumming; and E. Hearst. 1956. On the classification of reinforcement schedules. *Proceedings of the National Academy of Sciences 42* : 563–570.

Thompson, A.A.; M.P. Krupa; J.J. Andersen; and M.L. Commons. 1976. How time between reinforcement opportunities affects the discriminability and perceived value of a partial reinforcement schedule's reinforcement density. Paper presented at the Midwestern Association of Behavior Analysis, Chicago.

Weissman, A. 1961. Impairment of performance when a discriminative stimulus is correlated with a reinforcement contingency. *Journal of the Experimental Analysis of Behavior 4* : 365–369.

Wickelgren, W.A. 1974. Strength/resistance theory of the dynamics of memory storage. In D.H. Krantz, R.C. Atkinson, R.D. Luce, and P. Suppes, eds., *Contemporary Developments in Mathematical Psychology: Learning, Memory, and Thinking.* San Francisco: Freeman.

Williams, B.A. 1981. Do interactions in multiple and concurrent schedules have a common basis? In M.L. Commons, R.J. Herrnstein, and H. Rachlin, eds., *Quantitative Analyses of Behavior, Volume II: Matching and Maximizing.* Cambridge, Massachusetts: Ballinger (forthcoming).

III RESPONSE–REINFORCER RELATIONS AS DISCRIMINATIVE PROPERTIES OF REINFORCEMENT SCHEDULES

4 LEARNING AS CAUSAL INFERENCE

Peter R. Killeen

In the present set of experiments, it is suggested that reinforcement contingencies be viewed as signals embedded in a background of noise: It is the animal's task to discriminate what response brings about reinforcement. Such causal inference is held to underlie the action of both operant and respondent contingencies on behavior. It follows from this view that the effects of contingencies are not "hard wired" (as presumed by Hull [1943] and others), but are affected both by the detectability of the signal and by the payoffs contingent on relevant responses. In this chapter, I briefly discuss some current notions of causality and indicate that there is little consensus on a formal definition. But although there are many ways that the causal relation might be defined, situations that elicit a causal inference from naive humans are often seen to be consistent with the conditions that promote learning. Conversely, it is argued that learning would be maladaptive if it did not pay some attention to those relations that we intuitively label causal.

It is concluded that these two somewhat vague areas—theories of learning and theories of causality—might both be clarified by view-

This research was supported by Grant BNS 76-24534 from the National Science Foundation. I thank the Glass Bead Group for their comments and especially James Phillip Smith, who conducted the first experiment. The manuscript was greatly improved by the helpful comments of the editors.

ing them in terms of each other and in the light cast by a third theory, that of signal detectability. To that end an experiment was conducted to see if pigeons could discriminate whether they caused an event or whether it occurred independently of their behavior. They were very good at the task, and their behavior was shown to be a function of both detectability (response–reinforcer interval) and payoff. These data and considerations are shown to have radical implications for the concept of "superstitious" behavior.

THE CONCEPT OF CAUSALITY

To what extent may the laws of animal learning be viewed as algorithms for discerning causality? Such an interpretation is predicated upon an accepted definition of causality, but unfortunately there are many of those to choose from (Bunge, 1959; Cook and Campbell, 1979; Mackie, 1974; Simon, 1953; Sosa, 1975; Wallace, 1974). Hume's theory (1777) is a good place to start. Hume suggested three criteria for causality—temporal precedence, spatial contiguity, and constant conjunction (specifically, a sufficient relation: if C, then E). He later suggested that the first two conditions might serve merely as clues to help us infer the third condition more accurately. J.S. Mill (1959) suggested experimental methods for inferring causality, such as the Method of Differences (compare the results of a situation that has C and one that does not). This emphasis on replicability shifted the focus away from causal relations in unique events to the prediction of future conjunctions in classes of similar events (even though such prediction is often used to infer historical causality—e.g., "reconstructing the scene of the crime" and other tests of "plausibility").

As an empiricist, Hume held causation to be a relation between experiences rather than a connection between events. Bunge (1959) notes that there are many types of orderly connections between events, only some of which we opt to call "causal." For example, we do not call the position of a pendulum one inch above its nadir the cause of its moving to nine-tenths of an inch above nadir. Nor do we call the primeval fireball the cause of this symposium, although it was certainly necessary for it.

In the web of multiple causes, delayed effects, and types of logical relations that can be defined (e.g., necessity, sufficiency, insufficient but necessary events in the context of otherwise sufficient events), philosophers struggle for a mapping of parts of the world onto the label "causal relation." It is sometimes easy to forget that "causality" is a label and that while the universe seems orderly, it is not intrinsically "causal." Causality is an ascription whose appropriateness depends largely on its utility in making sense of parts of the world. In this light, it is easier to understand Hume, who did not deny connections between events, but did deny that we are privy to them: When we make a causal inference, it is an inference, based on a restricted set of experiences. We will see that the criteria Hume suggested for that inference are consistent with basic principles of learning.

THE CONDITIONS OF LEARNING

Organisms that can predict the future have an enormous evolutionary advantage over those that cannot. Endogenous clocks predict the rhythms of season and tide, but many important regularities exist on too short a time scale to make fixed clocks, calendars, or reflexes of any use. Since a good predictor of the near future is the near past, organisms that are sensitive to recent conjunctions are prepared to exploit future conjunctions. If an animal infers from a series of conditioning trials that two stimuli will continue to be paired in the future or that a response will continue to be paired with a reinforcer, we may say that it is making a causal attribution. Of course, it is questionable that even humans make inferences with any kind of consistency. Humans do come to conclusions and, when asked to defend them, will often cite conventional explanations that have little to do with the true controlling variables (Nisbett and Wilson, 1977). When explicitly asked to make logical inferences, they often fail, but their behavior can often be predicted on the basis of simple developmental (Piaget, 1954, 1974) or reinforcement principles. Jenkins and Ward (1965) found that subjects almost never tested the necessity of a putative cause by requesting data that might yield a "no" response; presumably, continued reinforcement of "yes" responses maintained the testing only of sufficient relations and did not lead to the evaluation of necessary relations. Kahneman and Tversky (1973) have eloquently pointed out many other errors of inference in human judgments.

But we cannot restrict the term "inference" to the ratiocination of experts. Humans often act as though they make inferences, even though the premises are often mistaken or the processes unconscious. We often take their resulting behavior as evidence of an inference, without direct evidence of a mediating rational process. We can do the same for nonverbal animals, finding the locution a convenient way of asserting that a certain type of learning has occurred, without at the same time insisting that it be contemporaneously manifest in overt behavior.

Temporal Precedence

The first of Hume's criteria is temporal precedence: A cause must precede its effect. Correspondingly, for conditioning to occur, a response must precede the reinforcer, a conditional stimulus (CS) must precede the unconditional stimulus (US). Backward conditioning does not work, although stimuli or responses that follow the reinforcer may predict the temporary absence of ensuing events and may then acquire inhibitory control (Rescorla and Wagner, 1972). Temporal precedence is affected by the delay between events: When the effect is delayed, people naturally look for mediating causes and speak of "chains of causality" (Staddon, 1973). Delay also has a deleterious effect on conditioning. Our estimates of the magnitude of this effect have increased steadily over the years (Renner, 1964). Watson (1917) found no differential effect on learning with delays of 0 and 30 seconds. In 1934, Wolfe found that the rate of learning declined to about half its asymptotic value when reinforcement was delayed about 10 seconds after the response. Skinner's (1938) research placed the half-maximal delay at 6 to 8 seconds. In research by Perin (1943) and Perkins (1947), the half-maximal delay decreased to about 5 seconds; in Grice's study (1948), it was pushed back to less than a second.

The shrinking of the gradient was due to the attempts by later investigators to minimize conditioned reinforcers that could mediate learning across the delay: In 1951 Miller could conclude that one of the general properties of conditioned reinforcers was their utility for bridging gaps in time. When the conditioned reinforcer does not completely span the interval between response and reinforcer, conditioning is impaired (Pearce and Hall, 1978), but not always ruined

(Kamin, 1965, 1969; Kendall and Newly, 1978; Lett, 1973; Revusky, 1974). Skinner (1938) imbued responses themselves with the power of conditioned reinforcers and used that power as the basis of his theory of response chaining, whereby long response sequences are maintained with the reinforcement offered by subsequent responses. But not all critics agree that these theories of conditioned reinforcers are adequate to explain the maintenance of persistent behaviors when the delay of reinforcement gradient is demonstrably so steep (e.g., Jenkins, 1970).

If one abandons the notion of reinforcement as strengthening, however, and accepts instead the notion that reinforcers both incite and direct behavior (Deluty, 1976; Eiserer, 1978; Killeen, 1975, 1979; LaJoie and Bindra, 1976; Staddon, 1977; Staddon and Simmelhag, 1971), then one can take for granted a given amount of behavior for a given amount of incitement. The time course of arousal is orders of magnitude longer than the delay of reinforcement gradient and adequate to maintain much diffuse behavior in most reinforcement contexts (Killeen, Hanson, and Osborne, 1978). We must then specify how this behavior gets allocated to instrumental rather than interim or adjunctive behavior; the problem becomes one of allocation, rather than one of motivation.

I have argued elsewhere that two simple mechanisms have evolved to mediate allocation of behavior—temporal control and sign tracking (Killeen, 1975; see also Bindra, 1974; Davis and Hurwitz, 1977; LaJoie and Bindra, 1978; Moore, 1973). When reinforcement is imminent, animals will approach signs of it (Hearst and Jenkins, 1974). Signs are stimuli (including proprioceptive stimuli) that are good predictors of incentives. Although not all predictors are causes, it is probably to an animal's advantage to treat them as such until disabused of the inference. There may be some differences between exteroceptive and proprioceptive signs: The very steep delay of reinforcement gradients that have been found for response–reinforcer asynchrony appear monotonic (but see Sizemore and Lattal, 1978), but the interstimulus interval functions for CS–US asynchrony often have a pronounced maximum at around 0.5 sec. Even so, Kimble notes that "the delay-of-reinforcement and the interstimulus interval functions appear to be quite similar" (1961: 159).

There are some events for which a short CS–US lag would be evidence against causation—for example, ingested food usually makes one sick only after minutes or hours, not seconds. Pari passu, taste aversions develop over delays of many minutes (Garcia, McGowan, and Green, 1972; Kalat and Rozin, 1972). One wonders if the delay gradient is not generally tuned to the time at which an effect is most likely: Are agonistic responses, which require a lag of several seconds to be processed by a conspecific, best reinforced at those lags? Do ponderous organisms or movements have shallower gradients than nimble ones?

Spatial Contiguity

Physical scientists have never entirely accepted the notion of action at a distance and have often searched for physical mediators of such action. One creative physicist went so far as to suggest that physical bodies are not so much attracted to each other as they are passively following geodesics in a non–Euclidean world. Behavioral scientists have seldom tested the psychological geometry of Skinner boxes, but have preferred to keep stimulus and response locations close to the site of reinforcement. Only recently have a few experimenters weakened that spatial contiguity. When the operandum is remote from the goal, competing sign-tracking and goal-tracking vectors must be resolved (Boakes, 1977), additional reward is necessary (Killeen, 1974), and conditioning may become impossible (Breland and Breland, 1966). Similar difficulties are found in auto shaping (e.g., Brandon and Bitterman, 1979) and other instances of Pavlovian conditioning (Rescorla and Cunningham, 1979; Testa, 1975), with these last two articles explicitly discussing causal principles in conditioning. One wonders if the field is about to witness the introduction of a new construct, a spatial conditioned reinforcer that can bridge physical discontiguities in the same way that traditional ("temporal") conditioned reinforcers bridge temporal discontiguities.

Constancy of Conjunction

A paradigmatic independent variable of learning theorists has been the number of pairings of CS and US or of response and reinforcer. As the number of trials increases and the evidence for the constancy of the conjunction mounts, learning inevitably improves. Conditioning may, of course, occur on a single trial. Here, spatial contiguity and temporal ordering are the cues that guide the inference of future conjunctions. When the effects (US) are salient, such as shock or poisoning, animals may be biased to presume causality with a minimal number of replications. Even here, though, conditioning is retarded if the organism has had previous experience with the stimulus or response not being followed by the US (Goodkin, 1976; Maier and Seligman, 1976; Revusky and Bedarf, 1967; Wheatley, Welker, and Miles, 1977).

During conditioning, the US need not always follow the CS (or the reinforcer the response) nor need the US always be preceded by the CS. These two different ways of weakening the correlation between events are, as might be expected, both disruptive of conditioning (Catania, 1971; Gibbon, Berryman, and Thompson, 1974). But whether such correlations are in any way a controlling variable (Baum, 1973) or whether their apparent effects are themselves merely a correlate of changes in spatiotemporal contiguity is not yet certain; small changes in contiguity seem to readily overwhelm otherwise strong correlations (Kamin, 1965; Sizemore and Lattal, 1977; Williams, 1976).

THE PERCEPTION OF CAUSALITY

Given the very steep delay of reinforcement gradients that have been found, how do we account for the large amounts of "superstitious" behavior that Skinner (1948) observed when he fed animals periodically? Much of it we now infer to be "adjunctive" behavior (Staddon and Simmelhag, 1971), stimulated by arousal cumulated over the course of periodic feedings (Killeen, Hanson, and Osborne, 1978). At some point in the interval between feedings, sign tracking will focus some of the behavior of organisms on some part of their environment, and that focus may even "backchain" to support a longer sequence of coordinated action. I suspect that it is the temporal parameters of sign tracking that sustain the inference of causality in most cases.

This explanation is, of course, hypothetical. We do not even know if animals can actually discriminate causal relations. Skinner noted that his "experiment might be said to demonstrate a sort of superstition. The bird behaves as if there were a causal relation between its behavior and the presentation of food . . ." (1948: 170)—that is, it responds vigorously. If the pigeons were indeed inferring causality, they were doing it very badly, given the fine temporal and visual discriminations that they can make. These considerations led to the following experiment, in which pigeons sometimes earned their food by key pecking and sometimes received it independently of their behavior. After each feeding, I asked them whether or not their behavior was responsible for the food.

In all of the experiments to be reported here, a simpler question was asked: A key light was turned off either when the bird pecked at it or independently of its behavior. The birds were asked to evaluate the cause of that stimulus change. The design was straightforward: Center-key pecks turned the light off with a probability of 5 percent. The computer that controlled the experiment also turned the key light off by generating invisible "computer pecks" at about the same rate that the pigeon was pecking. Each of the "computer pecks" also had a 5 percent probability of extinguishing the key light. Immediately after the darkening of the center key, two side keys were lit. If the pigeon's peck had caused the stimulus change, then a left-key peck would result in food; if a computer "peck" had caused the stimulus change, then a right-key peck would produce food. Errors led to 5 seconds of blackout. Could they solve this problem? Errors were inevitable, since effective computer pecks could coincide with pigeon pecks. It is not a simple discrimination, and people observing a pigeon perform often miscall the outcome.

The pigeons, however, mastered the discrimination within several days, and within a couple of weeks they were performing with 80 to 90 percent accuracy. Some of the pigeons developed strategies that improved their accuracy. One would peck at the center key at a high rate for 1 or 2 seconds. If a stimulus change occurred then, she would quickly peck the left key, indicating "I caused it." Between response bursts, she would spend several seconds in front of the right, "computer caused it" key. If that key came on while she was in front of it, she would immediately peck it. Because the computer "pecked" according to an exponentially weighted moving average of the pigeon's center-key rate, this strategy was effective not only in making the discrimination, but also in keeping events moving along at a brisk pace. It seemed that for most pigeons, the discrimination was made on the basis of the time delay between a pigeon peck and the stimulus change.

Sometimes it does not pay to tell the truth. I next determined to test the pigeons' pragmatism by rewarding "computer" responses more than "I" responses. Would they shift from their relatively even-handed attribution of causality to the presumption of an external locus of control (i.e., make more "computer caused it" decisions)? In Experiment 1 correct choice key pecks were reinforced after the completion of short interval schedules, and in Experiment 2 the amount of food a bird got for a correct peck on either choice key was varied (see Table 4–1). In both experiments I found large shifts in attribution of causality.

In these experiments, the detection of a causal relation may be viewed as the detection of a signal in a background of noise. The organism's response is guided both by the detectability of the signal and by the payoff it gets for the various responses. It is convenient to represent the behavior observed in the above experiments in the coordinates favored by signal detectability theorists. Figures 4–1 and 4–2 show the probability of a "hit" (saying "I caused it" when that is the correct response) versus the probability of a "false alarm" (saying "I caused it" when "the computer caused it" is the correct response). The plots look very similar to those published in Green and Swets (1966), where the task is the detection of a tone in a background of noise. The solid lines are derived from the presumption that the underlying distributions of signal and noise are Gaussian. That is improbable, but does not affect the interpretation here. The presumption of underlying exponential or log-normal distributions would generate curves only barely discriminable from the ones drawn.

Table 4–1. Experimental Conditions.

| | Experiment 1 | | Experiment 2 | |
| | Fixed Interval (seconds) | | Eating Time (seconds) | |
Condition	Left Key	Right Key	Left Key	Right Key
A	1.0	2.5	1.8	3.8
B	1.0	1.5	2.8	2.8
C	1.5	1.0	3.3	2.3
D	2.5	1.0	3.8	1.8

Figure 4–1. Receiver-operating-characteristic curves for three pigeons discriminating between peck-generated and computer-generated stimulus changes. Bias was manipulated by varying the fixed interval between the opportunity for the choice response and the payoff (food or time out). The smooth lines are based on hypothetical Gaussian distributions of unequal variance for signal and noise.

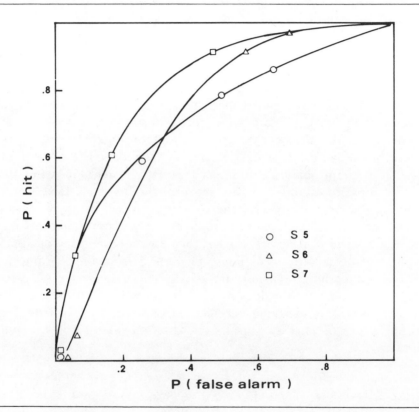

The data points in the upper right portions of the figures come from conditions in which the animals have been rewarded more (or sooner) for saying "I"; those in the bottom left come from conditions in which the animals have been rewarded more (or sooner) for saying "computer." The projected distance of the points along the positive diagonal (running from [0,0] to [1,1]) provides a measure of bias (see Nevin, Chapter 1, for a discussion of the theory of signal detectability and some measures of bias and discriminability). This distance (derived from Frey and Colliver's [1973] "RI") is plotted

Figure 4–2. Receiver-operating-characteristic curves for four pigeons discriminating between peck-generated and computer-generated stimulus changes. Bias was manipulated by varying the amount of food received for a hit or a correct rejection. The smooth lines are based on Gaussian distributions of unequal variance. (Source: Killeen, 1978; copyright by AAAS.)

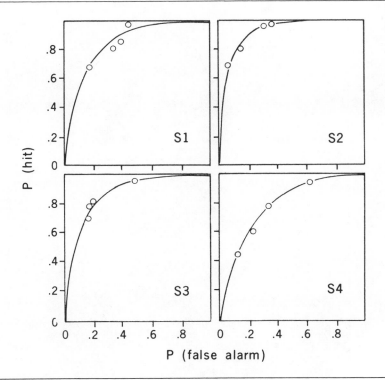

as a function of the relative value of reinforcers on the "I" key in Figure 4–3. Value (Rachlin, 1971) is defined as the number of rewards obtained times their magnitude (the duration of eating, Experiment 2) or immediacy (the reciprocal of the fixed interval, Experiment 1). There is clearly an orderly change in bias as a function of the relative payoff for saying "I" versus "it." Some of the correlation is due to the positive feedback in this design: The more the animals chose one alternative, the more they were rewarded for it. But the magnitude and direction of their preferences were clearly controlled by the independent variable; plots of bias against only immediacy or amount also revealed a very high correlation.

Figure 4–3. Bias (projections of the data points in Figures 4–1 and 4–2 along the positive diagonal) as a function of relative value (number of hits times the amount of immediacy of payoff for hits, divided by that quantity, plus the number of correct rejections times the amount or immediacy of payoff for rejections). Filled symbols are from Experiment 1, empty from Experiment 2.

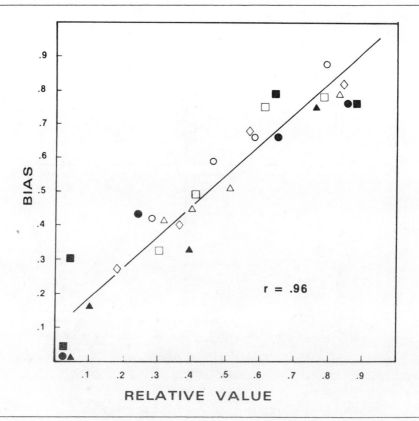

In the second experiment, the probability of an "I" response was recorded as a function of the delay between a response and the ensuing stimulus change. When the change was caused by the pigeon, it should have occurred immediately, but the computer (which ran this experiment in a time-share configuration) took about 50 milliseconds to disconnect the incandescent light, which in turn required about 10 milliseconds to drop to half-brightness. Expected delay for a signal is thus about 60 milliseconds. The "noise" events were lumped in 400 millisecond bins, centered at 200, 600, and 1000 mil-

Figure 4–4. Hypothetical discriminal dispersions underlying signals (left-most density) and noise (represented by the remaining density functions) at various lags. The distributions are log-normal: They were generated by exponential transformations of Gaussian distributions with standard deviations of 300 milliseconds and means at 60, 200, 600, and 1000 milliseconds. Events to the right of the vertical criterion lines are labeled "noise" (i.e., "computer generated") by the subject, and those to the left are labeled "signal." Criterion lines correspond to the various conditions of Experiment 1 listed in Table 4–1 and were inferred from the data in Figure 4–5.

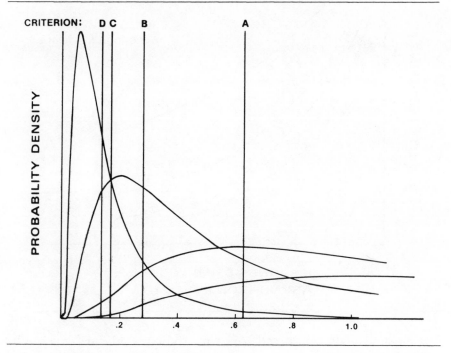

liseconds. For purposes of analysis, the noise may be treated as three distributions of events centered at those delays, as shown in Figures 4–4 and 4–5. The distributions are logarithmic-normal, because that construction accounted for the data better than the presumption of normal distributions (see Gibbon, Chapter 7). The standard deviation of the log-normal variants was presumed constant at 300 milliseconds. When transformed from the log-normal distributions, however, the standard deviation becomes proportional to the mean. The vertical lines are criterion lines inferred for each of the payoff conditions in the experiment. In condition A, saying "I"

Figure 4–5. The probability of saying "I" as a function of the delay between a key peck and the ensuing stimulus change. The data points in the leftmost column correspond to peck-generated events and are thus reinforced as hits. The remaining data points represent false alarms. The smooth lines were generated by the analysis in Figure 4–4.

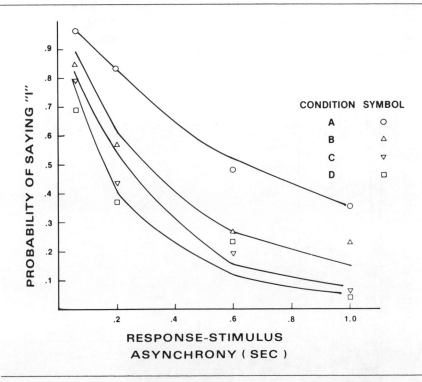

was most strongly reinforced, and thus the birds adopted a very liberal criterion: All events to the left of criterion A were called "signal" ("I caused it"), and only those to the right of the line were called "noise" ("the computer caused it"). In condition B, the payoffs were symmetric, and the pigeons adopted a moderate criterion. In conditions C and D, they were paid most for "computer" responses and adopted fairly strict criteria in those conditions. Figure 4–5 shows the obtained probabilities of saying "I" as a function of response–stimulus asynchrony; the psychometric functions were predicted from the analysis pictured in Figure 4–4 and provide an acceptable fit to the data.

Other treatments are possible. Davison and Tustin's (1978) analysis of signal detection performance in terms of the generalized matching law works quite well when applied to these data (see also Nevin, Chapter 1). But the point of this chapter is not the selection of one model of signal detectability to represent the obtained data. Signal detectability theory is essentially a philosophy that both motivation and discrimination are involved in choice behavior. Fleshing out that philosophy with models that have behavioral validity is a task that has only begun (cf. Nevin et al., 1975; Davison and McCarthy, Chapter 16). These data do establish the plausibility of applying models of signal detectability to the behavior of pigeons as they discriminate the degree of their control over the environment (see also Commons, 1979; Hobson, 1978; Joffe, Rawson, and Mulick, 1973; Lattal, 1975, 1979; and Chapter 5).

CAUSALITY OR MERELY CONTIGUITY?

Figures 4-4 and 4-5 suggest that the phenomenon we are studying is a mere temporal discrimination. This interpretation is abetted by more recent data, in which the delay of "signals" was reduced from 60 milliseconds to about 15 milliseconds: The pigeons became more accurate and could reliably discriminate between signals at 15 milliseconds lag and noise at 50 milliseconds lag.

But the data are double edged. The flexibility of criteria as a function of payoff suggests that temporal discrimination is modulated by a bias function—that is, that the pigeons were acting as model signal detectors. But should we not then infer that organisms also act as signal detectors in standard delay of reinforcement experiments? Many of those experiments are designed as "two-alternative forced choice," in which biases should cancel out. When they are not designed that way, however, we should expect steeper or shallower gradients as a function of the response cost and the relative payoffs. Usually the payoff for a hit is much more salient than the consequences for responses that fall in any of the other quadrants. This leads us to expect much "superstitious" responding when the intrinsic cost of the response is small, as is the case for key pecking (Neuringer, 1969, 1970; Osborne, 1977). Even though pigeons can make perfect discriminations between immediate reinforcement and reinforcement delayed by 80 milliseconds, the contingencies favor a strong bias toward the "I" part of the ROC curve. That behavior maximizes hit rates, and while it also elevates false alarm rate, that consequence is less important for foragers such as pigeons and rats.

The amount of behavior present in a situation is largely determined by the rate of incitement (Killeen, Hanson, and Osborne, 1978). If the baseline frequency of incentives is low, added "free" incentives may increase response rate, because their contribution to arousal has a greater effect than their contribution to directing behaviors "off key" (Boakes, Halliday, and Poli, 1975). If baseline frequency of incentives is high, added incentives decrease behavior. Thus, in extinction, where the baseline reinforcement frequency is minimal, response-independent incitement will prolong responding. Even when the reward is delayed by several seconds from the target response, there is some enhancement of responding (Rescorla and Skucy, 1969; Uhl, 1974). This is permitted by the relations shown in Figures 4-4 and 4-5, where the gradient may extend over several seconds depending on the subject's bias. This is not just a question of discrimination, which, for pigeons, can be perfect at temporal asynchronies of under 100 milliseconds. Thus Rachlin and Baum's (1972) paradoxical finding that "reinforcements for another response, reinforcements for not making Response A (for 2 seconds), and reinforcements delivered freely all had the same effect on Response A" (Rachlin, 1973: 229) now suggests that the alternate source of reinforcement was equally discriminable in all cases.

The notion of a flexible criterion for responding and its determination by the four contingencies summarized in the payoff matrix provide extra degrees of freedom with which to explain standard phenomena such as conditioned emotional response, contrast, learned helplessness, and the process of extinction. Response-incentive contiguity is important, but its effects cannot be understood without reference to the relative payoffs for other responses. There is no such thing as *the* delay of reinforcement gradient; there is a family of gradients whose parameters are the values of the organism's criterion.

If we treat an animal's responses to contingencies in terms of signal detection, what is the signal to be detected? In the present experiment, reinforcement was contingent on correctly determining whether or not a change in center-key illumination was caused by their key peck. The control of their choices was probably based on temporal asynchronies; in other designs, their choices may be based on other variables, such as a coefficient of conjunction (Baum, Chapter 10). Humans also base their inference of causality on those variables (Michotte, 1963), although there is a considerable overlay of control by intraverbals (Bem, 1972; de Charms, 1968; Kelley, 1973), which often debases their accuracy (Kahneman and Tversky, 1973; Nisbett and Wilson, 1977).

CAUSALITY, DECISION THEORY, ATTRIBUTION, AND BEHAVIOR

It is unlikely that there are strong evolutionary pressures on organisms that select for the ability to detect causal relations in any abstract sense (philosophers still have untoward difficulty at it). Animals are selected that can stay out of trouble and stay fed long enough to contribute genetic material to ensuing generations. Prediction and modification of future events that might impinge on their lifespace are important and will improve fitness. But unlike journal reviewers, Mother Nature does not attend primarily to the significance of the causal conjunction: Information or the amount of variance accounted for by a perceived relation, weighted by the impact of that relation on genetic fitness, are the variables most likely optimized.

The local emancipation from the genetic imperative that is permitted by language makes it possible to reinforce scientists for discerning and naming esoteric relations that have no intrinsic impact on their fitness. The marketplace of ideas (i.e., tenure and grant review committees, which dispense biologically important rewards) selects the type of causal inferences that scientists busy themselves with. Thus, the theory of general relativity has almost nothing to say about terrestrial phenomena, yet its invention was rewarded so strongly that it established the theory as a model for other scientists. The current pressures for "relevance" (i.e., for laws of inference that concern biological reinforcers) are now presumably biasing scientists' questions toward more mundane relations.

Whereas the arbitrary selection of issues permits scientists to attend to many types of relations and in turn permits semanticists to argue which of those many types they prefer to label "causal," nonverbal animals have been shaped by more consistent evolutionary pressures. They are seldom interested in action at a distance, and as the asynchrony between two events increases, so do the opportunities for alternate agents, alternative world lines, and more reliable predictors (Revusky, 1971; Williams, 1978). Conditioned reinforcement has evolved to provide changes of state; whereas it may be unlikely that a response was the cause of an event occurring 10 seconds later, an immediate stimulus change permits the causal inference of "change to state containing reward." The utility of the state containing the reward will be weakened by the 10 second delay of reward, but that weakening affects bias, which is a flexible and context-dependent type of control. The effects of delay on detectability are different and are usually much more acute (as in these experiments), but may depend on the nature of the presumptive cause (as in the taste aversion literature: Krane and Wagner, 1975). The two types of control must be unconfounded in order to be weighted appropriately. Eventually, however, they must be recombined, because behavior is a function of both.

Some philosophers (e.g., von Wright, 1974) have adopted an "interventionist" theory of causality, asserting causal efficacy in those situations in which we may act as an agent, interfering with the flow of events. There is evidence that nonverbal organisms also exhibit this philosophy, which emphasizes the role of necessary relationships in determining causality. To determine if a behavior is necessary for a reward, one must withhold the behavior and note if the reward is omitted or diminished. Spontaneous alternation, behavioral oscillation, and adjunctive behavior might all be interpreted as experiments—manipulations of the inferred cause even where the "proper" response is overlearned.

CONCLUSION

Organisms are bundles of negative entropy, Maxwell Demons that buy energy with information. The information is usually simple extrapolations of past conjunctions and is used to get them where food is and predators are not. Their behavior depends on both what they know (detectability effects) and what they need (bias effects). One cannot evaluate the appropriateness of behavior, such as that labeled superstitious, without first understanding the role that both factors play in controlling it. Indeed, if one insists on using the term superstition, it should be applied evenhandedly to behavior at both extremes of the curves of Figures 4-1 and 4-2; inaction can be as "superstitious" as overaction.

But an important implication of the current research is that the concept of superstitious behavior should be abandoned as an inappropriate and misleading simplification. Darwinian competition is seldom forgiving of such systematic and gratuitous waste of energy as is implied by the concept. That view of life encourages us to presume the adaptive value of such "abberations," and to use that presumption as leverage in understanding the nature of the environmental constraints that make such extreme behavior adaptive. This approach will be rejected by some as too dependent on the ubiquity of adaptation in the face of strong evidence for other types of evolutionary control, such as genetic drift, that might generate nonadaptive behavior (Gould, 1980). But the evolutionary-adaptive view is a scientific bias that has yielded many more hits than false alarms. I expect it will continue to be productive when addressed to philosophical issues such as causality, as well as to quantitative studies of operant behavior. Psychologists are in a unique position to exploit their experimental skills (which are specifically designed to uncover causal relations) in addressing both sets of issues.

REFERENCES

Baum, W.M. 1973. The correlation-based law of effect. *Journal of the Experimental Analysis of Behavior 20*: 137-153.

Bem, D.J. 1972. Self-perception theory. In L. Berkowitz, ed., *Advances in Experimental Social Psychology*, vol. 6. New York: Academic Press.

Bindra, D. 1974. A motivational view of learning, performance and behavior modification. *Psychological Review 81*: 199-213.

Boakes, R.A. 1977. Performance on learning to associate a stimulus with positive reinforcement. In H. Davis and H.M.B. Hurwitz, eds., *Operant-Pavlovian Interaction*, pp. 67-97. Hillsdale, New Jersey: Lawrence Erlbaum Associates.

Boakes, R.A.; M.S. Halliday; and M. Poli. 1975. Response additivity: Effects of superimposed free reinforcement on a variable-interval baseline. *Journal of the Experimental Analysis of Behavior 23*: 177-191.

Brandon, S.E., and M.E. Bitterman. 1979. Analysis of autoshaping in goldfish. *Animal Learning and Behavior 7*: 57-62.

Breland, K., and M. Breland. 1966. *Animal Behavior*. New York: Macmillan.

Bunge, M. 1959. *Causality: The Place of the Causal Principle in Modern Science*. Cambridge, Massachusetts: Harvard University Press.

Catania, A.C. 1971. Elicitation, reinforcement and stimulus control. In R. Glaser, ed., *The Nature of Reinforcement*. New York: Academic Press.

Commons, M.L. 1979. Decision rules and signal detectability in a reinforcement–density discrimination. *Journal of the Experimental Analysis of Behavior 32*: 101–120.

Cook, T.D., and D.T. Campbell. 1979. *Quasi-experimentation: Design and Analysis Issues for Social Research in Field Settings*. Skokie, Illinois: Rand McNally.

Davis, H., and H.M.B. Hurwitz. 1977. *Operant–Pavlovian Interactions*. Hillsdale, New Jersey: Lawerence Erlbaum Associates.

Davison, M.C., and R.D. Tustin. 1978. The relation between the generalized matching law and signal-detection theory. *Journal of the Experimental Analysis of Behavior 29*: 331–336.

De Charms, R. 1968. *Personal Causation: The Internal Affective Determinants of Behavior*. New York: Academic Press.

Deluty, M.Z. 1976. Excitatory and inhibitory effects of free reinforcers. *Animal Learning and Behavior 4*: 436–440.

Eiserer, L.A. 1978. Effects of food primes on the operant behavior of nondeprived rats. *Animal Learning and Behavior 6*: 308–312.

Frey, P.W., and J.A. Colliver. 1973. Sensitivity and responsivity measures for discrimination learning. *Learning and Motivation 4*: 327–342.

Garcia, J.; B.D. McGowan; and K.F. Green. 1972. Biological constraints on learning. In A.H. Black and W.F. Prokasy, eds., *Classical Conditioning II*. New York: Appleton–Century–Crofts.

Gibbon, J.; R. Berryman; and R.L. Thompson. 1974. Contingency spaces and measures in classical and instrumental conditioning. *Journal of the Experimental Analysis of Behavior 21*: 585–605.

Goodkin, F. 1976. Rats learn the relationship between responding and environmental events: An expansion of the learned helplessness hypothesis. *Learning & Motivation 7*: 382–393.

Gould, S.J. 1980. Wallace's fatal flaw. *Natural History 89* (1): 26–40.

Green, D.M., and J.A. Swts. 1966. *Signal Detection Theory and Psychophysics*. New York: Wiley.

Grice, G.R. 1948. The relation of secondary reinforcement to delayed reward in visual discrimination learning. *Journal of Experimental Psychology 38*: 1–16.

Hearst, E., and H.M. Jenkins. 1974. *Sign-tracking: The Stimulus–Reinforcer Relation and Directed Action*. Austin, Texas: Psychonomic Society.

Hobson, S.L. 1978. Discriminability of fixed-ratio schedules for pigeons: Effects of payoff values. *Journal of the Experimental Analysis of Behavior 30*: 69–81.

Hull, C. 1943. *Principles of Behavior*. New York: Appleton–Century–Crofts.

Hume, D. 1777. *Enquiries Concerning Human Understanding and Concerning the Principles of Morals*. Oxford: Clarendon, rpt. 1975.

Jenkins, H.M. 1970. Sequential organization in schedules of reinforcement. In N.W. Schoenfeld, ed., *The Theory of Reinforcement Schedules*. New York: Appleton–Century–Crofts.

Jenkins, H.M., and W.C. Ward. 1965. Judgment of contingency between responses and outcomes. *Psychological Monographs 79* (594).

Joffe, J.M.; R.A. Rawson; and J.A. Mulick. 1973. Control of their environments reduces emotionality in rats. *Science 180*: 1383–1384.

Kahneman, D., and A. Tversky. 1973. On the psychology of prediction. *Psychological Review 80*: 237–251.

Kalat, J.W., and P. Rozin. 1972. You can lead a rat to poison but you can't make him think. In M.E.P. Seligman and J.L. Hager, eds., *Biological Boundaries of Learning*. New York: Appleton–Century–Crofts.

Kamin, L.J. 1965. Temporal and intensity characteristics of the conditioned stimulus. In W.F. Prokasy, ed., *Classical Conditioning: A Symposium*. New York: Appleton–Century–Crofts.

_____. 1969. Predictability, surprise, attention, and conditioning. In B. Campbell and R. Church, eds., *Punishment and aversive behavior*. New York: Appleton–Century–Crofts.

Kelley, H.H. 1973. The processes of causal attribution. *American Psychologist 28*: 107–128.

Kendall, S.B., and W. Newly. 1978. Delayed reinforcement of fixed-ratio performance without mediating exteroceptive conditioned reinforcement. *Journal of the Experimental Analysis of Behavior 30*: 231–237.

Killeen, P.R. 1974. Psychological distance functions for hooded rats. *The Psychological Record 24*: 229–235.

_____. 1975. On the temporal control of behavior. *Psychological Review 82*: 89–115.

_____. 1978. Superstition: A matter of bias, not detectability. *Science 199*: 88–90.

_____. 1979. Arousal: Its genesis, modulation and extinction. In P. Harzem and M.D. Zeiler, eds., *Reinforcement and the Organization of Behavior*. New York: Wiley.

Killeen, P.R.; S.J. Hanson; and S.R. Osborn. 1978. Arousal: Its genesis and manifestation as response rate. *Psychological Review 85*: 571–581.

Kimble, G.A. 1961. *Hilgard & Marquis' Conditioning and Learning*. New York: Appleton–Century–Crofts.

Krane, R.V., and A.R. Wagner. 1975. Taste aversion learning with a delayed shock US: Implications for the "Generality of the Laws of Learning." *Journal of Comparative & Physiological Psychology 88*: 882–889.

LaJoie, J., and D. Bindra. 1976. An interpretation of autoshaping and related phenomena in terms of stimulus contingencies alone. *Canadian Journal of Psychology 30*: 157-173.

———. 1978. Contributions of stimulus-incentive and stimulus-response-incentive contingencies to response acquisition and maintenance. *Animal Learning and Behavior 6*: 301-307.

Lattal, K.A. 1975. Reinforcement contingencies as discriminative stimuli. *Journal of the Experimental Analysis of Behavior 23*: 241-246.

———. 1979. Reinforcement contingencies as discriminative stimuli: II. Effects of changes in stimuli probability. *Journal of the Experimental Analysis of Behavior 31*: 15-22.

Lett, B.T. 1973. Delayed reward learning: Disproof of the traditional theory. *Learning & Motivation 4*: 237-246.

Mackie, J.L. 1974. *The Cement of the Universe: A Study of Causation.* Oxford: Clarendon Press.

Maier, S.F., and M.E.P. Seligman. 1976. Learned helplessness: Theory and evidence. *Journal of Experimental Psychology: General 105*: 3-46.

Michotte, A. 1963. *The Perception of Causality.* New York: Basic Books.

Mill, J.S. 1959. *A System of Logic.* 8th ed. London: Longman.

Miller, N.E. 1951. Learnable drives and rewards. In S.S. Stevens, ed., *Handbook of Experimental Psychology.* New York: Wiley.

Moore, B.R. 1973. The role of directed Pavlovian reactions in simple instrumental learning in the pigeon. In R.A. Hinde and J. Stevenson-Hinde, eds., *Constraints on Learning: Limitations and Predispositions.* New York: Academic Press.

Neuringer, A.J. 1969. Animals respond for food in the presence of free food. *Science 166*: 399-401.

———. 1970. Supersitious key pecking after three peck-produced reinforcements. *Journal of the Experimental Analysis of Behavior 13*: 127-134.

Nevin, J.A.; K. Olson; C. Mandell; and P. Yarensky. 1975. Differential reinforcement and signal detection. *Journal of the Experimental Analysis of Behavior 24*: 355-367.

Nisbett, R.E., and T.D. Wilson. 1977. Telling more than we can know: Verbal reports on mental processes. *Psychological Review 84*: 231-259.

Osborne, S.R. 1977. The free food (contrafreeloading) phenomenon: A review and analysis. *Animal Learning and Behavior 5*: 221-235.

Pearce, J.M., and G. Hall. 1978. Overshadowing the instrumental conditioning of a lever-press response by a more valid predictor of the reinforcer. *Journal of Experimental Psychology: Animal Behavior Processes 4*: 356-367.

Perin, C.T. 1943. The effect of delayed reinforcement upon the differentiation of bar presses in white rats. *Journal of Experimental Psychology 32*: 95-109.

Perkins, C.C., Jr. 1947. The relation of secondary reward to gradients of reinforcement. *Journal of Experimental Psychology 37*: 377-392.

Piaget, J. 1954. *The Construction of Reality in the Child.* New York: Basic Books.

_____. 1974. *Understanding Causality.* New York: Norton & Co.

Rachlin, H.C. 1971. On the tautology of the matching law. *Journal of the Experimental Analysis of Behavior 15* : 249–251.

_____. 1973. Contrast and matching. *Psychological Review 80* : 217–234.

Rachlin, H.C., and W.M. Baum. 1972. Effects of alternative reinforcement: Does the source matter? *Journal of the Experimental Analysis of Behavior 18* : 231–241.

Renner, K.E. 1964. Delay of reinforcement: A historical review. *Psychological Bulletin 61* (5): 341–361.

Rescorla, R.A., and C.L. Cunningham. 1979. Spatial contiguity facilitates Pavlovian second-order conditioning. *Journal of Experimental Psychology: Animal Behavior Processes 5* : 152–161.

Rescorla, R.A., and J.C. Skucy. 1969. Effect of response-independent reinforcers during extinction. *Journal of Comparative and Physiological Psychology 67* : 381–389.

Rescorla, R.A., and A.R. Wagner. 1972. A theory of Pavlovian conditioning: Variations in the effectiveness of reinforcement and non-reinforcement. In A.H. Black and W.F. Prokasy, eds., *Classical Conditioning II. Current Research and Theory.* New York: Appleton–Century–Crofts.

Revusky, S. 1971. The role of interference in association over a delay. In W.K. Honig and H. James, eds., *Animal Memory.* New York: Academic.

_____. 1974. Long-delay learning in rats: A black–white discrimination. *Bulletin of the Psychonomic Society 4* : 526–528.

Revusky, S., and E.W. Bedarf. 1967. Association of illness with prior ingestion of novel foods. *Science 155* : 219–220.

Simon, H.A. 1953. Causal ordering and identifiability. In W.C. Hood and T.C. Loopmon, eds., *Studies in Econometric Method.* New York: John Wiley & Sons.

Sizemore, O.J., and K.A. Lattal. 1977. Dependency, temporal contiguity, and response-independent reinforcement. *Journal of the Experimental Analysis of Behavior 25* : 119–125.

_____. 1978. Unsignalled delay of reinforcement in variable-interval schedules. *Journal of the Experimental Analysis of Behavior 30* : 169–175.

Skinner, B.F. 1938. *The Behavior of Organisms: An Experimental Analysis.* New York: Appleton–Century.

_____. 1948. "Superstition" is the pigeon. *Journal of Experimental Psychology 38* : 168–172.

Sosa, E. 1975. *Causation and Conditionals.* London: Oxford University Press.

Staddon, J.E.R. 1973. On the notion of cause with application to behaviorism. *Behaviorism 1* (2): 25–63.

_____ . 1977. Schedule-induced behavior. In W.K. Honig and J.E.R. Staddon, eds., *Handbook of Operant Behavior*. Englewood Cliffs, New Jersey: Prentice–Hall.

Staddon, J.E.R., and V.L. Simmelhag. 1974. The "superstition" experiment: A reexamination of its implications for the principles of adaptive behavior. *Psychological Review 78*: 3–43.

Testa, T.J. 1975. Effects of similarity of location and temporal intensity pattern of conditioned and unconditioned stimuli on the acquisition of conditioned suppression in rats. *Journal of Experimental Psychology: Animal Behavior Processes 1*: 114–121.

Uhl, C.N. 1974. Response elimination in rats with schedules of omission training, including yoked and response-independent reinforcement. *Learning and Motivation 5*: 511–531.

Von Wright, G.H. 1974. *Causality and Determinism*. New York: Columbia University Press.

Wallace, W.A. 1974. *Causality and Scientific Explanation, Vol. 2: Classical and Contemporary Science*. Ann Arbor: University of Michigan Press.

Watson, J.B. 1917. The effect of delayed feeding upon learning. *Psychobiology I*: 51–60.

Wheatley, K.L.; R.L. Welker; and R.C. Miles. 1977. Acquisition of bar-pressing in rats following experience with response-independent food. *Animal Learning and Behavior 5*: 236–242.

Williams, B.A. 1976. The effects of unsignalled delayed reinforcement. *Journal of the Experimental Analysis of Behavior 26*: 441–449.

_____ . 1978. Information effects on the response–reinforcer association. *Animal Learning and Behavior 6*: 371–379.

Wolfe, J.B. 1934. The effect of delayed reward upon learning in the white rat. *Journal of Comparative Psychology 17*: 1–21.

5 REINFORCEMENT CONTINGENCIES AS DISCRIMINATIVE STIMULI
Implications for Schedule Performance

Kennon A. Lattal

INTRODUCTION

Schedule research most often concerns precise specification of reinforcement parameters such as frequency and dependency on one hand and response topography on the other. The operation of these variables may be labeled respectively as dynamic and differentiating effects of schedules (Catania, 1970). A third effect, and the focus of this book, is a discriminative one, described by Skinner (1958: 96) as follows: "A scheduling system sets up a performance and the performance generates stimuli which enter into the control of the rate of the responding, either maintaining the performance or changing it in various ways." According to this description, the discriminative effects of schedules can arise from the interaction between schedule arrangements and behavior. These interactions have been labeled indirect variables. If these indirect variables are to be assigned a causative role in schedule-controlled behavior, they must produce the effects they are assumed to exert indirectly when imposed directly (Zeiler, 1977).

Contingencies refer both to the procedures relating discriminative stimuli, responses, and reinforcement and to the specific functional

The research reported here was supported by a National Institute of Mental Health postdoctoral fellowship and by West Virginia University Faculty Senate research grants to the author.

relations between responding and reinforcement. In the former definition, contingencies describe the operations used to maintain behavior; in the latter they describe behavior, whether required or not, that precedes reinforcement (cf. Zeiler, 1972). By either definition, the relation between responding and other events, particularly reinforcement, is paramount in an analysis of behavior. The dynamic and differentiating effects of these relations on behavior is a central theme of most operant-conditioning research. The discriminative stimulus effects of such contingencies is the subject of this chapter. Its purposes are to suggest that contingencies, especially response–reinforcer relations, can be discriminated; to review experiments that attempt to isolate this function directly; to suggest some of the ways in which response–reinforcer relations might operate as stimuli in schedules; and to discuss some of the issues related to assigning a causative role in schedules to the indirect discriminative effects of response–reinforcer relations.

TYPES OF RESPONSE–REINFORCER RELATIONS AND THEIR EFFECTS ON BEHAVIOR

Considering experimenter-controlled arrangements at the time of delivery of a reinforcer, three response–reinforcer relations may be defined. A response can produce a reinforcer, it can delay a reinforcer, or the response and reinforcer can be unrelated to one another. The first relation includes both immediate and delayed reinforcement under conventional scheduling. Differential reinforcement of other behavior (DRO) schedules define the second relationship, and schedules of response-independent reinforcement define the third.

   Discrimination, or stimulus control, is invoked to describe behavior in situations that involve two or more stimuli. Thus, pecking a single, continuously illuminated red key while on a variable interval (VI) schedule is not a sufficient condition for describing behavior as being under the stimulus control of the red key light. Without variation in key light color, stimulus control cannot be assessed. Similarly, a discussion of behavior that is under the stimulus control of response–reinforcer relations is meaningful only in schedules that combine two or more different operational or functional relations.

The matrix in Table 5-1 provides some examples. Those combinations most germane to the present analysis are labeled 1, 2, and 3 in the matrix. Response-independent reinforcement arrangements are of interest to the extent that functional variations in response–reinforcer temporal contiguity occur.

A few experiments have examined the effects of some of these combinations of reinforcers delivered according to these different relationships. Lattal (1974) studied combinations of response-dependent and response-independent reinforcers (labeled 1 in Table 5-1). Reinforcers were arranged according to a variable schedule: The total number of reinforcers was constant (sixty per one hour session), and the percentage of each type of reinforcer was varied from 0 to 100 percent in different phases of the experiment. Response rates increased in proportion to the percentage of response-dependent reinforcers.

In another experiment (Lattal and Boyer, in press), pigeons were exposed to a concurrent schedule wherein key pecking was reinforced according to a fixed interval (FI) 300 second schedule and pauses in key pecking were reinforced under a DRO schedule. This schedule (labeled 2 in Table 5-1) subsequently will be referred to as a concurrent peck–pause schedule. Reinforcers under the DRO schedule were made available at variable time periods. They were delivered immediately if no key peck had occurred for at least 5 seconds or, if key pecking was occurring at the time the DRO reinforcer became available, after the first subsequent 5-second pause. The average time between DRO reinforcers was varied between 30 and 600 seconds in different phases of the experiment. Overall key peck response rates systematically increased as the frequency of DRO reinforcement decreased (cf. Rachlin and Baum, 1972). Similarly, the percent of the total session time spent pausing was less with less frequent DRO reinforcement.

These experiments suggest that combinations of different response–reinforcer relations result in response rates that differ from those occurring when a single response–reinforcer relation is present. Questions about variables that contribute to these differences in performance are therefore in order. In the concurrent peck–pause schedule example, dynamic effects operated through the temporal relations between response and reinforcer and the different reinforcement frequencies. Differentiating effects were arranged by requiring

Table 5–1. Examples of Combinations of Schedules Arranging Different Response Reinforcer Relationships.

		Schedule A	
Schedule B	Response Produces Reinforcer	Response-Independent Reinforcer	Response Delays Reinforcer
Response produces reinforcer	"conventional" schedules	1	2
Response-independent reinforcer	1	time schedules	3
Response delays reinforcer	2	3	DRO schedules

different forms of the response under the two schedules. In addition, it is suggested that the different response–reinforcer relations served as a source of indirect stimulus control over the two responses. It is to the assessment of this possibility that we now turn.

THE DISCRIMINATION OF RESPONSE–REINFORCER RELATIONSHIPS

To support the argument that response–reinforcer relationships are serving indirectly as discriminative stimuli in reinforcement schedules, it is necessary to demonstrate such discriminative control directly. Several procedures have been used to do this. They have used response rate measures in simple and multiple schedules, verbal reports, and probability or relative rates of response in a discrete or concurrent discriminative choice situation.

A simple measure of discriminative control is response rate under a schedule. Several studies have found that response rates are directly related to the relative frequency of response-dependent and response-independent or response-delayed reinforcement (Lattal, 1974; Lattal and Boyer, in press; Lattal and Bryan, 1976; Rachlin and Baum, 1972; Schoenfeld et al., 1973; Zeiler, 1976). Rachlin and Baum (1972) stated that their results "showed that pigeons can discriminate between response-dependent and response-independent reinforcement on the basis of dependency alone" (p. 237). While their conclusion subsequently was shown to be correct (Killeen, 1978), their conclusion based on the rate data should be questioned. The weakness in taking such rate changes as direct evidence of discrimination is that the discrimination measure may be seriously confounded by the dynamic, strengthening and weakening effects of the different reinforcement contingencies on response rate. It is not possible to obtain an independent measure of discriminative control using response rates in the different conditions, which disentangles such control from the dynamic and differentiating effects of the schedule.

Studies employing multiple schedules with different response–reinforcer relations in the components also are cited sometimes as evidence of discrimination of the relations. Appel and Hiss (1962) found that the FI component of a multiple FI fixed time (FT) schedule maintained higher rates than the FT component. Their conclusion was that the pigeons discriminated response-dependent from response-independent reinforcement. The problem with this interpretation is not only the confounding of dynamic and discriminative properties of the schedule but, more importantly, that in each component there were two sources of stimulus control that potentially interacted to produce rate differences—namely, the different key light colors and the different response–reinforcer relations. To demonstrate that the different response–reinforcer relationships differentially control responding would require that other discriminative stimuli be excluded.

Lattal (1973) examined whether different response–reinforcer relations differentially control responding in the absence of other discriminative stimuli. Rats' performances were compared under analogous multiple and mixed variable interval 1-minute, variable time 1-minute schedules. Components alternated randomly at 5-minute intervals under both schedules. Bright and dim levels of chamber illumination signaled the two components of the multiple schedule and an intermediate level of illumination occurred in both components of the mixed schedule. Under the multiple schedule, markedly different rates occurred in the VI and VT components. Under the mixed schedule, where the only potential discriminative stimulus was the response–reinforcer relationship, response rates were approximately equal in the two components after several sessions. Thus, the different response–reinforcer relationships did not differentially control responding. Even if differences in responding in the two components of the mixed schedule had occurred, as happened when the component duration was increased, it could not be taken as strong evidence of the discriminative properties of the response–reinforcer relationship because of the confounding of the response rate index of discrimination by the dynamic effects of the schedule.

Another way to determine whether different response–event relationships can be discriminated is to expose human subjects to the different relations and then ask them to describe the relationship between responding and the event. Poresky (1971) studied button pushing by children and adults. After developing responding under a short variable ratio schedule to earn points, half of the subjects received extinction and half received response-independent reinforcement. In a postexperiment interview, most of the adults, but few of the children, who received response-independent points verbalized the absence of a response–reinforcer relationship. The verbal reports were consistent with behavioral measures of performance under the different conditions. Gruber, Fink, and Damm (1957) had college students push a button that collapsed a bridge either simultaneously with the button push or at some delay after the button push. Verbal reports of a causal relation between button pushing and bridge collapsing were controlled by the temporal relation between the response and its effect—that is, reports of causality were more likely if the two events occurred closer together in time. However, reliability and validity problems of verbal reports that have unspecified consequences make them less useful than other behavioral measures of discrimination of response–event relationships.

The matching-to-sample procedure (Cumming and Berryman, 1965; Skinner, 1950) utilizes choice rather than response rate or verbal report as a discrimination measure. While choice responses may be influenced by dynamic reinforcement effects (i.e., biasing), these effects can be held constant to permit a more precise analysis of the stimulus control of choice.

Variations of the matching-to-sample procedure have proven useful in assessing the discriminative properties of different elements of a reinforcement schedule. Pliskoff and Goldiamond (1966) and Rilling and McDiarmid (1965) showed that different fixed ratio requirements could serve as discriminative stimuli controlling choice responses in a matching procedure; Stubbs (1968) and others have used the procedure to study the stimulus properties of time; Maki, Moe, and Bierley (1977) and Silberberg (1971) showed that the presence and absence of reinforcement could serve as discriminative stimuli for choice behavior; and Commons (1979) studied the discriminative function of variations in reinforcement frequency. Several chapters in the present volume have employed related procedures.

Figure 5-1 illustrates the use of this procedure by Lattal (1979) to show how reinforcement contingencies could serve as discriminative stimuli. The contingencies were the relation between responding in a sample component and the occurrence of a choice component. For convenience, these will be labeled response–reinforcer relations in that the choice component operationally served as a conditioned reinforcer for responding in the sample component. In the presence of an illuminated center key (the sample component), illumination of both side keys (the choice component) was produced either by a peck following a 10-second period of no pecking (a differential rein-

Figure 5–1. Schematic diagram of a trial in which different contingencies served as stimuli for choice responses. The sequence of events proceeds from left to right (*Source*: from Lattal, 1979).

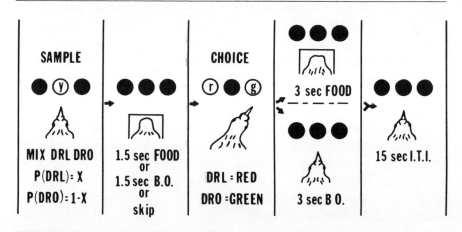

forcement of low rate [DRL] 10-second schedule) or by an absence of pecking for 10 seconds (a DRO 10-second schedule). The transition from the sample to the choice component was immediate (in the second panel in Figure 5–1, this is indicated by the word "skip").

The two relations were presented randomly in the sample component according to a mixed schedule (i.e., the center key was the same color whether DRL or DRO was in effect), and each occurred on half of the sample trials. Once in the choice component, a red choice key peck preceded by a peck that met the requirement in the sample component produced access to grain; similarly, a green choice key peck preceded by a pause that met the requirement in the sample component also produced grain access. Incorrect choices produced a 3-second blackout in the chamber. After a 15-second intertrial interval, the next trial was presented. Eighty to one hundred trials consisting of a sample and a choice component comprised a daily session. Figure 5–2 shows that the total percent of correct choices for both peck and pause requirements in the sample component ranged between 80 to 95 percent following acquisition and two subsequent reversals of the correct choice keys.

The DRL and DRO schedules were used in an attempt to equate as closely as possible indirect variables arising from the different contin-

Figure 5–2. Percent correct choice responses for two birds in the matching procedure. The last ten sessions of the initial training conditions (peck the red choice key for food after DRL in the sample component and peck the green choice key for food after DRO in the sample component) and all sessions during two reversals of the correct choice keys are shown (*Source*: from Lattal, 1975).

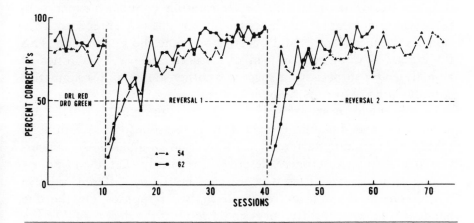

gencies. However, some differences between the two schedules did occur. Response rates and time per component were slightly greater when the DRL schedule was in the sample component during acquisition and both stimulus reversals. Their role in the discriminative control of choice cannot be excluded. However, it is difficult, if not impossible, to arrange different contingencies that equate all aspects of performance.

This experiment and a subsequent one by Killeen (1978) demonstrated that different response–event, or response–reinforcer, relations can serve as discriminative stimuli controlling choice responses in the absence of confounding by dynamic, response-strengthening or weakening effects of the different relationships. Thus, what was first identified as an indirect variable was converted to a direct variable and was shown to control behavior directly in the manner in which it is assumed to operate indirectly in schedules employing different response–reinforcer relations.

DISCRIMINATIVE PROPERTIES OF
RESPONSE-REINFORCER RELATIONS
AND SCHEDULE PERFORMANCE

The focus thus far has been on evaluating procedures and data offered as evidence of the discriminative control of behavior by response-reinforcer relations. Under carefully controlled experimental arrangements, animals' choices are determined by antecedent relations between responses and occurrence of the choice situation. This finding is of value not only in establishing sensory capabilities of animals, but also because it suggests another source of discriminative stimulus control of responding in reinforcement schedules.

One problem in assessing such control is the relative role of discriminative and dynamic effects of response-reinforcer relations in schedules combining different relations. For example, in the concurrent peck-pause experiment described previously (Lattal and Boyer, in press), behavioral differences were generated by different relative reinforcement frequencies for each of two responses. On the one hand, the behavioral differences could result if the degree of discriminability of, or stimulus control by, the different relations changed as their frequency of occurrence changed. Such changes in behavior also could result from changes in the dynamic function resulting from changes in reinforcement frequency of the two responses either independently of, or in conjunction with, changes in discriminability of the two relationships. While it is difficult to disentangle the dynamic and discriminative effects under the *in vivo* conditions of a schedule, one way to begin to bring the mountain to Mohammed is to create, and then separate, dynamic and discriminative effects in the matching procedure.

This possibility was examined by using a variation on the procedure shown in Figure 5-1 (Lattal, 1979). A matching procedure like that described previously was arranged in which pecking or pausing (DRL or DRO requirements) in the sample component produced 1.5-second access to food followed by a discrete choice situation in which correct choices, based on the response-reinforcer relation in the sample component, produced an additional 3 seconds of access to food. The probability of the sample component being a DRL (peck) requirement varied systematically between .07 and .93 in different conditions. A zero delay and a 1.5-second blackout replaced food as the contingent event following the sample component during two subsequent conditions. During the zero delay, both the food and blackout were omitted, so that the required response in the sample component immediately produced the choice component. Under both the zero delay and blackout conditions, the probability of the sample component being a DRL requirement was .50.

The isosensitivity curves in Figure 5–3 show that the conditional probability of a peck on the DRL choice key (given either type of response–reinforcer relation in the sample component) increased as the probability of a peck requirement in the sample component increased (filled circles; connected data points). The unconnected filled circles are replications of the P(DRL) = .50 condition. The unfilled circles show that omitting the food delivery that followed

Figure 5–3. Isosensitivity curves for each subject. Data points represent the probability of a peck on the DRL choice key (red key) given a DRL or a DRO contingency in the sample component during each condition. All points are the mean of the last five sessions at each condition (*Source*: from Lattal, 1979).

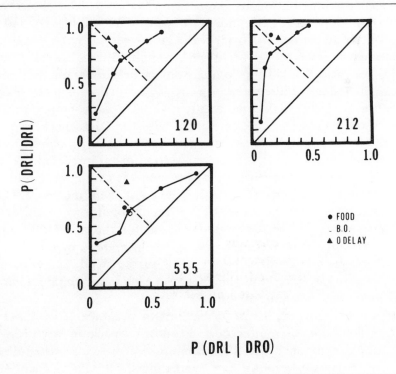

P (DRL | DRO)

the sample and preceded the choice component did not systematically alter performance relative to delivering it there for P (DRL) = .50 ("B.O." in panel 2 of Figure 5-1). Hence, turning on the side keys was salient enough that improvements were not obtained by terminating the sample component with food. Omitting the delay ("skip" in panel 2 of Figure 5-1) following the sample component increased discriminability of the two response-reinforcer relations for two birds, as indicated by the displacement of the data points from the positive diagonal toward 0,1.

According to signal detection theory (SDT), choice performance is determined jointly by variables affecting the discriminability of the stimuli (sensitivity) and by bias (Green and Swets, 1966). The parallel between the effects of these variables and the discriminative and dynamic effects in schedules has been noted by Nevin (1969, 1970, and Chapter 1) and others. SDT assumes that sensitivity and bias operate relatively independently, and it suggests procedures for isolating their contribution to performance. The analytic methods of SDT were applied to the present results in an attempt to identify the relative contribution of these two variables to the choice performance. Non-parametric indexes of sensitivity and bias, A' and B'' respectively, were derived from formulas suggested by Grier (1971). A parametric index of sensitivity, d', computed from Swets' (1964) tables was also derived for comparison to the nonparametric index. Figure 5-4 shows these three measures as a function of the probability of a DRL (peck) requirement in the sample component. Bias toward the red choice key, associated with the DRL (peck) requirement in the sample component, increased as the probability of a DRL (peck) requirement in the sample component increased. Neither A' or d' changed systematically across subjects as the probability of a DRL (peck) requirement in the sample component increased. These measures were constant across the different conditions for Bird 120 and respectively increased and decreased for the other two birds. This variability may reflect unmeasured differences in schedule or behavioral parameters arising from such uncontrolled sources of variation as response rates and time spent in each sample component, as described in the previous experiment.

In this experiment, the occurrence of each choice was a function of the likelihood of reinforcement following pecking or pausing in the sample component. In the concurrent peck-pause schedule described previously, response rates and time spent pausing changed as a function of the likelihood of reinforcement of the two responses.

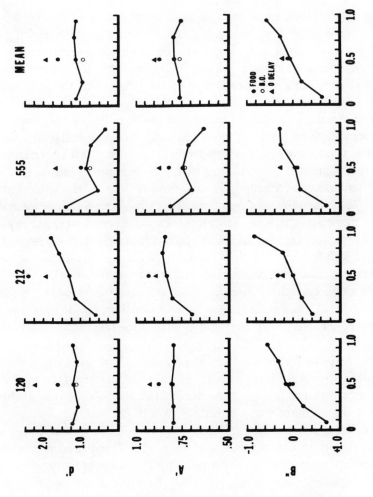

Figure 5–4. The indexes d', A', and B'' as a function of the probability of the DRL contingency during the sample component for each bird. All points are the mean of the last five sessions at each condition. Blackout data points (open circles) overlap with data points from the 1.5-second food access condition (filled circles) during the p(DRL) = 0.50 in the A' graph of Bird 120, in the B'' graphs for Birds 120 and 555, and the mean graph of B''. Filled unconnected circles represent the second exposure to the p(DRL) = 0.50 with a 1.5-second food access between sample and choice components (*Source:* from Lattal, 1979).

To step further out on a limb, it is suggested that there are certain parallels between making one choice or the other in the matching-to-sample procedure and making the choice of pecking or pausing in the concurrent peck–pause schedule. To the extent that these choices do parallel one another, performance differences in the concurrent peck–pause schedule produced here primarily reflect changes in bias or dynamic variables and not the discriminability of the response–reinforcer relations, which does not change systematically across changes in relative reinforcement frequency of the two alternatives.

In other schedules employing different response–reinforcer relations, there may be changes in discriminability of the different relations. Consider, for example, the repetitive temporal sequence of a reinforcement schedule—stimulus–response–reinforcer, stimulus–response–reinforcer, and so forth. Two temporal relations important to the present analysis of discriminability changes are those between the behavior and the reinforcer and those between the onset of reinforcement and the subsequent opportunity to respond. Both of these temporal relations suggest some limiting conditions on the stimulus control of responding by response–reinforcer relation in schedules.

In the response–reinforcer relation, something akin to what has been called a threshold of causality (Gruber, Fink, and Damm, 1957) might be considered. For example, Killeen (1978) studied choice responses in a matching procedure when the sample component arranged either immediate response-dependent or response-independent production of the choice component. Food reinforcement in the choice component depended on pecking the response key associated with the contingency that produced the choice component. Most false reports of a response-produced choice component were made when a response occurred within 0.5 to 2 seconds of a response-independent presentation of the choice component. In schedules, the discriminative control of behavior may be affected in a related manner depending on the consistency or predictibility of the time of reinforcement and the absolute value of the temporal separation of response and reinforcer under the different contingencies.

One situation where variations in discriminability of different response–reinforcer relations may occur is illustrated in an experiment where the required pause duration for DRO reinforcement was varied in a concurrent peck–pause schedule (Lattal and Boyer, in press). The key pecking of pigeons first was reinforced according to a FI 150-second schedule. Then the schedule was changed to a concurrent FI 150-second, VT 150-second schedule. When the concurrent schedule was introduced, the temporal distribution of responding changed from a positively accelerated one under the FI to a more linear one (cf. Lattal and Bryan, 1976). Next, a contingency was added such that once a VT reinforcer became available, it was delivered only if preceded by a pause of at least x seconds. The pause requirement was varied between 0 and 5 seconds during different phases of the experiment relevant to this discussion. Figure 5–5 illustrates how the percent of the total session time spent pausing (measured as any period of nonresponding $\geq$ 5 seconds) changed in two pigeons as a function of the pause requirement. There was little difference in time spent pausing between the 0-second conditions and pause requirements $\leq$ 2 seconds. When the pause requirement was increased to 5 seconds, the amount of time spent pausing increased.

As previously suggested, the discriminative and dynamic effects of the two response–reinforcer relations are confounded. However, one factor in explaining these findings is the notion of a threshold for distinguishing peck- and pause-produced reinforcers. For example,

Figure 5–5. Percent of total session time spent pausing by two birds under different required pauses for food reinforcement. Data points are the means of the last nine sessions at each condition. Ranges are also given.

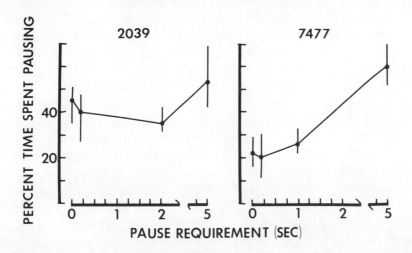

during the concurrent FI, VT schedule, the animals may have failed to distinguish peck- and pause-produced reinforcers and responded as though all were peck produced—namely, with little pausing. As the pause requirement increased, the pause prior to pause-produced reinforcers began to serve as a discriminative stimulus controlling increasing amounts of pausing. At the 5-second pause requirements, the two types of reinforcement contingencies were clearly distinguished; at required pauses in the shorter ranges, they were not distinguished as different from peck-produced reinforcers and therefore controlled little pausing. Thus, the threshold of distinguishing a nonzero delay response–reinforcer relation from a zero delay relation would be predicted to be in the same range as that suggested by Killeen's (1978) data.

The time between onset of reinforcement and the subsequent opportunity to respond is the other temporal relation in schedules to be considered in discussing stimulus control of behavior by response–reinforcer relations. Each response–reinforcer relation is separated from the next opportunity for it to exert discriminative control over responding by the duration of the reinforcer (assuming that food access is used, as it is in many studies of schedule performance). Lattal (1975) asked whether discriminative control by a response–reinforcer relation is affected by the temporal interval between its occurrence and the next opportunity to respond. This was answered by using a delayed matching procedure in which blackouts of different durations occurred between completion of the response requirement in the sample component and presentation of the choice component. Half of the sample components were terminated by completion of a DRL (peck) requirement and half by completion of a DRO (pause) requirement. The procedure was otherwise like that described in Figure 5–1. The effects of delays of 0 to 36 seconds on choice performance were similar to those found using other stimuli in the sample component of delayed matching procedures. That is, the percent correct choice responses decreased systematically with increasing delay values. Figure 5–6 shows that discriminability changed systematically with delay duration, as evidenced by the distance of the data points from the positive diagonal. Bias was unaffected, as shown by the distance of the data points from the negative diagonal. Thus, as the temporal separation increases between the occurrence of the response–reinforcer relation and subsequent opportunities to respond, discriminative control over behavior is weakened. Specifically, these data and those in Figures 5–3 and 5–4

Figure 5–6. Probability of a peck on the DRL choice key (red key), given a DRL or a DRO trial at each delay duration for two birds. The number above each data point is the delay duration in seconds. Triangles indicate the increasing duration sequence (0 seconds to 24 or 36 seconds), and circles indicate the decreasing duration sequence (36 or 24 seconds to 0 seconds). All points are based on the mean of the last five sessions at each condition (*Source*: from Lattal, 1975).

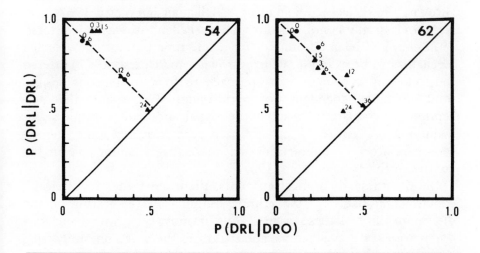

suggest that in schedules where reinforcement duration is fixed but greater than zero, discriminative control will be less than could occur if the reinforcement duration were shorter.

A related problem is the intermittent availability of the response–reinforcer relation. In standard operant-conditioning arrangements, discriminative stimuli are either present continuously or at least continuously available (e.g., as in observing–response procedures). The intermittent availability of the stimuli derived from response–reinforcer relations may also weaken, but not eliminate, stimulus control. Data from a variety of experiments, including the delayed matching data in Figure 5–5, suggest that trace stimuli can control responding. In this context, it also would be of value to know whether a systematic relation exists between overall frequency of different response–reinforcer relations and degree of stimulus control of responding. The A' and d' data in Figure 5–4 suggest that changes in the frequency of reinforcement of pecking and pausing does not systematically affect discriminability under those conditions.

THEORETICAL ACCOUNTS OF BEHAVIOR
BASED ON THE DISCRIMINATION OF
CONTINGENCIES

The discrimination of the relation between responding and reinforcers or other environmental events has been offered to explain a variety of behavioral phenomena. Self-punitive locomotor behavior (Brown, 1969), learned helplessness (Seligman and Maier, 1967), and certain classically conditioned responses (Peden, Browne, and Hearst, 1977) have all been accounted for at one time or another by such a mechanism. For example, Peden, Browne, and Hearst (1977) offered the following explanation of approach to food by pigeons despite food omission dependent on approaching: "We propose that perception of a relation between the signal and food engenders and maintains the entire orient-approach-peck sequence, and the response–reinforcer conjunctions play a relatively minor role in the control of this behavior" (p. 398).

Despite these theoretical accounts, there are rather few "clean" experimental data, by the criteria outlined above, bearing on the discriminability of these events. Thus, in most cases where such discriminations are assigned a causative role, there are no supporting experimental data showing that the events are in fact discriminated. Even where supporting data are provided, the contribution of the discrimination to control of the behavior often is unclear. Brown (1969) noted this problem:

> The . . . well nigh fatal weakness of the discrimination conception lies in its complete failure to provide precise statements concerning the theoretical relations holding between discriminations and behavior . . . The question now facing the theorist is that of predicting just what the animal will actually do, given that it has discriminated. . . . Knowing [the organism] is aware is of no use to the experimenter until the behavioral consequences of such awareness are explicitly formulated. (P. 505)

A final consideration is one of recognizing the multiple causes of schedule performance. In an attempt to simplify schedule-controlled behavior, operant research has emphasized the importance of dynamic and differentiating variables. The discriminative role of schedules and of contingencies operating within schedules only recently has sparked the interest of operant psychologists. However, without a consideration of discriminative effects in schedules, a complete accounting of schedule performance will not be forthcoming. How this knowledge of the discriminative properties of contingencies operating in schedules can contribute to an understanding of behavior was described quite well by Ferster and Skinner (1957):

> A more general analysis is also possible which answers the question of why a given schedule generates a given performance. It is in one sense a theoretical analysis, but it is not theoretical in the sense of speculating about corresponding events in some other universe of discourse. It simply reduces a large number of schedules to a formulation in terms of certain common features. It does this by a closer analysis of the actual contingencies of reinforcement prevailing under any given schedule. (P. 2)

SUMMARY

A rationale was developed for an analysis of the discriminative properties of response–reinforcer relations, and schedule arrangements in which these relations may serve as stimuli were defined. A review of the methods of assessing these discriminative properties directly suggested that the use of a matching procedure posed the fewest problems. Using this procedure, it has been demonstrated that animals discriminate between response-dependent and either response-independent or response-delayed reinforcers.

Since these relations potentially serve a discriminative function in certain reinforcement schedules, mechanisms of their operation in schedules were examined. Among the problems encountered in this analysis were those of separating bias and sensitivity effects, precise mechanisms of discriminative control, and the relation between the empirical evidence for reinforcement contingency discrimination and theoretical accounts of schedule performance.

REFERENCES

Appel, J.B., and R.H. Hiss. 1962. The discrimination of contingent from non-contingent reinforcement. *Journal of Comparative and Physiological Psychology* 55 : 37–39.

Brown, J.S. 1969. Factors affecting self-punitive locomotor behavior. In B.A. Campbell and R.M. Church, eds., *Punishment and Aversive Behavior*, pp. 467–511. New York: Appleton–Century–Crofts.

Catania, A.C. 1970. Reinforcement schedules and psychophysical judgment. In W.N. Schoenfeld, ed., *The Theory of Reinforcement Schedules*, pp. 1–43. New York: Appleton–Century–Crofts.

Commons, M.L. 1979. Decision rules and signal detectability in a reinforcement–density discrimination. *Journal of the Experimental Analysis of Behavior 32*: 101–120.

Cumming, W.W., and R. Berryman. 1965. The complex discriminated operant: Studies of matching-to-sample and related problems. In D.J. Mostofosky, ed., *Stimulus Generalization*, pp. 284–330. Stanford, California: Stanford University Press.

Ferster, C.B., and B.F. Skinner. 1957. *Schedules of Reinforcement*. New York: Appleton–Century–Crofts.

Green, D.M., and J.A. Swets. 1966. *Signal Detection Theory and Psychophysics*. New York: Wiley.

Grier, J.B. 1971. Nonparametric indexes for sensitivity and bias: Computing formulas. *Psychological Bulletin 75*: 424–429.

Gruber, H.E.; C.D. Fink; and V. Damm. 1957. Effects of experience on perception of causality. *Journal of Experimental Psychology 53*: 89–93.

Killeen, P. 1978. Superstition: A matter of bias, not detectability. *Science 199*: 88–90.

Lattal, K.A. 1973. Response–reinforcer dependence and independence in multiple and mixed schedules. *Journal of the Experimental Analysis of Behavior 20*: 265–271.

_____. 1974. Combinations of response–reinforcer dependence and independence. *Journal of the Experimental Analysis of Behavior 22*: 357–362.

_____. 1975. Reinforcement contingencies as discriminative stimuli. *Journal of the Experimental Analysis of Behavior 23*: 241–246.

_____. 1979. Reinforcement contingencies as discriminative stimuli: II. Effects of changes in stimulus probability. *Journal of the Experimental Analysis of Behavior 31*: 15–22.

Lattal, K.A., and S.S. Boyer. In press. Alternative reinforcement effects on fixed-interval responding. *Journal of the Experimental Analysis of Behavior*.

Lattal, K.A., and A.J. Bryan. 1976. Effects of concurrent response-independent reinforcement on fixed-interval schedule performance. *Journal of the Experimental Analysis of Behavior 26*: 495–504.

Maki, N.S.; J.C. Moe; and C.M. Bierley. 1977. Short-term memory for stimuli, responses, and reinforcers. *Journal of Experimental Psychology: Animal Behavior Processes 2*: 156–176.

Nevin, J.A. 1969. Signal detection theory and operant behavior. *Journal of the Experimental Analysis of Behavior 12*: 475–480.

_____. 1970. On differential stimulation and differential reinforcement. In W.C. Stebbins, ed., *Animal Psychophysics: The Design and Conduct of Sensory Experiments*, pp. 401–423. New York: Appleton–Century–Crofts.

Peden, B.F.; M.P. Brown; and E. Hearst. 1977. Persistent approaches to a signal for food despite food omission for approaching. *Journal of Experimental Psychology: Animal Behavior Processes 4*: 377–398.

Pliskoff, S.S., and I. Goldiamond. 1966. Some discriminative properties of fixed ratio performance in the pigeon. *Journal of the Experimental Analysis of Behavior 9*: 1–9.

Poresky, R.H. 1971. Noncontingency detection in children and adults. *Proceedings of the American Psychological Association*, pp. 691–692. Washington, D.C.: American Psychological Association.

Rachlin, H., and W.M. Baum. 1972. Effects of alternative reinforcement: Does the source matter? *Journal of the Experimental Analysis of Behavior 18*: 231–241.

Rilling, M.E., and C.G. McDiarmid. 1965. Signal detection in fixed-ratio schedules. *Science 148*: 526–527.

Schoenfeld, W.N.; B.K. Cole; J. Lang; and R. Mankoff. 1973. "Contingency" in behavior theory. In F.J. McGuigan and D.B. Lumsden, eds., *Contemporary Approaches to Conditioning and Learning*, pp. 151–172. Washington, D.C.: J.H. Winston & Sons.

Seligman, M.E.P., and S.F. Maier. 1967. Failure to escape traumatic shock. *Journal of Experimental Psychology 74*: 1–9.

Silberberg, A. 1971. A procedure for assessing pigeons' sensitivity to negative automaintenance procedures. Paper presented at Eastern Psychological Association, New York, April.

Skinner, B.F. 1950. Are theories of learning necessary? *Psychological Review 57*: 193–216.

_____. 1958. Reinforcement today. *The American Psychologist 13*: 94–99.

Stubbs, A. 1968. The discrimination of stimulus duration by pigeons. *Journal of the Experimental Analysis of Behavior 11*: 223–238.

Swets, J., ed. 1964. *Signal Detection and Recognition by Human Observers*. New York: Wiley.

Zeiler, M.D. 1972. Superstitious behavior in children: An experimental analysis. In H.W. Reese, ed., *Advances in Child Development*, pp. 1–29. New York: Academic Press.

_____. 1976. Positive reinforcement and the elimination of reinforced responses. *Journal of the Experimental Analysis of Behavior 26*: 37–44.

_____. 1977. Schedules of reinforcement: The controlling variables. In W.K. Honig and J.E.R. Staddon, eds., *Handbook of Operant Behavior*, pp. 201–232. Englewood Cliffs, N.J.: Prentice-Hall.

IV TEMPORAL FACTORS AS DISCRIMINATIVE PROPERTIES OF REINFORCEMENT SCHEDULES

6 TEMPORAL DISCRIMINATION
From Psychophysics to Reinforcement Schedules

D. Alan Stubbs and
Leon R. Dreyfus

Experiments on animals' temporal discrimination may be categorized in two general groups—one that uses reinforcement-scheduling procedures and the other, psychophysical procedures. Schedules of reinforcement often reveal regularities in performance that are a function of the temporal distribution of events, and some of these regularities suggest that a temporal discrimination may contribute to response output. Common findings that suggest the possibility of temporal discrimination include the gradually accelerated response rate observed under fixed interval schedules, the temporal spacing of responses under differential reinforcement of low rate and free operant avoidance procedures, and orderly relations between response output and schedule changes under a variety of temporal differentiation schedules (see Catania, 1970; Gibbon, 1972, 1977; Platt, 1979; for reviews).

To study temporal discrimination, animal psychophysical research has adapted the procedures of human psychophysics. In most of these experiments, an animal is presented with a stimulus that lasts for one of several durations; then one of two choice responses is reinforced depending on the duration of the prior stimulus. One

This chapter is dedicated to Israel Goldiamond for his influence in the area of schedules as discriminative stimuli. Many years ago he suggested placing fixed interval schedules within the context of psychophysics, the basic idea that gave rise to the present experiment.

response is reinforced if the duration was short, while the alternate response is reinforced if the duration was long. Research using psychophysical procedures has focused on issues such as accuracy of temporal discrimination, the comparison of discrimination at different durations, scaling of duration, and characteristics of the timing process (see Church, 1978; Stubbs, 1979; and Gibbon, Chapter 7).

Of the two approaches to temporal discrimination, the psychophysical approach is more direct and produces results that are easier to interpret. Psychophysical methodology permits experimental control of the stimuli to be discriminated and of the factors that might influence choice. Schedule performance, on the other hand, is influenced by many factors, so that it is not obvious to what extent temporal discriminations are involved. Although there are many promising and intriguing findings and excellent theoretical work that argue for a temporal discrimination interpretation of schedule performance, numerous authors have pointed to problems and have urged caution in giving too much weight to temporal discrimination interpretations (e.g., Dews, 1970; Morse, 1966; Platt, 1979). One has only to review the literature on fixed interval schedules, with the various explanations of Skinner (1938), Ferster and Skinner (1957), Schneider (1969), Dews (1970), Jenkins (1970), Staddon (1974), Killeen (1975), Hawkes and Shimp (1975), Gibbon (1977) and Roberts and Church (1978), to appreciate the variety of factors that contribute to schedule performance and to consider the complexity of assessing how temporal discriminations may be involved.

The research generated by these two methodologies raises certain issues that differ to some degree, depending on the individual's focus of interest. If the focus of study is temporal discrimination, the psychophysical methodology produces results that are more easily interpretable; the schedule results could be viewed as somewhat primitive, and as a result, one might be tempted to say, "let's just use psychophysical procedures and forget schedules." Such a position might have some merits, but it ignores a sizeable body of research that may provide supporting evidence or suggest possibilities overlooked in the psychophysical research. If, however, the focus is schedule performance, the interest is in those factors that influence schedule performance, one of which might be temporal discrimination. Researchers are forced in one sense to study temporal discriminations within the context of schedules, even though this approach may lead to findings that are difficult to interpret. In this context, the results of psychophysical experiments may be useful, but it is hard to integrate these results, since the two methodologies differ in so many ways. Researchers with these two different interests may face somewhat different issues when dealing with the two sets of data, but in a more general way their interests converge on the basic problem — how to integrate the two different sets of data.

The most frequent approach to integration is to search for common findings in the two sets of data. Examples of this approach include discussions of the relative timing process suggested by both psychophysics and schedules (e.g., Church, 1978; Gibbon, 1977; Stubbs, 1976b). This approach searches for common results but leaves the two methodologies separate. In contrast, the present work attempts to integrate the two methodologies by establishing a procedural transition between psychophysics and schedules. A psychophysical procedure was first arranged and then gradually modified across a series of conditions to more closely resemble a typical schedule procedure. The purpose was to establish a continuum of procedures that would allow for easier comparison and generalization of the two sets of data.

A free operant choice procedure (Mandell and Nevin, 1977; Stubbs, 1980) was chosen because it has elements both of psychophysics and of schedules. Stubbs used this procedure for duration discrimination, presenting pigeons with a series of time periods during which two key lights were on. One key was lighted blue while the other key was lighted either orange or green. Pecks on the blue (changeover) key changed the color on the alternate key, while pecks on the orange/green (main) key produced food intermittently. Food delivery depended both on the color of the main key and the time elapsed since the start of the key light period. Orange key responses were reinforced intermittently, but only during the first half of a time period (e.g., between 0 and 10 seconds), while green key responses were reinforced only during the second half (e.g., between 10 and 20 seconds). If food was delivered during a time period, the period ended. A blackout followed food, and then a new time period began. The procedure is similar to that of concurrent schedules (deVilliers, 1977) except that food availability depended on time elapsed as well as on key color in the discrimination task. Under this procedure, the pigeons pecked the orange main key for roughly the first half of a time interval, then pecked the blue changeover key, changing the color on the main key, and then pecked on the green main key for the second half.

The probability of a response being to green (long) and the probability that the animal was in the presence of green increased as a function of elapsed time. The probability functions for both responses and time were quite regular and ogival in form. Performance was assessed when the duration of the time periods was varied, and discrimination sensitivity, indexed by the slope of the probability function, remained constant across a wide range of durations. Under a different set of conditions having a closer bearing on the present study, the number of reinforcers for "short" (orange) and "long" (green) responses was varied, with relatively more reinforcers being delivered for one response. This change affected response bias while discrimination sensitivity remained relatively constant. All of these results are consistent with previous results of other procedures (Stubbs, 1979).

Basically, the free operant choice procedure is a psychophysical procedure, but since it involves free operant choice, it bears a procedural similarity to schedules. The purpose of the present experiment was to take the free operant procedure, modify it, and gradually make it even more schedulelike. Specifically, the procedure was made to resemble that of a fixed interval schedule. In Stubbs' (1980) experiment, one response produced food during the first half of some time periods while a second response produced food during the second half. In the present experiment, one response sometimes produced food early in the time period as before, while the other response would also sometimes produce food, but only after a certain interval had elapsed: Red key responses sometimes produced food between 0 and 20 seconds following key light onset, while during other time periods, the first green key peck after 20 seconds produced food. This procedure is similar to the previous one except that the reinforcement schedule for green key pecks resembles a conventional fixed interval schedule.

Basically, the procedure intermittently provides food for one response before a fixed interval has elapsed and intermittently provides food for a second response once the fixed interval has elapsed. This procedure was gradually modified over conditions to approximate a fixed interval schedule more closely by changes in the assignment of reinforcers for red key and green key, fixed interval responses.

Reinforcers were initially scheduled equally for red key and green key responses, but gradually the number of reinforcers for red key responses was reduced until only green key, fixed interval responses were reinforced. Choice data characteristic of psychophysics and rate data characteristic of schedules were recorded and compared as the procedure was modified from one that resembled the previous psychophysical procedure to one that resembled a fixed interval schedule.

METHOD

The subjects were three food-deprived pigeons. A standard pigeon chamber was used. Sessions were arranged by solid-state circuitry, with each session lasting until a pigeon received fifty food presentations.

Each session consisted of a series of key light time periods lasting a maximum of 30 seconds. The left key light was always white and the right key light red at the beginning of a time period. A peck to the white (changeover) key changed the color on the right (main) key from red to green; the changeover response also turned off the white light, making the changeover key inoperative for the remainder of the time period. Pecks to the main key intermittently produced food, depending both on the time elapsed and on the key color. During some time periods, food was scheduled for red key responses between 0 and 20 seconds following key light onset. During other time periods, food was scheduled for the first green key peck 20 seconds after the lights went on. Food was not scheduled during the remaining time periods; the lights simply remained on for 30 seconds, and then a 10 second blackout ensued, which was followed by a new time period. If a peck produced food, a blackout followed, and then a new time period began.

Reinforcers were arranged by a tape to occur irregularly for red key and green key responses only during one-third of the time periods. If the tape assigned a reinforcer, the reinforcer was assigned either for a red key response or for a green key response, never both. If food was assigned for a red key response, a random interval schedule operated while the key color was red to ensure a relatively uniform distribution of reinforcers across the first 20 seconds of the time period. If a reinforcer was missed—that is, if the animal did not respond in the presence of the appropriate key color at the appropriate time—the key light time period lasted the 30-second maximum; the blackout then ensued, and the reinforcer was again assigned during the following time period. The relative rate of reinforcement was changed across conditions so that gradually more and more reinforcers were provided for green key, fixed interval, responses. Table 6-1 summarizes the conditions. In the first four conditions, first 50, then 75, then 95, and finally 100 percent of the reinforcers were delivered for green key responses. Because reinforcers were available only during one-third of the time periods, a fifth condition was investigated in which a reinforcer was assigned for a green key peck every time period. This condition most closely resembled a standard fixed interval schedule, since food was available in every time period for the first green key response after 20 seconds. The final condition was a redetermination of the earlier 75 percent condition.

RESULTS

Three types of data were recorded for eight time classes: the number of red key and green key pecks; the time spent in the presence of red and green; and the number of reinforcers for pecks at different times following the onset of the key lights. Each of the first seven time classes was four seconds in duration (0-4 seconds, 4-8 seconds . . . 24-28 seconds), while the eighth was two seconds (28-30

Table 6-1. Summary of Experimental Conditions in Order of Presentation and Number of Sessions under Each.

Condition (percent of reinforcers delivered for green key responses)	#31	#32	#33
50	95	96	95
75	44	44	44
95	21	19	21
100	34	36	36
100[a]	20	20	17
75	42	37	35

a. Reinforcers were available during all time periods for this condition; for the remaining conditions reinforcers were scheduled only during one-third of the time periods.

seconds). Red key responses were reinforced during the first five time classes, while green key responses were reinforced during the remaining three. (Actually green key responses were reinforced primarily during the sixth time class [20–24 seconds]. Once the "fixed interval" had elapsed, however, reinforcers for green key responses remained available and were obtained occasionally in the seventh and eighth time classes.)

Figure 6–1 presents the probability of a green key response in each time class for the different conditions. The points represent probabilities that pecks, when they occurred, were to the green key as opposed to the red. The probability data were calculated by dividing the number of green key pecks by the total number of pecks, green key plus red key, in each time class.

The top portion of Figure 6–1 shows that when reinforcers were equally distributed for the two responses, probability of a green key peck was low during the first two time classes (0–8 seconds) and then increased across time classes. The functions are ogival in form and similar to other data obtained with animals discriminating stimulus duration (Stubbs, 1980). Similar functions were obtained when 75 and then 95 percent of the reinforcers were delivered for green key responses, with the major difference being a shift in the ogival functions to the left. This change indicates that the pigeons tended to change from red to green at earlier times. The filled and unfilled circles show that performance was quite similar in the two determinations of the 75 percent condition. The bottom portions show performance when 100 percent of the reinforcers were scheduled for green key responses, either on one-third of the time periods (fourth row) or on all of them (bottom row). Virtually all responses were on the green key under these latter two conditions, producing probability measures at or very near 1 in all time classes. Points were omitted in the first time class for Pigeons 32 and 33 and, in the bottom row, for the seventh and eighth classes for all three birds, since few responses were emitted during these times. Pigeons 32 and 33 did not peck during the first time class in either condition, and in the last condition, the animals always produced food during the sixth time class and thus never entered the last two time classes.

Figure 6–2 is comparable to Figure 6–1, but gives probability data for time rather than responses. Figure 6–2 shows the probability of time spent in green (as opposed to red). Data were calculated by dividing the time spent in green by the total time spent in that time

Figure 6–1. Probability of a green key response in different time classes across the different experimental conditions. Reinforcers were scheduled for red key responses during the first five time classes and for green key responses during the sixth (see text for details). Reinforcers were scheduled during one-third of the time periods in all conditions except the one shown in the bottom row; reinforcers were scheduled in every time period in this condition. Points represent averages of performance during the last five sessions under a condition.

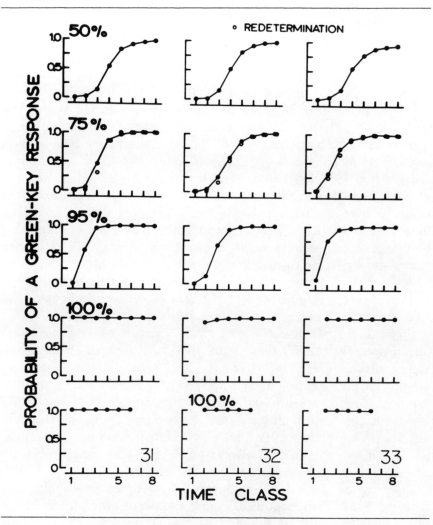

Figure 6−2. Probability of time spent in the presence of green in different time classes across different conditions. Reinforcers were scheduled for red key responses during the first five time classes and for green key responses during the sixth. Points represent means of performance during the last five sessions under each condition.

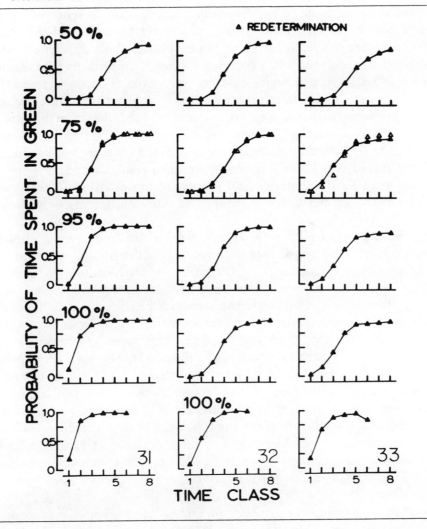

class (i.e., red time plus green time). The results are similar to those of Figure 6-1 in several respects. The functions in Figure 6-2 are ogival in form, indicating that the animals spent most of the time in the presence of red at early time classes and that the probability of time spent in green increased as a function of time. The ogival functions shifted to the left when relatively more reinforcers were delivered for green key responses. Unlike the response data, the time data show that the probability of spending time in the presence of green was low in the first time class even when 100 percent of the reinforcers were delivered for green key responses. This difference indicates that under the 100 percent conditions, the animals spent some time in red before changing to green even though they never pecked the red key. The difference stems from the fact that a time period always began with the key red, which exposed the animals to red even though no pecks were emitted.

Figure 6-3 directly compares response and time probability functions for Pigeon 32 in a single figure. The response and time functions were similar under the 50 percent conditions, but differed to a greater and greater degree as more and more reinforcers were delivered for green key responses.

The pigeons could peck at any rate in the free operant choice procedure, so response rate data could be calculated in addition to the probability data usually gathered in psychophysical experiments. Rate data provide more than just a supplement to the probability data. Response rates provide the standard measures in schedules, so the rate data here make closer contact with the data from more conventional schedules. Red key responses and green key responses in each time class were each separately divided by the total time spent in that time class. Figure 6-4 shows that red key response rates decreased as a function of time elapsed while green key response rates increased. In most conditions, the highest green key rate occurred in the sixth time class, the time class during which reinforcers were scheduled. Red key response rates declined as reinforcement conditions were changed from 50 to 100 percent. Green key response rates tended to increase across conditions, but the change was not consistent.

Figure 6-5 presents summary measures derived from the probability data that make contact with other psychophysical data. The top portion shows the time at which green key probability was 0.5 across conditions. The points indicate those times when red key and green

Figure 6–3. Comparison of response and time probability data for Pigeon 32 in each of the first four experimental conditions. The data are replotted from Figures 6–1 and 6–2.

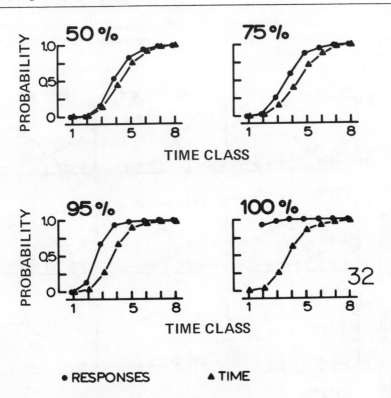

key probabilities were equal and is equivalent to the traditional psychophysical measure, the point of subjective equality (PSE). The points were interpolated from the probability data by the linear interpolation method (Guilford, 1954). The pattern of change differed from pigeon to pigeon, but the data for all three pigeons show that the PSE decreased from approximately 15 seconds to approximately 4 seconds as reinforcement conditions changed. Data for the cases in which green key response probability was above 0.50 in all time classes could not be computed and thus are not shown.

The bottom portions show Weber fractions, which provide a measure of sensitivity or discriminability across conditions. The Weber fraction for duration experiments is $\Delta T / T$, where T is some reference duration and ΔT is a second duration that can just be discriminated.

Figure 6–4. Response rate data in the different time classes across different experimental conditions. Unconnected points under the 75 percent condition show performance under the redetermination. Reinforcers were scheduled for red key responses during the first five time classes and for green key responses during the sixth. Points represent means of performance during the last five sessions under each condition.

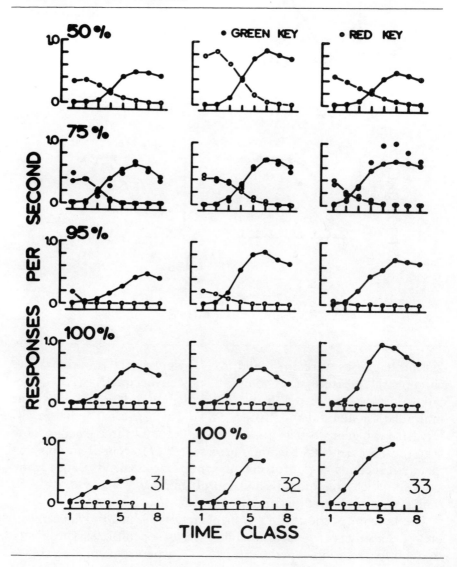

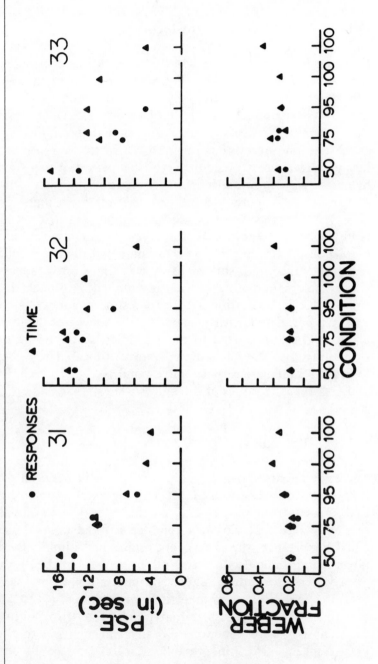

Figure 6–5. Summary measures of performance across conditions. The top portions show the point of subjective equality (PSE) or points at which green key probability equaled 0.50 both for responses and for time. The bottom portions show Weber fractions for both response and time data. See text for details on computation. Points represent means of performance during the last five sessions under each condition.

Under the present procedure, T was equivalent to the point of subjective equality. The value of ΔT was obtained in the following way (Stubbs, 1980): The times at which green key probabilities were 0.25 and 0.75 were calculated for each condition by the linear interpolation method. The time at which $P = 0.25$ was subtracted from the time at which $P = 0.75$ to define an interval of uncertainty. The resulting number was then divided by 2 to obtain a difference threshold, ΔT (see Guilford, 1954, for rationale). The Weber fractions were similar across conditions, indicating similar discrimination performance. The one exception occurred in the condition in which green key pecks were reinforced in every time period; Weber fractions were higher in this condition than in the others.

The data of Figure 6–5 indicate that the main change in performance was a change in response bias, while sensitivity remained relatively constant. The point of subjective equality acts as a measure of response bias by showing that the equal point for red and green responses (and time) shifted to shorter times across conditions. This change corresponds to an increasing tendency to peck to and spend time in green, indicating a bias to respond "long." The changes in PSE are correlated with changes in the ogives of Figures 6–1 and 6–2: As the PSE shifted to shorter times, so the entire ogival functions shifted to the left (toward shorter times). The Weber fractions indicating similar sensitivity correspond to the results in Figures 6–1 and 6–2 that the slopes of the ogives were similar.

DISCUSSION

The experiment reported here provided a link between psychophysics and schedule research by establishing a continuum of procedures that ranged from one similar to those used in psychophysical research to one that closely resembled a fixed interval schedule. Of equal importance, the experiment established a link between psychophysics and schedules in terms of the analysis of the results. The use of a choice procedure allowed computation of probability data, resulting in ogival psychometric functions leading to measures of sensitivity and response bias that are characteristic of a psychophysical analysis. These data were obtained in addition to the response data typically taken in schedule research and could be compared directly with rate data in all conditions.

The probability data demonstrate that ogival functions obtained across conditions, but that the functions shifted to earlier times as the relative reinforcement rate for green key responses increased. These results are similar to those obtained in other psychophysical experiments on duration discrimination. Similar changes in ogival functions have been observed when relative reinforcement rate has been manipulated both in a psychophysical trials procedure (Stubbs, 1976a) and in a free operant psychophysical procedure (Stubbs, 1980). The results of all three experiments agree that changes in relative reinforcement rate produce changes in response bias but not discrimination sensitivity. The results are consistent with the general findings of signal detection research that changes in the payoff structure influence response criterion or bias while sensitivity remains constant (e.g., Green and Swets, 1966).

The results demonstrate that fixed interval schedule performance can be placed within the context of psychophysics and suggest certain statements that can be made within this context. The probability data showed the most extreme degree of response bias under the fixed interval–like conditions, and the extreme degree of bias doubtlessly resulted from reinforcement of only one of the two choice responses. The findings agree with those of Stubbs (1976a), who used a psychophysical trials procedure in which reinforcers were provided for one response given one of a group of short durations and for a second response given one of a set of long durations. In the comparable condition of that experiment, all durations were presented, but only correct long responses were reinforced. The results were similar to those observed in the present experiment: The procedure led to an extreme degree of bias, evidenced by almost exclusive responding of one type; the pigeons primarily emitted long responses, even at the shortest durations.

Our results support a view of fixed interval schedule performance that is influenced by signal detection theory. The signal detection approach provides a way of viewing a variety of psychophysical and discrimination situations, separately analyzing sensitivity and response bias and the factors affecting each (Green and Swets, 1966; see also Nevin, Chapter 1). Sensitivity is affected by the signal-to-noise ratio (or difference between stimuli to be discriminated) and by organismic factors. Response bias is affected by the payoff structure for different stimulus–response combinations and by the a priori probability of presentations of different stimuli. A detection analysis of fixed interval schedules suggests that these schedules produce biased performance due to an asymmetric arrangement of response consequences. If a fixed interval schedule is considered as a temporal discrimination situation, the temporal stimuli may be grouped into durations less than and durations equal to or greater than the value of the fixed interval. The actions appropriate to these stimuli are, respectively, withholding a response and emitting a response. Although there are four stimulus–response combinations, there is an explicit consequence for only one. That is, only one class of action is reinforced in this situation—a key peck or lever press after a certain time. Other behavior associated with withholding a response is never explicitly reinforced. Further, there is no cost associated with emitting responses early (such as an analogous monetary loss for false alarm responses in some detection experiments). These factors combine to produce a stimulus–response payoff matrix favoring an extreme bias to respond. That such a bias occurs is suggested by the great number of early responses that normally characterize fixed interval performance. Such bias may be reduced by altering the stimulus–response matrix by providing reinforcement for some alternate response (as in the present study; see also Nevin, 1971) or perhaps by providing response-independent reinforcement (Rachlin and Baum, 1972). The bias normally seen and the changes in performance with alternative reinforcement are consistent with signal detection theory.

Although the present findings place fixed interval schedules within the context of psychophysics, the results suggest caution in speaking about temporal discriminations in fixed interval schedules. The probability data from the 100 percent condition revealed an extreme bias—so extreme, in fact, that green key response probability was at or near 1 in all time classes; ogives and resulting Weber fractions were obtained only with the time data. In contrast to the probability data, the rate data were characterized by a gradual increase as time elapsed, even in cases when probability data were at 1. Differences between the two sets of data raise the question of which is the better indicator of temporal discrimination. The difference could be taken as evidence that the response rate data provide a better measure, since these data showed changes in behavior even when the probability data were asymptotic. However, the probability data are consistent with those of the other conditions and agree with the findings of other psychophysical experiments; these consistencies argue in favor of the probability data when they seemingly differ from the response rate data. Also, fixed interval performance is influenced by many factors (e.g., Zeiler, 1977), so it could be that the changes in response rate have little to do with a temporal discrimination, but instead are influenced by some other factor or factors, such as delayed reinforcement effects. At the very least, the differences observed in the present experiment argue for extreme caution in use of rate data as an index of temporal discrimination.

The present experiment used both response and time probability measures and demonstrated a possible advantage of the time measure under the 100 percent conditions. By way of extension, the results suggest that time measures should be used to supplement the response rate measures typically used with fixed interval schedules. Time spent engaging in different classes of behavior—such as not responding, responding, or engaging in other specified behavior—could easily be recorded in addition to a number of responses.

The suggestion to place greater emphasis on time measures is in accord with three lines of evidence. First, Schneider (1969) and Schneider and Neuringer (1972) have performed a two-state analysis of fixed interval performance and observed that each interval is characterized by a period of time during which the animals paused followed by a period of time during which response rates were high. The time at which responding begins serves as a measure of performance, and perhaps the gradually accelerated response rate typically claimed to characterize fixed interval performance may be due in part to variability in time to start responding from interval to interval. A second line of evidence comes from research that has recorded behavior other than key pecks and lever presses (e.g., Killeen, 1975; Staddon, 1977). This research has shown that different classes of behavior are most likely at certain times during the interval. Third, experiments on concurrent schedules and the matching law have demonstrated not only that relative response rate matches relative reinforcement rate, but also that the relative amount of time spent on one of two schedules matches the relative reinforcement rate for that schedule. These results have led several authors to consider the possibility that time measures may be more fundamental and that response matching results from the way in which animals distribute their time to the different alternatives. These three lines of research, as well as the present experiment, indicate that response measures are not sufficient and should be supplemented by measures of the time spent engaging in different classes of behavior during fixed interval schedules.

Our experiment used the fixed interval schedule as a point of contact between psychophysics and schedules, but the method can be extended to other schedules as well. As one example, consider a differential reinforcement of low rate (DRL) schedule, which is similar to the fixed interval schedule in that the first response emitted after a certain time is reinforced, but differs in that each response emitted prior to that time resets the required time period. The new procedure could be like the fixed interval case, with red key responses reinforced during the first 20 seconds and the first green key response reinforced after 20 seconds has elapsed. To approximate the differential reinforcement of low rate schedule, green key responses that occur before 20 seconds would reset the time period. Reducing the number of reinforcers for red key responses would make the procedure more closely approximate a DRL schedule. The free operant choice procedure can easily be extended and applied to other schedules as well. The free operant psychophysical procedure can be used to supplement and complement the more common psychophysical trials procedures by providing an alternate set of procedures to examine the discriminative properties of schedules in a variety of settings.

REFERENCES

Catania, A.C. 1970. Reinforcement schedules and psychophysical judgements: A study of some temporal properties of behavior. In W.N. Schoenfeld, ed., *The Theory of Reinforcement Schedules*. New York: Appleton–Century–Crofts.

Church, R.M. 1978. The internal clock. In S.H. Hulse, H. Fowler, and W.K. Honig, eds., *Cognitive Aspects of Animal Behavior*. Hillsdale, New Jersey: Erlbaum Associates.

De Villiers, P. 1977. Choice in concurrent schedules and a quantitative formulation of the law of effect. In W.K. Honig and J.E.R. Staddon, eds., *Handbook of Operant Behavior*. Englewood Cliffs, New Jersey: Prentice–Hall.

Dews, P.B. 1970. The theory of fixed-interval responding. In W.N. Schoenfeld, ed., *The Theory of Reinforcement Schedules*. New York: Appleton–Century–Crofts.

Ferster, C.B., and B.F. Skinner. 1957. *Schedules of Reinforcement*. New York: Appleton–Century–Crofts.

Gibbon, J. 1972. Timing and discrimination of shock density in avoidance. *Psychological Review 79* : 68–92.

_____. 1977. Scalar expectancy theory and Weber's law in animal timing. *Psychological Review 84* : 279–325.

Green, D.M., and J.A. Swets. 1966. *Signal Detection Theory and Psychophysics*. New York: John Wiley & Sons.

Guilford, J.P. 1954. *Psychometric Methods*. 2nd ed. New York: McGraw–Hill.

Hawkes, L., and C.P. Shimp. 1975. Reinforcement of behavioral patterns: Shaping a scallop. *Journal of the Experimental Analysis of Behavior 23* : 3–16.

Jenkins, H.M. 1970. Sequential organization in schedules of reinforcement. In W.N. Schoenfeld, ed., *The Theory of Reinforcement Schedules*. New York: Appleton–Century–Crofts.

Killeen, P. 1975. On the temporal control of behavior. *Psychological Review 82* : 89–115.

Mandell, C., and J.A. Nevin. 1977. Choice, time allocation, and response rate during stimulus generalization. *Journal of the Experimental Analysis of Behavior 28* : 47–57.

Morse, W.H. 1966. Intermittent reinforcement. In W.K. Honig, ed., *Operant Behavior: Areas of Research and Application*. New York: Appleton–Century–Crofts.

Nevin, J.A. 1971. Rates and patterns of responding with concurrent fixed-interval and variable-interval reinforcement. *Journal of the Experimental Analysis of Behavior 16* : 241–247.

Platt, J.R. 1979. Temporal differentiation and the psychophysics of time. In M.D. Zeiler and P. Harzem, eds., *Advances in Analysis of Behavior: Vol. 1: Reinforcement and the Organization of Behavior*. Chichester, England: Wiley.

Rachlin, H.C., and W.M. Baum. 1972. Effects of alternative reinforcement: Does the source matter? *Journal of the Experimental Analysis of Behavior 18* : 231–241.

Roberts, S., and R.M. Church. 1978. Control of an internal clock. *Journal of Experimental Psychology: Animal Behavior Processes 4* : 318–337.

Schneider, B.A. 1969. A two-state analysis of fixed-interval responding in the pigeon. *Journal of the Experimental Analysis of Behavior 12* : 677–687.

Schneider, B.A., and A.J. Neuringer. 1972. Responding under discrete-trial fixed-interval schedules of reinforcement. *Journal of the Experimental Analysis of Behavior 18* : 187–199.

Skinner, B.F. 1938. *The Behavior of Organisms*. New York: Appleton–Century–Crofts.

Staddon, J.E.R. 1974. Temporal control, attention, and memory. *Psychological Review 81* : 375–391.

_____. 1977. Schedule-induced behavior. In W.K. Honig and J.E.R. Staddon, eds., *Handbook of Operant Behavior*. Englewood Cliffs, New Jersey: Prentice–Hall, Inc.

Stubbs, D.A. 1968. The discrimination of stimulus duration by pigeons. *Journal of the Experimental Analysis of Behavior 11* : 223–258.

_____ . 1976a. Response bias and the discrimination of stimulus duration. *Journal of the Experimental Analysis of Behavior 25* : 243–250.

_____ . 1976b. Scaling of stimulus duration by pigeons. *Journal of the Experimental Analysis of Behavior 26* : 15–25.

_____ . 1979. Temporal discrimination and psychophysics. In M.D. Zeiler and P. Harzem, eds., *Advances in Analysis of Behavior: Vol. 1: Reinforcement and the Organization of Behavior.* Chichester, England: Wiley.

_____ . 1980. Discrimination of stimulus duration and a free-operant psychophysical procedure. *Journal of the Experimental Analysis of Behavior 33* : 167–185.

Zeiler, M.D. 1977. Schedules of reinforcement: The controlling variables. In W.K. Honig and J.E.R. Staddon, eds., *Handbook of Operant Behavior.* Englewood Cliffs, New Jersey: Prentice–Hall.

7 TWO KINDS OF AMBIGUITY IN THE STUDY OF PSYCHOLOGICAL TIME

John Gibbon

INTRODUCTION

At least two distinct sets of data in the animal timing literature suggest that the subjective time scale may not be linear in real time. One set of experimental results could be termed time "estimation" or "reproduction" data by analogy to similar procedures with humans. They consist largely of temporal differentiation procedures where subjects are rewarded for placing an index response at a given delay from a start signal. Catania (1970) has argued that a variety of such temporal estimation data suggests a subjective time scale that is a power function of real time with an exponent less than one. Zeiler and his co-workers (DeCasper and Zeiler, 1977; Zeiler, 1977) have pursued this line with a variety of results taken largely from procedures that reward all index responses delayed more than some minimum time. Zeiler's results also have been interpreted as implying a power function having an exponent less than one.

A second data base comes from time discrimination studies (Church and Deluty, 1977; Church, Getty and Lerner, 1976; Stubbs, 1976). These data have suggested a logarithmic subjective time scale

This work was supported by NSF grants BNS76–01229 and BNS78–23616. I am indebted to Mr. Stephen Fairhurst for the development and execution of the computer programs used to obtain the maximum ω^2 bisection functions. I thank Russell Church for many fruitful discussions of these ideas.

157

largely on the basis of three features: First, psychometric functions are approximately symmetric when plotted against the logarithm of real time; second, Weber's Law has been confirmed in a variety of psychophysical contexts; and third, the subjective "middle" between two time values appears to lie at the geometric mean of those values (see also Stubbs and Dreyfus, Chapter 6).

On the other hand, I have argued (Gibbon, 1977) that both time estimation data and time discrimination data are compatible with a linear representation of time but with a ratio comparitor for telling times apart. Platt (1979) and Platt, Kuch and Bitgood (1973) have shown that with the appropriate experimental technique, the exponent in temporal differentiation procedures may approach one—the veridical scale. My purpose in this chapter is to contrast implications of curvilinear and linear subjective time scales for both kinds of experiment. The arguments will be largely theoretical rather than data based, though some recent analysis of the temporal discrimination data of Church and Deluty (1977) will be summarized (Gibbon, 1981). The results are less than totally satisfactory for discriminating alternative theories. The reasons for the ambiguities, however, differ in the two data bases. The time estimation or time production procedures suffer from an interpretive difficulty that might be characterized as the experimenter "getting what he pays for." Ambiguities in the time discrimination area do not reflect this problem. Rather, they arise from the possibilities for different response strategies to handle unreinforced trials.

ESTIMATION

In the simplest temporal differentiation procedure, subjects are rewarded for an index response when it falls beyond some minimum time after a start signal. The start signal may be the last instance of the behavioral index (as in DRL) or some different kind of behavior—for example, onset of lever depression—or it may be an exteroceptive stimulus event. In any case, we imagine that the subject's history with this procedure has built up an appreciation of the time values above the minimum that have been reinforced. Typically after long training, distributions of time since the start signal to the index response look like those in Figure 7–1 for a short minimum (S) and a long minimum (L). In the short minimum case, responses tend to

Figure 7-1. Schematic representation of index response distributions under a temporal differentiation schedule that rewards responses exceeding a minimum time. The distribution on the left corresponds to a short minimum (S), and the distribution on the right corresponds to a long minimum (L).

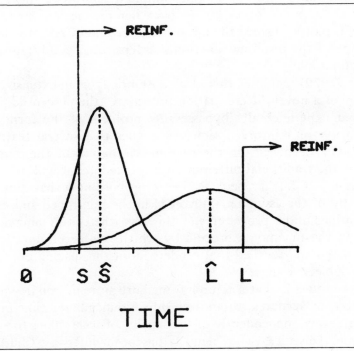

cluster around the minimum value, with most frequent responding occurring just above this minimum. If the minimum is long (L), then the most frequent index response tends to go unreinforced with the mode lying to the left of the minimum reinforced duration. This feature of empirical temporal differentiation response distributions is reflected in a slope less than one when central tendency in the index response is plotted against the experimentally programmed minimum. At some intermediate value (T ≃ 10 seconds), the center of the estimation distribution lies at the programmed minimum. Results of this kind have led several theorists to argue that subjective time grows as a power function of real time with an exponent less than one. Short times are "overestimated" and long times are "underestimated" on this view because their subjective representations are over and under the real time values.

There are several difficulties with this interpretation of the results. One objection is that subjects are never presented with the minimum time value, but rather with a band of reinforced values, all of which lie above that minimum. It thus behooves subjects to estimate the reinforced times rather than the minimum reinforced time. I have argued elsewhere (Gibbon, 1977) that when the mean index response latency is plotted against the mean reinforced index response latency, the slope of the resulting function sharpens considerably, sometimes up to about one.

Platt (1979) amplifies this idea substantially in an extensive investigation of a novel differentiation procedure (the percentile procedure) that experimentally bypasses the problem of the form of the distribution of reinforced time. He argues that several features of timing data devolve from the asymmetric nature of the reinforced band in the traditional differentiation procedures. I will not pursue that argument further here. Rather, I propose now that quite independently of the asymmetry involved in the reinforced and emitted distributions under procedures of this sort, there is an inherent symmetry in the mnemonic process by which reinforced durations are remembered and recalled that renders moot the spacing of scale values for subjective time.

The key idea is that a temporal memory system, well designed by evolution for accuracy, should reproduce remembered time in about the same way independently of the spacing of scale values for subjective time. This idea is not new. It has been noted by Church and Deluty (1977) and discussed also by Platt (1979). Here it is given somewhat more emphasis and an explicit form, illustrated in Figure 7-2. Subjective time is shown growing as the curvilinear growth function in the figure. This is a power function with an exponent of 0.9, but the argument I wish to make holds for arbitrary function forms, provided they are monotone.

Imagine that after considerable training on the estimation procedure, a value to be remembered and reproduced that is short, S, (or long, L) is encoded into memory via the growth function. In the procedures discussed above, this value would be most reasonably viewed as the mean of reinforced times, rather than the minimum reinforced time. In any case, the target time, S (or L), has a subjective representation, $\mu(S)$ (or $\mu(L)$), indicated by the solid (encode) arrows mapping real time into subjective time.

Figure 7–2. Subjective remembered time as a function of real time. A power function representation of the growth of subjective time is shown, with the solid arrows indicating encoding of the memory for a short (S) or a long (L) time. The dashed arrows represent the implausible decoding mechanism required to generate estimates, $\hat{S}$ and $\hat{L}$, which are larger and smaller, respectively, than the target times.

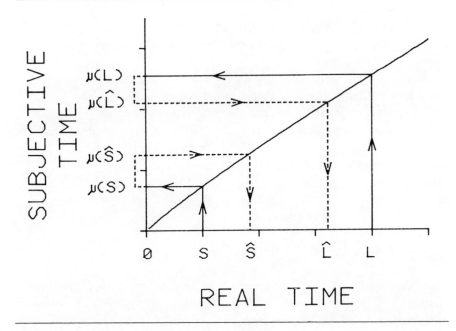

One way to conceive of the reproduction process is to think of time during a particular trial as a particle moving up the growth function. When it is sufficiently close to $\mu(S)$, a response is initiated. That is, the decoding process ought to approximate the encoding process in the reverse direction. In the extreme case in which decoding was precisely symmetric with encoding, the form of the subjective translation function would make no difference whatever (provided it was monotone). Subjects would deliver what they were paid for, independently of the spacing of subjective time values.

In fact, the data corresponding to Figure 7–1 are at variance with such a view. Rather, the time estimate, $\hat{S}$, for a short value, S, is somewhat larger than S, while the time estimate, $\hat{L}$, corresponding to a long target time, L, is somewhat shorter than L. In Figure 7–2, this curious situation is sketched. The encoding and decoding processes are shown as fundamentally different. For the decoding system to match the data, one would have to imagine that remembered time on the subjective scale moves up as it is stored (or decoded) when it is a short time value, and moves down as it is stored (or decoded) when it is long. Such a mysterious decoding system (indicated by dashed arrows) seems to me entirely implausible. While one might imagine a monotone distortion during memory storage or retrieval, it is difficult to imagine a system in which long times are distorted down and short times are distorted up.

The encode–decode symmetry problem remains no matter what the form of the subjective transformation of real time. The fact that in many time estimation procedures, the estimates tend to be approximately a power function of the target time is not evidence that the subjective scale has the same form. In fact, I will go further in the next section and argue that under certain assumptions, a power function for the subjective scale leads to a linear function relating estimates to real time.

Power Law $\mu(T)$ Implies Linear $\hat{T}$

One way in which the overestimation of short times and underestimation of long times might arise is shown in Figure 7–3. Imagine that as time during the trial elapses, subjects pick a threshold or time window edge to initiate responding that is somewhat below the remembered target time. That is, imagine that subjects respond when trial time is "close enough" to the remembered target time, where "close enough" is a high percentage. In the diagram in Figure 7–3, the encode arrows over S and L show the target time translation to memory. The dotted arrows below $\mu(S)$ and $\mu(L)$ are set at a proportion, $A = 0.8$, of the remembered time value. When trial time crosses this 80 percent window edge, responding is initiated. However, responding is not immediate, but takes some fixed time, M. This is indicated at the base of the dashed decode lines, so that the final response execution occurs at an estimate time ($\hat{S}$ or $\hat{L}$) that is M seconds greater than the initiation time. It is this feature that can produce overestimates of short times and underestimates of long times. Suppose that a short time is the target, with $S = 5$ seconds, and that the percentage window is the 80 percent value shown here. The re-

Figure 7–3. Subjective time as a function of real time for a more plausible encoding and decoding scheme. The curvilinear growth function again is a power function of real time, and the solid arrows indicate the encoding into memory of the rewarded values. The decoding scheme (dashed arrows) begins at a percentage (A) of the encode value, but requires a fixed additive component (M) before the index response (estimation) is made at $\hat{S}$ or $\hat{L}$. With this scheme, overestimates occur for short times but underestimates occur for long times.

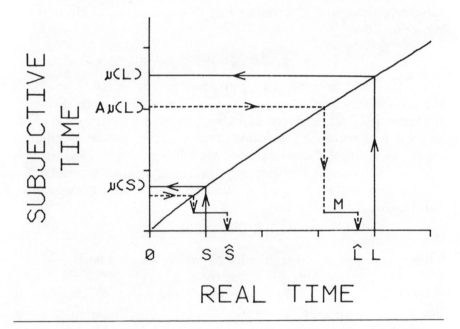

sponse should then be initiated on the average at 4 seconds into the trial. If the response requires 2 seconds to complete, then the result is an overestimate by about 1 second ($\hat{S}$ = 6 seconds). But consider a long target value, say L = 20 seconds. Now, the same percentage window edge would initiate a response at 16 seconds. With the same execution time of 2 seconds, the estimate would occur at $\hat{L}$ = 18 seconds, which is an underestimate of the long target value. A hypothetical system like this would then produce the observed over- and underestimation.

While it is a speculative account, it has the advantage that the percentage window edge idea corresponds directly to similar theorizing of mine for FI performance (Gibbon, 1977).[a] It also has the conceptual advantage that the decode process distorts in only one direction—namely, pushing index responses toward lower times. It is only at quite short target times that response execution time (or some other additional fixed component) could result in over-estimation.

Now with a system like this, we may ask what the form of the mean estimate time, $\hat{T}$, should be as a function of real target time, T. To be as general as possible, we adopt the following rules. Let the subjective time, $\mu(T)$, corresponding to real time, T, be given by the power function

$$\mu(T) = (T - T_0)^p \mu , \qquad T > T_0 .$$ (7.1)

The x intercept value, T_0, is a refractory period for the beginning of the growth function. That is, it is a small time below which subjective time is effectively zero and above which subjective time begins to grow with real time. The slope of the function, μ, may be thought of as the mean of the unit timer (when $T - T_0 = 1$). Now, we may use our percentage threshold for initiating the response. Letting elapsed time within the trial be denoted by t, its subjective counterpart reaches threshold when

$$\mu(t) = A \mu(T)$$ (7.2)

where A is the percentage value at which responding is initiated. With these conventions the estimate, $\hat{T}$, is made up of the t satisfying Equation (7.2) plus some fixed response time, M. That is, $\hat{T} = t + M$.[b] With these assumptions, substituting Equation (7.1) for t ($\mu(t) = [t - T_0]^p \mu$) into Equation (7.2), it is readily seen that μ plays no role, since it multiplies both sides of the equality, and

$$t = A^{\frac{1}{p}} T + \left(1 - A^{\frac{1}{p}}\right) T_0$$ (7.3)

a. The percentage value indicated as A here corresponds to $1 - 1/b$ where b is the response evocation threshold.

b. This kind of theorizing is appropriate to many other situations as well and has received extensive treatment in the avoidance area (Gibbon, 1979). M is thought of as some fixed component in the response latency, at least a portion of which is the actual time required to physically execute the response. However, from observations in other contexts (e.g., Libby and Church, 1974; cf. Gibbon, 1979), execution time may be only part of the duration of the fixed component.

so that

$$\hat{T} = A' T + C \qquad (7.4)$$

where

$$A' = A^{\frac{1}{p}}$$

and

$$C = (1 - A') T_0 + M \ .$$

The estimated time should be linear, not curvilinear, in the real time values being estimated. The exponent of the power function is absorbed into the slope of the estimate function. It is thus completely confounded with the size of the percentage threshold. The intercept represents mainly the fixed component in each latency. Note that when $M \simeq 0$ and the percentage threshold is 100 percent ($A' = 1.0$), $\hat{T} = T$, the veridical scale. This is true for any exponent value for the power law.

The encode–decode logic forces the disappearance of the exponent of the power function. That is, the percentage response rule (Equation [7.2]) has subjective time on both sides of the equation, and so the exponent appears (encode) and disappears (decode) from both sides to result in the linear Equation (7.4). The version of the power law (Equation [7.1]) is a quite general form, so that the insensitivity of $\hat{T}$ to curvature in the translation to subjective time is properly taken to reflect a fundamental property of the decoding process.

Logarithmic $\mu(T)$ Implies Power Function $\hat{T}$

The above analysis showed that the form of the estimate function on a simple scheme for producing these estimates was linear, independently of curvature in the power function. We now can consider the same kind of scheme but applied to a logarithmic transform. That is, imagine that subjective time, $\mu(T)$, is related to real time, T, by

$$\mu(T) = K\left[\log_B T^p - \log_B T_0^{\ p}\right] \ , \quad T > T_0 \qquad (7.5)$$

where B is the base of the subjective log transform, and $\log_B T_0^{\ p}$ is the refractory period, the x intercept as in Equation (7.1). Equation

(7.5) is the analogue of Equation (7.1) for a logarithmic transform of subjective time. It says that subjective time is linear in the logarithm of real time to some power, p. It is readily apparent, however, that Equation (7.5) may be translated to natural logs with the exponent and intercept incorporated into a two-parameter system. That is, subjective time is proportional to the natural log of real time divided by the real time unit, T_0.

$$\mu(T) = K' \ln(T/T_0) \tag{7.6}$$

where

$$K' = \frac{Kp}{\ln B}$$

With this rule for the growth function, the remainder of the analysis goes through as above, using Equation (7.6) for t and T on the left and right of Equation (7.2). This gives the initiation time, t, as

$$t = T_0 (T/T_0)^A \tag{7.7}$$

so that

$$\hat{T} = T_0^{1-A} T^A + M \tag{7.8}$$

Equation (7.8) says that the estimates should be linear in a power of T where the exponent is the percentage window value for the target time (not a subjective scale exponent). Note again that for $M = 0$, a 100 percent threshold implies a veridical estimate function, $\hat{T} = T$. In fact, data are never fit to the full Equation (7.8), but rather to Equation (7.8) setting $M = 0$ — that is, to a two-parameter power function.

At first blush, then, Equation (7.8) or Equation (7.8) with $M = 0$ would appear to be consonant with the data presented by a variety of authors (cf. Catania, 1970; Eisler, 1975). However, if we set $M = 0$, then there is no crossover point in this function. That is, there is no point at which estimates match real time value for the stimulus except at the beginning of the function, when $T = T_0$, the unit in the log system. This is readily seen by solving for T_0 as a function of T_e, the value when $\hat{T} = T \equiv T_e$ (for equality). Obviously, $T_0 = T_e$. Intuitively this makes sense because it is when $T = T_0$ (that is, when T equals the time unit) that the exponent does not alter the estimate value. Thus, the accurate estimate occurs at the unit for the log system. But there are no function values (negative subjective times) below this value. Therefore, if we are to believe the data fits requiring $M = 0$, the log system does not accommodate the linearity in double log coordinates, either. The boundary conditions are violated.

In summary, our preceding analysis shows that the reproduction data cited so widely by proponents of the power law are not evidence for an exponent on the subjective time scale. But by the log timing analysis, they are also not evidence for a log scale, since equality occurs only for the smallest perceivable objective time (the unit).

It is not my purpose here to propose a solution to this dilemma, but rather to emphasize that there is a dilemma requiring solution. It seems to me that the simple solution depicted in Figure 7–3 deserves more scrutiny. It may well be that the data many authors have cited as evidence for a power law are about as well fit by a linear function. Alternatively, fits to Equation (7.8) with $M > 0$ may be feasible with M large enough that the accurate estimate point does not entail negative subjective times below it. On the other hand, it seems to me likely that additional processes may be involved that tend to push estimates to lower and lower values as the time being estimated grows (cf. Platt, 1979).

DISCRIMINATION

There are several features of data on time discrimination that suggest a logarithmic subjective scale. One is that psychometric functions are roughly symmetric when plotted against the logarithm of real time (Church and Deluty, 1977; Stubbs, 1968). Another property is Weber's Law, which in a temporal discrimination context means that discriminability of two durations remains constant at constant ratios of these durations, irrespective of their absolute values. Weber's Law may be taken to favor a log scale, since constant absolute differences on this scale correspond to constant ratios in real time. If subjects discriminate time values by taking differences, the log scale is consonant with Weber's Law.

A third feature of recent time discrimination results represents a more compelling argument for a logarithmic scale. It is the observation that the "middle" between two time values lies at their geometric mean. The finding arises both in operant contexts (Stubbs, 1976) and in choice procedures modeled on signal detection methods (Stubbs, 1968). The study by Church and Deluty (1977) provides the most extensive data. Elsewhere I have analyzed the Church and Deluty data in light of four different models of the discrimination process (Gibbon, 1981). The four models arise from the two different constructions of the subjective time scale we have been considering (power law and log timing) combined with two different response rules. The remainder of this chapter summarizes this analysis. Before treating the theoretical material, the temporal bisection function, which provides the primary data obtained from the Church and Deluty (1977) procedure, is described.

Bisection Function

The bisection function relates the discriminability of a sample duration (T) to two training durations, one short (S), and the other long (L). Rats were first trained to report "short" ("S") by responding on the left of two levers and "long" ("L") by responding on the right of two levers after experiencing a sample tone signal that lasted either S or L seconds, respectively. Subjects came to report "S" and "L" with high accuracy when the training stimuli were S and L, respectively. After this preliminary training, testing was conducted on sample durations, T, with $S \leqslant T \leqslant L$ with neither report reinforced except when the sample was $T = S$ or L. Subjects showed a graded report probability for the intermediate stimuli, as indicated in Figure 7-4. The data points represent the probability of reporting "short" as a function of the sample duration, T, averaged over four rats. The five functions correspond to five S,L pairs used—four in a 1:4 ratio and one (the filled squares) in a 1:2 ratio.

There are three notable features of these data. First, for the 1:4 data, the functions stay in about the same accuracy range on the ordinate. That is, the 1 second versus 4 second task shows the same level of performance at the endpoints as the 2 second versus 8 second, and so forth, while the 4.2 versus 8.4 task shows (appropriately) less accuracy at the endpoints. Second, the functions are steeper for shorter absolute values of S and L (e.g., 1 versus 4 seconds) and begin to flatten when the time ranges are increased (e.g., 4 versus 16 seconds).

Both of these features—that the slopes tend to flatten and that the range covered is about the same when S/L remains in the same ratio—are consonant with Weber's Law, which for this situation

Figure 7–4. Short report probability, $P("S")$, as a function of stimulus value, T, for five conditions. Four of the conditions had the rewarded short value and the rewarded long value in a 1:4 ratio (open points), and the fifth condition had the rewarded short value ($S = 4.2$) and the rewarded long value ($L = 8.4$) in a 1:2 ratio (filled squares).

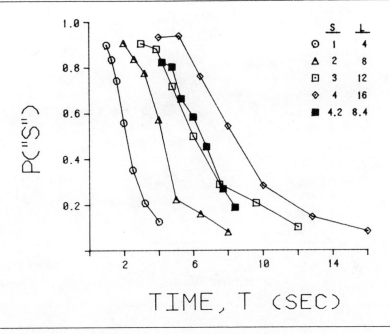

requires that report probability remain constant at constant ratios of T to either endpoint, when the endpoints are held in a given ratio. That is, short report probability for, say, 2 seconds in the 1 to 4 second range should equal short report probability at 6 seconds for the 3 to 12 second range, and so forth. Equivalently, all of the functions with $S/L = 1/4$ should superimpose when plotted as a function of T/S.

The third feature of these data to note is that the indifference points, $T_{1/2}$, where the functions cross $P("S") = 0.5$, occur at about the geometric mean, $\sqrt{SL}$. This may be seen graphically in Figure 7–5, which plots indifference points taken by interpolation from these functions against the geometric mean for each of the five sets of data and also for data from a similar procedure studied by Stubbs (1968) with pigeons. The solid line is the regression function, which

Figure 7–5. Indifference $T_{1/2}$, as a function of the geometric mean of the short and long duration values. Data are interpolated indifference points from Figure 7-4 and from a procedure studied by Stubbs (1968). The dashed line represents equality and the solid line represents the best fit linear regression.

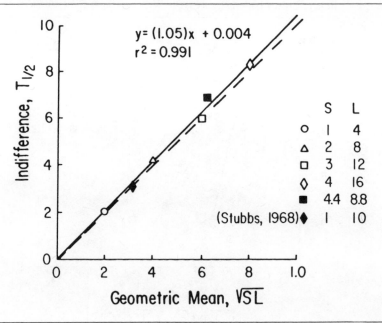

accounts for better than 99 percent of the variance. It is clear that the slope does not differ from one (represented by the dashed line).

Weber's Law and the geometric mean finding may be exemplified by plotting short report probability as a function of T normalized by the geometric mean—that is, $P(``S")$ against $T/\sqrt{SL}$. The reason that normalizing for indifference at the geometric mean superimposes all of these functions is that the differing slopes produced by the 1 to 2 range versus the 1 to 4 range are appropriately rescaled. Weber's Law says that the functions should superimpose at constant ratios of T to either endpoint. But since $T/\sqrt{SL} = (T/S)/\sqrt{L/S}$, the normalization by $\sqrt{SL}$ should provide superimposition. This is shown in Figure 7-6, with $P(``S")$ plotted against a log time axis. To a first approximation, the data do indeed superimpose. Note also that the psychometric function is nearly symmetric on the log scale. All of these features—Weber's Law, the geometric mean, and

Figure 7–6. Short report probability as a function of the log of the probe duration normalized by the geometric mean, log $(T/\sqrt{SL})$.

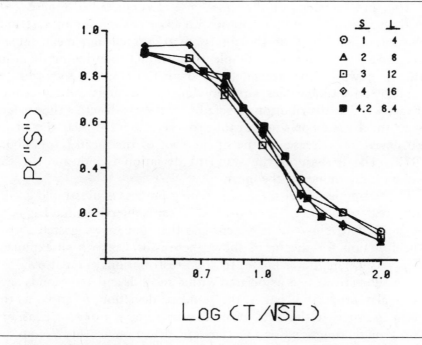

approximate symmetry on the log scale — on their face would appear to argue for a logarithmic time sense. However, some quantitative analysis is required to rule out alternatives. We will see that when these ideas are examined in quantitative detail, viable alternatives remain.

Six Models

Three differing versions of the structure of subjective time will be examined in combination with two different response rules, to generate six models of the manner in which the data in Figure 7–5 might have been generated. The first response rule is one familiar from signal detection theory — the likelihood ratio or "odds ratio." Essentially, this rule has subjects compare the odds that the sampled percept generated by T on a particular trial was in fact likely to have been generated by S or L. The other response rule is a similarity rule.

For this rule, subjects ask whether their percept of T is more similar to their memory of S or of L.

The three versions of the time sense are depicted in Figure 7–7. In the top panel, a simple counter model or Possion timing system is illustrated. Real time on the abscissa is translated into mean subjective time, $\mu(T) = \mu T$, via a simple proportional counting mechanism. This is shown by the straight line growth function. On the ordinate, the subjective time values corresponding to 4 seconds and 16 seconds are shown. The distributions erected over these subjective time values obey the Poisson or square root property—namely, that the standard deviation increases as the square root of the mean (cf. Gibbon, 1977). The growth of the standard deviation is indicated by the dashed function below the mean.

In the middle panel the Scalar timing process is illustrated on the same real time scale. The growth of mean subjective time has been generalized to allow an exponent less than one, as suggested above. The function for the mean shown here is drawn with an exponent of $p = 0.9$. On the ordinate, the two distributions erected over the mean subjective times associated with 4 seconds and 16 seconds have the scalar property. That is, the standard deviation, σ, grows as the mean, μ, so that the coefficient of variation, $\gamma = \sigma/\mu$, is constant. The growth function for the standard deviation in this example is indicated by the dashed curve below the mean function. Finally, in the bottom panel, still more extreme curvature of subjective time is indicated for a Log timing system. In this system, subjective time grows as the logarithm of real time, and the two distributions erected over subjective 4 seconds and subjective 16 seconds have the same variance.

Likelihood Ratio Rule

The first discrimination rule studied is the likelihood ratio rule familiar from signal detection theory. According to this rule, subjects do the equivalent of comparing the odds that the sample percept in fact generated by T was really generated by S or L. That is, for a signal duration of T, giving rise to a percept on the subjective time scale, subjects compare the probabilities that that percept arose as a random sample from the S or the L distributions. The response rule

Figure 7–7. Three alternative subjective time scales. In the top panel, a Poisson timing process is shown in which mean subjective time (on the ordinate) is proportional to real time (on the abscissa) but variability increases as the square root of the mean. In the middle panel, the Scalar process is sketched in which subjective time grows as a power function of real time and variability grows directly with real time, so that the coefficient of variation is constant. In the bottom panel, the Log timing process is shown in which subjective time grows as the logarithm of real time and variance on the subjective scale is constant. The dashed curve in each panel is the standard deviation function. The distributions have been drawn so that $\mu(4) = 3$ and $\gamma(4) = 0.3$ for each timing process. The solid line from the point where the two probability density functions intersect represents the predicted indifference point for a likelihood ratio rule. This occurs at the geometric mean for Poisson timing, at the harmonic mean for Scalar timing, and at the geometric mean for Log timing.

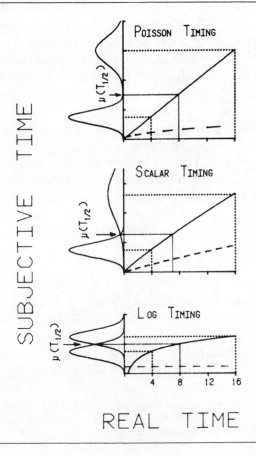

requires a response in favor of S ("S") whenever the likelihood exceeds a potentially biased criterion. There was virtually no bias in these data (Gibbon, 1981), and so this rule has one immediate prediction—the indifference point ($T_{\frac{1}{2}}$) should lie at the point at which the two probability density functions intersect. This is the point at which the odds are equal that the percept arose from either endpoint distribution. The implication is illustrated graphically for the three constructions of subjective time in Figure 7-7.[c] The point of intersection on the subjective time scale, $\mu(T_{\frac{1}{2}})$, is translated back out to the real time scale via the function for the mean subjective time.

$T_{\frac{1}{2}}$ lies at the geometric mean for the Poisson timing system in the top panel and for the Log timing system in the bottom panel. But for the Scalar timing system in the middle panel, the predicted $T_{\frac{1}{2}}$ value lies not at the geometric mean but somewhat lower. In this example, with $S = 4$ and $L = 16$, the geometric mean is 8 seconds and the predicted $T_{\frac{1}{2}}$ value for the scalar timing system lies below this, at about 7.2 seconds. This is approximately the harmonic rather than the geometric mean. In Appendix I of this chapter, the derivations in Gibbon (1981) are summarized. It is shown formally there that the $T_{\frac{1}{2}}$ value is indeed the geometric mean for the Poisson system and the Log system and a power law version of the harmonic mean for the Scalar system. It is also shown that Weber's Law does not hold for the Poisson system, but does hold for the other two.

Thus, to summarize for the likelihood model, Poisson timing has the wrong kind of sensitivity, in that long times are better discriminated than they should be, but it has the right temporal middle between the short and long value. Scalar timing has the right kind of sensitivity in that Weber's Law holds, but the wrong temporal middle, which is predicted to be too low.

Of the three scales, Log timing is the only one consonant with both Weber's Law and geometric mean. This is all the more impressive in the light of a wide variety of effects in other timing situations that are consonant with the Scalar timing process with a ratio rule for discriminating different time values. I have shown elsewhere (Gibbon, 1977) that the expectancy ratio formulation reduces to the like-

---

c. In fact, for $\sigma_S \neq \sigma_L$ there are two intersections—the principal one, shown in Figure 7-7, and another at very small values of probability density (at subjective zero for Scalar timing and at negative subjective times for Poisson timing).

lihood ratio rule under certain assumptions about the discrimination process. Thus, potentially, these data argue against the expectancy ratio formulation, which accommodates a rather extensive data set in other contexts. In the next section, an alternative response rule that is in some sense more feasible than the likelihood ratio is examined for each of the three time scales.

Similarity

There is reason to doubt that the likelihood ratio rule is in fact a feasible one for the time values studied by Church and Deluty (1977). Consider an 8-second probe stimulus when the short value is 4 seconds and the long value 16 seconds. The 8-second stimulus is at the geometric mean of S and L and is equally "confusable" with either endpoint. Referring to Figure 7–7 for log timing, note that the probabilities on both distributions are small at 8 seconds, where they intersect. That is, within variance estimates common from other settings, a percept as extreme as (subjective) 8 would be generated by the endpoint stimuli quite infrequently (in the example in Figure 7–7, about fourteen times in one hundred). Given long experience with intermediate stimuli that were actually experienced on one-half of the trials (the other one-half were endpoint trials), it seems on its face unreasonable that subjects should respond as though intermediate values were in fact generated by the reinforced S and L stimuli.

Another way to put this issue is to argue that it is not the confusability of T with S or L that results in intermediate report probabilities, but rather the similarity of T to S or L. Similarity response rules are readily constructed by considering the (normalized) distance of T from either end on the subjective scale. Several of such rules are shown graphically in Figure 7–8. In each panel, the abscissa represents subjective time (corresponding to the ordinate in Figure 7–7), and the subjective referents for the short value $\mu(S)$ and for the long value $\mu(L)$ are shown at 2 and 8 units on this scale. On the ordinate, the subjective distance between the probe duration, T, and either the short or the long endpoint is shown (scaled with double the unit size for clarity). Consider the two straight line functions in the top panel: They are simply the distance in subjective time between the probe stimulus and the short endpoint, $D(S,T) = \mu(T) - \mu(S)$, and the

Figure 7–8. Similarity-dissimilarity measures at intermediate subjective times between $\mu(S)$ and $\mu(L)$. In the top panel, the two pairs of subjective distance measures are equal at the arithmetic mean (dashed line). In the middle panel, the two measures are equal at the harmonic mean; and in the bottom panel, the two pairs of measures are equal at the geometric mean.

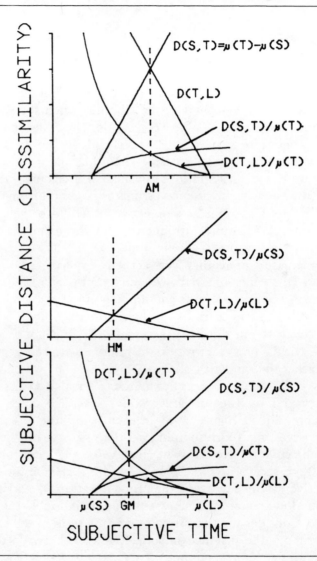

distance between the probe value and the long endpoint, $D(T,L) = \mu(L) - \mu(T)$. They intersect at the arithmetic mean of the short and long values indicated by the dashed vertical line (AM). Thus, if subjects are regarded as taking the subjective distance between the probe and one endpoint and comparing it to the subjective distance between the probe and the other endpoint, one would expect indifference—equality between these two subjective distances—at the arithmetic mean on the subjective time scale.

The other pair of curves in the top panel are normalized distance measures. The shallow rising curve labeled $D(S,T)/\mu(T)$ is the distance of T from S normalized for T, and the steep falling curve is the distance to L normalized for T. If these distances normalized for the probe value were the basis for indexing similarity of the probe to either endpoint, then again, indifference should occur where they intersect, at the arithmetic mean. Thus, the top panel represents two dissimilarity measures—either the simple difference or this difference normalized for T—that both result in indifference at the arithmetic mean on the subjective scale.

An alternative dissimilarity measure is shown in the middle panel. Here, the distance on the subjective scale between the probe and the endpoint is normalized by the endpoint (rather than by the probe, as in the upper panel). When this kind of normalization is used, indifference is predicted at the harmonic mean (HM) rather than the arithmetic mean. The indifference point is again indicated by the dashed line.

In the bottom panel, two dissimilarity measures are shown in which normalization is directional—that is, the norming value is either the smaller of the two or the larger of the two. The former case is represented by the falling curve labeled $D(T,L)/\mu(T)$ and the straight rising line labeled $D(S,T)/\mu(S)$. The latter, norming by the larger of the two values, is represented by the two lower functions. For both of these directional rules, which preserve the order of the norming value, indifference is predicted at the geometric mean, again shown by a dashed vertical line.

The three panels thus represent three different constructions of a similarity–dissimilarity metric. For the upper panel, indifference is predicted at the arithmetic mean in subjective time. This means that these similarity measures would be consonant with the data only if the arithmetic mean in subjective time translated to the geometric mean in reai time. It is readily seen from Figure 7–7 that this is true for the Log timing process and not for the other two. Similarly, the measure in the middle panel would require that the harmonic mean in subjective time have a real time counterpart at the geometric mean. I know of no system with that property. Certainly none of the three timing processes considered here have it.

Finally, in the bottom panel, the directional norming measures have an indifference point at the geometric mean in subjective time. It is readily shown that as long as the refractory period on the subjective time scale is negligible ($T_0 \simeq 0$ in Equation [7.1]), the geometric mean in the power law version of subjective time is the geometric mean in real time. If

$$\mu(T) = \mu T^p \qquad (7.9)$$

then

$$\mu(T_{1/2}) = [\mu(S)\mu(L)]^{1/2}$$

implies

$$T_{1/2}^{\,p} = (SL)^{p/2}$$

or

$$T_{1/2} = \sqrt{SL} \qquad (7.10)$$

Therefore, these similarity measures would be appropriate for the Scalar or Poisson timing processes and not appropriate for the Log timing process.

Two Similarity Response Rules

The above analysis for the indifference point forces either one of the pairs of dissimilarity measures in the top panel with Log timing or one of the pairs of measures in the bottom panel with Poisson or Scalar timing. We will now see that while there are two distinct similarity measures in the top panel and two distinct similarity measures in the bottom panel, they in fact reduce to one response rule each if the criterion is to respond "S" if T is more similar to S than L. The two measures in the top panel are quantitatively identical, since the requirement to respond "S" when

$$\frac{D(S, T)}{\mu(T)} < \frac{D(T, L)}{\mu(T)}$$

is obviously equivalent to

$$D(S,T) < D(T,L) \qquad (7.11)$$

For the directional rules in the bottom panel, the requirement to respond "S" when

$$\frac{D(S,T)}{\mu(T)} < \frac{D(T,L)}{\mu(L)}$$

is equivalent to requiring that

$$\frac{\mu(S)}{\mu(T)} > \frac{\mu(T)}{\mu(L)} \qquad (7.12)$$

Normalization by the smaller is also equivalent to Equation (7.12), so that both work out to be equivalent to the requirement that the ratio of subjective S to subjective T be greater than the ratio of subjective T to subjective L. Thus, both measures are equivalent to a simpler one—namely, one in which similarity of I to J equals the ratio of the smaller of (I, J) to the larger of (I, J). This number is small when I and J are widely separated and approaches one as they become close. These two rules—a difference for Log timing and a ratio for Scalar or Poisson timing—are thus the only possible ones that are consistent with the geometric mean finding as the subjective middle between the short and the long real time values.

Referents Known Exactly

The two rules (Equations [7.11] and [7.12]) potentially include three random variables. The percept for the current time probe, T, and the remembered values of the endpoints, the percepts associated with S and L, are all potentially variable, so that discrimination rules are complex. However, a simplification is obtained by considering the case in which the referents for the short and long endpoints are known exactly, so that all the variance is in the sample percept generated by T. This case is the simplest mathematically, though perhaps not psychologically, since it requires perfect memory for the reinforced durations. (The reverse case is considered later.) The mathematics summarized in Appendix II of this chapter show that for Log timing, the psychometric function takes the simple form

$$P(\text{"}S\text{"}) = \Phi\left(\frac{1}{2}d'_{SL} - d'_{ST}\right) \qquad (7.13)$$

where Φ is the unit normal distribution function and d'_{IJ} is the stand-ard normal distance between means of I and J on the subjective scale. Since $\Phi(0) = \frac{1}{2}$, indifference occurs when subjective $T_{\frac{1}{2}}$ lies at $\frac{1}{2}$ the distance from S to L—that is, when $d'_{ST_{\frac{1}{2}}} = \frac{1}{2}d'_{SL}$ or $T_{\frac{1}{2}} = \sqrt{SL}$. Weber's Law is also accommodated, since distances on the log scale correspond to ratios in real time. Report probability is constant at constant ratios of T to S (d'_{ST}), given a constant ratio of S to L (d'_{SL}).

For the other two time scales, the psychometric function takes the form (cf. Appendix II of this chapter)

$$P(\text{``}S\text{''}) = F_\lambda[C(T)] \qquad (7.14)$$

where F_λ is the distribution function for a noncentral chi-square vari-ate with one degree of freedom and noncentral parameter, λ. This rather forbidding terminology has a straightforward interpretation for the single degree of freedom case:

$$F_\lambda(C) = \Phi(\sqrt{C} - \sqrt{\lambda}) - \Phi(-\sqrt{C} - \sqrt{\lambda}) \qquad (7.15)$$

The criterion, C, and the noncentral parameter, λ, are interpreted differently for Poisson and Scalar timing. For Poisson timing

$$\sqrt{\lambda} = (\sqrt{T})/\gamma \qquad (7.16)$$

and

$$\sqrt{C} = (\sqrt{SL/T})/\gamma \qquad (7.17)$$

where $\gamma = \sigma/\mu$ is, as before, the sensitivity of the unit timer ($T = 1$). For Scalar timing,

$$\sqrt{\lambda} = 1/\gamma \qquad (7.18)$$

and

$$\sqrt{C} = (\sqrt{SL})/T\gamma \qquad (7.19)$$

where γ for the Scalar timing system is constant for all T.

Comparing the two λ and C definitions, it is clear that those for Scalar timing are constant for constant ratios, T/S and S/L (cf. argu-ment earlier on normalizing by $\sqrt{SL}$). This system thus satisfies Weber's Law. The definitions in Equations (7.16) and (7.17) are not constant at constant T/S and S/L (e.g., let $T = S$). Thus their sum and difference (Equation [7.15]) are not either, and so Weber's Law is violated. This violation is intuitively appropriate, since the coefficient of variation for the Poisson system decreases with the absolute size of the intervals (cf. Gibbon, 1977).

The Scalar timing and Log timing alternatives both remain viable for the similarity rules. Log timing has a somewhat different form than Scalar timing, but the differences are of form only. A computer program fit the data normalized for $\sqrt{SL}$ with an iterative program for both psychometric functions (Equations [7.13] and [7.14]). The program iterated the sensitivity parameters assuming no bias and an exponent for Scalar timing of $p = 1$. The results are displayed in Figure 7–9. For both models, the variance accounted for was virtually identical ($\omega^2 = 0.97$). A second fit of the Scalar timing function allowing p to vary resulted in $\hat{p} = 0.64$, but with a negligible improvement in variance accounted for ($\omega^2 = 0.972$ versus $\omega^2 = 0.970$). Thus, the data are insensitive to exponent value.

Figure 7–9. Bisection data (Figure 7–6) fit with the Log timing and Scalar timing psychometric functions.

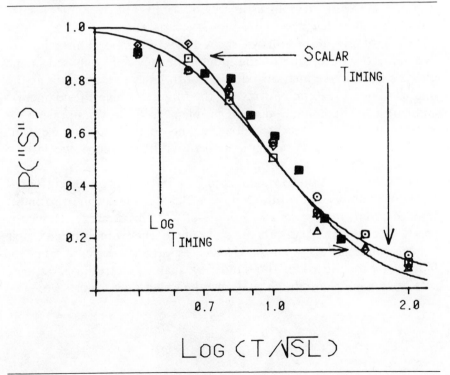

The exponent of the power law plays a role in the Scalar timing and Log timing models that is quite similar to the sensitivity index, γ. For Log timing, in fact, p and γ are entirely confounded. The exponent does not determine the location of the bisection function but does change its slope. Thus, the question of whether $p = 1$ or $p < 1$ remains unresolved. It may be that variance in the data preclude observation of finer precision with this parameter. On the other hand, it may be that here as elsewhere in animal time discrimination (Gibbon, 1977), p may be set at one with no loss in predictive power.

The estimates of sensitivity, γ, were in the neighborhood of 0.4, a value that is high relative to previous fits to time discrimination data with rats. I have argued elsewhere (Gibbon, 1981) that this sensitivity estimate may be too large. This would be the case if all the variance came from the memory for the endpoints while the sample percept of T was precisely $\mu(T)$. The analysis used an approximation that showed that the variance estimates in this case would reduce γ by a factor of $1/\sqrt{2}$. This interpretation brings the sensitivity values more in line with previous estimates. It seems intuitively more sensible also to allow recency to produce less variability.

In conclusion, the results of the analysis of temporal bisection are in a sense the other side of the indeterminacy coin exposed in the analysis of time estimation data. In both cases, a close look at the implications of different forms for the time scale reveal fundamental ambiguities. The encode–decode problem arises in temporal reproduction procedures because subjects tend to tell us what we want them to. In a sense, reinforcement corrupts the inferences we wish to draw about the underlying scale.

One way around this problem is to base inferences on unreinforced behavior. The bisection function, or at least the location of its indifference point, represents an example of just this strategy. However, partly because subjects are unconstrained when unrewarded, their behavior may reflect several different response strategies. This possibility, as exemplified in the similarity analysis, introduces another sort of ambiguity in inferences about the underlying scale.

APPENDIX I: LIKELIHOOD RATIO

General Case: $\sigma_S \neq \sigma_L$

Let f_J normal, $J = S, T, L$ with mean and standard deviation, μ_J, σ_J and $\gamma_J = \sigma_J / \mu_J$. The likelihood ratio rule requires a report of "S" when

$$\frac{f_S(x_T)}{f_L(x_T)} > b\beta \qquad (7.20)$$

where x_T is the subjective percept generated by T, and $b\beta$ is a biased motivational parameter (Gibbon, 1977). No bias or reinforcement differential has $b\beta = 1$. I show elsewhere (Gibbon, 1981) that the likelihood ratio rule (Equation [7.20]) is equivalent to

$$\chi'^2(1, \lambda) < C \qquad (7.21)$$

where χ'^2 is a noncentral chi-square variate with one degree of freedom. The noncentral parameter, λ, and the criterion, C, are both functions of S, T, and L on the subjective scale. They may be expressed as

$$\sqrt{\lambda} = \frac{1}{\gamma_T} - \frac{A}{\sigma_T B} \quad , \qquad (7.22)$$

and

$$C = \frac{1}{\sigma_T^2}\left[\left(\frac{D}{B}\right)^2 - \frac{E}{B}\right] \quad , \qquad (7.23)$$

where

$$A = \frac{1}{\sigma_S \gamma_S} - \frac{1}{\sigma_L \gamma_L} \quad ,$$

$$B = \frac{1}{\sigma_S^2} - \frac{1}{\sigma_L^2} \quad , \qquad (7.24)$$

$$D = \frac{1}{\sigma_S \gamma_L} - \frac{1}{\sigma_L \gamma_S} \quad ,$$

$$E = 2\ln(b\beta\,\sigma_S/\sigma_L) \quad .$$

The bisection function is therefore given by the distribution function for this family of noncentral chi-square variates (Patnaik, 1949).

$$P(\text{``}S\text{''}) = P(\chi'^2 < C)$$

$$= \Phi(\sqrt{C} - \sqrt{\lambda}) - \Phi(-\sqrt{C} - \sqrt{\lambda}) \tag{7.25}$$

Indifference, $T_{1/2}$. The form (7.22) may be shown positive for μ_J, σ_J monotone in the same direction with J. Also, the normal assumption for x_J requires γ_J relatively small, so that negative subjective times are negligible. For this case, $\sqrt{\lambda}$ is relatively large, and Equation (7.25) implies that $P(\text{``}S\text{''}) \simeq \frac{1}{2}$ when

$$\sqrt{C} = \sqrt{\lambda} \tag{7.26}$$

From Equation (7.25), the error in this approximation is

$$\Phi(-2\sqrt{\lambda}) = P(\text{``}S\text{''}) - \frac{1}{2} \ .$$

The condition (7.26) is equivalent to

$$\mu_{T_{1/2}} = \frac{A}{B} + \left[\left(\frac{D}{B}\right)^2 - \frac{E}{B} \right]^{\frac{1}{2}} \tag{7.27}$$

Poisson Timing. Let $\mu_T = \mu T$, $\sigma_T = \sigma\sqrt{T}$, $\gamma_T = \gamma/\sqrt{T}$ where μ, σ, $\gamma = \sigma/\mu$ are these parameters for the unit timer. For this process the assignments (Equation [7.24]) give

$$A = 0, \quad \left(\frac{D}{B}\right)^2 = \mu^2 \, SL$$

and

$$\frac{E}{B} = \sigma^2 \left(\frac{\ln(S/L)}{1/S - 1/L} \right) ,$$

Equation (7.27) then may be shown equivalent to

$$\mu_{T_{1/2}} = \mu \left[SL \left(1 - \gamma^2 \, \frac{\ln(S/L)}{L - S} \right) \right]^{\frac{1}{2}} \tag{7.28}$$

Since γ for all three systems must be small, we may ignore the γ^2 term and find that $T_{1/2} \simeq \sqrt{SL}$, the geometric mean.

The Poisson process does not accommodate Weber's Law, however. To see this, consider only $T = S$. Weber's Law requires that report probability be constant for constant S/L. But the noncentral parameter and criterion (Equations [7.22] and [7.23]) depend on S and L. For $T = S$,

$$\sqrt{\lambda} = \frac{1}{\gamma} \sqrt{S}$$

and

$$\sqrt{C} = \frac{1}{\gamma} \sqrt{L}$$

Ignoring terms with the factor, γ^2, substitution in (Equation [7.25]) provides the counterexample.

Scalar Timing.   Let $\mu_T = \mu T^p$, $\sigma_T = \sigma T^p$, $\gamma_T = \gamma$ where μ, σ, $\gamma = \sigma/\mu$ are again these parameters for the unit timer. The assignments (Equation [7.24]) for this system imply

$$\sqrt{\lambda} = \frac{1}{\gamma} \left[1 - \frac{(S/T)^p}{1 + (S/L)^p} \right] , \tag{7.29}$$

and

$$C = \left(\frac{(S/T)^{2p}}{1 - (S/L)^{2p}} \right) \left(\frac{1}{\gamma^2} \left[\frac{1 - (S/L)^p}{1 + (S/L)^p} \right] - 2 \ln b\beta \, (S/L)^p \right) . \tag{7.30}$$

Weber's Law holds, since both λ and C are constant at constant T/S for constant S/L. The indifference point, however, is not the geometric mean. Equating $\sqrt{\lambda}$ and $\sqrt{C}$ from Equations (7.29) and (7.30) and ignoring terms with the factor γ^2,

$$T_{\frac{1}{2}} \simeq \left[\frac{1}{2} \left(\frac{1}{S^p} + \frac{1}{L^p} \right) \right]^{\frac{-1}{p}} \tag{7.31}$$

For $p = 1$, this is the harmonic mean (HM). Note that for $p = 1$,

$$\sqrt{\lambda} = \frac{1}{\gamma} \left[1 - \frac{1}{2} \left(\frac{HM}{T} \right) \right] ,$$

so that the approximation error is $\Phi(-1/\gamma)$. (For example, if $\gamma = \frac{1}{2}$, $\Phi(-1/\gamma) = .02$; if $\gamma = \frac{1}{3}$, $\Phi(-1/\gamma) = .001$.)

Constant Variance: $\sigma_S = \sigma_T = \sigma_L \equiv \sigma$

This is the familiar Thurstone Case V. Standard techniques give the likelihood ratio rule (7.20) as

$$z < C ,\qquad (7.31)$$

where z is unit normal. The criterion, C, is

$$C = \frac{1}{2} d'_{SL} - d'_{ST} - \frac{\ln b\beta}{d'_{SL}} \qquad (7.32)$$

where

$$d'_{IJ} = \frac{\mu_J - \mu_I}{\sigma} ,\qquad I \neq J = S, T, L \qquad (7.33)$$

is the standardized distance measure along the perceptual continuum. The bisection function is therefore

$$P(\text{``}S\text{''}) = \Phi(C) . \qquad (7.34)$$

Indifference (at $T_{\frac{1}{2}}$) occurs when $C = 0$. For no bias, this implies

$$d'_{ST_{\frac{1}{2}}} = \frac{1}{2} d'_{SL} ,$$

or

$$\mu_{T_{\frac{1}{2}}} = \frac{1}{2}(\mu_L + \mu_S) . \qquad (7.35)$$

Log Timing. Let $\mu_T = K' \ln(T/T_0)$, $T > T_0$, as in Equation (7.6). Then $d'_{IJ} = \frac{K'}{\sigma} \ln(J/I)$, so that

$$C = \frac{K'}{\sigma} \ln\left(\frac{\sqrt{SL}}{T}\right) - \frac{\ln b\beta}{\frac{K'}{\sigma} \ln(L/S)} . \qquad (7.36)$$

The criterion is thus constant at constant T/S for constant S/L, so Weber's Law holds. The indifference point, from Equation (7.24) is given by

$$K' \ln(T_{\frac{1}{2}}/T_0) = K' \ln\left(\frac{\sqrt{SL}}{T_0}\right)$$

or

$$T_{\frac{1}{2}} = \sqrt{SL} .$$

APPENDIX II: SIMILARITY

Referents Known Exactly

Let the percept for the endpoints, $\hat{\mu}_J = \mu_J$, $J = S, L$. Assuming no bias, the directional rule (7.12) for Poisson and Scalar timing may be written

$$x_T^{\,2} < \mu_S \mu_L \tag{7.37}$$

where x_T is normal (μ_T, σ_T). This rule implies

$$P(\text{``}S\text{''}) = P(\chi'^2[1, \lambda] < C) \ , \tag{7.38}$$

where

$$\sqrt{\lambda} = \frac{1}{\gamma} \ , \tag{7.39}$$

and

$$C = \frac{\mu_S \mu_L}{\sigma_T^{\,2}} \tag{7.40}$$

Approximate indifference again requires $\sqrt{\lambda} \simeq \sqrt{C}$, or

$$\mu_{T_{\frac{1}{2}}} = \sqrt{\mu_S \mu_L} \ . \tag{7.41}$$

Poisson Timing. Let $\mu_T = \mu T$, $\sigma_T = \sigma\sqrt{T}$, $\gamma_T = \gamma/\sqrt{T}$, as before. Indifference is appropriately at the geometric mean (from Equation [7.41]), but Weber's Law does not hold. Substitution in Equations (7.39) and (7.40), letting $T = S$, gives $\sqrt{\lambda} = \sqrt{S}/\gamma$ and $\sqrt{C} = \sqrt{L}/\gamma$, so that again the parameters depend on S and L, not their ratio.

Scalar Timing. Let $\mu_T = \mu T^p$, $\sigma_T = \sigma T^p$, $\gamma_T = \gamma$ as before. From Equation (7.41), indifference is appropriately at the geometric mean. Now Weber's Law holds. Substituting in Equations (7.39) and (7.40) gives

$$\sqrt{\lambda} = \frac{1}{\gamma} \ ,$$

and

$$C = \frac{1}{\gamma^2}\left(\frac{\sqrt{SL}}{T}\right)^{2p}$$

which are constant at constant T/S for constant S/L.

Log Timing. Assuming no bias, the difference rule for Log timing (Equation [7.11]) may be written

$$x_T < \frac{1}{2} (\mu_S + \mu_L) \ ,$$

or

$$z < \frac{1}{2} d'_{SL} - d'_{ST} \equiv C \ . \tag{7.42}$$

Thus

$$P (\text{"}S\text{"}) = \Phi(C) \ , \tag{7.43}$$

and indifference occurs when

$$d'_{ST_{\frac{1}{2}}} = \frac{1}{2} d'_{SL} \tag{7.44}$$

as for the likelihood ratio formulation. The only differences between the two predictions appear in bias effects (Gibbon, 1981). Thus, Weber's Law and the geometric mean are accommodated with both response rules for Log timing.

Sample Known Exactly

I have shown elsewhere (Gibbon, 1981) that assuming variance in the memory for the referents, but no variance in the percept of the current time ($x_T = \mu_T$), results in a change in the interpretation of the sensitivity parameters. For Log timing,

$$\hat{\sigma}_{Sam} = \hat{\sigma}_{Mem} \sqrt{2} \ , \tag{7.45}$$

and for Scalar timing

$$\hat{\gamma}_{Sam} = \hat{\gamma}_{Mem} \sqrt{\hat{\gamma}^2_{Mem} + 2} \ . \tag{7.46}$$

The form assumed for these interpretations was the Log timing psychometric function (Equation [7.34]) but with criterion (Equation [7.32]) multiplied by $\sqrt{2}$.

REFERENCES

Catania, A.C. 1970. Reinforcement schedules and psychophysical judgments. In W.N. Schoenfeld, ed., *The Theory of Reinforcement Schedules.* New York: Appleton–Century–Crofts.

Church, R.M., and M.Z. Deluty. 1977. Bisection of temporal intervals. *Journal of Experimental Psychology: Animal Behavior Processes 3*: 216–228.

Church, R.M.; D.J. Getty; and N.D. Lerner. 1976. Duration discrimination by rats. *Journal of Experimental Psychology: Animal Behavior Processes 2*: 303–312.

De Casper, A.J., and M.D. Zeiler. 1977. Time limits for completing fixed ratios. IV. Components of the ratio. *Journal of the Experimental Analysis of Behavior 27*: 235–244.

Eisler, H. 1975. Subjective duration and psychophysics. *Psychological Review 82*: 429–450.

Gibbon, J. 1977. Scalar Expectancy Theory and Weber's Law in animal timing. *Psychological Review 84*: 279–325.

_____. 1979. Timing the stimulus and the response in aversive control. In M.D. Zeiler and P. Harzem, eds., *Reinforcement and Organization of Behaviour.* New York: Wiley.

_____. 1981. In Press. On the form and location of the psychometric bisection function for time. *Journal of Mathematical Psychology.*

Libby, M.E., and R.M. Church. 1974. Timing of avoidance responses by rats. *Journal of the Experimental Analysis of Behavior 22*: 513–517.

Patnaik, P.B. 1949. The non-central X'^2, and F–distributions and their applications. *Biometrika 36*: 202–232.

Platt, J.R. 1979. Temporal differentiation and the psychophysics of time. In M.D. Zeiler and P. Harzem, eds., *Reinforcement and Organization of Behaviour.* New York: Wiley.

Platt, J.R.; D. Kuch; and S.C. Bitgood. 1973. Rats' leverpress durations as psychophysical judgments of time. *Journal of the Experimental Analysis of Behavior 19*: 239–250.

Stubbs, A. 1968. The discrimination of stimulus duration by pigeons. *Journal of the Experimental Analysis of Behavior 11*: 223–238.

_____. 1976. Scaling of stimulus duration by pigeons. *Journal of the Experimental Analysis of Behavior 26*: 15–26.

Zeiler, M. 1977. Schedules of reinforcement: The controlling variables. In W.K. Honig and J.E.R. Staddon, eds., *Handbook of Operant Behavior*, pp. 201–232. Englewood Cliffs, New Jersey: Prentice–Hall.

V RESPONSE-BASED CUES AS DISCRIMINATIVE PROPERTIES OF REINFORCEMENT SCHEDULES

8 FIXED-RATIO-COUNTING SCHEDULES
Response and Time Measures Considered

Sally L. Hobson and
Frederic Newman

The present volume contains a number of studies that directly examine the discriminability of reinforcement schedules for infrahuman organisms. The approaches reflect both the operant tradition and the influence of sensory psychology and yield a quantitative analysis of reinforcement schedules that is quite straightforward. What distinguishes this work from animal psychophysics in general is simply the dimension defining the stimuli to be discriminated: Instead of exteroceptive stimuli such as lights and sounds, a set of schedule values (e.g., differences in response requirements, stimulus durations, or reinforcement probabilities) is programmed. Hence, it is not surprising that the signal detection approach to psychophysics (Green and Swets, 1966) has been a major factor in the development of the entire area (Nevin, Chapter 1). Some of the other antecedents may be less well known.

In the response domain, consider Ferster and Skinner's (1957) work on fixed ratio (FR) schedules, where every nth response was reinforced. When different ratio sizes were mixed within sessions, the

The authors wish to thank William M. Baum, A. Charles Catania and D. Alan Stubbs for supplying unpublished data from their own studies for comparison to ours. Marc Davis, Mitchell Foster, Marilyn Schneck, James Slezak, John Tillou, and Scott Valentine did a splendid job running the experiments. Susan Dottavio and John Southard helped with the computer analysis. Reprints can be obtained from Sally L. Hobson, Department of Psychology, Adelphi University, Garden City, New York 11530.

results suggested that the number of emitted responses functions as a discriminative stimulus and thus could be studied like any other. At the time that Ferster and Skinner's work appeared, Mechner (1958a, 1958b) had just completed a parametric study of fixed ratio "counting" (FRC) schedules with rats in order to analyze response sequences. In a counting procedure, the subject must make a minimum number of consecutive responses (a run) on one lever before a report response on a second lever is reinforced. Brandon (Chapter 9) refers to these schedules as response-terminated counting schedules. Because response differentiation is required, reinforcement plays a shaping role in this procedure (see also Lattal, Chapter 5). The procedure is formally equivalent to the method of production in classical psychophysics. Thus, the subject's run length provides an estimate of its sensitivity to the required value. However, the psychophysical parallel was not exploited until much later (Hobson, 1975; Platt and Johnson, 1971; Platt and Senkowski, 1970).

In the temporal domain, a similar research trend appears. Mechner and Guevrekian's (1962) early work on timing schedules, where response time rather than number was selectively reinforced, did not initially take hold. Perhaps one reason the psychophysical implications of Mechner's work were ignored is that behavioral research was focused elsewhere — on motivational effects in particular (e.g., Mechner and Latranyi, 1963) and on the dynamics of reinforcement schedules generally (e.g., Morse, 1966; Lattal, Chapter 5). The alternative to studying temporal control using timing schedules has been to use temporal discrimination procedures (i.e., by arranging experimenter-controlled differences in stimulus duration). However, this too failed to attract much research interest until the late 1960s (see Stubbs, 1968).

Meanwhile, Rilling and McDiarmid (1965) developed a two-alternative choice procedure to examine the discriminability of fixed ratio schedules for pigeons and included a signal detection account of the data. Brandon (Chapter 9) refers to this ratio discrimination procedure as a stimulus-terminating counting schedule. Stubbs' (1968) work on stimulus duration followed. Thus, two of the earliest demonstrations of the applicability of signal detection methods to animal behavior involved response-based or temporal cues rather than conventional stimuli. (For a general review of animal psychophysics, see Blough and Blough 1977.)

Our present study extends the ratio discrimination work to ratio-counting schedules. In this chapter, the psychophysical properties of ratio schedules will be emphasized, as measured under the two types of procedures (response differentiation and stimulus discrimination). The results will be compared to the equivalent results for time-based schedules. The relevant studies are outlined in Table 8–1, which summarizes the procedures used and how the results were analyzed. While the list is not exhaustive, the table emphasizes the parametric studies that are similar to ours, and it also contains single-valued studies to indicate the extent to which different procedures, species, and schedules have been examined. In addition, Table 8–1 includes studies (e.g., Le Fevre, 1973) which address the issue of how different reinforcement schedules are processed, the mechanisms involved, and so forth. Because no obvious schedule-detecting receptors exist, some researchers have considered response dimensions other than time and number (see Notterman and Mintz, 1965, on response force; also, McCullough, Le Buffe, and Gerding, 1979, on local response rates). Here, we consider the possibility of a reductionist account for time and number. Perhaps ratio performance really depends on timing processes rather than on count-related features of the task. Or, to reverse directions, perhaps temporal discriminations are actually based on some sort of counting process that subjects use to occupy the required interval.

To address the process question properly requires, first, a clear understanding of the procedures used in these studies and their variants and, second, parametric data on schedule size and transfer tests from one class of schedules to another. As the studies discussed below indicate, a single experiment rarely resolves a given issue, but a set of converging results may come closer and, at the same time, suggest new research strategies. These issues will be discussed later. For now, the point of the present study is that an organism's ability to discriminate its own behavior in a choice situation may be closely related to the way in which its performance is controlled under response differentiation procedures.

FIXED RATIO DISCRIMINABILITY

To determine the discriminability of fixed ratio schedules, Rilling and McDiarmid (1965) required their subjects to indicate which of

Table 8–1. Summary of the Procedures Used to Study Response-based and Time-based Reinforcement Schedules. The first half of each section lists discrimination studies and the second half, response differentiation studies.

Studies	Subjects	Task	Schedule Size	Individual Results
Response-based schedules				
Rilling and McDiarmid (1965)	2 pigeons	FR discrimination	FR 50	Yes
Rilling (1967)	3 pigeons	FR discrimination	FR 50	Yes[c]
Hobson (1975)	12 pigeons	FR discrimination	FR 10–30	Yes[a]
Hobson (1978)	3 pigeons	FR discrimination	FR 10–30	Yes[d]
Mechner (1958 a, b)	6 rats	Minimum ratio	FR 4–16	Yes[a, b]
Mechner and Guevrekian (1962)	7 rats	Minimum ratio	FR 4	Yes[c]
Brandon (1969)	8 rats	Ratio bands	FR 8	Yes
Platt and Senkowski (1970)	8 rats	Minimum ratio	FR 4–16	No[a, b]
Platt and Johnson (1971)	12 rats	Minumum ratio	FR 4–24	Some
Laties (1972)	4 pigeons	Minimum ratio	FR 8	Yes[c]
LeFevre (1973)	4 rats	Minimum ratio	FR 8	Some[c]
Time-based schedules				
Rilling (1967)	3 pigeons	FI discrimination	FI 45 sec	Yes[c]
Stubbs (1968)	3 pigeons	Duration discrimination	10–40 sec	Yes[a]
Kinchla (1970)	7 pigeons	Duration discrimination	5 sec	Yes[d]
Elsmore (1972)	2 monkeys	Duration discrimination	100 sec	Yes[d]
Church, Getty, and Lerner (1976)	3 rats	Duration discrimination	0.5–8.0 sec	Yes[a]
Stubbs (1976)	3 pigeons	Duration discrimination	22 sec	Yes[d]
Church and Deluty (1977)	8 rats	Duration discrimination	4–16 sec	No[a]

Mechner and Guevrekian (1962)	4 rats	Minimum R time	5 sec	Yes
Malott and Cumming (1964)	2–3 rats	Minimum IRT	0.4–100 sec	Yes
Staddon (1965)	3 pigeons	Minimum IRT	5.7–31.5 sec	Yes[b]
Catania (1970)	4 pigeons	Minimum R latency	1.3–24.4 sec	Yes[a,b]
LeFevre (1973)	4 rats	Minimum R time	3.2 sec	Some[c]
Platt, Kuch, and Bitgood (1973)	5 rats	Minimum R duration	0.4–6.4 sec	Yes[a,b]
Kuch (1974)	4 rats	Duration bands	4–16 sec	Yes[a,b]
DeCasper and Zeiler (1974)	8 pigeons	Minimum time	16–300 sec	Yes[a,b]
DeCasper and Zeiler (1977)	4 pigeons	Minimum pause	10–80 sec	Yes[a,b]
DeCasper and Zeiler (1977)	4 pigeons	Minimum R time	20–100 sec	Yes[a,b]
Stubbs (1980)	3 pigeons	FI hybrid	0.8–200 sec	Yes[a]

Note: Studies that analyze temporal aspects of performance under simple FI schedules and in aversive control situations have been reviewed elsewhere (Gibbon, 1977) and are excluded.

a. These parametric studies, on the effect of schedule size, provide estimates of $\Delta I/I$ or the data required for the calculation. The results from both types of procedures (differentiation and discrimination) can be so analyzed. Details available upon request.

b. Response differentiation studies showing the relation between emitted and required values and thus whether a power function obtains.

c. Only these studies report measures of both run length and time. However, Laties (1972) does not include variability estimates for the latter, and LeFevre (1973) for the most part presents frequency distributions without citing specific values.

d. Signal detection studies emphasizing response bias rather than sensitivity measures.

two different-sized ratios they had just completed on a center key by pecking the appropriate side key to obtain reinforcement. The results, and those of subsequent studies, showed that performance was similar to that obtained along other stimulus dimensions.

When payoffs for correct choices were varied, the receiver operating characteristics (ROCs) obtained were consistent with a generalized model of signal detection theory (Hobson, 1978). When one ratio was held constant and the other varied, the psychometric functions relating measures of sensitivity to schedule difference were orderly for a wide range of ratio sizes (Hobson, 1975; Pliskoff and Goldiamond, 1966; Rilling and McDiarmid, 1965). An analysis of relative discriminability showed that performance improved with absolute ratio size (Hobson, 1975). That is, in ratio discrimination, the difference threshold, divided by ratio size ($\Delta I/I$, the Weber fraction in classical psychophysics), decreased as ratio size increased. The same trend in discriminability was found to characterize the results from ratio-counting studies (Mechner, 1958a; Platt and Senkowski, 1970) when they were reanalyzed (see Hobson, 1975).

It is not surprising that the trend in Weber fractions agrees for both ratio discrimination and ratio counting. Similar results were found across different methods in visual and auditory psychophysics with human subjects (Engen, 1971). There are some generalizations to be tested, however. The ratio sizes studied did not entirely overlap. The ratio-counting work extends from FRC 4 to FRC 16 only, while the range for ratio discrimination is wider, but does not include the smaller sizes (see Table 8-1). Also, note the clear division of labor. Rats served as subjects exclusively in the parametric studies on ratio counting, while pigeons served in the ratio discrimination studies. This division is undesirable because it may confound procedural differences with species differences of the sort sometimes reported for timing schedules (e.g., Hemmes, 1975; Richardson and Loughead, 1974). Thus, research on ratio counting with pigeons is indicated.

TEMPORAL DISCRIMINABILITY

In the case of time-based schedules, a large number of studies now exist that have procedures similar to the ratio work just described.

Differentiation procedures will be considered first. In the timing equivalent of Mechner's ratio-counting schedule (e.g., Mechner and Guevrekian, 1962), the subject's response initiates the time interval, and a second response terminates it. Thus, it is a two-key version of the more familiar interresponse time (IRT) procedure (e.g., Malott and Cumming, 1964; Staddon, 1965), where reinforcement occurs only if the time between responses exceeds some minimum value. Subsequent research has shown that other temporal properties of responding can be selectively reinforced—response latency (Catania, 1970); response duration (e.g., Platt, Kuch, and Bitgood, 1973); and certain temporal features of fixed ratio responding (e.g., De Casper and Zeiler, 1977).

A most interesting and controversial finding in this literature is that subjects, especially pigeons, tend progressively to underestimate the required interval as schedule size increases. Hence, a power function with an exponent less than one obtains. Also, in some tasks, subjects tend to respond in "bursts," which makes their responding bimodal. Generally, the time requirements used are minima rather than maxima or bands of reinforced values. Time ranges in the parametric temporal differentiation research include the sizes used in temporal discrimination studies (see Table 8-1). The latter are discussed next.

The work on experimenter-controlled differences in duration uses discrimination procedures that are similar to the choice task that Rilling and McDiarmid (1965) developed for ratio schedules. Typically, the subject is required to indicate whether a stimulus of long or short duration has just occurred, but need not otherwise respond to obtain reinforcement (see especially Church and Deluty, 1977; Church, Getty, and Lerner, 1976; Stubbs, 1968). In the fixed interval (FI) version of a temporal discrimination task, the subject must respond at the end of the preset interval before indicating its duration (Rilling, 1967).

Recently, Stubbs and his co-workers have developed a set of hybrid procedures that combine some of the features of a free operant FI task with choice possibilities (see Stubbs and Dreyfus, Chapter 6). For all three types (differentiation, discrimination, hybrid), the results show that time is a well-behaved stimulus dimension: The psychophysical functions are just as orderly as the results for ratio tasks. However, a straightforward translation of Mechner's (1958a) original schedule into its fixed-interval-timing equivalent has not appeared, though Baum (1978) has performed relevant research, and his unpublished data are available. The lack of research on this type of timing is unfortunate because FI contingencies are widely used, and the results are frequently compared to FR (see Nevin, 1973). One result in particular should be noted: Both FR and FI generate similar, highly stereotyped patterns of responding.

COMPARING RATIO- AND TIME-BASED PERFORMANCE

When performance under ratio schedules is compared in detail to performance under time-based schedules, several differences are found. First, in discrimination tasks, the ROCs have somewhat different forms (cf. Hobson, 1978; Stubbs, 1976). At present, it is unclear whether this difference is independent of schedule size. Second, for time-based schedules, but not for ratio schedules, it appears that the Weber fraction remains reasonably constant across a large range of sizes—from 1.3 to 24.4 seconds in Catania's (1970) study and from 10 to 40 seconds in Stubbs' (1968). Both studies are widely cited. The consistency of the results is discussed later. Third, for ratio-counting schedules, a linear relation between emitted and required values is found, while for timing schedules, power functions rule (e.g., DeCasper and Zeiler, 1977; Lowe, Harzem, and Spencer, 1979; but see Gibbon, 1977). However, a larger range of schedule sizes is required for more precise comparisons. Fourth, Fetterman (1979) suggests that the scaled size of ratio schedules may differ from those involving stimulus duration. These sorts of parametric differences are difficult to explain unless one assumes that performance under ratio- and time-based schedules reflects different behavioral processes.

Three studies have directly compared performance under time-based and response-based (ratio) schedules. All are single-valued studies and used between subjects designs. The first study (Mechner and Guevrekian, 1962) found a difference in run time variability between an FRC 4 schedule and a 5-second timing one. In the latter schedule, a rat starts a timer with a press on bar 1 and stops it with a press on bar 2. The difference in run time variability was not discussed, probably because mean run times differed (see Table 8-3, below). Thus, the difference is difficult to interpret in the absence of other data.

The second study (Rilling, 1967) compared FI and FR performance using the discrimination procedure described above. The results (session averages) suggested that when pigeons discriminated a pair of large-sized schedules, number of responses was the controlling factor on both FR and FI. The third study (LeFevre, 1973) extended Mechner and Guevrekian's comparisons of ratio counting and timing to a trial-by-trial analysis of number of responses (i.e., run length) and the corresponding temporal measure (run time) on both schedules. The results with this procedure differed from Rilling's (1967) discrimination finding. Le Fevre concluded that his rats were not "counting" when response time was differentially reinforced nor were they "timing" under the equivalent ratio schedule (FRC 8). However, Le Fevre noted that subjects on the timing schedule rarely made more than one or two bar 1 responses after initiating the interval. Apparently, this is not an isolated finding for response-initiated timing schedules (see Mechner and Latranyi, 1963; also, Catania, 1979).

Clearly, no general conclusion about the relation between counting and timing can be made from the available data. The Le Fevre (1973) and Rilling (1967) studies may disagree simply because of differences in procedures, species, schedule values, or performance measures. Because these are single-valued studies, the results serve to reemphasize the importance of additional research across a range of ratio sizes, with both temporal and response measures examined. The parametric work, reviewed above, leads to the same conclusion. The fact that extra responses do not routinely develop on a response-initiated timing schedule suggests that other timing tasks ought to be examined and transfer tests included.

THE PRESENT STUDY

In view of the limited parametric data on performance under different-sized ratio-counting schedules, the present study extended the early work on rats to another species (pigeons) and to larger ratio sizes (FRC 4 to FRC 50), so that the results may be compared to those obtained using ratio discrimination procedures. To facilitate comparisons, subjects from Hobson's (1975) earlier study were included and tested along with new birds trained under Mechner's (1958a) original procedure. Temporal measures were obtained along with run length distributions to determine whether performance on either dimension (response time or number) resembled the results for time-based tasks (Catania, 1970; Stubbs, 1968). The second phase of the study examined performance under several fixed interval equivalents of ratio-counting schedules, using a within subjects transfer design. In this way, the notion that a common process underlies both types of response differentiation was directly tested by switching subjects from FRC to FI and vice versa. Thus, the present study extended the research on temporal differentiation to a set of timing schedules not previously examined. The analysis includes Baum's unpublished data on FRC and FI.

Method

A total of twelve White Carneaux pigeons served, including four from an earlier ratio discrimination study (Hobson, 1975) and four naive subjects. Only the left and center keys of a standard three-key pigeon chamber were used. The keys were lit (center green, left white) except during reinforcement. However, for Bird 352, the key lights were turned out for five seconds (time out) after each unreinforced run and after reinforcement.

The fixed ratio counting procedure is described first. After several days of preliminary training, a procedure like Mechner's (1958a) was introduced. This Mechner counting procedure was a mixed one-key FR and a two-key ratio-counting schedule. On some cycles (one-key FR), completion of a certain number of consecutive center-key pecks directly produced access to grain, while on others (two-key FR or ratio counting), the first side-key report response occurring after the center-key minimum had been met was reinforced. The two types of cycles were programmed in an irregular sequence and occurred equally often. On both, underestimates (i.e., side-key pecks before completion of the required ratio) immediately reset the ratio. Sessions lasted until eighty reinforcements had been obtained.

Table 8-2 summarizes the procedural details. Most subjects were tested in different orders across a wide range of ratio sizes, with one or more replications. For example, Bird 380 was tested and retested at all six sizes (FRC 4, 7, 10, 16, 30, and 50) after initial training at relatively small ratios. Column 4 of the table shows the number of different ratio sizes replicated, with the total number of replications in parenthesis. In the results section (below), most of the data

Table 8–2. Summary of Ratio-counting Procedures for Individual Subjects. The three subjects (Birds 101, 102, and 352) that were initially trained on fixed interval schedules are listed last, and those trained under both types of schedules (FRC and FI) are marked (*). For this last group of subjects, trial-by-trial measures of ratio run time and total time were obtained along with mean values. For further details, see text and Table 8–3.

Bird	Ratio Sizes Tested	Number of Different Ratios	Replications	Initial Test Order	Response Measures for Ratios
359*	FRC 4–50	3	2 (2)	FRC 50, 7, 4, 4, 50; FI 15	Run length, time
362	FRC 4–50	6	6 (9)	FRC 10, 7, 16, 10, 16, 4	Run length, mean time
363	FRC 4–16	4	2 (2)	FRC 10, 7, 16, 7, 4, 10	Run length
364	FRC 4–50	6	5 (9)	FRC 10, 7, 16, 16, 10, 4	Run length, mean time
365*	FRC 4–50	2	0 (0)	FRC 50, 4; FI 3	Run length, time
370	FRC 4–50	6	2 (2)	FRC 10, 30, 7, 50, 4, 16	Run length, mean time
377*	FRC 4–50	6	5 (9)	FRC 10, 7, 16 ... FI 9, FI 3	Run length, mean time
380	FRC 4–50	6	6 (8)	FRC 10, 7, 16, 7, 10, 30	Run length, mean time
422*	FRC 30	1	1 (1)	FRC 30; FI 12; FRC 30	Run length, time
101	none	0	0 (0)	FI 15	none
102*	FRC 14	1	0 (0)	FI 9; FRC 14	Run length, time
352*	FRC 10	1	0 (0)	FI 9; FI 9; FRC 10	Run length, time

shown are means, based on the last five sessions of each determination after several weeks of training at a given ratio size. Note that
relevant data were obtained on two-key cycles only, where run length
is free to vary.

The last column of Table 8–2 summarizes the response measures
obtained. On FRC, distributions of run length (number of center-key
pecks between each side-key report) were recorded to reflect performance along the reinforced dimension as ratio size was varied. In
most cases, the results included the corresponding means for run
time (from first center-key peck to side-key report) and total time
(time between side-key reports excluding reinforcement time—that
is, pause time plus run time). Pause times were separately recorded,
but are not treated in detail here. For our transfer subjects (e.g.,
Bird 365), all three distributions (run lengths, run times, total times)
were recorded along with the means. This phase of the study is
described next, along with Baum's procedures.

Generally, the present FI timing task was like the one used for
ratio counting, and the equivalent response measures were derived.
Reinforcement was programmed either for the first center-key peck
occurring after the specified interval had elapsed (one-key FI) or for
the first side-key report following such a center-key peck (FI timing). Each side-key report reset the timer. This constitutes the basic
FI timing procedure in our study and in Baum's. Again, only the FI
timing portion is reported. In our work, two FI values were examined. Birds 102 and 352 were trained at FI 9.3 seconds, a value just
below the point where Catania (1970) found a match between emitted and required times when response latency was differently reinforced in a single key situation. Birds 101 and 359 were trained at a
larger size (FI 15 seconds). Three of the subjects also received ratio
training. Test order appears in Table 8–2. Baum trained two birds at
FI 12 and FI 30 seconds and two others at comparable ratio sizes
(FRC 40 and FRC 80). Otherwise, his procedures are much like ours.

In addition to the basic FI procedure, two variations were examined to determine whether "counting" could explain performance on
a wider variety of timing tasks than heretofore examined. In one
type (a partial reset procedure), reinforcement contingencies were
"relaxed" as follows. On those occasions when a "correct" side-key
peck occurred after the end of the interval without a terminal center-
key peck preceding it, the timer was not reset; instead, the subject
was merely required to satisfy the center-key response requirement

(one peck) before a side-key peck (at any time) would produce reinforcement. Three subjects were tested at two FI sizes under this type of procedure. Then, one of them (Bird 352) was switched to the basic FI timing schedule previously described. FRC data were also obtained (see Table 8-2).

In the second variation (response-initiated FI), the basic center-side key sequence was retained, but a center-key peck was required to start the timer. In this respect, the procedure was like the response-initiated timing schedule that Mechner and Guevrekian (1962) introduced: Both selectively reinforce long run times instead of long total times as in our other versions. The one subject (Bird 422) tested under this procedure was trained before and after on FRC 30. The transfer value chosen was FI 12 seconds, to match the subject's mean run time on the prior (ratio) schedule. The same sort of match was made for other subjects when they were switched from one class of schedules to the other. That is, total time on FRC was used to determine schedule size on basic FI and on the partial reset version, and run length on FI was used to determine the equivalent FRC value.

Results

Figure 8-1 shows examples of the frequency distributions obtained from pigeons exposed to ratio-counting schedules of several different sizes. Baum's results, which are similar to ours, are summarized in Table 8-3 below. First, consider the subjects' performance along the reinforced dimension (FRC run length—filled circles in Figure 8-1). Basically, the distributions are unimodal and nearly symmetrical, with their means and medians falling just above the required size. The distributions flatten and widen with increasing ratio size. Thus, the run length results for pigeons closely replicate the findings for rats (e.g., Mechner, 1958a) and extend them to a much wider range of ratio sizes—up to FRC 80 with Baum's data included.

Second, the frequency distributions for FRC time generally look much like those for FRC run length. In Figure 8-1, total times have been shown in order to prepare the reader for subsequent FRC-FI comparisons. Run times have been omitted to simplify the figure. Both time measures appeared to follow the reinforced dimension (run length). To determine whether the correspondence between frequency distributions held across individual trials, correlation coef-

Figure 8-1. Typical examples of relative frequency distributions obtained using ratio-counting schedules. The results for total time are shown along with those for run length, the reinforced dimension (filled circles). The mean and standard deviation for the latter are listed beside each set of distributions. Sample size (*N*) is also shown.

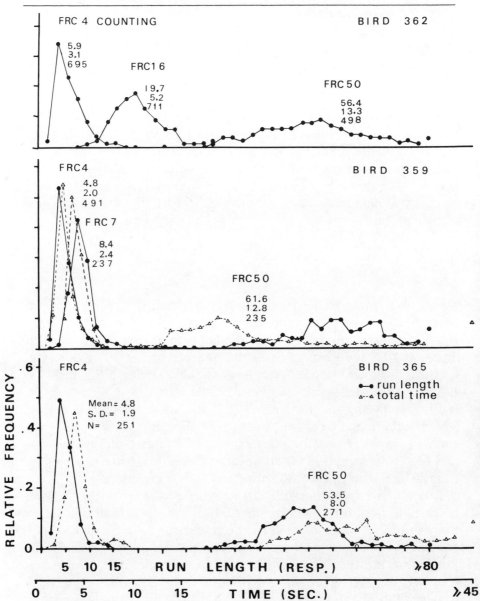

ficients were computed. Rather than reproduce the entire set of correlation matrixes, let us describe the relation between run length and run time, which LeFevre (1973) also examined. In several cases, the correlations turned out to be much stronger than LeFevre's, even when the data were rank ordered to control for extreme values. For example, two of our subjects (Bird 365 at FRC 4 and Bird 422 at FRC 30) had run time–run length correlation coefficients of about 0.9. Does this mean that subjects (at least pigeons) are using time as the basis for terminating their response runs in ratio-counting schedules? Apparently not. As subsequent sections make clear, we failed to find other, more direct evidence of response time parallels to bolster the correlational data. The results for FI timing schedules are a case in point.

The frequency distributions shown in Figure 8–2 are typical of the results obtained in our laboratory and in Baum's when FI timing schedules are used. The figure shows performance on the reinforced dimension (time) and performance on a collateral dimension (run length). For Bird 422, run times were selectively reinforced (response-initiated FI), and for the remaining subjects, total times were reinforced (basic FI timing and partial reset FI timing). The most interesting feature of Figure 8–2 is not the similarity of the response and time distributions on a given schedule, but the difference between performance on both the FI variants (top panel) and performance on the basic FI schedules (middle and bottom panels). Only the former is bimodal. That is, a tendency to respond much too soon (to make quick side-key reports after only one or two center-key pecks) developed when FI reset contingencies were relaxed or when response-initiated timing was imposed. This tendency to burst coexisted with another pattern of responding—the tendency to wait out the scheduled minimum. The location of this second mode depended upon schedule size. In this respect, performance on the FI variants resembled performance on basic FI timing schedules.

Bimodality is a fairly common result in other sorts of timing tasks, but not a universal finding. Thus, the heterogeneity of our FI results replicates the complex pattern of data in the timing literature. The results for response-initiated FI in particular call out for further study, because though based on a single subject, they suggest that response bursting occurs in some two-key timing situations and not in others (not in basic FI). The results for the partial reset procedure are interesting because the procedure does not require time and

Figure 8–2. Typical examples of relative frequency distributions from the basic FI timing schedule (middle and bottom panels) and two variants of that schedule (top). As in Figure 8-1, the parameters shown are for the reinforced dimension, time (open symbols). See text for further details.

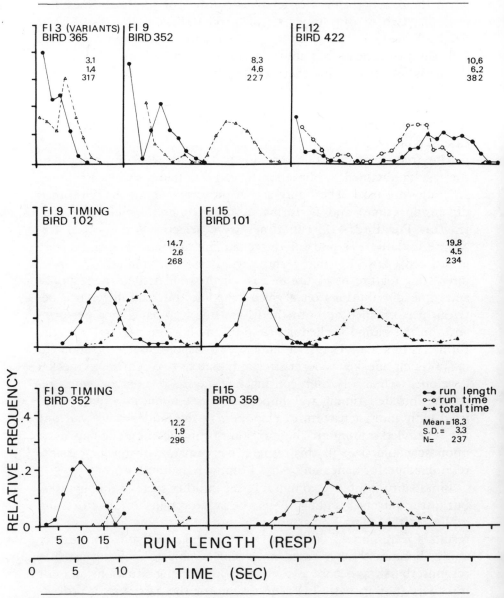

response requirements to be satisfied together and thus will reinforce a sequence of long followed by short response times should they occur while the response-initiated procedure (like other, full reset procedures) will not. Yet, both procedures produce bursting and, hence, a sizable number of errors (see Table 8–3).

In contrast to the results for timing, the ratio-counting results appear much simpler. None of the ratio subjects—neither ours nor any others we know of—have ever shown bimodal responding. Instead, at each ratio size, the subjects all develop finely "tuned," unimodal run length distributions (see also Brandon, Chapter 9). Figure 8–3 shows the relation between mean run length (R) and ratio size (r) on logarithmic coordinates (filled circles). The individual results are for all determinations, while the group data are based only on those tests where time measures were also obtained. For each subject, the corresponding means for either ratio run time or total time (open circles or squares) are also shown. In addition, the figure shows the run length means from two other pigeon studies—Baum's at FRC 40 and Laties' at FRC 8 (triangles, bottom right-hand panel). For a summary of Laties' procedure, see Table 8–1. In each case, the run length data fall just above the minimum requirement line (dotted line), which indicates that at all ratio sizes, subjects tended to exceed ("overestimate") the minimum requirements for reinforcement.

The solid line function in the figure is a least squares fit to the group data and shows, for the reinforced dimension, that the average transformed data are linear. The same relation appears at the individual level. Typically, the fits to the individual data account for more than 99 percent of the variance. Figure 8–3 shows the exact amounts in parenthesis. Thus, a power function provides a good description of the run length means. For the subjects shown, the equation for the group is:

$$R = 1.60\,r^{0.92} \tag{8.1}$$

In this equation, mean length (R) and ratio size (r) are expressed in terms of number of responses. Transformed into logarithms, the exponent of the equation appears as the slope of the function in Figure 8–3 and the coefficient appears as its intercept. For our pigeons, all the exponents are close to unity, and the coefficients range from one to two. Thus, the individual results, like the parameters of Equation (8.1), suggest that the crossover from overestimation to underestimation must occur at large ratio sizes, well beyond FRC 100 for

Figure 8–3. Mean run length (filled circles) as a function of ratio size, on logarithmic coordinates. The corresponding means for ratio run time (open circles) and/or for total time (open squares) are also shown. The left-hand ordinate shows the scale for run length in responses. The right-hand ordinate, unlabeled, has hash marks at 5, 10, 20, and 50 seconds for run time and at twice these values (10–100 seconds) for total time. Due to cropping of the ordinate below 5 seconds, one data point was omitted—Bird 380, total time = 2.4 seconds at FRC 4.

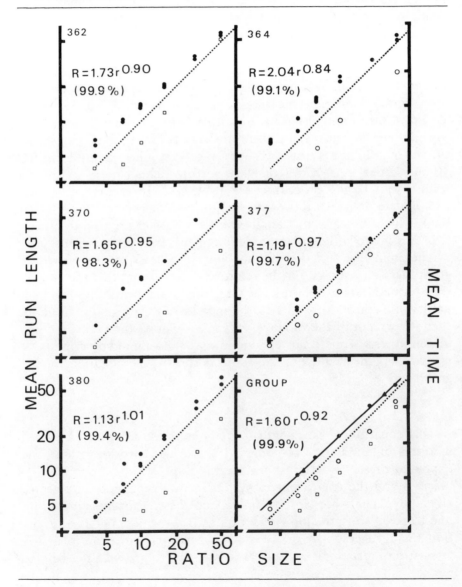

most subjects. Baum's data at FRC 80 (Table 8–3) are consistent with this conclusion. The similarity in results for rats and pigeons is discussed later.

As for the nonreinforced collateral dimensions, ratio run time and total time increased with schedule size, as expected, though not in parallel with run length. As Figure 8–3 indicates, the results appeared J shaped on logarithmic coordinates. Pause times (not shown) looked similar though more irregular. The difference in function form for run length and concomitant temporal measures suggests that ratio counting can not simply be explained as a by-product of timing.

For FI timing, the relevant data (means) appear in Table 8–3. Examination of the table suggests that on basic FI, total times overestimated the FI requirements in a fashion similar to the overestimate of the FR requirement by run length in FRC schedules. Apparently, this is not a typical finding. Comparable overestimation has not been reported in previous work on related temporal tasks. However, there are insufficient parametric data to define the FI functions with the same precision as the ratio functions in Figure 8–3.

Considered in isolation, the mean data do not themselves support a claim of basic differences between ratio schedules and time-based schedules. Variability measures must also be considered. Hence, coefficients of variation were determined for all our data by dividing the standard deviation of each frequency distribution by its mean. The result is equivalent to the Weber fraction and provides a convenient measure of relative sensitivity. The ratio-counting results are described first.

Figure 8–4, bottom panel, shows the Weber fractions for ratio run length, all subjects, as a function of ratio size. Solid lines connect the results for subjects tested at several adjacent values. The results for Birds 359 and 365 are shown with triangles. The top panel of Figure 8–4 includes group data (means) from four other ratio-counting studies (Baum, 1978; Laties, 1972; Mechner, 1958a; Platt and Senkowski, 1970) for comparison to our own data. For our study, medians are plotted as well as means, but only for those determinations where time measures were also obtained. The individual results (lower panel) are for all determinations. The Weber fraction for fixed ratio discrimination is also shown (Hobson, 1975), so the results from the two types of procedures may be directly compared. The

Table 8–3. Weber Fractions for Individual Subjects Under Several Counting and Timing Schedules. Mean values (responses or time in seconds) are listed in parenthesis. Percent errors, number of sessions trained, and sample size (N) for the last five sessions are also shown. The first two sections of the table contain results for subjects directly transferred from one type of schedule to the equivalent version of the other type (e.g., Bird 365, FRC 4 versus FI 3 seconds). The last section shows results for other determinations. For replications, test order is shown in parenthesis (Bird 359, FRC 50 (1), and so forth). Results (means) for Baum's subjects and for Mechner and Guevrekian's (1962) subjects appear in the rightmost columns.

Fixed Ratio Counting Schedules	Bird 365	Bird 352	Bird 102	Bird 422	Bird 359	Results of Other Studies	
	FRC 4	FRC 10	FRC 14	FRC 30 (1)	FRC 50 (2)	FRC 40 (Baum)	FRC 4 (M&G)
Run length	0.38 (4.8)	0.22 (12.1)	0.23 (18.5)	0.13 (33.7)	0.14 (55.1)	0.19 (46.1)	0.23 (4.3)
Run time	0.42 (2.9)	0.21 (7.5)	0.20 (7.6)	0.15 (12.5)	0.17 (12.1)	0.19 (14.7)	0.37 (2.0)
Total time	0.36 (4.1)	0.25 (8.8)	0.20 (11.7)	0.32 (17.9)	0.22 (16.8)	0.26 (16.5)	— (5.1)
Errors	24%	18%	9%	14%	28%	23%	—
Sessions/N	41/251	10/248	11/221	31/227	39/277	52/384	—

Fixed Interval Timing Schedules	Bird 365	Bird 352	Bird 102	Bird 422	Bird 359	Results of Other Studies	
	FI 3[a]	FI 9	FI 9	FI 12[b]	FI 15	FI 12 (Baum)	Time 5 (M&G)[c]
Run length	0.61 (3.7)	0.32 (10.3)	0.30 (14.7)	0.59 (25.7)	0.22 (28.2)	0.42 (20.6)	—
Run time	0.56 (2.1)	— (9.7)	— (7.0)	0.59 (10.6)	0.29 (10.3)	0.41 (9.9)	0.11 (4.9)
Total time	0.46 (3.1)	0.16 (12.2)	0.17 (12.1)	0.55 (19.1)	0.18 (18.3)	0.25 (15.7)	— (11.6)
Errors	39%	24%	21%	50%	20%	22%	—
Sessions/N	29/317	33/269	37/269	32/382	36/237	52/394	—

Replications and Other Determinations	FRC 50		FI 9[a]		FRC 30 (2)		FRC 50 (1)		FRC 80 (Baum)		FI 30 (Baum)	
Run length	0.14	(53.5)	0.70	(5.8)	0.19	(33.7)	0.20	(61.6)	0.25	(87.8)	0.60	(19.0)
Run time	0.46	(23.8)	0.68	(6.1)	0.23	(12.3)	0.87	(15.3)	0.30	(24.3)	0.46	(15.9)
Total time	0.24	(34.0)	0.56	(8.3)	0.38	(19.0)	0.58	(23.7)	0.30	(29.1)	0.24	(31.9)
Errors	24%		56%		15%		12%		30%			
Sessions/N	60/263		23/327		31/240		63/235		28/468		29/515	

Note: Except for the timing schedules noted below, within each class of schedules (FRC or FI), procedures are quite similar, or else they involve minor variations (e.g., 5-second time outs for Bird 352) with no effect on the trends shown here.

a. Modified version of the basic FI timing schedule (partial reset contingency).

b. Response-initiated FI timing schedule. Main key response required to start and end the interval.

c. Mechner and Guevrekian's timing schedule. This is response initiated (as in b above) but requires no further main key responding.

Figure 8–4. Weber functions for ratio-counting schedules. The results for individual subjects appear in the lower half. Group data are shown above, along with the results from other studies, including Baum's at FRC 40. The function for fixed ratio discrimination is also shown (Hobson, 1975). Note the logarithmic abscissa.

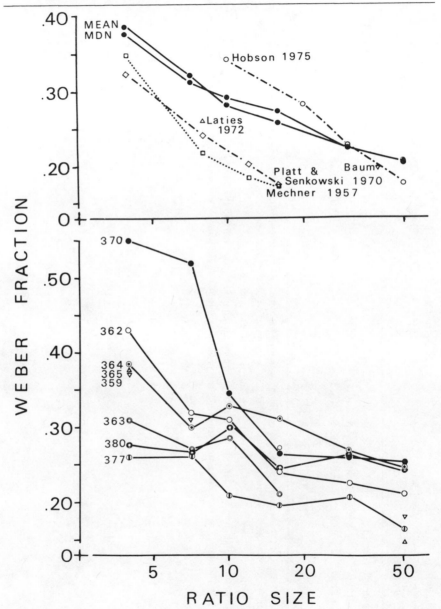

discrimination results are based on the standard deviation of the psychometric function divided by the mean and include Rilling and McDiarmid's (1965) results at FR 50. In each study and for both procedures, the effect of ratio size was clear: The Weber fraction decreased as response requirements increased. Rat N4 in Mechner's (1958a) study provided the sole exception, showing a flat function.

As a group, the results indicate that a strict version of Weber's Law ($\Delta I/I = k$), such as Gibbon (1977) proposes for time, does not hold for ratio-counting schedules or for ratio discrimination, even when quite large sizes (FRC 40 or 50) are included. At still greater values, either the procedures (and results) are not comparable (Pliskoff and Goldiamond, 1966), or else the data base is too small to support firm conclusions (Baum, 1978). The Weber fraction may level off in this region (see Table 8-3). For our purposes, though, the important finding is that for ratio schedules, a decreasing trend is generally found.

To illustrate the difference between the trends for ratio-based and time-based contingencies, we replotted the results for ten parametric studies of temporally defined dimensions on the same set of coordinates and then overlaid the Weber fractions computed for ratio run length distributions, using mean ratio run times as the abscissa for the latter. Thus, a comparison was made in terms of reinforced dimensions. The group results (medians) appear in Figure 8-5. For temporal differentiation (e.g., Catania's 1970 study of response latencies), Weber fractions are plotted as a function of the required interval, while for temporal discrimination (e.g., Stubbs, 1968), the results are shown as a function of the duration of the larger of the two stimuli in each discriminative pair. Plotted in this fashion, the results for reinforced dimensions show the kind of schedule difference mentioned earlier. In the middle region (from 3 to 30 seconds, roughly), the Weber functions for various time-based tasks appear relatively flat and thus cut across the ratio run length data. For the entire range, a broad U-shaped time function appears. The difference does not appear to depend upon selection of a particular temporal dimension for comparison. For example, consider the three studies (Catania, 1970; Church and Deluty, 1977; Kuch, 1974) whose time ranges overlap ours, given the abscissa scale in the figure. Each used a different set of temporal contingencies, but the results are similar among them and different from ours. Generally in these studies, the group results hold at the individual level. In other words, in the time

Figure 8–5. Weber functions from several timing studies. The results for both temporal differentiation and temporal discrimination procedures appear. The Weber fractions for the ratio run length are plotted here as a function of mean run time for the ratio, rather than as a function of ratio size as in Figure 8-4. The time data come from the following studies: (a) Church, Getty, and Lerner (1976); (b) Platt, Kuch, and Bitgood (1973) and Kuch (1974); (c) Catania (1970); (d) Church and Deluty (1977); (e) Stubbs (1968); (f–h) DeCasper and Zeiler (1974; 1977); and (i) Stubbs (1980). See text and Table 8–1 for details.

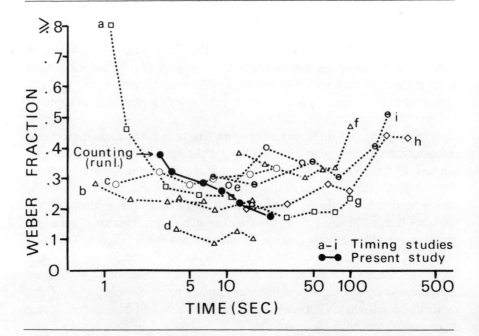

region occupied by performance on our ratio-counting schedules, we found few if any data for temporally defined tasks showing decreasing Weber fractions like those for ratio run lengths.[1]

The difference shown in Figure 8–5 means that relative sensitivity improves with schedule size for ratio-based, but not for time-based, schedules. So from several vantage points, the reductionist argument

---

1. Exceptions to the group data in Figure 8-3 include Rat 3 in Church et al. (1976), Bird 101 in DeCasper and Zeiler (1974), Rat 10 in Platt, Kuch, and Bitgood (1973), and Bird 11 in Stubbs (1968). In the latter two studies, interquartile ranges and medians were used to estimate Weber fractions. Elsewhere, standard deviations and means were used.

looks weak. For more direct evidence, transfer data must be considered. The top two sections of Table 8-3 show data from subjects transferred from one class of schedules to the other. The bottom section of the table shows other, related determinations. A few cases have been omitted (e.g., Bird 359, FRC 4) to save space, but these are no different than the data shown. Comparable results (between group data) from other studies (Baum, 1978; Mechner and Guevrekian, 1962) are included. Sensitivity measures are considered first.

The Weber fractions in Table 8-3 indicate that on both FRC and basic FI, responding was relatively less varied on the dimension specified by reinforcement than on other, nonreinforced dimensions. In some cases, the difference favored the reinforced dimension quite dramatically: On the first determination at FRC 50, Bird 359 showed considerable variability in run times and in total times, but relatively little variability in run lengths (Weber fraction = 0.20). Later, when the subject was retrained on FRC 50 and then transferred to FI 15 seconds, the run length measure increased, while the total time measure decreased, though not symmetrically. The exceptions are confined to some of the smaller ratio sizes (FRC 4, FRC 14). In any case, the general trend in our study and in the others is that subjects tend to be most sensitive to the reinforced dimension, whether that be time or number. The results for Bird 352, FRC 10, suggest that subjects can detect a schedule change within the first ten days of transfer (see Table 8-3), which deserves further study.

Since sensitivity appeared to be contingency-specific, a reductive account of one type of performance in terms of the other is implausible. An analysis of the subjects' means (Table 8-3) reinforces this conclusion. In our study and in Baum's (1978), the basic FI timing schedules produced shorter run lengths and also lower rates of responding than their fixed ratio equivalents. For example, after transfer from FRC 50 to FI 15, Bird 359 averaged only 28.2 responses per run and dropped its pecking rate to nearly half of its former (ratio) value. A similar change occurred in the opposite direction for Birds 352 and 102 soon after they were switched to ratio counting. Also, Bird 422 recovered its previous FRC 30 performance after interpolated training on response-initiated FI.

SUMMARY AND CONCLUSIONS

Both our results and Baum's (1978) indicate that when response number is differentially reinforced under ratio-counting schedules, using pigeons, a systematic shift in the run length distribution occurs with absolute schedule size, so that even at ratios as large as FRC 80, performance closely approximates schedule size (Figure 8-1). Of course, the match is not exact: Subjects tend to overshoot the required minimum by a small margin. In quantitative terms, the relation appears as a steep power function between the obtained means and the required size (Figure 8-3). The exponent is close to one, implying that a linear function would provide almost as good an account of the data. In other words, our functions are virtually indistinguishable from those of other (rat) studies (e.g., Mechner, 1958a), where most subjects have shown linearity for the ranges studied. In each, the projected crossover point, if any, falls beyond one hundred responses.

Compared to our ratio-counting results, most temporal differentiation studies yield relatively flat functions (exponents < 0.9) and show early transitions from over- to underestimation even when reponse bursting has been eliminated (e.g., Catania, 1970). Apparently, for basic FI timing, overestimation occurs across a wider range of values (Table 8-3). In this respect, our timing results are ratio-like. Yet what appeared to be small changes in the basic procedure (FI variants) produced bimodal responding (Figure 8-2), a fairly common finding in the timing literature. Here, however, the focus is ratio counting as a separate process, so we confine these matters to a footnote,[2] urging additional research to be undertaken.

In terms of sensitivity, the Weber functions for both ratio discrimination and ratio counting (Figure 8-4) cut across the ones for time-based schedules (Figure 8-5). This difference indicates that under both times of psychophysical procedures, the precise effects of schedule size depend upon which dimension (response number or time) is programmed for reinforcement. The FRC results in particular support an earlier suggestion (Hobson, 1975) that a decreasing

2. The results for FI variants looked a lot like those for IRT schedules—a different type of timing task—and not like those for two-key timing tasks (e.g., Mechner and Guevrekian, 1962), despite close procedural parallels to the latter. Thus, further research with both rats and pigeons is clearly indicated.

Weber function characterizes ratio performance generally. The conclusion is that the processes governing ratio discrimination and ratio counting are to an important extent quite similar.

A within subjects comparison of run length and time measures indicated that differentiation along one dimension does not produce a parallel set of changes along other, nonreinforced dimensions even though statistically significant response–time correlations are obtained. Specifically, the comparison showed (1) that on FRC, mean times were not a power function of ratio size, unlike run lengths; (2) that Weber fractions for the reinforced dimension (on FRC or basic FI) were smaller than those for the other dimensions measured (Table 8–3); and (3) that both run length and response rate changed after transfer. Thus, our results extend LeFevre's (1973) comparisons from rats to pigeons and from a single pair of schedules to several. Here, however, a different kind of timing schedule was examined, and sensitivity measures were included, increasing the generality of LeFevre's conclusions. Baum's (1978) unpublished data on FRC and basic FI timing schedules are consistent with these conclusions.

Equally important, for the first time the possible equivalence of conting and timing schedules was directly assessed by transfer training techniques. The consistency of the transfer results with the more usual types of comparisons rounds out Mechner and Guevrekian's (1962) original report. In addition, our finding that subjects tend to be most sensitive to the reinforced dimension is much like their finding regarding deprivation: Changes in deprivation levels did not affect performance on the reinforced dimension. Together, these results strongly suggest that ratio- and time-based schedules require separate accounts. Because this possibility has not been pursued to date, it deserves some further comment.

First, it should be pointed out that while an assumption of separate processes preserves the traditional classification of reinforcement schedules in terms of programmed contingencies, it does not rule out the existence of behavioral mechanisms that cut across schedule class. Indeed, our results demonstrate the power of reinforcers to shape behavior in specific directions, despite the subjects' earlier histories, some of which included noncontingent reinforcement (autoshaping). Second, we caution readers against construing our analysis of performance in various time-based tasks as demonstrating that this class is necessarily homogeneous. If anything, the ratio results for differentiation and discrimination look more consistent. Certainly, there is as yet no suggestion of a species difference in counting of the sort that concerns the timing literature, as mentioned earlier. However, even if there were not some controversy, species generality ought to be more widely demonstrated. For example, ratio discrimination could easily be studied using rats, to complete the present set of comparisons. Also, estimates of sensitivity (Weber fractions) under IRT reinforcement are not generally available. The only IRT studies we know of with an appropriate range of schedule sizes (Malott and Cumming, 1964; Staddon, 1965) do not report variability measures, which limits their usefulness as testing grounds for quantitative accounts of schedule discriminability. The fact that our analysis turned up some exceptional results at the individual level (i.e., not all the Weber functions for time were similar) should issue a clear call to researchers to use sample sizes larger than two or three subjects wherever possible.

In any case, to date, theoretical work on schedule discriminability and related areas (scaling) has focused on time-based tasks and thus on one particular set of empirical relations. For this reason, existing models do not seem well-equipped to handle the ratio findings. For example, Gibbon's "scalar" theory of temporal control encompasses a variety of experimental findings, but requires additional assumptions to account for the apparently nonscalar aspect of temporal differentiation (i.e., underestimation of schedule size in timing). Similarly, Church, Getty, and Lerner (1976) are able to account for the initially steep (nonscalar) segment of the Weber functions they obtained by assuming the existence of an added source of variance for temporal discrimination. In both cases, the same sort of question arose: Why wasn't performance more scalar (more Weber-like)?

In contrast, the ratio data do not present this kind of problem, for they appear fundamentally nonscalar (i.e., the Weber functions decrease across a wide range of ratio values). This means that accounts of ratio performance need not be burdened with scalar assumptions. Instead, researchers might do well to proceed from an entirely different set of principles. One possibility is a Poisson-based ("neural counting") model (see Church, Getty, and Lerner, 1976, for a recent discussion). This model predicts increased sensitivity at larger schedule sizes, as required by ratio discrimination and ratio-counting data. However, the model does not predict steep power functions, as in Figure 8–3. Thus, alternative models should be explored.

Meanwhile, is there any reason to believe that subjects adopt a time-based strategy on counting schedules or vice versa? Our results, it could be argued, do not entirely rule out this possibility, for they do not directly address Rilling's (1967) finding that number of responses was the controlling variable in both fixed ratio and fixed interval discrimination tasks. However, the present data suggest an interpretation of Rilling's results. The fact that the Weber function for ratios cuts across the function for time-based schedules (Figure 8–5) means that at large schedule sizes, where Rilling's work was done, sensitivity to response number improves while time does not. A subject trying out a count-related strategy in this region may, in effect, discover a more reliable indicator of the extant schedule value than a time-based strategy can provide and may thus continue "counting." Possibly, this is what Rilling's FI subjects discovered. If so, then subjects trained like Rilling's ought to show positive transfer when switched from FI to an equivalent FR discrimination. An experiment of this kind would constitute an attempt both to replicate and to extend Rilling's study as well as ours.

Lest this scenario sound far fetched, let us remind the reader, as Blough and Blough (1977: 524) have, that animals like humans have an uncanny ability to "devise response strategies different from those intended by the experimenter," provided there are payoffs. More generally, the experiment would demonstrate to what extent known facts—in this case, psychophysical relations—may be used to account for other research findings.

REFERENCES

Baum, W. 1978. (Unpublished data).

Blough, D.S., and P.M. Blough. 1977. Animal psychophysics. In W.K. Honig and J.E.R. Staddon, eds., *Handbook of Operant Behavior*, pp. 514–539. Englewood Cliffs, New Jersey: Prentice–Hall.

Brandon, P.K. 1969. The effects of error-contingent time out on counting behavior in rats. Doctoral dissertation, University of Michigan.

Catania, A.C. 1970. Reinforcement schedules and psychophysical judgments. In W.N. Schoenfeld, eds., *The Theory of Reinforcement Schedules*, pp. 1–42. New York: Appleton–Century–Crofts.

_____. 1979. Differential reinforcement of counting and timing in pigeons: Implications for response-chaining accounts of temporal judgment. Paper presented at the Eastern Psychological Association meetings, Philadelphia.

Church, R.M., and M.A. Deluty. 1977. Bisection of temporal intervals. *Journal of Experimental Psychology: Animal Behavior Processes 3* : 216–228.

Church, R.M.; D.J. Getty; and N.D. Lerner. 1976. Duration discrimination by rats. *Journal of Experimental Psychology: Animal Behavior Processes 2*: 303–312.

DeCasper, A.J., and M.D. Zeiler. 1974. Time limits for completing fixed ratios. III. Stimulus variables. *Journal of the Experimental Analysis of Behavior 22*: 285–300.

_____. 1977. Time limits for completing fixed ratios. IV. Components of the ratio. *Journal of the Experimental Analysis of Behavior 27*: 235–244.

Elsmore, T.F. 1972. Duration discrimination: Effects of probability of stimulus presentation. *Journal of the Experimental Analysis of Behavior 18*: 465–469.

Engen, T. 1971. Psychophysics. I. Discrimination and detection. In L.A. Riggs and J.W. Kling, eds., *Woodworth and Schlosberg's Experimental Psychology*, 3rd ed., pp. 11–46. New York: Holt, Rinehart and Winston.

Ferster, C.B., and B.F. Skinner. 1957. *Schedules of Reinforcement.* New York: Appleton–Century–Crofts.

Fetterman, G. 1979. Scaling of response-produced stimuli. Paper presented at the Association for Behavioral Analysis meetings, Dearborn, Michigan.

Gibbon, J. 1977. Scalar expectancy theory and Weber's Law in animal training. *Psychological Review 84*: 279–325.

Green, D.M., and J.A. Swets. 1966. *Signal Detection Theory and Psychophysics.* New York: Wiley.

Hemmes, N.S. 1975. Pigeons' performance under differential reinforcement of low rate schedules depends upon the operant. *Learning and Motivation 6*: 344–357.

Hobson, S.L. 1975. Discriminability of fixed-ratio schedules for pigeons: Effects of absolute ratio size. *Journal of the Experimental Analysis of Behavior 23* : 25–35.

_____. 1978. Discriminability of fixed-ratio schedules for pigeons: Effects of payoff values. *Journal of the Experimental Analysis of Behavior 30*: 69–81.

Kinchla, J. 1970. Discrimination of two auditory durations by pigeons. *Perception and Psychophysics 8* : 299–307.

Kuch, D.O. 1974. Differentiation of press duration with upper and lower limits on reinforced values. *Journal of the Experimental Analysis of Behavior 22*: 275–283.

Laties, V.G. 1972. The modification of drug effects on behavior by external discriminative stimuli. *Journal of Pharmacology and Experimental Therapeutics 183* : 1–13.

LeFevre, F.F. 1973. Instrumental response chains and timing behavior. Doctoral dissertation, New York University.

Lowe, C.F.; P. Harzem; and P.T. Spencer. 1979. Temporal control of behavior and the power law. *Journal of the Experimental Analysis of Behavior 31*: 333–343.

Malott, R.W., and W.W. Cumming. 1964. Schedules of interresponse time reinforcement. *Psychological Record 14*: 211–252.

McCullough, T.A.; P.A. LeBuffe; and J.D. Gerding, Jr. 1979. Local rate variation in the fixed-ratio run. Paper presented at the Eastern Psychological Association meetings, Philadelphia.

Mechner, F. 1958a. Probability relations within response sequences under
ratio reinforcement. *Journal of the Experimental Analysis of Behavior 1*:
109–121.

_____ . 1958b. Sequential dependencies of the lengths of consecutive response
runs. *Journal of the Experimental Analysis of Behavior 1*: 229–233.

Mechner, F., and L. Guevrekian. 1962. Effects of deprivation upon counting
and timing in rats. *Journal of the Experimental Analysis of Behavior 5*:
463–466.

Mechner, F., and M. Latranyi. 1963. Behavioral effects of caffeine, methamphetamine and methylphenidate in the rat. *Journal of the Experimental
Analysis of Behavior 6*: 331–342.

Morse, W.H. 1966. Intermittent reinforcement. In W.K. Honig, ed., *Operant
Behavior: Areas of Research and Application*, pp. 52–108. New York: Appleton–Century–Crofts.

Nevin, J.A. 1973. The maintenance of behavior. In J.A. Nevin, ed., *The Study
of Behavior*, pp. 201–236. Glenview, Illinois: Scott, Foresman and Company.

Notterman, J.M., and D.E. Mintz. 1965. *Dynamics of a Response*. New York:
Wiley.

Platt, J.R., and D.M. Johnson. 1971. Localization of position within a homogeneous behavior chain: Effects of error contingencies. *Learning and Motivation 2*: 386–414.

Platt, J.R., and P.C. Senkowski. 1970. Response-correlated stimulus function-
ing in homogeneous behavior chains. In J.H. Reynierse, ed., *Current Issues
in Animal Learning*, pp. 195–231. Lincoln: University of Nebraska Press.

Platt, J.R.; D.O. Kuch; and S.C. Bitgood. 1973. Rats' lever-press durations as
psychophysical judgments of time. *Journal of the Experimental Analysis of
Behavior 19*: 239–250.

Pliskoff, S.S., and I. Goldiamond. 1966. Some discriminative properties of
fixed-ratio performance in the pigeon. *Journal of the Experimental Analysis
of Behavior 9*: 1–9.

Richardson, W.K., and T.E. Loughead. 1974. Behavior under large values of
the differential-reinforcement-of-low-rate schedule. *Journal of the Experimental Analysis of Behavior 22*: 121–129.

Rilling, M. 1967. Number of responses as a stimulus in fixed interval and fixed
ratio schedules. *Journal of Comparative and Physiological Psychology 63*:
60–65.

Rilling, M., and C. McDiarmid. 1965. Signal detection in fixed-ratio schedules.
Science 148: 526–527.

Staddon, J.E.R. 1965. Some properties of spaced responding in pigeons. *Journal of the Experimental Analysis of Behavior 8* : 19–27.

Stubbs, D.A. 1968. The discrimination of stimulus duration by pigeons. *Journal of the Experimental Analysis of Behavior 11* : 222–238.

_____. 1976. Response bias and the discrimination of stimulus duration. *Journal of the Experimental Analysis of Behavior 25* : 243–250.

_____. 1980. Discrimination of stimulus duration and a free-operant procedure. *Journal of the Experimental Analysis of Behavior 33* : 167–185.

9 A SIGNAL DETECTION ANALYSIS OF COUNTING BEHAVIOR

Paul K. Brandon

Schedules of reinforcement may have both strengthening and shaping properties. In general, time-based schedules of reinforcement have been used to study strengthening effects, while number-based schedules have been used to study shaping effects. Differential reinforcement in number-based schedules may be studied in a two-lever procedure, where a response on lever B may be reinforced depending on the length of a run of consecutive responses on lever A.

This chapter explores the determinants of sensitivity to run length differences and of the bias to under- or overestimate the run length required for reinforcement. The procedures used to identify these determinants necessarily differ from procedures reported elsewhere in this book. In most of these other studies, the subject was required to discriminate between different reinforcement contingencies—that is, some properties of relationships between responses and reinforcers function as antecedent events that control future behavior. For example, Rilling and McDiarmid (1965), Hobson (1975, 1978), and others have trained pigeons to use the number of responses emitted during a stimulus period as a discriminative stimulus for making the

The experiments reported in this chapter were supported in part by grants from the Faculty Research Council of Mankato State University. Scott Doss assisted in the preparation of this chapter. The data for subject SD1 on the chronic RC 3+ schedule presented here will be included in his forthcoming masters' thesis. He has provided a helpful sounding board for many of the arguments presented here.

225

correct response in a following choice period. The precise number of responses emitted in that period, which is analogous to a specific value on a stimulus dimension, was determined by the experimenter, not by the subject. Thus, the procedure is analogous to conventional stimulus control procedures, since it involves the manipulation of external stimulus events by the experimenter.

This chapter analyzes a situation in which the subject determines the number of responses emitted without the aid of exteroceptive controlling stimuli. While the removal of stimulus presentation from the control of the experimenter weakens the analogy with conventional stimulus control procedures, some of the technology developed for the analysis of stimulus control may still be applied. The definition of stimulus control is based on conditional probabilities — the probability of the subject emitting the defined response in the presence of the discriminative stimulus and the probability of the subject emitting the same response in the absence of the discriminative stimulus. The evidence for the existence of stimulus control consists of the observed difference between these probabilities. Signal detection analysis, which was derived from decisions theory, may be applied in any setting in which a subject must decide which of two reponses is correct for a given stimulus presentation (see Swets, 1973). The actual application of a signal detection analysis to subject-controlled counting behavior will be developed later in the chapter.

THE RESPONSE-TERMINATED COUNTING SCHEDULE

Mechner (1958) introduced a procedure that he termed "Fixed Consecutive Number." In that schedule, after a subject emits a number of consecutive responses — that is, a run length (RL) — that is greater than or equal to a specified lower limit on one lever, N, and then emits a second (teminating) response, reinforcement is delivered (see also Hobson and Newman, Chapter 8). Here, this procedure will be denoted $RC+$ (response-terminated counting with no upper limit, $RL \geq N$), to distinguish it from the similar procedure that requires a subject to emit an exact number of responses on the first lever for reinforcement on the second. Thus, an upper as well as a lower boundary for reinforced run lengths is set. This second procedure will be denoted RC ($RL = N$). In both versions of the schedule, all terminating responses reset the count to zero. This resetting function further differentiates the RC schedules from simple ratio schedules. In either case, the subject is required to control the length of the response run by emitting the terminating response only after the appropriate number of counting responses, thus producing a run of the specified length. The tendency to overrun or underrun the lower run length limit should be affected by whether or not there is an upper limit.

To see the effect of setting an upper boundary on reinforced run length, Berryman, Wagman, and Keller (1960) compared the behavior of rats on RC 8 and RC 8+ schedules. Setting an upper boundary lowered the mode and reduced the variability of the run length distributions. To interpret this result, the authors pointed out the analogy between the stimulus aspects of the response sequence and the psychophysical method of ascending limits. They regarded run length as a stimulus that increased in intensity. At some point, the subject responded by switching from the counting response to the terminating response. This application of traditional psychophysical tools to a response-oriented experimental procedure presages the later application of signal detection methods to response number discrimination tasks.

EXTENSION OF SIGNAL DETECTION ANALYSIS FROM FIXED RATIO SCHEDULES TO RC SCHEDULES

Rilling and McDiarmid (1965) first applied the theory of signal detection to a fixed ratio (FR) discrimination situation derived from the matching-to-sample procedure that is used widely in the study of stimulus control. Subjects completed either of two fixed ratio schedules on the center key. The completion of the experimentally determined ratio is signaled by the center-key light being turned off and the two side keys being illuminated; thus, the schedule is designated SC, for stimulus-terminated counting schedule. A response on the left-hand key was reinforced if the subject had just emitted the lower of the two ratios; a response on the right-hand key was reinforced if the higher of the two ratios had just been emitted. The results were well suited to signal detection analysis, since there were two possible responses (left key and right key) with independently specifiable outcomes and two stimulus situations—high fixed ratio and low fixed ratio. Hobson (1975, 1978) went on to study the effect of fixed ratio size and choice outcomes on both discriminability and bias using a signal detection analysis.

The basic difference between the stimulus-terminated counting paradigm and the response-terminated counting paradigm is that the former has the subject report how many responses it has emitted in a run terminated by the experimenter while the latter has the subject report whether it has reached the specified number by either switching to the terminating response or continuing to count. Reinforcement in the *RC* procedure is contingent upon a response sequence of the specified length being produced. There are no terminating stimuli presented by the experimenter before the switch terminates the run. In the *SC* procedure, on the other hand, the size of the ratio is controlled by the experimenter terminating a run by starting the choice period. Reinforcement depends only upon the subject's accurate report of whether the ratio was high or low. Therefore, the *SC* procedure is less applicable to questions that concern the subject's ability to produce a response sequence of a specified length and to the general question of the internal dynamics of response sequences.

SIGNAL DETECTION AS APPLIED
TO RC SCHEDULES

After each response in the *RC* sequence, the subject may either continue its run or emit the terminating response. Different consequences follow the terminating response, depending upon the particular sequence of responses that the subject has produced. In applying signal detection analysis to *RC* behavior, two particular choice points are examined—first, the subject has just emitted one less than the specified number of consecutive responses; second, the subject has just completed the specified number of responses. In each of these two situations, two possible responses are considered—first, the subject may emit another counting response (continue to count); second, the subject may emit the terminating response (end the counting run). This yields the 2 × 2 decision matrix central to the theory of signal detection (Table 9-1).

A run of the specified length is considered the stimulus, while a run of one less than the specified length is considered to be the

Table 9−1. Schematic Representation of the Signal Detection Paradigm Applied to Response Counting.

	$RL = RC$	$RL = RC - 1$
Terminate	Hit	False alarm
Continue to count	Miss	Correct rejection

Notes: RL = run length;   RC = required count.

absence of the stimulus or "noise" (these are verbal analogies and are not intended to imply underlying processes). A terminating response that is made when run length is one less than the specified number is considered a "false alarm," while a terminating response that is made when the run is the specified length is considered a "hit." Continuing to count when run length is one less than the specified number is termed a "correct rejection," and continuing to count when the run has reached the specified length is a "miss." The probabilities of the first two outcomes (hits and false alarms) are used to plot points on the receiver-operating-characteristic (ROC) graph and to calculate indexes of detectability and response bias. False alarm probability is calculated by dividing the number of runs of one less than the specified number by the number of runs greater than or equal to one less than the specified number (i.e., the number of times the count has reached or exceeded the specified consecutive number minus one, which defines total opportunities to emit the terminating response in the presence of a count of one less than the specified number). Hit probability is calculated by dividing the number of runs of the specified length by the number of runs greater than or equal to the specified length.

The extent to which the probability of a hit exceeds the probability of a false alarm is the basis for measuring the subject's sensitivity to the difference between the two run lengths. The overall size of both probabilities is the basis for measuring response bias. If most of the run length distribution is above the specified number, the probabilities of both hits and false alarms (terminating responses under both conditions) will be low, indicating an overall bias away from the terminating response (overcounting). Similarly, if most of the run length distribution is below the specified number, the response bias will be toward terminating the sequence (undercounting). A distribution producing no response bias will be skewed somewhat toward undercounting, with a mode less than the specified number.

A symmetrical run length distribution with its mode at the specified number will show a moderate positive response bias (toward overcounting). An increase in the variability of the run length distribution will generally result in a decrease in detectability.

Since the form of the "signal" and "noise"distributions is not known, the nonparametric indexes of sensitivity and bias (Grier, 1971) A' and B'' are used rather than the more usual d' and β. The formulas for their computation are:

$$A' = \frac{1}{2} + \frac{(y - x)(1 + y - x)}{4y(1 - x)} \ ,$$

and

$$B'' = \frac{y(1 - y) - x(1 - x)}{y(1 - y) + x(1 - x)}$$

where x is the probability of a false alarm (the lesser probability) and y is the probability of a hit (the greater probability). A' varies between 0.50 and 1, and indicates the subject's sensitivity to the difference between signal and noise or, in this case, the subject's ability to discriminate between adjacent correct and incorrect run lengths. B'' varies between +1 and –1 and indicates the subject's bias toward responding or not responding under both signal and noise conditions. In the RC counting paradigm, a positive B'' indicates a bias toward continuing the counting run and away from the terminating response. Taken together, A' and B'' can be used to characterize a subject's performance on an RC schedule under a given set of experimental conditions. Plotting ROC points on normal probability axes is an effective way of comparing results from a number of different sources or conditions.

The signal detectability analysis is valuable because it separates the effects of reinforcement contingencies (response bias) from the inherent limitations on the subject's performance on a given task (sensitivity). Data obtained from different experimental variations on the same basic task can be summarized and compared within a common format. However, there are some uncertainties in the application of signal detection analysis to response-terminated counting. First, the use of normal probability coordinates assumes underlying Gaussian signal and noise distributions. The data to be presented below suggest that any violations of this assumption are not extreme.

Second, since the subject's run length determines whether signal or noise is presented on each trial, the a priori probabilities of these events cannot be determined. Thus, one cannot readily generate iso-bias curves, which describe performance when signal strength varies while biasing variables such as signal probability and outcomes are held constant. Nevertheless, the tools of signal detection analysis can be effective on at least a descriptive level and can be useful in clarifying results that otherwise are difficult to fit into a unifying framework.

The following hypothetical examples illustrate the way different run length distributions affect the location of ROC points and the indexes of corresponding sensitivity and bias, A' and B''. Figure 9-1 shows the location of points representing the hypothetical run

Figure 9-1. An ROC graph containing points representing the results of several hypothetical run length distributions produced by an RC 3 schedule. The horizontal axis represents the conditional probability of emission of a run of length 2 given that the run has reached at least that length. The vertical axis represents the conditional probability of emission of a run of length 3, the specified length. These probabilities are equivalent to the conditional probabilities of the emission of the terminating response after runs of lengths 2 and 3.

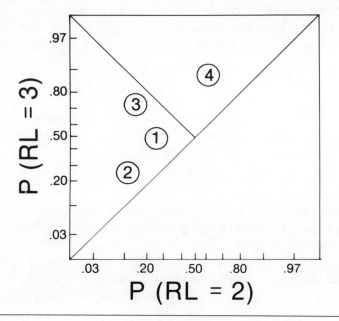

Figure 9–2. The hypothetical relative frequency distributions of run lengths for the ROC points in Figure 9-1.

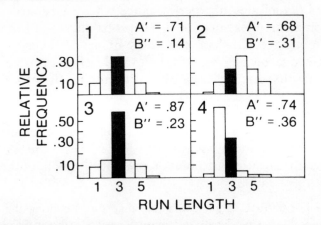

length distributions that appear in Figure 9-2, which represents several possible outcomes from a basic *RC* 3 procedure. It does not matter whether the schedule is *RC* 3 or *RC* 3+; the procedure for calculating the indexes and the ROC points is the same, since both are based on the relative conditional probabilities of occurrence of the adjacent nonreinforced (*RL* = 2) and reinforced (*RL* = 3) run lengths. In this case, the probability of a hit is the number of runs of length 3 divided by the number of runs of lengths 3 through 6:

$$P(RL = 3 | RL \geq 3) = \frac{\#(RL = 3)}{\#(RL \geq 3)} \ .$$

The probability of a false alarm is equal to the number of runs of length 2 divided by the number of runs of lengths 2 through 6:

$$P(RL = 2 | RL \geq 2) = \frac{\#(RL = 2)}{\#(RL \geq 2)} \ .$$

Thus, each distribution is represented by a point whose horizontal component is determined by the probability of a false alarm and whose vertical component is determined by the probability of a hit, derived as above. While these points have been defined in terms of the counting responses, the conditional probabilities of the emission of the terminating response after runs of lengths 2 and 3 are in fact being calculated. These conditional probabilities may be calculated from the run length distributions and conditional probability distributions presented by Mechner (1958) and by Berryman, Wagman, and Keller (1960), although they did not themselves apply a signal detection analysis.

Point 1 on the ROC graph in Figure 9–1 represents a moderate level of performance on an RC–3 counting task, indicated by the displacement from the major diagonal and an A' value of 0.71. There is a small amount of positive response bias, indicated by the displacement below the minor diagonal, and a B'' value of 0.14. Note that this ROC point is produced by a run length distribution (1 in Figure 9–2) that is symmetrical with its mode at the specified number of 3. As mentioned above, this form of run length distribution is evidence of some response bias. Point 2 in Figure 9–1 represents a shift of the distribution toward overcounting. A' has not changed substantially, but B'' has increased considerably, indicating the increased bias away from emitting the terminating response. Point 2 on the ROC graph thus shows about the same displacement above the major diagonal, but a substantially increased displacement below the minor diagonal. This type of shift is typical of that produced by a change in reinforcement contingency (payoff matrix in signal detection terms) while leaving the basic task unchanged. Point 3 illustrates a different process—a change in task difficulty rather than reinforcement contingency. Response bias for point 3 ($B'' = 0.23$) has not increased greatly compared to point 1 ($B'' = 0.14$), but the detectability of the difference between run lengths of 2 and 3 has increased from $A' = 0.71$ to $A' = 0.87$.

Point 4 illustrates the change in the form of the run length distribution necessary to produce a strong negative response bias. The mode has shifted to a run length of 2. Compared to the first distribution, it shows a strong skewing toward the low end. Note that A' (and the displacement above the major diagonal) have increased slightly even though the mode is now at a nonreinforced run length. Points 2, 1, and 4 illustrate the pattern produced on an ROC graph when reinforcement contingencies are manipulated while task difficulty is held constant. Note that the sensitivity index shows relatively little change ($A' = 0.68, 0.71, 0.74$) while bias shows a major shift from positive to negative ($B'' = 0.31, 0.14, -0.36$).

These examples illustrate the great strength of the signal detectability analysis—its ability to separate the biasing effects of reinforcement contingencies from the capability of the subject to discriminate between adjacent run lengths. Run length distributions that are very different in form (i.e., distributions 1 and 4) are seen to demonstrate the same degree of detectability once the difference in response bias has been controlled.

REANALYSIS OF PREVIOUSLY PUBLISHED DATA

The ability of a signal detectability analysis to compare data from different experimental situations is illustrated in Figure 9–3, which

Figure 9–3. ROC points derived from data originally published by Berryman, Wagman and Keller (1960), Brandon (1969), Mechner (1958) and Mechner and Latranyi (1963).

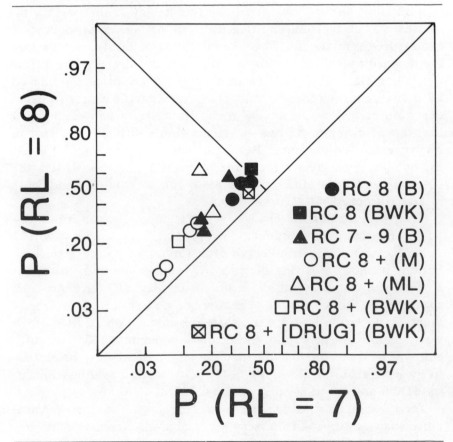

replots data from RC schedules originally presented in run length distribution form by Mechner (1958), Mechner and Latranyi (1963), Berryman, Wagman, and Keller (1960), and Brandon (1969).

Most of the points from the RC 8 schedules have about the same displacement above the major diagonal, indicating equivalent task difficulty. However, the change in reinforcement contingencies produced by setting an upper as well as a lower boundary on reinforced sequence lengths reduces the bias toward overcounting. This can be seen clearly by comparing the two points from Berryman, Wagman, and Keller (filled and unfilled squares). Performance on RC 8 shows little effect of response bias ($A' = 0.65$, $B'' = 0$). Performance on RC 8+, while equivalent in sensitivity, is clearly biased toward overcounting ($A' = 0.68$, $B'' = 0.35$), as would be predicted by the change in reinforcement contingencies. The administration of chlorpromazine to subjects on RC 8 had little effect on response bias, but clearly affected the subjects' detection of the difference in run lengths ($A' = 0.60$, $B'' = 0.02$). The fact that the effect of the drug was restricted to sensitivity is not evident from the original run length distributions, since the distribution after the administration of chlorpromazine is skewed further to the left than is the run length distribution for the same schedule without the drug.

SOME CURRENT DATA

Figure 9-4 shows the results for four rats run on an RC 3 schedule (daily sessions run to one hundred reinforced trials) and for one rat run on an RC 3+ schedule (chronic situation; 24 hr/day averaging about 600 reinforcers, with free water and unrestricted opportunity to count for food). These results corroborate the conclusions drawn from the results of previous research. The discriminability of adjacent run lengths can be assessed independently from the differing biasing effects produced by the various experimental procedures. In particular, the RC and RC+ procedures produce a specified run length equally well, but they differ in the extent to which they introduce response bias. The run length distributions appear similar, both with a mode at the RC of 3. The most significant difference is that the distribution produced by $RC-3+$ is skewed to the right, since this schedule reinforces overcounting but not undercounting. The ROC point is displaced well below the minor diagonal, clearly indi-

Figure 9-4. ROC points, indexes of sensitivity and bias (A' and B'') and run length distributions for four rats on an RC 3 schedule (Ss 11-14) and for one rat run continuously on an RC 3+ schedule (SD1). the points represent the means of 4 or 5 day's sessions for each subject. A' and B'' for RC 3 are the means for the four subjects.

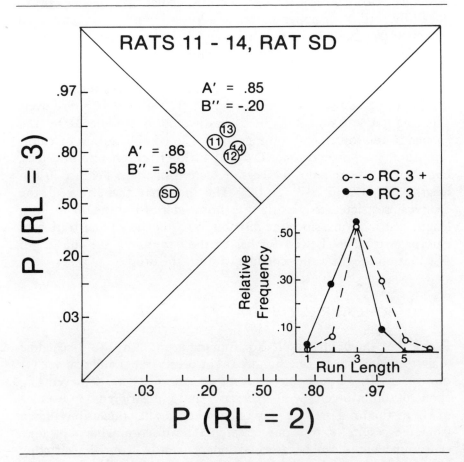

cating this bias. The run length distribution for *RC* 3, on the other hand, is skewed to the left, taking a form that produces relatively unbiased performance. The distribution and indexes for *RC* 3 are based on means of the four individual subjects whose data are plotted on the ROC graph (the ROC graph is the most efficient way to present the data from a number of sources in a format that permits direct comparison). The sensitivity index A' is virtually the same for

RC and *RC+*, which is consistent with the equal displacement of the points on the ROC graph from the major diagonal. This suggests that an ROC curve (a straight line on the normal probability coordinates used here) could be generated by systematically reducing the upper boundary of reinforced run length (for instance, varying the schedule from *RC* 3 to *RC* 3+, with *RC* 3-4, *RC* 3-5, and *RC* 3-6 as intermediate steps). The data from Brandon (1969) indicate that specifying an upper as well as a lower limit can produce an intermediate amount of response bias.

One possible objection to this procedure for generating ROCs from run length distributions is that it disregards some of the information available in the raw frequency distributions of run lengths. However, the selective analysis presented here concentrates on those particular aspects of *RC* behavior that are most directly under reinforcement control. Run lengths of zero are generally produced by consecutive emissions of the terminating response, often after nonreinforced counts. They are certainly of interest, but they are not necessarily comparable to counting runs of lengths greater than zero. Overcounting beyond the required minimum run length, on the other hand, produces no change in the probability of reinforcement; thus there is little differential reinforcement control over the different run lengths above the specified number. This is a justification for lumping together the total number of runs of lengths greater than the *RC*, as is done in the analysis described here.

The result of the selective nature of the analysis presented here is to focus attention on the decision points in the schedule where different responses (choices) lead to different consequences. Changes in behavior at these choice points as a function of changes in experimental conditions can be seen more clearly through signal detection analysis than it can through the comparison of run length distributions.

THE GENERATION OF ROC CURVES
FROM LATENCY DISTRIBUTIONS

The preceding material has illustrated one way to apply signal detection methods to the analysis of behavior on *RC* schedules. Some of the power of the ROC analysis is that it has shown the subject's competence in producing a response sequence that meets quantitatively specified requirements. However, complete ROC curves have not been generated for single subjects under a given set of experimental conditions. In addition, since the technique described above yields only one measure of the probability of a hit, only a single pair of run lengths can be compared. Finally, the inability to specify the form of the stimulus and noise distributions a priori raises questions about the use of normal probability coordinates for plotting ROC curves. Despite these limitations, the data presented here indicate that signal detection methods can be productively applied to RC performance using the relative probabilities of occurrence of adjacent run lengths. An alternative approach that may strengthen this analysis will now be considered.

Moody (1970) suggests that one alternative method useful in generating psychophysical data is to use the variation in response latency as an index of changes in stimulus intensity. The difference between a given run length and the run length required for reinforcement may be construed as analogous to an intensity difference. Thus, the latency for RC behavior, as measured by the time elapsing between the last counting response in the run and the emission of the terminating response, might be used as a measure of choice certainty analogous to a rating scale and be recorded separately for several different run lengths occurring during the same session.

The general approach follows Blough's (1967) study of stimulus generalization in the pigeon. Blough transformed the traditional response rate data into rating data of the sort used in signal detection analysis to get multiple decision criteria (and thus a complete ROC curve) from a single stimulus generalization experiment. Effectively, this was equivalent to the systematic manipulation of response bias for a range of stimulus values, achieved through the analysis of one set of data.

Blough's procedure was to view the pigeon as detecting a difference between a given wavelength of light and the positive discriminative stimulus. By using different response rates as decision criteria, he was able to generate families of ROC curves showing stimulus generalization independently of response bias factors. Yager and Duncan (1971) extended this analysis to response latencies generated by goldfish in a stimulus generalization task, producing families of ROC curves similar to those derived from human subjects using rating methods.

Green, Terman, and Terman (1979) generated both latency-based and yes-no ROC curves for rats on an auditory intensity discrimination task. They found that the latency-based measure of detectability showed less variability across conditions than did the yes-no-based measure, strengthening the case for latency as an index of stimulus value. Their data also showed that the latency differentiation was primarily a function of the difference in intensity between the stimuli to be discriminated, rather than an unconditioned energizing effect of stimulus intensity.

DERIVING RUN LENGTH ROC CURVES FROM TERMINATING RESPONSE LATENCY

Figure 9-5 presents data showing that run length behaves as an intensive dimension. Latencies between the last counting response and the terminating response were recorded in 200 millisecond bins for the four rats whose run length distributions were presented in Figure 9-4. During a given session, two latency distributions were recorded—latencies for the required run length of 3 and latencies after the incorrect runs of length 1, 2, or 4. Points on the ROC curves were derived by comparing the relative frequency of latencies less than a given criterion after a run length of 1, 2, or 4 and after a run length of exactly 3. These relative frequencies were then plotted on normal probability coordinates. Thus, only one ROC curve was generated during a given session; the families of curves presented in Figure 9-5 represent the means of three different sets of sessions.

In Figure 9-5, the rats' latencies, while producing run lengths of the required number, $RL = N = 3$, are compared to latencies produced for runs of lengths 1, 2, and 4, $RL \neq 3$. For runs of lengths 1 and 2, the ROC curves are similar to those derived by Blough (1967), Yager and Duncan (1971), and Green, Terman, and Terman (1979), and are ordered in their displacement from the main diagonal according to stimulus disparity. The fact that ROC curves derived from run length latencies resemble conventional ROC curves and are appropriately ordered indicates that the number of responses in a sequence functions as an intensive stimulus dimension. The ROC curves appear to deviate from a straight line of unit slope mainly at the high end. The raw latency distributions shown for subjects $S11$ and $S12$ in Figure 9-5 show that this is due at least in part to a cluster of long-latency-terminating responses after runs of lengths 1 and 2.

Latencies for the terminating response after runs of length 4 were consistently shorter than latencies after runs of the required length

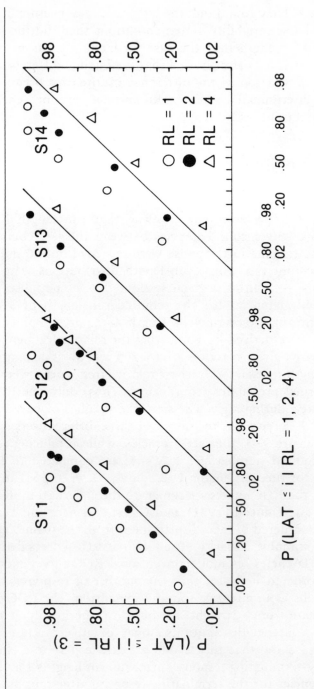

Figure 9–5.   ROC curves derived from latency distributions for subjects S11–S14. The horizontal axis has been collapsed. Raw latency distributions are also presented for subjects S11 and S12. For each subject, each ROC curve is derived from a different set of 4 or 5 sessions.

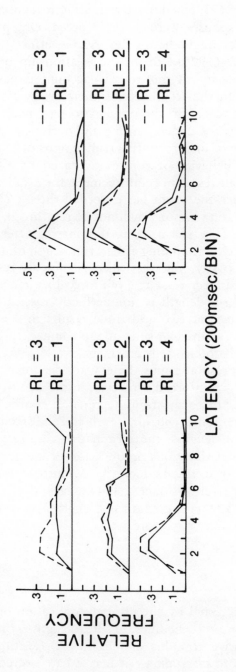

of 3. Since this was an *RC* 3 schedule, terminating responses after runs of four counting responses were not reinforced. One possible explanation for this effect might be an "energizing effect" of the sort described by Moody (1970)—an inverse relationship between latency and stimulus intensity. A more likely account is based on response consequences. On the *RC* schedule, there are two alternatives. One is to continue to count; the other is to terminate. There are different consequences for undercounting and overcounting (terminating late). In the case of undercounting (run lengths of 1 or 2 on the *RC* 3 schedule), the behavior of continuing to count after the run has reached 1 or 2 can result in reinforcement for a subsequent terminating response. Once the count has exceeded three ($RL > 3$) however, the next terminating response will not be reinforced. Which error is most serious—a false alarm, (i.e., terminating after a run length of 2) or a miss (i.e., terminating after a run length of 4)? The latter error may be less costly, since it will most quickly reset the schedule and enable the subject to start a reinforceable sequence. In other words, given that run length is not perfectly discriminated, uncertainty between counts of two and three results in a conflict between continuing and terminating, since if the count is three, the terminating response will produce reinforcement, while if the count is two, another counting response must be emitted in order for the terminating response to be reinforced. However, in the case of uncertainty between counts of three and four, there is no conflict, since an additional counting response will not result in reinforcement in either case. For both run lengths, the terminating response is the best one available. Conflict situations produce longer latencies than nonconflict situations. Hence, this asymmetry of reinforcement contingencies would account for the fact that latencies after runs of length 4 are shorter than latencies after runs of length 3, even though the former are not followed by a reinforcer.

SUMMARY

Three conclusions are suggested by the present application of signal detection analysis to counting schedules: (1) Run length is functionally similar to an intensive stimulus dimension. (2) Contingencies used to get an organism to discriminate it may create overcounting or undercounting without affecting sensitivity. A lower limit alone produces a bias toward overcounting, while an upper limit reduces that bias. An exact limit does not produce unbiased counting, but a slight amount of overcounting. (3) When the required count is specified exactly, latency data indicate that undercounting produced more conflict than overcounting, as reflected by the different latencies associated with each.

A signal detectability analysis based on the latency of the terminating response shows promise as a measure of the relative detectability of run length as it varies in distance and direction from the specified run length. Generating a complete ROC curve in a single session under a fixed set of conditions is an effective way to control for possible response biases.

The signal detectability analysis based on the conditional probabilities of different run lengths seems best suited to the study of sensitivity at a single point within the counting sequence—the transition from a nonreinforceable run length to the specified minimum run length. In addition, the analysis measures the extent and direction of response bias and is thus a valuable tool for studying experimental manipulations involving reinforcement contingencies. Finally, generating ROC points and indexes of sensitivity and bias provides a means of comparing results from different sources involving the same basic counting task. It is clear that these analytical techniques, originally developed for stimulus control situations, can effectively be applied to the study of how a subject assesses its own performance on a task that does not involve control by external stimuli.

REFERENCES

Berryman, R.; W. Wagman; and F. Keller. 1960. Chlorpromazine and the discrimination of response-produced cues. In L. Uhr and J.C. Miller, eds., *Drugs and Behavior*. New York: Wiley.

Blough, D.S. 1967. Stimulus generalization as signal detection in pigeons. *Science 158*:-940–941.

Brandon, P.K. 1969. The effects of error-contingent time out on counting behavior in rats. Doctoral dissertation, University of Michigan.

Green, M.; M. Terman; and J.S. Terman. 1979. Comparison of yes-no and latency measures of auditory intensity discrimination. *Journal of the Experimental Analysis of Behavior 32*: 363–372.

Grier, J. 1971. Nonparametric indexes for sensitivity and bias: computing formulas. *Psychological Bulletin 75*: 424–429.

Hobson, S.L. 1975. Discriminability of fixed-ratio schedules for pigeons: Effects of absolute ratio size. *Journal of the Experimental Analysis of Behavior 23*: 25–35.

_____. 1978. Discriminability of fixed-ratio schedules for pigeons: Effects of payoff values. *Journal of the Experimental Analysis of Behavior 30*: 69–81.

Mechner, F. 1958. Probability relations within response sequences under ratio reinforcement. *Journal of the Experimental Analysis of Behavior 1*: 109–121.

Mechner, F., and N. Latranyi. 1963. Behavioral effects of caffeine, methamphetamine and methyphenidate in the rat. *Journal of the Experimental Analysis of Behavior 6*: 331–342.

Moody, D.B. 1970. Reaction time as an index of sensory function. In W.C. Stebbins, ed., *Animal Psychophysics*, pp. 277–302. New York: Appleton–Century–Crofts.

Rilling, M., and C.G. McDiarmid. 1965. Signal detection in fixed-ratio schedules. *Science 148*: 526–527.

Swets, J.A. 1973. The relative operating characteristic in psychology. *Science 182*: 990–1000.

Yager, D., and T. Duncan. 1971. Signal-detection analysis of luminance generalization in goldfish using latency as a graded response measure. *Perception and Psychophysics 9*: 353–355.

VI | DISCRIMINATIVE FACTORS AFFECTING PERFORMANCE ON COMPLEX SCHEDULES

10 DISCRIMINATION OF CORRELATION

William M. Baum

Recent theoretical work on reinforcement distinguishes two views—the molecular and the molar (Baum, 1973; Rachlin, 1976). Molecular views in general describe behavior and the environment as composed of discrete events that can be assigned to given times. Applied to reinforcement, the molecular view focuses on measurements that can be made at the moment a reinforcer is presented, such as the qualities of the preceding response and the delay between the response and reinforcer. From such variables, the molecular view proposes to account not only for molecular phenomena, but also for variation in measures like average response rate that cannot be assessed at any moment and hence are referred to as molar.

The molar view begins with the idea that order in behavior often only appears at the molar level; when analysis proceeds to a molecular level, experimental findings become contradictory and uninterpretable (e.g., Nevin, 1979). In the molar view, for example, a relation between response rate and rate of reinforcement need not necessarily be reduced to underlying molecular phenomena. Since molecular analysis could sometimes shed further light, the relationship between molar and molecular analysis could be complementary, rather than contradictory.

The research described was supported by grants from NIH and NSF to Harvard University. Preparation of this manuscript was supported in part by NSF Grant No. BNS–7906852 to the University of New Hampshire.

247

Being newer, the molar view has had to prove itself. Although the weight of knowledge accumulating at a molar level has supported it (e.g., de Villiers, 1977), a crucial test would make the basic premise more convincing. Such a crucial test would lie in the results of an experiment that required an organism to discriminate between two situations that could only be distinguished at a molar level.

A number of experiments have aimed at this mark but have failed to hit it clearly. Rachlin and Baum (1972), Killeen (Chapter 4), and Lattal (Chapter 5) found evidence that pigeons distinguish reinforcers that are produced by pecks from those that are response-independent. A molecular view could argue that the discrimination depended on the inevitable delay between pecks and response-independent reinforcers, as distinct from the immediacy of response-produced reinforcers. Commons (1979, and Chapter 3) and Mandell (Chapter 2) came closer by finding evidence that pigeons can distinguish one rate of reinforcement from another. Proponents of the molecular view, however, might argue that the discrimination depended on the intervals between reinforcers and therefore resembled any other discrimination of temporal duration (Stubbs, 1980; Stubbs and Dreyfus, Chapter 6).

MOLAR ANALYSIS OF MIXED-SCHEDULE PERFORMANCE

Perhaps the most direct test of molar-based discrimination would make use of mixed schedules—schedules in which contingencies are changed without accompanying stimuli (Ferster and Skinner, 1957). Mixed schedules have been studied relatively little. Some have followed up on Ferster and Skinner's (1957: 620–625) finding that pigeons can distinguish between a fixed ratio and a fixed interval in a mixed schedule. Their bird ran off the fixed ratio after reinforcement and, if another reinforcer failed to occur, switched to fixed interval performance (cf., Chapters 8, Hobson and Newman; and 9, Brandon). Since the switch depended on the number of responses or the time spent responding, either of which could be construed as a molecular cue, this finding cannot provide the crucial test.

Mixed schedules in which reinforcement alternates with extinction fail to be crucial for similar reasons. Bullock and Smith (1953) trained rats in sessions that consisted of forty reinforced lever presses followed by an hour of extinction. The rats improved in discrimination across sessions: the number of responses during extinction decreased. One could argue that the discrimination depended on the absence of the reinforcer following each press or simply the absence of the reinforcer—molecular cues—rather than the switch in contingency. Boren and Sidman (1957) trained rats in a similar manner, but with free operant avoidance maintaining lever pressing in the first part of the session. In their experiment, absence of shock could indicate either successful avoidance or extinction (i.e., disconnecting the shock). That discrimination improved, just as in Bullock and Smith's experiment, may indicate that molar aspects of the components controlled performance. Doubt remains, however, because the switch in contingency always occurred at a fixed time in the session—a regularity that could have produced the discrimination just as well.

To be certain that molar variables control discrimination in a mixed schedule, one must remove all regularities that could serve as molecular cues. Lattal (1973) studied a procedure that might satisfy this requirement. He trained rats in mixed schedules in which variable-interval reinforcement alternated at random with response-independent reinforcement at the same rate. Each component lasted for a certain minimum time, usually 5 minutes. The procedure still contained potential molecular cues: each response-dependent reinforcer immediately followed a response, and, as often as not, components changed after the fixed minimum duration. Even so, Lattal found little evidence of discrimination, except when components lasted for 30 or 60 minutes—durations that might be regarded simply as retraining based on whether or not responses produced immediate reinforcement.

The failure of Lattal's procedure suggests a further requirement besides removal of regularity. The discrimination ought to vary with respect to changes in procedure in a manner readily understood by the molar account. If we describe Lattal's experiment as an attempt to train a discrimination between a positive response-reinforcer correlation (the variable-interval schedule) and a zero response-reinforcer correlation (response-independent reinforcers), then we would expect that the degree of such a discrimination would depend on variables that might make a correlation better or worse. In particular, discrimination between two correlations should worsen as the rate of reinforcement decreases, because any molar factors that distinguish the two components should become more variable and hence less distinct.

The study described here represents an attempt to achieve the procedure necessary for the crucial test of the molar account. No single molecular event could serve as a cue, because responses were never clearly tied to reinforcers, and components changed in a highly unpredictable manner. Discrimination occurred and, moreover, varied in the way that the molar account would predict.

EXPERIMENTAL METHOD

All general features of the procedure were standard. Four experienced homing pigeons, maintained in the usual way, served as subjects. The apparatus consisted of a standard operant chamber connected to a computer. Experimental sessions, which were conducted almost every day, ended as described below after an irregular number of reinforcers, each of which consisted of 2-second access to grain.

Each session presented a mixed schedule composed of two types of component—one requiring pecks at the response key for reinforcement and one requiring absence of pecks for reinforcement. The two schedules were designed to be as symmetrical as possible in their requirements. The first could be called a conjunctive fixed-ratio 1 variable-time schedule (cf. Zeiler, 1976). A variable-interval programmer advanced continuously, except during reinforcement. Whenever an interval timed out, a reinforcer was delivered if a peck had occurred sometime during that interval; if no peck had occurred, no reinforcer was presented, and a new interval was begun. For brevity, we can call this the peck component. The second component could be called a conjunctive DRO (differential reinforcement of other behavior) variable-time schedule. It operated exactly like the other, except that at the end of an interval, a reinforcer was delivered only if no peck had occurred during the interval; if a peck had occurred, no reinforcer was presented, and a new interval was begun. For brevity, we call this the DRO component.

Each session consisted of three components—a peck component first, followed by a DRO component, and then another peck component. Components terminated after presentation of a certain required number of reinforcers, this number varying irregularly from component to component, with a minimum of fourteen and a maximum of forty-six reinforcers (an arithmetic series averaging thirty).

The various conditions differed in the variable-time schedule that was joined with the DRO and peck requirements. The sequence appears in Table 10-1. The VT schedules contained fourteen intervals drawn from the progression specified by Fleshler and Hoffman (1962). Each condition continued until three measures appeared stable—the two response rates calculated over the last seven inter-reinforcer intervals of the DRO component and the final peck component and the ratio of those two response rates.

RESULTS AND DISCUSSION

The degree of discrimination was estimated from the response rates that prevailed during the last seven interreinforcement intervals of the DRO component and final peck component. The initial peck component was ignored because the beginning of the session served as a cue for pecking. Figure 10-1 shows a discrimination index— relative response rate—calculated by dividing the rate for the peck component by the sum of the two rates, as a function of the programmed rate of reinforcement. A relative rate of 0.5 would indicate no discrimination; the two rates would be equal. The values shown

Table 10-1. Order and Number of Sessions of Conditions.

	VT (seconds)	Number of Sessions
1	5	33
2	7.5	14
3	10	55
4	15	25
5	20	69
6	30	42
7	20	33
8	15	70
9	10	28

Figure 10–1. Discrimination as a function of programmed rate of reinforcement. Lines connect the points to show order of conditions.

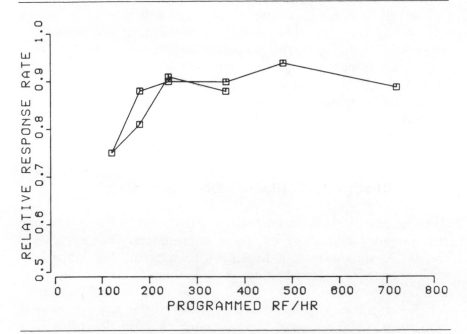

are averages across the four birds of the medians across the last seven sessions. They were representative of individual performances. Discrimination was good and increased across the first two conditions.

As the programmed rate of reinforcement was decreased below 240 reinforcements per hour (VT 15 seconds), discrimination tended to lessen. There was still some evidence of discrimination for 120 reinforcements per hour (VT 30 seconds), but the response rates were so low and variable as to make the result uncertain. When the VT was shortened again, increasing the programmed rate of reinforcement, discrimination improved again. The increased relative response rate at 180 reinforcements per hour (VT 20 seconds) fell below the earlier value. Such hysteresis suggests that the discrimination, once formed, tended to persist and, once disrupted, tended to remain disrupted.

Figure 10–2 shows cumulative records, one for each pigeon, from the last seven sessions of exposure to VT 10 seconds (the third condition). The records show varying degrees of discrimination and dif-

Figure 10–2. Cumulative records of sessions with *VT* 10 seconds. Pecks were totaled every 30 seconds of the session. Vertical lines indicate component changes.

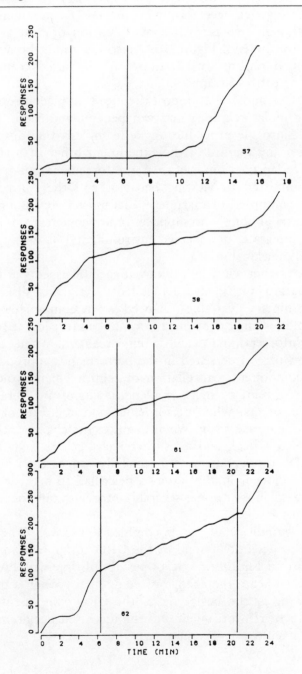

ferent patterns of performance. All show the positive acceleration in the third component that would be expected if some extended sample of the peck component were necessary for pecking to recommence. Negative acceleration in the DRO component was less evident, although two records show cessation or near cessation of responding by the end. Figure 10–2 also illustrates the way that the components' durations varied; those shown varied from just over 2 minutes to nearly 15 minutes.

Figures 10–1 and 10–2 support the idea that pigeons can discriminate among molar relations between pecking and food. The irregularities built into the procedure make it unlikely that discrimination depended on any feature of the experiment other than the positive and negative correlations between reinforcement and responding. Anyone committed to viewing behavior and the controlling environment as composed of discrete events must find this a remarkable conclusion. To anyone who supposes that living creatures are mechanisms that integrate and average environmental happenings, it must seem entirely reasonable.

Inquiring further, we might ask what specific aspects of the experimental situation might have controlled the pigeons' discrimination. What environmental variables changed when components changed? Two possibilities emerge at once—rate of reinforcement (or interval between reinforcers) and delay of reinforcement. When components changed, if a pigeon persisted in the performance appropriate to the preceding component, cancellation of reinforcement would cause a drop in rate of reinforcement or a lengthening of the average interval between reinforcers. When performance adjusted, rate of reinforcement would increase again. When components changed, the average delay between a peck and a reinforcer changed as well. The delays in the DRO component were necessarily longer than in the peck component. Indeed, in the latter, a peck had to precede each reinforcer, whereas in the former several reinforcers could occur in a row with no pecks at all.

The two variables could act in combination as well. When a pigeon had ceased to peck at the end of the DRO component, only the decrease in rate of reinforcement, or passage of time with no reinforcement, could indicate the change of component. When a pigeon continued pecking at the beginning of the DRO component, both the drop in rate of reinforcement and the increased peck-reinforcer delays could signal the new component.

Whichever variable controlled performance, the pigeons performed the equivalent of a statistical test of significance. When inappropriate performance persisted at the beginning of a new component, the interreinforcement intervals preceding the first reinforcers could be longer than the longest interval in the VT schedule. In practice, this rarely occurred, probably because the preponderance of short intervals enabled a short pause in pecking often to produce reinforcement (in the DRO component) or an isolated peck soon to produce reinforcement (in the peck component). It is as if the pigeon had to answer the question, Are these intervals too long to have been drawn from the population comprising the schedule? Since the lengthened intervals generally fell in the range of programmed intervals, the decision could not be considered a simple temporal discrimination; it had to depend on probability and, therefore, accumulated past experience.

Similar reasoning applies to the possible signaling function of peck-reinforcer delays at the beginning of a new component. Although the delays differed in central tendency (median) from DRO to peck component, sometimes by a factor of twenty to one, the frequency distributions always overlapped. Isolated pecks at the beginning of the peck component would produce reinforcers at delays that usually were shorter than the delays in the DRO component. Pauses at the beginning of the DRO component would produce reinforcers at delays that usually were longer than in the peck component.

One conclusion seems inevitable: No cue at one instant of time could have controlled the performance. Some process equivalent to averaging, sampling, and guessing had to occur. Further analysis and experimentation may reveal whether delay, rate of reinforcement, or some combination of the two controls discrimination of correlation. For now, we note only that such discrimination apparently can occur.

REFERENCES

Baum. W.M. 1973. The correlation-based law of effect. *Journal of the Experimental Analysis of Behavior 20*: 137–153.
Boren, J.J., and M. Sidman. 1957. A discrimination based upon repeated conditioning and extinction of avoidance behavior. *Journal of Comparative and Physiological Psychology 50*: 18–22.

Bullock, D.H., and W.C. Smith. 1953. An effect of repeated conditioning-extinction sessions upon operant strength. *Journal of Experimental Psychology 46*: 349–352.

Commons, M.L. 1979. Decision rules and signal detectability in a reinforcement-density discrimination. *Journal of the Experimental Analysis of Behavior 32*: 101–120.

De Villiers, P. 1977. Choice in concurrent schedules and a quantitative formulation of the law of effect. In W.K. Honig and J.E.R. Staddon, eds., *Handbook of Operant Behavior*, pp. 233–287. Englewood Cliffs, New Jersey: Prentice–Hall.

Ferster, C.B., and B.F. Skinner. 1957. *Schedules of Reinforcement.* New York: Appleton–Century–Crofts.

Fleshler, M., and H.S. Hoffman. 1962. A progression for generating variable-interval schedules. *Journal of the Experimental Analysis of Behavior 5*: 529–530.

Lattal, K.A. 1973. Response-reinforcer dependence and independence in multiple and mixed schedules. *Journal of the Experimental Analysis of Behavior 20*: 265–271.

Nevin, J.A. 1979. Overall matching versus momentary maximizing: Nevin (1969) revisited. *Journal of Experimental Psychology: Animal Behavior Processes 5*: 300–306.

Rachlin, H. 1976. *Behavior and Learning.* San Francisco: Freeman.

Rachlin, H., and W.M. Baum. 1972. Effects of alternative reinforcement: Does the source matter? *Journal of the Experimental Analysis of Behavior 18*: 231–241.

Stubbs, D.A. 1980. Temporal discrimination and a free-operant psychophysical procedure. *Journal of the Experimental Analysis of Behavior 33*: 167–185.

Zeiler, M.D. 1976. Conjunctive schedules of response-dependent and response-independent reinforcement. *Journal of the Experimental Analysis of Behavior 26*: 505–521.

11 REINFORCEMENT AS INPUT
Temporal Tracking on Cyclic Interval Schedules

Nancy K. Innis

INTRODUCTION

The temporal pattern of food presentation plays an important role in the organization of behavior on many reinforcement schedules. One of the most distinctive and reliable behavior patterns generated by a reinforcement schedule is the fixed interval (FI) scallop (Ferster and Skinner, 1957). Animals exposed to FI schedules soon come under the control of the temporal properties of the schedule, pausing for a relatively constant proportion of the interreinforcement interval before beginning to perform the required operant (Schneider, 1969). The operant or terminal response, usually key pecking for pigeons, is confined to the later portion of each fixed interval, while earlier in the interval, a variety of other activities may occur (Staddon, 1977; Staddon and Simmelhag, 1971). The postreinforcement

Experiments 2a, 3, 4a, 5 and 6 were carried out at Dalhousie University and funded by National Research Council Grant APT–102, W. K. Honig, principal investigator. Experiment 1 was supported by the Ontario Addiction Research Foundation and carried out in the laboratory of J. D. Keehn. Experiments 2b and 4b (carried out at the University of Western Ontario) and preparation of the manuscript were supported by Natural Sciences and Engineering Research Council Canada Grant A–9945, N. K. Innis, principal investigator. I thank W. K. Honig and J. D. Keehn for supporting the research; R. H. I. Dale and D. Reberg for commenting on the manuscript; and especially W. A. Mills for invaluable discussions and criticism and J. E. R. Staddon for advice and encouragement over the many years this research was in progress.

pause on FI schedules represents the time the bird is engaged in interim activities (cf. Innis and Honig, 1979). Depending on the criterion for defining the onset of the terminal response, the post-reinforcement pause is typically one-half to two-thirds of the duration of the fixed interval. Schneider (1969) reported pauses of about two-thirds of the interval on schedules ranging from 16 to 512 seconds.

The generality of temporal control by interval duration can be assessed by considering studies in which intervals of more than one duration are programmed during an experimental session. Staddon (1967, 1969) exposed pigeons to four repetitions (cycles) of a series of twelve 1-minute intervals followed by four 3-minute intervals (12 FI1, 4 FI3) for a large number of sessions. During 1-minute intervals, the postreinforcement pause was about 30 seconds—half the duration of the interval—and thus consistent with the findings reported for simple FI schedules. However, during the 3-minute intervals, pauses were also approximately 30 seconds, much shorter than would be expected if the duration of the longer interval were controlling the animals' behavior. On other two-valued cyclic interval schedules, in which a series of either 2 or 6-minute intervals (FI2 or FI6) alternated with a series of 1-minute intervals (FI1), pauses during FI1 were again about 30 seconds. Very slight increases above this 30-second basic pause were observed across successive 2-minute intervals, and pauses shorter than 30 seconds often occurred during 6-minute intervals (Innis and Staddon, 1970; Kello and Staddon, 1974). Occasionally during the longer intervals on these two-valued schedules, pauses would occur after about 1 minute had elapsed, suggesting that the birds' behavior was under the control of some sort of 1-minute "timer."

The lack of differential temporal control reported by Staddon and his associates was surprising given Harzem's (1969) finding that rats exposed to progressive interval schedules, during which successive interreinforcement intervals gradually increased in duration across the session, showed increased postreinforcement pauses as the session progressed. Was the finding reported by Staddon and his associates simply a species difference, or was it a result of the properties of the schedule?

In an attempt to answer this question, I combined the progressive interval and cyclic interval procedures described above, presenting pigeons with four daily cycles of a series of intervals that increased and then decreased according to an arithmetic progression (Innis, 1970). Each cycle comprised intervals of seven different durations, presented in an ascending followed by a descending sequence. The intervals ranged from 30 to 120 seconds, and with the exception of the longest and shortest intervals, each interval differed from the preceding and succeeding interval by a constant value, t, with $t = 15$ seconds. Thus, each cycle consisted of the following sequence of interval presentations—30, 45, 60, 75, 90, 105, 120, 120, 105, 90, 75, 60, 45, and 30 seconds.

The data revealed that the shortest pause in any given cycle was about 12 seconds in duration and that pause durations gradually increased and decreased across successive intervals in a pattern that closely resembled the pattern of increasing and decreasing interval requirements. Changes in postreinforcement pause, then, can be described as "tracking" changes in interval value. There was, however, a phase lag of about one interval between the pattern of pause durations observed and the pattern of intervals presented. For example, pauses during the second 120-second interval of a cycle were typically longer than pauses during the first 120-second interval. Finally, the data indicated that although pause durations associated with the 30-second intervals of a cycle were only slightly shorter than might be expected on the basis of Schneider's (1969) findings (e.g., about 12 seconds), pauses during the 120-second intervals were considerably shorter (e.g., about 27 seconds) than might be expected. Thus, while postreinforcement pauses showed differential control by interval duration on this schedule, some loss of control relative to simple, single value FI schedules was apparent. Performance on similar seven-valued cyclic interval schedules (with interval durations changing from $2t$ to $8t$ and with the values of t for different schedules ranging from 2 to 40 seconds) was subsequently examined, and similar tracking behavior was observed (Innis, 1970; Innis and Staddon, 1971). The performance of pigeons on one of these schedules is described in more detail in Experiment 1, below.

The fact that pigeons, like Harzem's rats, came under the control of the temporal properties of a progressively changing interval schedule while displaying little or no control by the longer interval on two-valued cyclic schedules was intriguing. The following series of studies was designed to identify the conditions under which temporal control develops and when it is constrained and to determine the factors underlying the differences in performance observed on various cyclic interval schedules. The variables examined include the number of intervals per cycle, repetition of specific intervals, the duration of the shortest interval, the ratio of short to long intervals, and the progression or pattern of changes in interval duration.

GENERAL METHODS

Although the experiments described below were carried out over a number of years in several laboratories, the same general procedures were followed in all cases. The procedural details for all six experiments are outlined in Table 11-1.

The seven birds in Experiments 2b and 4b were Silver Kings, and the other 39 birds were White Carneaux. All birds were housed individually, maintained at approximately 80 percent of their free-feeding weights, and had free access to water in their home cages. The birds in Experiments 2, 3, and 4 had previous experience on a variety of reinforcement schedules. The birds in Experiment 1 were auto-shaped to key peck, while those in Experiments 5 and 6 were shaped by hand.

In most of the studies, standard commercial operant conditioning chambers were used. The homemade box used in Experiments 2b and 4b was smaller (32 by 35 by 46 cm) than the usual enclosure, and that used in Experiment 6 was somewhat larger (50.8 by 38.1 by 35.6 cm). The latter box, designed for observation of the birds, had two walls and the roof made of Plexiglas and was located on a countertop in a lighted room. The other chambers were entirely enclosed. In all cases, pecks on the center response key, located directly above the opening to the feeder, provided brief access to mixed grain. The durations of the magazine cycle, which ranged from 3 to 5 seconds across studies, are reported in Table 11-1. The center keys were illuminated with either white, red, or green light (see Table 11-1) from in-line projectors mounted behind the keys. If a box had more than one key, the side keys were dark and inoperative. During food presentation the key light was turned off, and the houselight was either turned off or dimmed (Experiments 2a, 4a, and 5). In all studies, white noise was continuously present to help mask extraneous sounds.

Table 11-1 lists the schedules of reinforcement programmed for each bird and the number of sessions under each condition. The value of t, number of intervals of different durations, number of intervals per cycle, and number of cycles per session are also reported. Experiments were terminated when each bird's performance was stable over several consecutive sessions, as determined by visual inspection of cumulative records and printout data. In most cases, postreinforcement pause data from the last five sessions of a condition were analyzed in detail.

The degree of temporal control exerted by these cyclic schedules can be assessed in two ways. In the first, performance on simple FI schedules as reported by Schneider (1969) may be taken as a standard against which to evaluate performance during intervals of particular durations on these cyclic schedules. If pauses during intervals of the different durations were about half the interval duration, satisfactory temporal control would be established. Data from previous studies indicate that this is not the case; even pauses during the shortest interval of the cycle were often less than half its duration, and pauses in longer intervals were relatively shorter.

Another measure of the degree of temporal control is the amplitude of the pause cycle (the relative difference between the longest and shortest pause). Generally, the larger the amplitude of the cycle, the greater the degree of temporal control by the schedule. This measure is independent of the absolute duration of the shortest pause.

In all the figures presented here, postreinforcement pauses are plotted as a proportion of the duration of the shortest interval in the cycle. This relative measure allows for easy comparison of the data across different-valued schedules and permits a ready assessment of how closely the pause in the shortest interval of a cycle corresponds to the shortest pause predicted from simple FI schedule data.

STUDIES OF CYCLIC INTERVAL SCHEDULES

Experiment 1

Innis and Staddon (1971) trained five pigeons on the seven-valued cyclic interval schedule represented schematically in the top panel of Figure 11–1. As shown, the sequence of interval durations was determined by the arithmetic progression $2t$, $3t$, $4t$, $5t$, $6t$, $7t$, and $8t$, presented first in ascending and then in descending order. Since the

Table 11-1.   Procedural Details for Six Experiments.

Experiment	Subjects	Interval Durations (seconds)	t Value (seconds)	Different Durations
1	1220, 1987 5429, 7153	8→32, 32→8	4	7
2a	32, 33 91, 92	5(40)→5(120)→5(40)	20 20	5 5
2b	5001, 5290 5250, 5371	4(10)→4(40)→4(10) 4(40)→4(160)→4(40)	5 20	7 7
3-1	40, 70 07, 95 06, 37	10, 30, 30, 10 30, 90, 90, 30 60, 180, 180, 60	5 15 30	2 2 2
3-2	40, 70 07, 95 06, 37	5→35, 35→5 15→105, 105→15 30→210, 210→30	5 15 30	7 7 7
4a	402, 410 407, 408	20, 60 60, 180	10 30	2 2
4b	122, 123, 126	60, 180	30	2
5	13, 14, 23 24, 33, 34 11, 12, 21 22, 31, 32	40, 200, 360, 200, 40 40, 280, 360, 280, 40	40 40	3 3
6	54, 55, 56 57, 58, 59 51, 52, 53	10→30, 30→10 (FI) 10→30, 30→10 (FRI FT) 10→30, 30→10 (FT)	5 5 5	5 5 5

Table 11–1. continued

Intervals in Cycle	Cycles in Session	Sessions	Key Color	Duration of Reinforcement (seconds)
14	4	64	White	4
45	1	28	Red	5
45	1	40	Red	5
52	1	32	Green	4
52	1	32	Green	4
4	14	31	White	3
4	14	31	White	3
4	14	31	White	3
14	4	32	White	3
14	4	32	White	3
14	4	32	White	3
2	20	65	Red	5
2	20	65	Red	5
2	25	25	Green	4
5	4	52	Red	5
5	4	52	Red	5
10	4	92	White	3
10	4	92	White	3
10	4	92	White	3

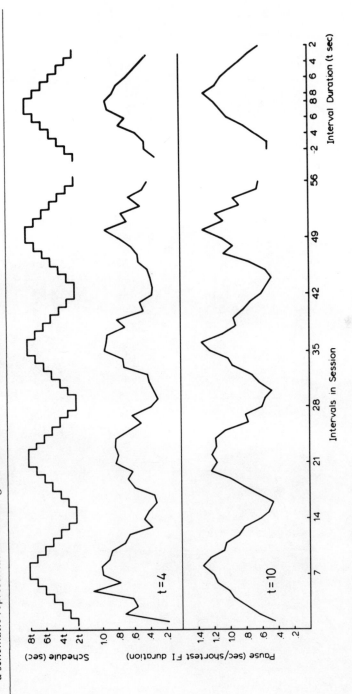

Figure 11-1. Mean postreinforcement pause during each interval of the experimental session for two seven-valued cyclic interval schedules in which interval durations changed according to an arithmetic progression. Data at the bottom are means of five birds over five sessions for a schedule based on $t = 10$ seconds. Data at the top are means of four birds over five sessions for a schedule based on $t = 4$ seconds. On the right are average pause cycles; means across the four cycles of the sessions are to the left. Pauses are plotted as a proportion of the duration of the shortest interval in a cycle. At the top of the figure is a schematic representation of changes in interval duration in each cycle.

value of t was set at 10 seconds, each of the four cycles presented in a session consisted of the following sequence of intervals—20, 30, 40, 50, 60, 70, 80, 80, 70, 60, 50, 40, 30, and 20 seconds. The birds were then given two test sessions during which the sequence of intervals was determined by a different progression. In one of the test sessions, the sequence was determined by a logarithmic progression, while in the other test session, the sequence was determined by a geometric progression. During both the logarithmic and the geometric test sessions, the number of reinforcements per cycle (fourteen) and the total cycle time (700 seconds) were the same as they had been during the baseline, arithmetic progression schedule. To satisfy these requirements, the interval values for the logarithmic test session were determined by the equation $\log_{10} x + \log_{10} 2x + \log_{10} 3x + \log_{10} 4x + \log_{10} 5x + \log_{10} 6x + \log_{10} 7x = 5.822$, which yields $x = 2.01$. Multiplying each term in the equation by 60 seconds and arranging the intervals in both an ascending and descending series generated the following sequence for each of the four interval cycles in the test session—18, 38, 47, 55, 60, 65, 69, 69, 65, 60, 55, 47, 38 and 18 seconds. For the geometric test session, the interval values were determined by the equation $t + \theta t + \theta^2 t + \theta^3 t + \theta^4 t + \theta^5 t + \theta^6 t = 350$, which yields $t = 2.76$ and $\theta = 2.0$. Arranging the intervals in an ascending and descending series generated the following sequence for each of the four cycles in the geometric test session — 3, 6, 11, 22, 44, 88, 176, 176, 88, 44, 22, 11, 6 and 3 seconds. A schematic representation of the sequence of interval durations presented during the logarithmic test session and the geometric test session is shown in Figure 11–2.

The procedure employed in the present experiment was similar to that described for the Innis and Staddon (1971) study. Four birds were trained on a seven-valued, cyclic interval schedule where the ascending and descending sequence of interval values was determined by the arithmetic progression $2t$, $3t$, $4t$, $5t$, $6t$, $7t$, and $8t$. Whereas t was 10 seconds in the Innis and Staddon (1971) study, t was set at 4 seconds in the present experiment. Further procedural details are given in Table 11–1. Following training on the arithmetic progression schedule, the birds received a test session in which the interval values were determined by a logarithmic progression and a test session in which these values were determined by a geometric series. The test sessions were separated by six sessions of reexposure to the baseline, arithmetic progression schedule. Interval durations for the

Figure 11–2. Mean postreinforcement pause during each interval of test sessions for groups of birds exposed to schedules in which interval durations changed according to a logarithmic (upper panel) or a geometric (lower panel) progression. The post-t = 10 curves are means of five birds with baseline training on the t = 10 schedule and the post-t = 4 curves are means of four birds following baseline training on the t = 4 schedule. Pauses are plotted as a proportion of the duration of the shortest interval in the cycle. A schematic representation of the changes in interval duration is shown for each test schedule. The ordinate for the logarithmic schedule is in logarithmic units.

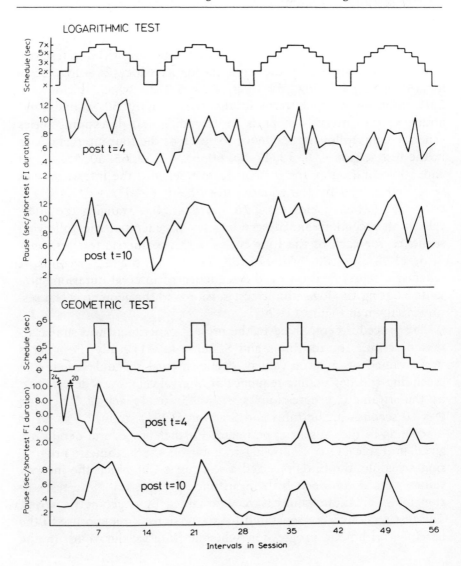

tests were generated by the formulae described above. To keep the cycle time the same as that provided by the baseline schedule (i.e., 280 seconds), each term in the equation describing the logarithmic progression was multiplied by 24 seconds. Thus, arranging the intervals in an ascending and descending order provided the following sequence of intervals for each of the four cycles of the logarithmic test session—7.2, 14.4, 18.8, 22, 24, 26, 27.6, 27.6, 26, 24, 22, 18.8, 14.4, and 7.2 seconds. Similarly, for the geometric progression the value of t was 1.1, and the interval values in an ascending and descending series were 1.1, 2.2, 4.4, 8.8, 17.6, 35.2, 70.4, 70.4, 35.2, 17.6, 8.8, 4.4, 2.2 and 1.1 seconds.

The data of interest from the present experiment and from the Innis and Staddon (1971) experiment are presented in Figures 11–1 and 11–2. Figure 11–1 shows the performance of birds trained on the $t = 4$ (top) and the $t = 10$ (bottom) baseline, arithmetic progression schedules. Postreinforcement pauses averaged across all birds in each group during five sessions of asymptotic performance are plotted as a function of each interval in the session on the left of Figure 11–1. Mean pause times, averaged across cycles, are shown for each interval on the right of Figure 11–1.

In general, postreinforcement pauses tracked changes in interval duration with a phase lag of about one interval. The shortest pause was about half the duration of the shortest interval for birds trained on the $t = 10$ schedule and about one-third of the shortest interval for birds trained on the $t = 4$ schedule.

Mean postreinforcement pauses for each group of birds during the logarithmic and geometric test sessions are presented in Figure 11–2. When exposed to a single test session during which intervals changed according to a logarithmic progression, the pigeons in both the $t = 4$ and $t = 10$ groups continued to track changes in interval duration with changes in postreinforcement pause. The performance of birds trained on the $t = 4$ schedule was somewhat more variable, but on the average, the amplitude of the pause cycles shown for both groups of birds was quite similar. Since the interval durations determined by the logarithmic progression did not differ greatly from those experienced on the baseline, arithmetic-progression schedule, it is perhaps not surprising that pausing displayed control by the temporal properties of the logarithmic progression schedule. The intervals determined by the geometric progression, on the other hand, differed considerably from those experienced during baseline training. Nevertheless, as shown in the bottom half of Figure 11-2, postreinforcement pauses during the geometric test session tracked changes in interval duration. The tendency of pauses to track changes in interval duration was apparent even though the amplitude of the pause cycles decreased across the geometric test session.

The duration of the shortest pause on the geometric progression schedule constituted a larger proportion of the shortest interval experienced than did the duration of the shortest pause on the logarithmic progression schedule. In absolute terms, however, the duration of the shortest postreinforcement pause on the geometric progression schedule was substantially reduced relative to the shortest pause obtained during baseline, arithmetic progression training. In this regard, it may be important to note that the geometric progression schedule programmed a relatively large proportion of very short intervals compared to the proportion of short intervals provided during the arithmetic progression schedule.

When the baseline arithmetic progression schedule was restored following the geometric test session, tracking comparable to that observed during initial baseline training was immediately recovered. However, pauses at each interval were initially shorter than those observed prior to the test session and only gradually rose to pretest levels. The latter finding suggests that during baseline training, the birds learned more than simply to respond on the basis of absolute interval duration. Rather, some more general rule involving the production of slight adjustments in pause length across successive intervals of a cycle seems to be involved.

The finding that, for both the $t = 4$ and the $t = 10$ groups, tracking tended to deteriorate across successive cycles of the geometric test session suggests a variable of possible importance to the occurrence of tracking. That is, unlike the cyclic interval schedules generated by an arithmetic or logarithmic progression, both of which produced stable tracking, the cyclic interval schedule generated by the geometric progression programmed rather large and abrupt changes in the durations of successive intervals. Perhaps small, gradual changes in the duration of successive intervals are necessary for tracking. If so, two-valued schedules such as those employed by Staddon (1967), which program large, abrupt changes in interval duration, would not be expected to result in tracking.

Experiment 2

Another difference between the two-valued and the seven-valued schedules described in the introduction concerns the repetition of specific intervals. In the two-valued schedules, each cycle consisted of twelve consecutive presentations of the 1-minute interval followed by several consecutive presentations of the longer interval. In contrast, with the exception of the shortest and longest intervals, each interval comprising the seven-valued schedules occurred only once during the ascending and once during the descending series of a cycle (see schematic schedule representation at the top of Figure 11-1).

In the present study, I examined performance on multivalued schedules in which intervals were presented in an ascending and a descending arithmetic progression, but each specific interval was presented a number of times in succession. Each session consisted of a single presentation of the interval cycle. This procedure is diagrammed schematically in Figure 11-3.

In Experiment 2a, four birds were trained on a schedule in which interval durations progressed from 40 seconds to 120 seconds and then back to 40 seconds. Since the difference between successive interval values (i.e., t) equalled 20 seconds, the progression can be expressed as proceeding from $2t$ to $6t$ and back to $2t$. Each of the five interval values in the ascending and descending series occurred five times in succession (see Table 11-1).

The mean postreinforcement pause for the four birds over the last five sessions of training is presented for each interval in the session in Figure 11-3. Postreinforcement pauses clearly tracked changes in interval duration. An average pause cycle that combines the data from all five intervals of a given duration in the ascending and descending series is shown on the right of Figure 11-3. The performance represented here was very similar to that observed on the seven-valued schedules described in the introduction and in Experiment 1.

In Experiment 2b, performance on a schedule in which interval durations progressed from $2t$ to $8t$ and back to $2t$ was examined. Each of the seven intervals presented in the ascending and the descending series was repeated four times in succession. For two of the birds, t equalled 5 seconds, while for the remaining two, t equalled 20 seconds (see Table 11-1).

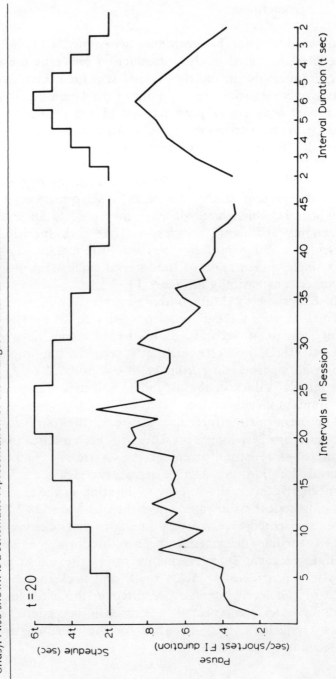

Figure 11-3. Mean postreinforcement pauses across the forty-five intervals of the session (left) for Experiment 2a, and an average pause cycle (right) for all five intervals of each duration in the series. Data are means across four birds over the last five sessions of the study and are presented as a proportion of the value of the shortest interval duration in the cycle (40 seconds). Also shown is a schematic representation of the changes in interval duration.

Average pause cycles for the $t = 5$ and the $t = 20$ birds are shown on the left in Figure 11–4. Each point represents the mean pause over the four intervals of each duration for the last five sessions of training. As in Experiment 2a, postreinforcement pauses tracked changes in interval duration. In fact, comparing the data of Experiment 2 with those of Experiment 1 (Figure 11–1) suggests that tracking was not greatly influenced by the repetition of specific intervals.

A comparison of the average pause cycles for birds on the $t = 5$ and $t = 20$ second schedules, shown in Figure 11–4, indicates that in terms of the amplitude measure, tracking was less efficient on the schedule with the larger interreinforcement intervals. This reduction in temporal control by schedules based on large values of t was also observed on the typical seven-valued cyclic interval schedule when t values were greater than 10 seconds (Innis, 1970; Innis and Staddon, 1971).

Experiment 3

As noted previously, Staddon (1967) found that birds trained on a two-valved, 12 FI 1-minute, 4 FI 3-minute schedule failed to track changes in interval duration with changes in postreinforcement pause. Innis and Staddon (1970), on the other hand, found that birds trained on a two-valued, 12 FI 1-minute, 6 FI 2-minute schedule displayed some evidence of tracking. Postreinforcement pauses during the 2-minute intervals were, on the average, slightly longer than pauses during the 1-minute intervals. According to the argument presented in Experiments 1 and 2, one difference between the schedule employed by Staddon (1967) and that used by Innis and Staddon (1970) is the magnitude of the shift in interval duration. That is, temporal tracking may occur on cyclic interval schedules only when the magnitude of the change in interval duration is relatively small. Clearly the FI 1-minute, FI 3-minute schedule examined by Staddon (1967) programmed a larger change in interval duration than did the FI 1-minute FI 2-minute schedule examined by Innis and Staddon (1970). A second difference between the 12 FI 1-minute 4 FI 3-minute and the 12 FI 1-minute 6 FI 2-minute schedules that may contribute to the different behavioral outcomes is the ratio of the number of short to long intervals within each

Figure 11–4. Mean postreinforcement pause cycles for groups of birds exposed to various cyclic interval schedules. Schematic representations of the schedules are presented at the top of each panel. Data are means of the last five sessions of each experiment. The curves on the left are from two groups of two birds in Experiment 2b that received a single cycle of interval durations changing according to an arithmetic progression for schedules based on $t = 5$ and $t = 20$ seconds. The pauses are averages of four intervals of each duration in the cycle. The average pause cycles in the center are data for two groups of two birds in Condition 2 of Experiment 3. Data are means over the four cycles of the last five sessions of exposure to an arithmetic progression schedule for which the value of t was either 5 or 15 seconds. On the right are average pause cycles for two groups of six birds exposed to three-valued cyclic interval schedules in Experiment 5. In all cases, pauses are plotted as a proportion of the duration of the shortest interval in a cycle.

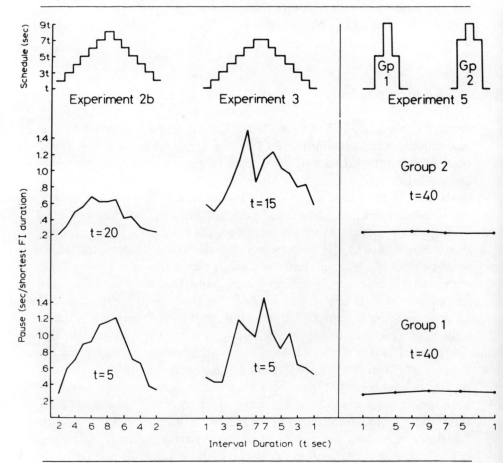

cycle. In Staddon's (1967) study this ratio was 3:1, while in the Innis and Staddon (1970) study the ratio was 2:1. The present experiment was conducted to examine the possibility that tracking on a two-valued, cyclic interval schedule is facilitated when the ratio of the number of short to long intervals in a cycle is low, even though the magnitude of the change in interval duration may be relatively large.

In Condition 1 of Experiment 3, pigeons were trained on a two-valued, cyclic interval schedule in which the short and the long intervals were both presented twice in every cycle, first in ascending and then in descending order. The interval values employed were designated $2t$ and $6t$. Thus, as diagrammed schedmatically at the top of Figure 11-5, each of the fourteen cycles presented in a session comprised the following sequence of intervals—$2t$, $6t$, $6t$, and $2t$. Three groups of two birds were trained, and for each group, t was set at 5, 15, or 30 seconds (see Table 11-1). Note that the group for which t was set at 30 seconds was exposed to intervals of the same duration as those employed by Staddon (1967)—namely, FI 1-minute and FI 3-minute. In Condition 2, all birds were trained on a seven-valued, cyclic interval schedule in which the intervals progressed from t to $7t$ and then back to t seconds. This schedule is graphically represented in the lower panel of Figure 11-5. Since for each group, the value of t during Condition 2 was identical to that experienced in Condition 1 (i.e., 5, 15, or 30 seconds), the mean rate of reinforcement programmed for each bird was constant between conditions.

Mean postreinforcement pauses for the two birds that experienced schedules based on $t = 30$ seconds are shown in Figure 11-5. In the left panel, mean postreinforcement pauses over the last five sessions of each condition are plotted for each interval in the session. The curves in the right panel represent mean pauses at each interval value in the ascending and in the descending series averaged across cycles. Data obtained in Condition 1 are presented in the top panels, while data from Condition 2 are presented in the bottom panels.

Although there was some tendency for pauses to track changes in interval duration during the first two cycles in Condition 1, pauses during the remaining cycles were not systematically related to interval duration. Indeed, the curve representing mean pauses at each interval value experienced is quite flat. In contrast, during exposure to the seven-valued schedule in Condition 2, pauses tracked changes

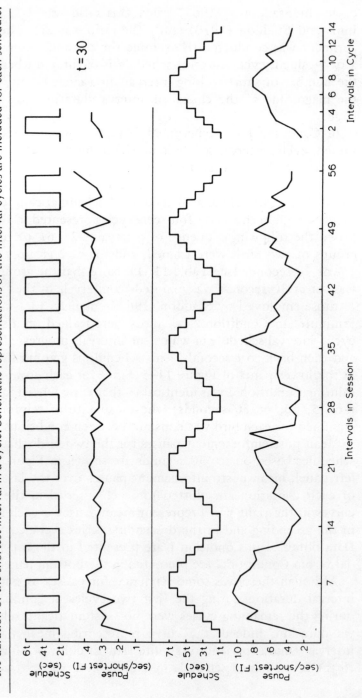

Figure 11–5. Mean postreinforcement pauses over the last five sessions of Condition 1 (upper panel) and Condition 2 (lower panel) of Experiment 3 for two birds exposed to the $t = 30$ second schedules. In Condition 1 there were fourteen cycles of the series, $2t$, $6t$, $6t$, $2t$. In Condition 2 there were four cycles of a seven-valued schedule with intervals ranging from t to $7t$, $7t$ to t. Data on the right are means across cycles of the session shown on the left. Pauses are plotted as a proportion of the duration of the shortest interval in a cycle. Schematic representations of the interval cycles are included for each schedule.

in interval duration throughout each of the four cycles presented every session.

The results obtained for birds in the $t = 5$ and $t = 15$ seconds groups were essentially identical to those described for the $t = 30$ seconds birds. Mean postreinforcement pauses at each interval in the ascending and descending series over the last five sessions of Condition 1 training were averaged across cycles and are presented for individual birds in the left panels of Figure 11-6. Data from the $t = 30$ seconds birds are shown at the bottom of the panel for purposes of comparison. Mean postreinforcement pauses at each interval value in the ascending and descending series over the last five sessions of Condition 2 training were averaged across both cycles and birds and are shown for the $t = 5$ and $t = 15$ birds in the center panels of Figure 11-4. As can been seen, pauses did not track changes in interval duration on the two-valued schedule experienced in Condition 1, but did track on the seven-valued, cyclic interval schedule experienced in Condition 2.

The major conclusion to be drawn from the results of Experiment 3, then, is that programming a low ratio of short to long intervals will not induce tracking on a two-valued, cyclic interval schedule. Presumably, then, the difference between the Innis and Staddon (1970) and Staddon (1967) experiments that was responsible for the occurrence or nonoccurrence of tracking was the difference in the magnitude of the change in interval duration employed. The results of Condition 2, like those from Experiment 1, lend some support to this conclusion in that tracking was observed on a seven-valued, cyclic interval schedule involving small changes in the duration of successive intervals.

It may, however, be argued that the two-valued schedule used in Experiment 3 constituted a double alteration problem and, as such, reduced the likelihood of differential control by interval duration. Although the results from Experiment 2 suggested that increasing the number of consecutive occurrences of a specific interval duration had little or no impact on tracking, it may be that simply alternating the short and long intervals of a two-valued schedule would induce temporal tracking. This possibility was investigated in Experiment 4.

Figure 11−6. The histograms on the left represent mean postreinforcement pauses for individual subjects in Condition 1 of Experiment 3 in which birds were exposed to a two-valued cyclic schedule, providing a double alternation of intervals. Each column is the mean across fourteen cycles of each of the last five sessions for each schedule. Schedules with t = 5, 15, and 30 seconds were studied. The histograms on the right represent mean postreinforcement pauses for individual subjects in Experiment 4. For birds in the bottom panel (126, 123, 122), data are means over twenty-five cycles for each of the last five daily sessions on a two-valued cyclic schedule in which short ($2t$) and long ($6t$) interval durations simply alternated. For the other birds there were twenty cycles per session. Schedules based on t = 10 and t = 30 seconds were studied. The pauses from the $2t$ intervals are represented by the open bars and from the $6t$ intervals by the solid bars. All pauses are plotted as a proportion of the duration of the shortest interval in the cycle ($2t$). Schematic representations of the pattern of changes in interval duration are shown at the top of the figure.

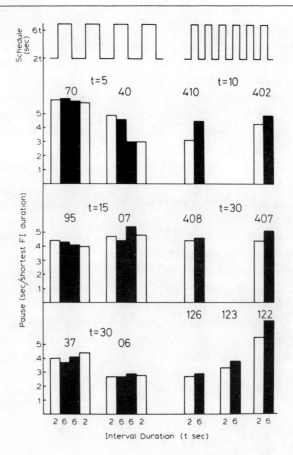

Experiment 4

In Experiment 4a and b, pigeons were exposed to two-valued schedules in which intervals designated $2t$ and $6t$ simply alternated. For two of the seven birds studied, the value of t was set at 10 seconds, while for the remaining five birds, it was set at 30 seconds. As in Experiment 3, it should be noted that the intervals generated by setting $t = 30$ seconds were identical to those employed in Staddon's (1967) experiment—namely, FI 1 minute and FI 3 minute. The minor differences in procedure between Experiment 4a and 4b are noted in Table 11-1.

Mean postreinforcement pauses for each interval averaged across all cycles of the last five sessions of training are presented for individual birds in the panels on the right of Figure 11-6. Although pause durations in the $6t$-second interval were consistently longer than those in the $2t$-second interval, the differences were extremely small—about $0.02t$ to $0.1t$ seconds. Thus, while it remains possible that simply alternating the intervals of a two-valued schedule may facilitate tracking relative to the double alternation procedure of Experiment 3, the present results do not provide strong evidence for this hypothesis. Moreover, the small pause differences obtained in the present study suggest, consistent with the results of Experiment 3, that the ratio of the number of short to long intervals in a cycle is, at best, of minor significance to the occurrence of tracking.

Experiment 5

The results of the preceding studies indicate that tracking of changes in interval duration by changes in pause time develops on five-valued (Experiment 2) and seven-valued (Experiments 1 and 3), cyclic interval schedules but does not appear (Experiment 3) or develops poorly (Experiment 4) on two-valued, cyclic interval schedules. An experiment conducted in my laboratory by Robert Fitzner (1974) suggests that three-valued, cyclic interval schedules may, like two-valued schedules, fail to support temporal tracking.

Two groups of six birds were trained on the schedules indicated in Table 11-1. For Group 1, the four cycles presented each session contained the following sequence of intervals—40, 200, 360, 200, and

40 seconds. For Group 2, the interval sequence was 40, 280, 360, 280, and 40 seconds. A representative cycle of each schedule is shown at the top of Figure 11-4.

Mean pause times for each interval averaged across all cycles of the last five sessions of training are presented for Groups 1 and 2 in the panels on the right of Figure 11-4. As can be seen, neither group displayed temporal tracking. In both groups, pause times appear to be unrelated to the interval durations presented, averaging about one-third of the shortest interval duration in Group 1 and about one-quarter of that duration in Group 2.

While the results of Experiment 5 suggest that temporal tracking may not occur on three-valued, cyclic interval schedules, a possible source of confounding should be noted. It was argued in Experiment 1 that tracking may occur only when the magnitude of the change in successive interval durations is relatively small. Since relatively large changes in the duration of successive intervals were programmed in the present experiment, the absence of tracking may be attributable to this variable rather than to the small number of intervals employed.

Experiment 6

An attempt was made in the preceding experiments to examine the effect on tracking of variables such as the number of interval values in a cycle, the number of consecutive presentations of the same interval value, and the ratio of short to long intervals in a cycle. The present experiment was conducted, first, to determine if pause durations on cyclic interval schedules are related to consistent patterns of behavior that emerge within each interval and, second, to determine if the response contingency specified by fixed interval schedules is a prerequisite of temporal tracking.

Nine birds were exposed to a five-valued, cyclic interval schedule in which the interval sequence was determined by the arithmetic progression $2t$, $3t$, $4t$, $5t$, and $6t$, presented in ascending followed by descending order. Since t was set at 5 seconds, all birds received the interval series 10, 15, 20, 25, 30, 30, 25, 20, 15, and 10 seconds in each of the four cycles comprising a daily session. For three of the birds (an FI group), reinforcement was contingent upon the first response to occur at the end of the interval in effect. For three birds in a second group (a fixed time or FT group), reinforcement occurred at the end of each interval, independently of responding. For the remaining three birds (the conj FR1 FT group) a conjunctive fixed ratio 1, fixed time contingency was in effect in each interval presented (Powers, 1968; Shull, 1970; cf. also Baum, Chapter 10; Commons, Paul, and Tallon, 1967). That is, reinforcement occurred at the end of each interval specified by the cyclic schedule, provided that at least one response had occurred within that interval. Further procedural details are given in Table 11-1.

In addition to recording pause times and responses, each bird's behavior was monitored and recorded on videotape. Data from the last five sessions of training were subjected to detailed analysis.

Mean postreinforcement pauses, averaged over the last three cycles of the last five training sessions, are presented for each bird in Table 11-2. For the FI and conj FR1 FT groups, pauses represent the time that elapsed between reinforcement and the first peck in the succeeding interval. For the FT group, pause times were determined through observation of the videotapes. With the exception of Bird 53, all birds displayed two distinct patterns of activity in each interval — interim activities that occurred in the period immediately following reinforcement and terminal responses that began sometime after reinforcement and increased in frequency up to the occurrence of the next scheduled reinforcement (cf, Staddon and Simmelhag, 1971). For the FT birds, then, pauses were defined as the time elapsing between reinforcement and the onset of the terminal response.

The data in Table 11-2 show that for birds in Groups 1 and 2, and to a lesser degree Birds 51 and 52 of Group 3, pauses tracked changes in interval duration. Moreover, inspection of the videotapes revealed that as tracking occurred, it was the time allocated to the ongoing interim activity (usually pacing along or orienting toward the magazine wall) that increased as a function of interval duration. In no case did the increases in postreinforcement pause result from the addition of new responses to the behavior sequence.

As noted previously, the behavior of Bird 53 was atypical. This bird spent the whole of each interval pacing along the side wall of the experimental chamber. The pause times at each interval for Bird 53 represent the time required to withdraw from the feeder and begin pacing.

Two major conclusions may be drawn from the results of the present study. First, temporal tracking for the conj FR1 FT birds dif-

Table 11–2. Average Postreinforcement Pauses (seconds/shortest interval duration) for Individual Subjects During the Ten Intervals of a Cycle (mean of three cycles, five sessions) of Experiment 6. On the right the relative amplitude of the pause cycle is given.

Birds	Interval Duration (seconds/shortest interval duration)										Amplitudes (sec/10)
	10	15	20	25	30	30	25	20	15	10	
Group 1 (FI)											
54	.69	.52	.55	.60	.63	.93	.76	.65	.74	.66	.41
55	.51	.44	.46	.56	.64	.60	.69	.63	.49	.53	.25
56	.71	.58	.75	.84	.89	.86	.78	.94	.64	.69	.31
$\overline{X}$	.64	.51	.59	.67	.72	.79	.74	.74	.64	.63	.32
Group 2 (FRIFT)											
57	.85	.73	.97	1.01	1.09	.91	.91	.96	.91	.99	.36
58	.59	.45	.57	.73	.61	.91	.91	.88	.83	.61	.47
59	.60	.74	.76	.64	.86	.96	.96	.92	.94	.90	.37
$\overline{X}$	.68	.64	.77	.79	.85	.93	.93	.92	.89	.83	.40
Group 3 (FT)											
51	.24	.25	.38	.33	.32	.46	.31	.34	.33	.32	.22
52	.48	.43	.45	.58	.61	.56	.52	.54	.54	.51	.18
53	.21	.14	.15	.16	.14	.17	.16	.17	.19	.16	.07
$\overline{X}$	.31	.27	.33	.36	.36	.40	.33	.35	.35	.33	.16

fered little from that observed for birds in the FI group, suggesting that the response contingency at the end of an interval, as specified by fixed interval schedules, is not a necessary condition for temporal tracking. This finding suggests that pausing on cyclic interval schedules is not controlled by features of the reinforced response that are systematically related to interval duration (i.e., number of pecks emitted in the preceding interval). Second, the finding that increments in interval duration increased the amount of time allocated to interim behavior rather than the number of different interim responses suggests that pausing on cyclic interval schedules is not a product of a response-chaining mechanism (i.e., Laties, Weiss, Clark, and Reynolds, 1965). In short, these results suggest that pausing may be determined by the interreinforcement interval per se and may be mediated by some kind of endogenous clock.

GENERAL DISCUSSION

When pigeons are exposed to simple FI schedules of reinforcement, a stereotyped pause and respond pattern of behavior develops (Ferster and Skinner, 1957). The duration of the postreinforcement pause on such schedules is determined by the duration of the interreinforcement interval and is typically about one-half to two-thirds this value (cf., Schneider, 1969). When intervals of more than one duration are presented during the same experimental session, different degrees of temporal control have been observed. On the typical mixed reinforcement schedule, the duration of the postreinforcement pause in all intervals is determined by the value of the shortest interval (Catania and Reynolds, 1968). A similar finding was recorded by Staddon (1967) with a two-valued FI 1-minute FI 3-minute cyclic interval schedule. He found that while performance during the 1-minute intervals was very similar to that observed on simple FI 1-minute schedules, performance during the 3-minute intervals differed from the typical FI 3-minute pattern. The short pauses observed by Staddon during the FI 3-minute intervals of the two-valued schedule were essentially the same duration (30 seconds) as the 1-minute interval pauses. However, on other cyclic interval schedules, which programmed a number of regularly changing interval durations, some degree of temporal control by durations other than that of the shortest interval has been observed (Innis, 1970;

Innis and Staddon, 1971). The surprising finding that pigeons could "track" changes in interval duration when intervals of several different durations were presented, but not when intervals of only two durations were presented, led to the series of studies reported in this chapter.

There were several differences between the schedules studied by Staddon (1967) and by Innis and Staddon (1971), which suggested the following as possible determiners of the performance differences observed—the number of different-valued intervals per cycle, the size of the increment (or decrement) between successive intervals, the absolute durations of the intervals, the ratio of short to long intervals, the repetition of consecutive intervals in a cycle, and the pattern or progression in which interval duration changed. Perhaps the most obvious variable is the number of different interval durations in a cycle. In the studies reported here, performance was examined on schedules programming two, three, five, and seven different interval durations. A comparison of the pause cycles obtained in the six experiments described here indicates a greater degree of temporal control on the five and seven-valued schedules. In fact, little if any control by the longer intervals was observed on the two and three-valued schedules (Experiment 3, 4, and 5). For schedules programming three or more interval durations, Keller (1973) obtained similar results. He trained pigeons on sinusoidal cyclic interval schedules in which the number of different intervals per cycle ranged from two to nineteen and interval durations fell between 20 and 180 seconds. With the exception of the two-valued schedule, the pigeons showed more efficient temporal tracking as the number of interval values in a cycle increased. Contrary to the results of Experiments 3 and 4, Keller found much longer pauses during the 180-second than during the 20-second intervals of his two-valued schedule.

While the number of intervals in a cycle seems to be an important variable for producing temporal tracking, it should be noted that in both the experiments reported in this chapter and in Keller's (1973) study, the size of the increment (or decrement) between successive intervals covaried with the number of interval durations in a cycle. When fewer different-valued intervals were programmed, the change in duration between adjacent intervals was greater or more abrupt. In the two-valued schedules in Experiments 3 and 4, the longer interval was always three times the duration of the shorter interval; and in Experiment 5 the differences between the first and second intervals of a cycle were even greater than this. On all these schedules, pigeons showed little or no temporal control by the longer intervals, pausing for approximately the same amount of time during all intervals of the cycle. The only data presently available that contradict the view that a large and abrupt change in interval duration limits the pigeon's ability to track schedule changes are from the birds trained on Keller's two-valued schedule.

Although changes in postreinforcement pause tracked changes in interval duration on the five- and seven-valued cyclic interval schedules examined in Experiments 1, 2, 3, and 6, there was some loss of temporal control if performance on simple FI schedules is taken as a standard. Pauses during intervals of the shortest durations in a cycle came closest to matching those characteristic of simple FI schedules of the same duration. This was true for intervals ranging from 5 to 40 seconds. Pauses during subsequent intervals, however, constituted a relatively smaller proportion of interval durations as the intervals in a cycle became longer. The duration of the longest pause during a particular cycle was generally no more than twice the duration of the shortest pause, whereas the duration of the longest interval of a cycle ranged from three (Experiment 6) to seven (Experiment 3) times the duration of the shortest interval. Thus, relative to the standard pauses characteristic of particular FI values, temporal control was reduced during most intervals of the cycle.

The amplitude of the pause cycle (difference between the shortest and longest pause) was to some extent determined by the absolute durations of the intervals programmed, as can be seen by comparing the data for the $t = 5$ and $t = 20$ subjects from Experiment 2 shown in Figures 11-3 and 11-4. The amplitude of the pause cycle was reduced on the $t = 20$ seconds schedule. Innis and Staddon (1971) reported a similar reduction in the amplitude of the pause cycle for birds trained on cyclic interval schedules with values of t greater than 10 seconds.

The difference in performance on Staddon's (1967) two-valued schedule and the Innis and Staddon (1971) seven-valued schedule does not seem to be related to the repetition of intervals in a cycle or to the ratio of short to long intervals over the range of interval numbers and ratios examined here. The results of Experiment 2 show that pigeons will continue to track changes in interval duration on multivalued schedules when four or five intervals of each duration are presented consecutively.

On the other hand, when intervals of two different durations simply alternated (Experiment 4), control by the longer interval was minimal; and when short and long intervals were presented in double alternation (Experiment 3), no temporal tracking was observed. Although short and long intervals were presented equally often on these two-valued schedules, tracking behavior was similar to that observed by Staddon (1967) when the ratio of short to long intervals was 3:1.

SUMMARY

The results of the six experiments reported here, along with the previous findings of Staddon and his associates, suggest that two factors are important in determining the duration of postreinforcement pauses on cyclic interval schedules—the absolute duration of the shortest interval in a cycle and the relative magnitude of the increment (or decrement) in interval duration across successive intervals of a cycle. The first factor is important in establishing the duration of the shortest pause. This pause was typically about one-third to one-half the duration of the shortest interval, slightly shorter than the pause characteristic of simple FI schedules with intervals of comparable values.

The second factor is important in determining the degree of control exerted by the longer intervals of a cycle on the pauses occurring during those intervals. In most of the studies reported here, the size of the increment in interval durations covaried with the number of intervals in a cycle so that the two- and three-valued schedules programmed relatively larger increments than the five- and seven-valued schedules. On the latter schedules, where the increments in interval duration were usually 50 percent or less, temporal tracking was always observed, while on the former schedules, on which the longer intervals were at least three times the duration of the shorter intervals, there was little or no temporal tracking. The results reported for the geometric test schedule in Experiment 1, during which several interval durations were programmed but increments in interval duration were large, support the view that it is the gradual change in interval durations, rather than the number of different intervals in a cycle, that allows for the development of temporal tracking.

The main conclusion to be drawn from the results reported here, then, is that if a gradually changing series of interval durations is presented repeatedly to a pigeon, the bird will be able to alter its performance in response to changes in the temporal pattern of food presentations. At present, studies are being carried out to determine the range of changes in interval value to which the pigeon is sensitive and to establish the limits of temporal control on cyclic interval schedules.

REFERENCES

Catania, A.C., and G.S. Reynolds. 1968. A quantitative analysis of the responding maintained by interval schedules of reinforcement. *Journal of the Experimental Analysis of Behavior 11*: 327–383.

Commons, M.L.; S.M. Paul; and R.R. Tallon. 1967. Combining trial and free operant designs using response contingent reinforcement delivered at the end of a predetermined interval. Eastern Psychological Association, Boston.

Ferster, C.B., and B.F. Skinner. 1957. *Schedules of Reinforcement.* New York: Appleton–Century–Crofts.

Fitzner, R. 1974. Effect of lighting conditions on postreinforcement pause in two cyclic-interval reinforcement schedules. Honours thesis, Dalhousie University.

Harzem, P. 1969. Temporal discrimination. In R.M. Gilbert and N.S. Sutherland, eds., *Animal Discrimination Learning.* New York: Academic Press.

Innis, N.K. 1970. Temporal tracking on cyclic-interval reinforcement schedules. Doctoral dissertation, Duke University.

Innis, N.K., and W.K. Honig. 1979. Stimulus control of behavior during the postreinforcement pause on FI schedules. *Animal Learning and Behavior 7*: 203–210.

Innis, N.K., and J.E.R. Staddon. 1970. Sequential effects in cyclic-interval schedules. *Psychonomic Science 19*: 313–315.

_____. 1971. Temporal tracking on cyclic-interval reinforcement schedules. *Journal of the Experimental Analysis of Behavior, 16*: 411–423.

Keller, J.V. 1973. Responding maintained by sinusoidal cyclic-interval schedules of reinforcement: A control-systems approach to operant behavior. Doctoral dissertation, University of Maryland.

Kello, J., and J.E.R. Staddon. 1974. Control of long-interval performance on mixed cyclic-interval schedules. *Bulletin of the Psychonomic Society 4*: 1–4.

Laties, V.C.; B. Weiss; R.L. Clark; and M.D. Reynolds. 1965. Overt "mediating" behavior and the discrimination of time. *Journal of the Experimental Analysis of Behavior 8*: 107–116.

Powers, R.B. 1968. Clock-delivered reinforcers in conjunctive and interlocking schedules. *Journal of the Experimental Analysis of Behavior 11*: 579–586.

Schneider, B.A. 1969. A two-state analysis of fixed-interval responding in the pigeon. *Journal of the Experimental Analysis of Behavior 12*: 677–688.

Shull, R.L. 1970. The response-reinforcer dependency in fixed-interval schedules of reinforcement. *Journal of the Experimental Analysis of Behavior 14*: 55–60.

Staddon, J.E.R. 1967. Attention and temporal discrimination: Factors controlling responding under a cyclic-interval schedule. *Journal of the Experimental Analysis of Behavior 10*: 349–359.

_____. 1969. Multiple fixed-interval schedules: Transient contrast and temporal inhibition. *Journal of the Experimental Analysis of Behavior 12*: 585–590.

_____. 1977. Schedule-induced behavior. In W.K. Honig and J.E.R. Staddon, eds., *Handbook of Operant Behavior*, pp. 125–152. Englewood Cliffs, New Jersey: Prentice–Hall.

Staddon, J.E.R., and V.L. Simmelhag. 1971. The "superstition" experiment: A reexamination of its implications for the principles of adaptive behavior. *Psychological Review 78*: 3–43.

VII DISCRIMINATIVE EFFECTS OF RESPONDING AND REINFORCEMENT IN STUDIES OF STIMULUS CONTROL

12 THE ANALYSIS OF MEMORY FOR SIGNALS AND FOOD IN A SUCCESSIVE DISCRIMINATION

Mark Rilling and
R.C. Howard

INTRODUCTION

A fundamental problem in research on schedules of reinforcement is to determine what aspect of the stimulus controls the response pattern. Some years ago Rilling and McDiarmid (1965) attacked this problem directly within a psychophysical framework. A discrimination was established between two different values of a schedule of reinforcement, and an attempt was made to identify the effective stimulus that controlled the discrimination. Choice responses provided the index of discrimination.

More specifically, the psychophysical paradigm was derived from the theory of signal detectability. In the first component of a behavioral chain, pigeons responded on one of two alternative fixed ratios (or fixed intervals) presented in a pseudorandom sequence on the center key. When the given requirement was fulfilled, the center key light was turned off, and the two side key lights were turned on initiating the second component. There a single left key peck produced immediate reinforcement if the shorter ratio had been completed on the center key, and a single right key peck produced immediate reinforcement if the longer ratio had been completed on the center key. Errors delayed reinforcement without correction. In other words, during the first component the programmed stimulus was a performance on a reinforcement schedule, and during the second component the choice behavior provided a measure of discrimination between these two performances. Rilling and McDiarmid (1965) demonstrated that as the difference between two fixed ratios was reduced, the number of errors in discrimination increased. A second experiment, with interval as well as ratio schedules (Rilling, 1967), indicated that the number of responses rather than the passage of time was the stimulus that acquired control over the choice response. Fortunately, after these early experiments, the psychophysical paradigm began to be used by other investigators. Much of the work is represented in other chapters in this volume.

Since the original work on discrimination between schedules of reinforcement, there has been an increase in the study of memory and cognition as an area of research in animal learning. The recent publication of two books devoted to research on these topics is an indicator of this development. Spear's (1978) book deals with the processing of memories, with emphasis on forgetting and retention, while the book by Hulse, Fowler, and Honig (1978) consists of papers reflecting the common view that cognitive processes in animal behavior are an appropriate subject for experimental analysis.

Stimulus control may be defined as a change in a dependent variable, such as the rate of responding, that is produced by a change in a particular property of a stimulus (Rilling, 1977). The familiar stimulus generalization gradient is a typical example of stimulus control. In stimulus control procedures, the stimulus is physically present at the time that the indicator response is observed. Behavior is also controlled by stimuli not physically present when the indicator response occurs. Memory may be defined as trace stimulus control when behavior is controlled by stimuli that have terminated before the indicator response occurs. All of the events included in conventional stimulus control paradigms, such as schedules of reinforcement or discriminative stimuli, may be investigated with trace control procedures.

The experiment by Rilling and McDiarmid (1965) described above may be considered as a procedure for analyzing trace stimulus control. In this case the trace stimulus was response-produced stimuli generated by a specific schedule of reinforcement. That is, the birds had to "remember" whether they just completed a long or short fixed ratio. In another experiment, Rilling (1968) established a discrimination between two fixed ratio schedules of reinforcement. In one, fixed ratio 25, the reinforcer was delivered after the twenty-fifth response; on the other, fixed ratio 50, the fiftieth response was reinforced. During test trials, a time out was introduced after the twenty-sixth response on fixed ratio 50. The accuracy of the discrimination rapidly decreased to chance as the duration of the time out was increased. The time out weakened control over the indicator response by the response-produced stimuli that preceded the time out. In other words, trace stimulus control by the response-produced stimuli of the first half of the fixed ratio 50 may have been weakened by inserting a delay interval within the schedule. The birds' memory for their recent behavior is disrupted by the insertion of a retention interval.

Our more recent work also employs a paradigm of trace stimulus control. All of the experiments in this chapter have in common a procedure in which the discriminative stimuli are terminated prior to the time when the rate of pecking is used as an index of stimulus control. Schedules of reinforcement involve complex compound stimuli such as a light, food, and response-produced stimuli. The experiments follow the strategy of separating these stimuli into elements to determine how each element affects retention. An experimental analysis of trace stimulus control might reveal how events within schedules acquire control over behavior. The research is atheoretical and may be interpreted equally well within the traditional behavioristic framework or within the cognitive framework that has recently become popular.

The research strategy has been to ask questions rather than test theories. The results of five experiments are reported here. These experiments were designed to answer the following five questions. 1. In Experiment 1, does food overshadow a discriminative stimulus on the key when the compound is a signal preceding reinforcement in discrimination learning? 2. In Experiment 2, does food overshadow a discriminative stimulus on the key when the compound is a signal preceding nonreinforcement in discrimination learning? 3. In Experiment 3, does food retain its stimulus control function over longer delays than a stimulus on the key? 4. In Experiment 4, is a discriminative stimulus paired directly with food effective over a longer trace interval than a discriminative stimulus not directly paired with food? 5. In Experiment 5, is intermittent reinforcement of a discriminative stimulus a determinant of retention? By comparing the results of Experiments 1 and 2, it is possible to determine if overshadowing occurs independently of whether the compound stimulus is associated with reinforcement or extinction. Experiments 4 and 5 provide different procedures for manipulating the associative value of a stimulus as a determinant of retention.

GENERAL PROCEDURE

Each of the five experiments reported in this chapter employs the same basic procedure. The origin of the procedure was the application of psychophysical methods to the study of the discrimination of temporal intervals by Reynolds and Catania (1962). More recently, the procedure has been refined by Weisman and Dodd (1979) to answer the question of whether the order of two events functioned as a discriminative stimulus for successive operant behavior.

An operant unconditional discrimination consisting of two components was employed. The discriminative stimulus was presented in the first component, and the response period was the second component. Stimuli presented in the first component that precede periods of reinforcement were designated positive stimuli (S+), while those stimuli that precede periods of extinction were designated negative stimuli (S−). Differential responding was measured in the second component. By analogy with a psychophysical procedure, the independent variable consisted of the presentation of the stimulus in the first component, and the dependent variable was the rate of responding in the second component. The advantage of this procedure is that a wide range of stimuli may be presented in the first component and a wide range of response rates may be observed in the second component.

More specifically, the second component was a response period initiated by the presentation of a white key light. Key pecking during the white key light was differentially reinforced depending upon the stimulus presented during the first component. On positive trials, after the presentation of the stimulus in the first component, responding during the white key light was reinforced with food after a variable interval of 15 seconds had elapsed. In the absence of the positive stimulus, extinction was in effect, and the white key light terminated automatically after 15 seconds. The exception to this procedure was Experiment 2, where these contingencies were reversed so that the discriminative stimulus in the first component was followed by extinction in the second component. Testing began after the acquisition of the discrimination in which a high rate of responding was observed on reinforced trials and a low rate of responding was observed on nonreinforced trials.

The two different testing procedures were sequence generalization testing and a retention test. In research on stimulus control (see Rilling, 1977), an experimenter administers a stimulus generalization test by systematically varying a physical property of the training stimulus across the test stimuli presented during the stimulus generalization test. Physically different stimuli that produce the same rates of responding on the stimulus generalization test are assumed to have acquired equal stimulus control over behavior. In a sequence generalization test, the animal is first trained with one sequence during training and then tested for responding to all possible sequences. The rationale for the sequence generalization test is that equivalent sequences should produce equal rates of responding during the generalization test. For example, if food overshadows the key light following training with a two-element sequence consisting of food and key light, then sequences containing food in either the first or second position should produce higher rates of responding than sequences containing only the key light without food. The assumption of the sequence generalization test is that functionally equivalent stimuli produce equal rates of responding. In retention testing, a retention interval is inserted between the two components.

OVERSHADOWING BY FOOD OF A SIGNAL PRECEDING REINFORCEMENT IN DISCRIMINATION LEARNING

Pavlov (1927) discovered overshadowing when he found that the strength of responding to a conditional stimulus was reduced when the stimulus was presented as a compound as compared to the condition when the stimulus was presented alone. Overshadowing of a stimulus, A, may be defined as a reduction in stimulus control produced after training in which A is always presented together (concurrently or serially) with another stimulus, B. The design of an overshadowing experiment requires a comparison of an experimental condition involving the AB compound with the control condition in which A is presented alone. Overshadowing is measured on test trials in which stimulus A is presented alone. Overshadowing is obtained if the experimental condition shows less stimulus control by element A than a control group trained with element A alone.

Data summarized by Mackintosh (1974) demonstrate that overshadowing occurs in operant discrimination learning as well as the Pavlovian paradigm. More recently, Hall, Mackintosh, Goodall, and Martello (1977) employed a compound stimulus consisting of a stimulus imperfectly correlated with reinforcement and a stimulus highly correlated with reinforcement. The compound stimulus signaled that responding during S+ was reinforced, while the absence of the compound stimulus signaled extinction. They found that a less valid predictor of reinforcement lost control when it was presented simultaneously with a better predictor of reinforcement.

The concept of overshadowing formed the basis of Staddon's (1974) theory of the temporal control of operant behavior. His two basic assumptions were that food overshadowed the stimulus presented on the key and that food was more memorable than a neutral stimulus such as a key light. Staddon explained the scallop obtained on fixed interval schedules by assuming that the delivery of food overshadowed the stimulus presented on the key. These assumptions led Staddon to interpret, as an example of overshadowing, the finding that food was more effective than a key light presented in place of food in inhibiting the onset of pecking on a fixed interval schedule. The purpose of Experiment 1, carried out by Rilling, Howard, and Johnson (1980), was to verify Staddon's assumption that food overshadows a key light.

In previous work on overshadowing, the discriminative stimuli were usually presented concurrently and were often lights and tones adjusted in intensity so that one element of the compound was relatively more salient than the other. Serial presentation of the compound stimulus was selected for the present studies because much less is known about overshadowing in the case of nonoverlapping stimuli. One of the most common sequences in conditioning is the two-event sequence in which a neutral stimulus is paired with an unconditioned stimulus. In research on autoshaping, a pigeon is typically presented with a key light followed by food. The present research employed a key light and food as the elements of a compound stimulus to determine if food overshadowed a discriminative stimulus on the key. An additional theoretical rationale for the study was to answer the question of whether a stimulus normally employed as an unconditioned stimulus overshadowed a stimulus normally employed as a conditioned stimulus.

Two orders of successive presentation are possible: The key light may be presented first or second. When the key light is presented first, the procedure corresponds to a forward conditioning or autoshaping trial in which the stimulus on the key is followed immediately by food. When the key light is presented second, the stimuli are ordered as in a backward conditioning trial in which food is followed by the key light.

Weisman and Dodd (1979) employed two different colors of key light as sequential compound discriminative stimuli. The results of their research demonstrated that the second element acquired more stimulus control over the discrimination than the first element when the elements had equal salience. The present experiments extend the research of Weisman and Dodd to the case where one element of the compound is food. One prediction is that control by the second element is reduced when the first element is food.

The procedure for this experiment is based upon that of Weisman and Dodd (1979). The elements of the compound stimulus employed in the first component of the schedule are food and a colored key light. The element that is presented first at the beginning of a trial is designated A, while the second element is designated B. An X designates the replacement of an absent A or B by an interval of the same length, but without an illuminated key or food. For example, the designation XX, the designation for an extinction trial or S–, refers to the procedure in which the key is illuminated white without a preceding AB compound.

Reinforcement or extinction of pecking on a white key in the second, response component, of the schedule was dependent upon the stimulus presented in the first component. Discrimination training consisted of S+ trials in which, after presentation of the AB sequence, responding to the white key light was reinforced with food, which terminated the trial. On S– trials, also designated as XX trials, responding to the white key was extinguished, and the trial terminated automatically after 15 seconds.

An S+ trial began with a 3-second presentation of stimulus A, followed by a 0.5-second interstimulus interval, which in turn was followed by a 3-second presentation of stimulus B. Following the

AB sequence, after a 0.5-second interval, the white key was illuminated, and pecking was reinforced on a variable interval schedule (VI 15 seconds). The delivery of the programmed reinforcer terminated the particular trial. An extinction or S− trial began with the presentation of the white stimulus without a preceding AB sequence. After S−, key pecks were not reinforced, and the trial terminated automatically after 15 seconds. The S+ and S− trials were presented randomly. Four groups with eight pigeons per group were employed.

In Experiment 1, for one group of pigeons, an autoshaping trial served as the S+ in a forward conditioning arrangement—that is, a colored key light was followed by food. For another group of pigeons, a backward conditioning trial served as the S+—that is, food was presented first, followed by a colored light on the center key. These autoshaping sequences were discriminative stimuli signaling that following the termination of the discriminative stimulus, pecking the white center key would be reinforced with food.

To demonstrate sequential overshadowing with these sequences, it is necessary to show that food reduces the amount of stimulus control by the key light as compared to control conditions in which the key light is presented in the absence of food. Selecting appropriate control conditions for a sequential overshadowing experiment is especially difficult, and perhaps no single comparison on overshadowing is without problems. Two control groups were employed in an effort to meet the criteria for overshadowing. For the forward conditioning control group, lighting the key red and then green served as the discriminative stimulus. This provided a condition in which food was not part of a compound employed as a discriminative stimulus. As compared to the experimental groups in which food was employed as part of a discriminative stimulus, there should be more stimulus control over behavior by the neutral stimulus in the control group than by the neutral stimulus overshadowed by food in the experimental group.

For the backward conditioning control group, two different types of positive trials were employed in which a single element was presented alone as a discriminative stimulus. On half the positive trials, the discriminative stimulus was food followed by an interval equal to the duration of the stimulus on the key for the backward conditioning group. On the other half of the positive trials, the discriminative stimulus was a colored light on the key followed by the onset of the white key. If food overshadows the discriminative stimulus on the key in a backward conditioning paradigm, then less control should be obtained by the key light in the backward conditioning group than in the control group in which the key light was presented alone.

The pigeons received daily sessions of discrimination training. The rates of responding during the final white period were computed daily for both positive and negative trials. From these response rates, a discrimination index was computed using the following equation: Discrimination index = (mean response rate on positive trials)/(mean response rate on positive trials + mean response rate on negative trials). A discrimination index of 0.50 indicates chance performance, whle a discrimination index of 1 indicates perfect discrimination. The criterion for completion of discrimination training was a discrimination index of 0.90 for two consecutive days.

After the birds reached criterion, test trials were randomly introduced into the regular discrimination sessions in order to determine how much control each of the elements of the compound stimulus had acquired over the discrimination. Each test stimulus consisted of the successive presentation of two stimulus elements for 3 seconds each consisting of all possible combinations of A, B, and X with each presented in the first and second position. Since A, B, and X were each presented in the first and last position, the test trial plan was a 3 X 3 matrix with nine cells. These nine stimuli indicated as follows:

AA	AB	AX
BA	BB	BX
XA	XB	XX

A test trial consisted of the presentation of one of the nine stimuli, followed by 15 seconds of the white center key component, which was terminated without reinforcement. The dependent variable was the rate of white center key pecking following each of the nine test stimuli averaged over the nine sessions of testing.

Figure 12–1 shows the average response rate following each of the nine test stimuli for the four groups. For both experimental groups, displayed in the upper panels of Figure 12–1, sequences containing food generally led to a higher rate of responding than sequences not containing food. For the forward conditioning group, displayed in the upper right panel of Figure 12–1, the two event sequences con-

Figure 12–1. Mean rates of responding averaged across all subjects in an associative generalization test in extinction for each of the nine test stimuli. The test followed discrimination training in which responding during the white choice period was reinforced following the *AB* sequence (*S+*) and was extinguished during the white choice period following *XX* (*S-*).

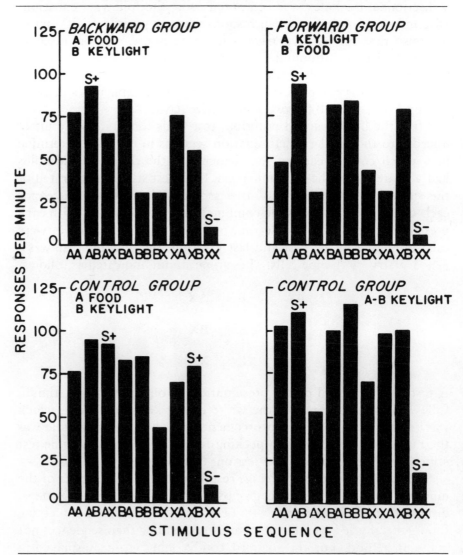

taining food as one of the elements (AB, BA, BB) and the sequence with food alone in the training position (XB) showed significantly more responding than the sequences in which neither element contained food (AA, XA, AX, and XX). The rate of responding to the sequences containing the key light alone without food (AA, AX, and XA) was significantly less than the rate to the S+(AB), but significantly greater than the rate of responding to the S-(XX). The key light gained some control over responding, but demonstrated less control than food, which was thus shown to be the dominant stimulus.

For the backward conditioning group, the upper left panel of Figure 12-1, the two event sequences containing food as one of the elements (AA, AB, BA) each led to significantly more responding than the sequences in which neither element contained food (BB, BX, XB, and XX). Again, the key light alone acquired some stimulus control over responding. The rate of responding to the sequences containing the key light alone (BB, BX, and XB) was significantly less than S+(AB), but greater than S-(XX).

The data for the two control groups are displayed in the lower panel of Figure 12-1. For the key light–key light control group, presented in the lower right panel of the figure, there were no significant differences among the two event sequences containing A and B (AA, AB, BA, BB) and the sequences in which either A or B was contiguous with white (XA and XB). Each of the preceding sequences showed a significantly higher rate of responding than was obtained to the negative stimulus (XX). Intermediate rates of responding, less than AB and greater than XX, were only obtained when X was inserted between A (AX) or B (BX) and white.

For the overshadowing control group, two positive stimuli were employed during discrimination training prior to the introduction of test stimuli. The stimuli associated with reinforced pecking during discrimination training were food X (AX) and X key light (XB). This control procedure was effective in generating rates of responding that were not significantly different among the following stimuli (AA, AB, AX, BA, BB, XA, and XB). Only sequence BX generated a significantly lower rate of responding than each of the preceding stimuli. All of the sequences were significantly greater than XX.

In terms of the overshadowing hypothesis, the most relevant comparison is between the backward pairing group (upper left panel of Figure 12-1) and the backward pairing control group (lower left panel of Figure 12–1). The question is whether stimulus control by the colored key light, element B, is reduced for the backward group. Sequences containing B alone (BB, BX, and XB) showed lower rates of responding in the experimental group (upper panel) than in the control group (lower panel). Therefore, our conclusion is that food overshadowed the key light.

For the forward conditioning group, control of responding by the key light, A, was significantly reduced as compared to the stimulus control demonstrated by the key light in the key light–key light control group. Test sequences AA and XA, but not AX, demonstrated significantly less control over discriminative pecking in the forward pairing group than in the key light–key light control group. In summary, the major effect of the addition of food as one element of an AB sequence is to reduce stimulus control by the other element when that element is a key light.

OVERSHADOWING BY FOOD OF A SIGNAL PRECEDING EXTINCTION IN DISCRIMINATION LEARNING

For all four groups receiving discrimination training in Experiment 1, the AB sequence preceding the white key light functioned as a discriminative stimulus for the reinforcement of pecking with food. The absence of the AB sequence preceding the white key light functioned as a discriminative stimulus for extinction during white. In Experiment 2, carried out by Rilling, Howard, and Johnson (1980), the contingencies of reinforcement were reversed from those of Experiment 1, so that key pecking during white was reinforced only following the absence of the AB sequence at the beginning of a trial. The occurrence of an AB sequence at the beginning of a trial indicated that responding during white was extinguished.

Previous work has established that stimuli associated with extinction acquire inhibitory control over responding (see Rilling, 1977, for a review). Food itself quite often serves as a discriminative stimulus for nonreinforcement. The low rates of responding obtained after reinforcement on fixed ratio and fixed interval schedules are in part a reflection of the effectiveness with which food functions as a discriminative stimulus for nonreinforcement.

In previous research on overshadowing, the compound stimulus was associated with reinforcement. Blocking is defined as reduced stimulus control by one element of a compound stimulus produced by prior training with the other element of the compound stimulus. Using a go/no-go discrimination with pigeons, vom Saal and Jenkins (1970) found that the acquisition of stimulus control by one element of a compound stimulus signaling nonreinforcement was blocked by pretraining with the other element of the compound stimulus. Overshadowing has not been demonstrated when the compound is a discriminative stimulus for nonreinforcement. The purpose of this experiment was to employ a two-element compound, with food and a signal on the key as the elements, to determine if food overshadows a signal on the key when each event signals nonreinforcement.

Three groups of eight pigeons per group were employed. In the forward conditioning experimental group, element A was a key light, and element B was food. In the backward conditioning experimental group, element A was food, and element B was the key light. In the control group, each element of the AB sequence served as a discriminative stimulus for not responding. Elevated rates of responding to the test sequences containing the key light for the experimental groups as compared to the control group provides evidence of overshadowing.

Figure 12–2 shows the average key-pecking rate for each of the nine test stimuli for the three groups. As a result of discrimination training, a high rate was observed following S+(XX) and a low rate was observed following S–(AB). For the forward and backward experimental groups, the test sequences can be divided into two sets. Test sequences containing food were associated with a relatively low key peck rate, while test sequences without food were associated with relatively high key peck rates. In other words, food was more effective as a discriminative stimulus for nonreinforcement than a signal on the key for both experimental groups.

For the control group in which each element was a red or green color on the key, low key peck rates were obtained for all test sequences containing the two elements of S– (AA, AB, BA, and BB). Test sequences in which one of the elements was S– (AX, BX, XA, XB, and XX) each maintained key peck rates that were relatively higher than S–(AB).

By comparing the forward and backward conditioning groups individually with the control group it is possible to determine if food overshadowed the signal on the key as a discriminative stimulus for nonreinforcement. Since the key-pecking rates for the birds in the control group were higher than for the animals in the experimental

Figure 12-2. Mean rates of responding averaged across all subjects in an associative generalization test in extinction for each of the nine test sequences. The test followed discrimination training in which responding during the white choice period was reinforced following *XX* (*S*+) and responding was extinguished following *AB* (*S*-).

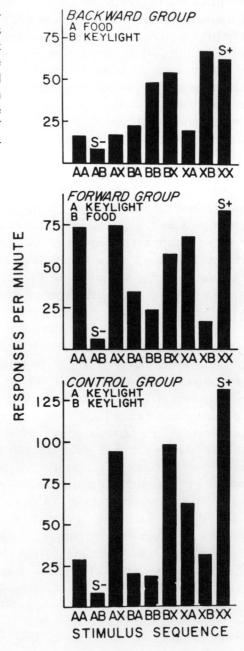

groups, the data were transformed into percent of maximum rate by arbitrarily assigning the XX stimulus a value of 100 percent and expressing the data for the other test stimuli in terms of the percentage of the rate to S+. The comparison of the backward conditioning group, in which A was food and B was the colored key, with the control group demonstrated that sequences that contained either B alone or B immediately preceding the white key period (BB and XB) controlled significantly more pecking for the backward conditioning group than for the control group. When food was an additional element in the sequence in the backward conditioning group, it overshadowed the colored key light.

For the forward conditioning group, test sequences containing either A alone or A immediately preceding the white key (AA and XA) led to significantly more pecking than in the colored light–colored light control group. These data suggest that the presence of food in the forward conditioning group overshadowed the colored light on the key. Therefore, the major effect of the addition of food was to substantially reduce the colored light's function as a discriminative stimulus for nonreinforcement.

In summary, the data from these two experiments demonstrate that food overshadows a colored light independently of whether the sequence is a discriminative stimulus for reinforcement or nonreinforcement.

RETENTION OF FOOD VERSUS A KEY LIGHT

Experiments 1 and 2 demonstrate that food overshadowed a colored light on the key. Experiments 3 through 5 are based on Howard (1979). The purpose of Experiment 3 was to verify Staddon's (1974) assumption that food retains its trace stimulus control over longer delays than a stimulus on the key by comparing retention functions for food and a key light color over a wide range of intervals using a within subjects design. In his discussion of forgetting in animal learning, Shimp (1978) assumed that the occurrence of food is more salient than a key peck. One implication of Shimp's view is that memory for food is better than memory for the color of the stimuli on the key.

It seems likely that one of the differences between the biologically relevant events employed as USs in conditioning experiments and the biologically irrelevant events employed as CSs is that trace stimulus control by a US is superior to that by a CS. For example, food delivered to a pigeon in a food hopper is an extremely salient multidimensional stimulus consisting of food, a lighted hopper, and the sound produced by the operation of the magazine. Furthermore, food is a biologically relevant stimulus ingested by the animal. The aftereffects of ingestion may exert stimulus control over the pigeon's behavior after the food hopper has been released. Such aftereffects may persist long enough to span the retention interval. In contrast, the presentation of a color on the key is less effective than food in producing stimulus control, as demonstrated in the preceding experiments.

An experiment by Maki, Moe, and Bierley (1977) suggested that trace stimulus control by food is superior to trace stimulus control by the visual stimulus on the key. Their basic procedure was to reinforce a left-side-key-peck when it followed a given stimulus and to reinforce a right-side-key-peck after it followed the other stimulus. For example, after the prior presentation of food for 2 seconds, the side keys were illuminated red and green. A peck on the red key was reinforced with additional food, while a peck on the green key went unreinforced. Birds consistently discriminated correctly above 87 percent of the time across delays that ranged between 8 and 15 seconds. When the conventional visual sample stimulus was used, the retention intervals for similar discriminability were between 3 and 7 seconds.

Experiment 3 was designed to compare retention functions for food and a key color. The same basic procedure was used again with eight pigeons. The discriminative stimulus presented in the first component was a single element—either food or a colored light on the key. An S+ trial began with either access to grain for 3 seconds or illumination of the key light with green for 3 seconds. After a 0.5-second interval, the key was illuminated white at the beginning of the response period. Pecking the center key was reinforced on a variable interval schedule (VI 15 seconds), so that the average duration of the response period was 15 seconds. The delivery of the programmed reinforcer terminated the particular trial. An extinction or S− trial began with the presentation of the response period and the white key without either the preceding food or the colored key light. After S−, key pecks were not reinforced, and the trial terminated automatically after 15 seconds. After the pigeons discriminated between S+ and S-, retention functions were obtained by varying the delay between food or the key light and the response period. Access to food is defined to be better retained in memory than the presentation of a key light when the former leads to responding after S+ over a longer retention interval than the latter.

After training until a discrimination index of 0.90 was reached for two consecutive sessions, a retention test was begun. Each pigeon received seven sessions of testing, with the order of delay intervals counterbalanced across sessions and pigeons. A retention session consisted of forty S+ and forty S- trials as in training, with fourteen additional probe trials inserted between training trials in a semirandom order. On a probe trial, either food or the colored key light was followed by a delay interval of either 0, 2, 4, 8, or 12 seconds. Then the response period was initiated by the white key light coming on for 15 seconds. Key pecks in this response period were not reinforced. Trials beginning with food and with the key light were tested at each delay interval during each session.

The results shown in the left portion of Figure 12–3 demonstrate that food and the colored key light were equally effective as positive discriminative stimuli, since response rates following either S+ were not significantly different. The right portion of Figure 12–3 shows the retention functions for food and the stimulus on the key. Control by food is retained better than control by the key light at all retention intervals. In other words, key pecking during the response period dropped off more slowly when the S+ trial began with food than when the trial began with the illumination of the key with a colored light. A difference in stimulus control between food and the key light was not present during discrimination training and emerged only during the retention test, when a true delay followed each stimulus. These data suggest that food and the key light were equally discriminable, but not equally memorable. The data provide confirmation for the assumptions of Shimp (1978) and Staddon (1974) that food is more memorable than a colored stimulus on the key.

RETENTION OF A STIMULUS PAIRED WITH FOOD

The finding that food is retained better than a key light provides empirical confirmation for Staddon's assumption that food is more effective in acquiring control over subsequent behavior than "neu-

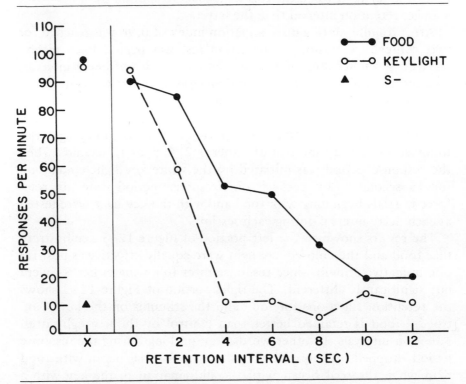

Figure 12–3. Retention curves for food and a key light following discrimination training in which each event separately functioned as a discriminative stimulus for reinforcement during the white choice period.

tral" stimuli such as the color of the light on the key. This outcome is hardly surprising, since the delivery of food involved many stimulus elements from more than one sensory modality, whereas the key light was a simple visual stimulus. The present experiment raises a more theoretically significant question: Is retention determined by the associative value of a stimulus apart from its sensory properties? In this research, the associative value of a stimulus is defined by the relationship between the stimulus and food. More specifically, the question is whether a discriminative stimulus directly paired with food is retained longer than a discriminative stimulus not directly paired with food.

Data obtained by Stubbs, Vautin, Reid, and Delehanty (1978) suggest that a brief color paired with food is more effective in controlling subsequent choice behavior than a brief stimulus that was not paired with food. Stubbs et al. (1978) interrupted a fixed interval schedule with a psychophysical choice procedure following either a short or a long time after either of two prior events—food or a colored light on the key. Using a complicated procedure, Honig (1978: 233–236) also found that the pairing of a sample stimulus with food improved retention as compared with a similar stimulus not paired with food. These experiments suggest that the operation of pairing a stimulus with food is a promising procedure for asking questions about memory.

The present experiment was also designed to differentiate between active and passive models of animal memory. An example of a passive model of animal memory is the trace decay theory of Roberts and Grant (1976). Trace strength theory assumes that the strength of a memory trace is determined by the physical properties of the sample stimulus (e.g., duration and intensity). The sample stimulus is the to be remembered event. Once the sample stimulus has terminated, the memory trace passively decays in the absence of the sample stimulus. The choice response is determined by the strength of the memory trace. The theory is consistent with data showing a decline in matching-to-sample accuracy as a function of increases in the retention interval. Trace decay theory predicts identical retention functions for two colored lights of equal salience and is silent about the associative value of a stimulus as a determinant of retention.

In contrast with the passive point of view, other theorists (e.g., Honig 1978; Wagner, 1978) assume that active processing may occur after the termination of the sample stimulus, so that retention is not inexorably dependent upon the passage of time. Honig's view is that the sample stimulus establishes an "instruction" so that the pigeon remembers "what to do" rather than "what it saw." In the present experiment, the instructional hypothesis predicts that a stimulus paired with food is a more effective instruction for subsequent pecking than a stimulus not paired with food. Alternatively, Wagner's view is that a stimulus paired with food is "rehearsed" during the retention interval more than a stimulus not paired with food. Increased rehearsal increases the maintenance of trace stimulus control. The subjects in this experiment were eight White Carneaux pigeons.

In order to clarify the three different sequences employed in the first component as discriminative stimuli on S+ trials, a diagram of the procedure is presented in Figure 12–4. Red and green key lights

Figure 12–4. Diagram of the procedure used during Experiment 4. The discriminative stimulus labeled *DS* was unpaired on 100 percent of its presentations. The discriminative stimulus labeled conditioned stimulus (*CS*) was paired with food on 75 percent of its presentations and unpaired with food on 25 percent of its presentations. Each of these three types of discriminative stimuli was followed by the white choice period after an interval of 2 seconds.

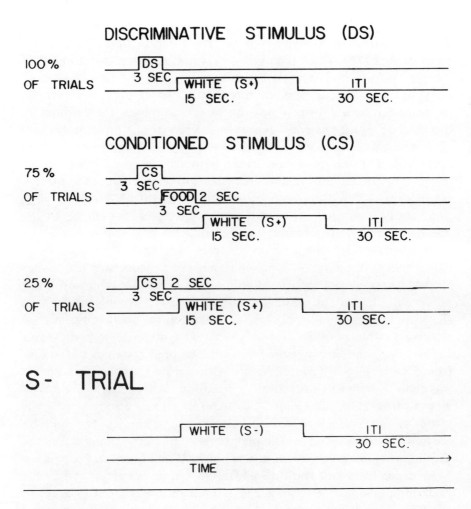

were presented for 3 seconds in the first component. One color of the key (DS) was never directly paired with food, but consistently preceded the white choice period by 2 seconds on 100 percent of the presentations. The other color (CS) was immediately followed by food for 3 seconds on 75 percent of the presentations and was unpaired with food on 25 percent of the presentations. For example, for half of the birds, S+ trials began with three different types of events—red key light alone, green key light alone, and green key light followed immediately by food. The green key light is labeled a conditioned stimulus (CS) because it was paired with food, while the red key light is simply labeled a discriminative stimulus (DS). The roles of red and green key colors were reversed for the other birds.

Food was a redundant element in the first component, since a colored key light alone predicted food on 100 percent of the trials. Presentation of food following the key light was designed to alter the associative value of the color paired with food, while a partial reinforcement condition of 75 percent was selected to reduce the possibility of generalization decrement during testing.

Each of the three types of discriminative stimuli in the first component was followed after 2 seconds by the white response period. Each trial following S+ terminated with food when a peck was reinforced on the variable interval 15-second schedule. The absence of one of the three positive stimuli preceding the onset of the white choice period signaled an S- trial. An S- trial terminated automatically after 15 seconds without reinforcement. The ITI was 30 seconds.

The three different stimuli presented during the retention test were the CS alone, the CS plus food, and the DS alone. Retention functions were obtained for each of the three stimuli at retention intervals of 2, 4, 6, 8, 12, and 16 seconds.

The left portion of Figure 12-5 shows the average rate of responding during the white choice period as a function of the three events employed as positive discriminative stimuli. Prior to the test for retention, the rate of responding among the stimuli did not differ significantly over the last three days of training. The filled triangle indicates that a low rate of responding was obtained during the white choice period on S- trials.

The right portion shows the ratio of responding during the white response period following each of the three positive stimuli as a function of the interpolated retention interval. The major finding was

Figure 12–5. Retention curves for a discriminative stimulus (*DS*), a conditioned stimulus presented alone (*CS*), and a conditioning trial in which the *CS* always paired with food. Data were obtained during test trials following discrimination training in which the three positive stimuli were a key light color (*DS*), or a different key light color (*CS*) that was always paired with food.

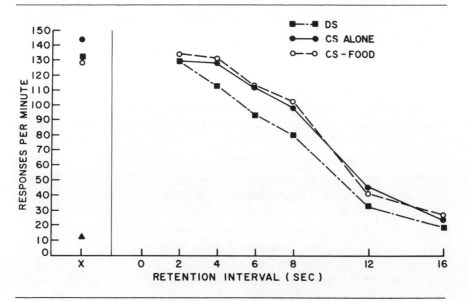

that response rate following the stimulus never paired with food (the DS) decreased more rapidly across all the retention intervals than responding to either the CS alone or the CS followed by food. Trace stimulus control was more effectively maintained by a color paired with food than by a color not paired with food. Also interesting was the finding that on trials when the CS was presented alone, it controlled the same rate of responding as when it was paired with food.

A within subjects analysis of variance showed responding during the white response period to differ significantly as a function of the positive stimulus presented during the first component, $F(2, 14) = 9.12$, $p < .005$, and as a function of the retention interval tested, $F(3, 35) = 39.2$, $p < .001$. A Duncan's multiple range test showed that the CS (the key light paired with food) was followed by the same rate of responding whether it was presented alone or paired with food, but this key light maintained a higher rate of responding than the key light (DS) that was never paired with food, $F(2, 14)$ = 9.12, $p < .005$. A test for simple main effects comparing the CS and DS key lights showed that responding differed significantly at 4 seconds, $F(1, 40)$ = 10.6, $p < .005$; 6 seconds, $F(1, 40)$ = 17.6, $p < .001$; 8 seconds, $F(1, 40)$ = 15.8, $p < .001$; and 12 seconds, $F(1, 40)$ = 7.4, $p < .01$. Responding did not differ significantly at 0 seconds and 16 seconds—$Fs < 1$. This analysis clearly demonstrates that retention of a stimulus is improved by pairing the stimulus with food.

RETENTION AND INTERMITTENT REINFORCEMENT

In the preceding experiment, a colored key light paired immediately with food on 75 percent of the trials was retained better than a colored key light never immediately paired with food. These data suggest that trace stimulus control is determined in part by the associative value of the stimulus controlling responding. The associative value of a stimulus controlling responding can be manipulated either by pairing the stimulus with food prior to the choice period or by intermittent reinforcement. In all of the preceding experiments, each S+ trial terminated with food. The independent variable in this experiment is the probability that the stimulus presented in the first component on S+ trials is followed by the white response period and food in the second component. It seems likely that the higher the percentage of trials in which the first component is followed by the second component, the less likely it is that interpolated retention intervals will disrupt trace stimulus control.

The present experiment is relevant to Nevin's (1974) concept of response strength as resistance to change. Nevin found that control by stimuli correlated with higher reinforcement probabilities was less affected by disrupting events—for example, response-independent food presented between components—than was control by stimuli correlated with lower reinforcement probabilities. The insertion of a retention interval within a discrimination can be considered a disrupting event. Therefore, Nevin's concept of response strength leads to the prediction that trace stimulus control is especially susceptible to disruption or forgetting when reinforcement of the sample stimulus is intermittent.

Six pigeons were used in Experiment 5. Each pigeon was presented with three different colored key lights as discriminative stimuli in the first component of the basic procedure. On each trial, only one of the colors was presented as a single element. The associative value of the key light is manipulated by varying the percentage of trials (S1 = 90 percent, S2 = 50 percent, and S3 = 10 percent) on which the key light was followed by the white response period and food. When a stimulus was not followed by the white key, it was followed by the standard 30-second ITI. A within subjects design was employed, so each of the six pigeons was exposed to all three percentages and color (red, green, and yellow) was counterbalanced across subjects.

The positive discriminative stimuli were the colored key lights presented for 3 seconds prior to the onset of the white response period. The negative discriminative stimulus, S−, was the absence of a colored light prior to the onset of the response period. A session of discrimination training consisted of twenty presentations of each color for a total of sixty trials. The S− was also presented sixty times. Training ended when a pigeon obtained a 0.90 discrimination index for two consecutive sessions.

The retention intervals were 2, 4, 6, 8, 10, and 12 seconds. All three discriminative stimuli were tested at each retention interval during each session. Six sessions were required to obtain the retention functions.

The left portion of Figure 12–6 shows the average rate of responding during the response period over the last three days of training when S+ was signaled by S1 (filled circles), S2 (open circles), or S3 (filled squares). The rates of responding did not differ statistically between the three positive stimuli. Responding to S− is also presented (filled triangle).

The right portion of Figure 12–6 shows the rate of responding during the response period preceded by either S1, S2, or S3 as a function of the interpolated retention interval. The figure shows that S1 (90 percent) was superior to S2 (50 percent) and that S2 was superior to S3 (10 percent). Thus, even though rates of responding to the stimuli were identical when the retention interval was zero, significant differences among the conditions emerged when a retention interval was inserted between the sample and the response period. These results provide further confirmation for the view that

Figure 12–6. Retention curves for the rate of responding during the white choice period as a function of the probability that the discriminative stimulus was followed by food.

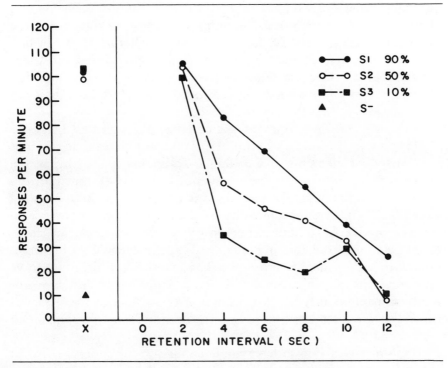

the associative value of a stimulus is an important determinant of retention.

DISCUSSION

In Experiments 1 and 2, food and a key light were presented in a serial compound as discriminative stimuli for successive operant behavior. Food overshadowed the key light and was the primary determinant of stimulus control. Two types of serial compounds were employed, with food presented in a forward or backward pairing arrangement. In the backward pairing condition, the key light had a more favorable temporal relationship with the events that terminated the trial. Nevertheless, food still predominated over key light in the backward pairing arrangement, demonstrating the potency of food in overshadowing control by the color of the stimulus on the key. If a two-element serial compound contains one element normally employed as a US (e.g., food) and another element normally employed as a CS (e.g., a key light), these data suggest that the US will overshadow the CS independently of whether the CS is presented as the first or second element. The overshadowing that was obtained in these experiments occurred independently of whether the compound stimulus signaled reinforcement (as in Experiment 1) or extinction (as in Experiment 2).

Data from previous research such as that of Foree and Lo Lordo (1975) and Jacobs and Lo Lordo (1977) demonstrates that stimulus control by the elements of a compound stimulus depends upon the reinforcer associated with the compound stimulus. A constraint on overshadowing may be the reinforcer associated with the compound stimulus. Therefore, the generality of the present data to other stimuli is a matter for additional empirical work. For example, shock could be substituted for food as one of the elements in the AB compound to determine if shock overshadows the key light. Negative reinforcement on an avoidance schedule could be substituted for reinforcement with food to determine if the results of the sequence generalization test depend upon the reinforcer used to maintain responding.

These results may also have implications for our understanding of the role of various stimuli in controlling behavior in schedules of reinforcement. In the typical procedure with a pigeon, the three stimulus elements of a schedule of reinforcement are—food, the stimulus on the key, and pecking. In analyzing the temporal control produced by schedules of reinforcement, Staddon (1974) made two assumptions: (1) food overshadows other stimuli such as the key light, and (2) food is retained longer than a neutral stimulus, such as a key light. Experiments 1 and 2 confirmed Staddon's first assumption, while Experiment 3 demonstrated that food retained its trace stimulus control function over longer delays than a stimulus on the key. The strategy of separating the complex events of a schedule of reinforcement into elements is a useful tool for determining which elements of the stimulus control the pattern of responding.

The associative value of a stimulus emerged as an important determinant of retention in Experiments 4 and 5. The procedure employed to manipulate the associative value in Experiment 4 was immediate pairing of the key light with food in the first component, while the procedure in Experiment 5 was to vary the percentage of trials in which a single element in the first component was followed by the second component, which ultimately terminated with food. The results suggest that the higher the associative value of a stimulus, the more effectively the stimulus maintains responding across the retention interval. These data are also consistent with Nevin's (1974) view that the greater the response strength associated with a stimulus, the more resistant trace stimulus control is to disruption by a retention interval.

The results of Experiment 4 demonstrated that a stimulus associated with food was more memorable than a stimulus that was not associated with food, even on trials when food was not presented in conjunction with the former. In fact, Figure 12–5 shows that the CS alone was just as effective in controlling responding on the retention test as was the CS–food compound. This equivalence between the CS alone and the CS–food compound is not surprising when the experimental procedure is recalled. Experiment 3 was designed so that food was a redundant element, since the stimulus paired with food on 75 percent of the trials was presented alone on 25 percent of the trials. This feature was incorporated to reduce the generalization decrement during the retention test. The CS alone and the CS–food compound maintained the same rates of responding during discrimination training, and this lack of difference was maintained during generalization testing.

In Experiments 1 and 2, pairing a key light with food produced overshadowing by the key light; yet in Experiment 4, pairing a key light with food improved retention. These results are not paradoxical when the difference in procedures between these experiments is considered. In Experiments 1 and 2, the key light was the redundant element, since the more salient element, food, always accompanied the key light. On the other hand, in Experiment 4, the redundant element was food, since the key light paired with food itself predicted food when presented alone on 25 percent of the trials.

The finding in Experiment 4 that a stimulus paired with food was retained almost as well as the CS–food compound is relevant to Konorski's theory of classical conditioning, which has been described by several authors in a book edited by Dickinson and Boakes (1979). According to Konorski, excitatory conditioning involves the formation of an association between an internal representation of the CS and an internal representation of the US. Therefore, the presentation of the CS not only retrieves a representation of the CS, but also retrieves a representation of the US. The finding that the CS alone was as effective as the CS–food compound is consistent with Konorski's theory that the key light was retrieving a representation of food.

The results of these experiments are also relevant to theories of animal memory and cognitive processes in animal behavior. These theories can be divided into active and passive theories depending upon the type of control assumed after the termination of the sample stimulus. The trace decay theory of Roberts and Grant (1976) cannot handle the data obtained in Experiment 4. In trace decay theory, retention is determined by the strength of a passive memory trace dependent upon the physical properties of the sample stimulus. Subsequent behavior is based upon the relative strengths of the memory traces. In Experiment 4, the two key light colors had similar physical properties, yet retention was superior for the key light color that was paired with food.

Honig's (1978) instruction hypothesis — a theory applicable to all the data presented in this chapter — is that the discriminative stimulus in the first component establishes an "instruction" that determines whether the pigeon will or will not peck the white choice key during the second component. It is only necessary for the pigeon to remember the instruction to peck or not to peck during the white response period, and it is not necessary for the pigeon to remember the discriminative stimulus. The overshadowing experiments demonstrate that food was a more effective instruction than the key light for pecking during the response period in Experiment 1 and for withholding pecking during Experiment 2. Similarly, in Experiment 4, a stimulus paired with food was more effective in controlling pecking during the white response period than was a stimulus not paired with food.

An unconditional procedure was employed in all of the experiments, so that each discriminative stimulus was associated exclusively with either reinforcement or nonreinforcement. In a conditional discrimination such as the matching-to-sample procedure, reinforcement is dependent upon a relationship between two stimuli, so that the discriminative stimulus by itself is insufficient for predicting reinforcement. As Honig (1978) points out, the instructional hypothesis applies only to unconditional discriminations and is not applicable to conditional discriminations. The instructional hypothesis could be eliminated as an explanation for the data obtained in Experiment 4 by employing a conditional discrimination. The procedure in Experiment 4 could be redesigned as follows: Responding is reinforced during the white response period when a CS–food sample is followed by a vertical line on the white key during the response period; and responding is extinguished during the response period when a CS–food sample is followed by a horizontal line on the white key during the response period. With this refined procedure food does not provide a unique instruction for any response. By extending the unconditional procedure employed here to the conditional case, it should be possible to assess the generality of the finding that the associative value of a stimulus is a determinant of retention.

SUMMARY AND CONCLUSIONS

Five experiments were reported using a paradigm of trace stimulus control in which the discriminative stimulus was presented in the first component and responding was measured in the second component. Experiments 1 and 2 demonstrated that food overshadows a colored light on the key independently of whether the sequence is a discriminative stimulus for reinforcement or nonreinforcement. Experiment 3 compared retention functions for food and a key light as discriminative stimuli for pecking and demonstrated that key pecking during the response period declined more slowly when the discriminative stimulus was food than when the discriminative stimulus was a colored key light. Experiment 4 demonstrated better retention for a discriminative stimulus—a colored key light—paired with food than for a discriminative stimulus not paired with food. Experiment 5 demonstrated that retention decreased as a function of the probability that a discriminative stimulus in the first component was followed by food in the second component. Experiments 4 and 5 demonstrated that the associative value of a discriminative stimulus was an important determinant of retention. The advantage of the trace stimulus control procedure for the experimental analysis of behavior is that it provides a bridge for unifying research on schedules of reinforcement with research on memory and cognitive processes.

REFERENCES

Dickinson, A., and R.A. Boakes. 1979. *Mechanisms of Learning and Motivation*. Hillsdale, New Jersey: Lawrence Erlbaum Associates.

Foree, D.D., and V.M. LoLordo. 1975. Stimulus–reinforcer interactions in the pigeon: The role of electric shock and the avoidance contingency. *Journal of Experimental Psychology: Animal Behavior Processes 1*: 39–46.

Hall, G.; N.S. MacKintosh; G. Goodall; and M. Martello. 1977. Loss of control by a less valid or by a less salient stimulus compounded with a better predictor of reinforcement. *Learning and Motivation 8*: 145–158.

Honig, W.K. 1978. Studies of working memory in the pigeon. In S.H. Hulse, H. Fowler, and W.K. Honig, eds., *Cognitive Processes in Animal Behavior*. Hillsdale, New Jersey: Lawrence Erlbaum Associates.

Howard, R.C. 1979. Effects of stimulus relevance on short-term memory in the pigeon. Doctoral dissertation, Michigan State University.

Hulse, S.H.; H. Fowler; and W.K. Honig. 1978. *Cognitive Processes in Animal Behavior*. Hillsdale, New Jersey: Lawrence Erlbaum Associates.

Jacobs, W.J., and V.M. LoLordo. 1977. The sensory basis of avoidance responding in the rat. *Learning and Motivation 8*: 448–466.

Maki, W.S.; J.C. Moe; and C.M. Bierley. 1977. Short-term memory for stimuli, responses, and reinforcers. *Journal of Experimental Psychology: Animal Behavior Processes 3*: 156–177.

MacKintosh, N.J. 1974. *The Psychology of Animal Learning*. London: Academic Press.

Nevin, J.A. 1974. Response strength in multiple schedules. *Journal of the Experimental Analysis of Behavior 21*: 389–408.

Pavlov, I.P. 1927. *Conditioned Reflexes*, T.V. Anrep, translator. London: Oxford University Press.

Reynolds, G.S., and A.C. Catania. 1962. Temporal discrimination in pigeons. *Science 135*: 314–315.

Rilling, M.E. 1967. Number of responses as a stimulus in fixed-interval and fixed-ratio schedules. *Journal of Comparative and Physiological Psychology 63*: 60–65.

_____. 1968. Effects of timeout on a discrimination between fixed-ratio schedules. *Journal of the Experimental Analysis of Behavior 11*: 129–132.

_____. 1977. Stimulus control and inhibitory processes. In W.K. Honig and J.E.R. Staddon, eds., *A Handbook of Operant Conditioning*. Englewood Cliffs, New Jersey: Prentice–Hall.

Rilling, M.E., and C.G. McDiarmid. 1965. Signal detection in fixed-ratio schedules. *Science 148*: 526–527.

Rilling, M. E.; R. C. Howard; and C. Johnson. 1980. Overshadowing by food of stimulus control by a keylight in a two-element compound preceding S+ or S- during discrimination learning. *Animal Learning and Behavior 8*: 601–608.

Roberts, W. A., and D. S. Grant. 1976. Studies of short-term memory in the pigeon using the delayed matching-to-sample procedure. In D. L. Medin, W. A. Roberts, and R. T. Davis, eds., *Processes of Animal Memory*. Hillsdale, New Jersey: Lawrence Erlbaum Associates.

Shimp, C. P. 1978. Memory, temporal discrimination, and learned structure in behavior. In G. H. Bower, ed., *The Psychology of Learning and Motivation*. New York: Academic Press.

Spear, N. E. 1978. *The Processing of Memories: Forgetting and Retention*. Hillsdale, New Jersey: Lawrence Erlbaum Associates.

Staddon, J. E. R. 1974. Temporal control, attention, and memory. *Psychological Review 81*: 375–391.

Stubbs, D. A.; S. J. Vautin; H. M. Reid; and D. L. Delehanty. 1978. Discriminative functions of schedule stimuli and memory: A combination of schedule and choice procedures. *Journal of the Experimental Analysis of Behavior 29*: 167–180.

Vom Saal, W., and H. M. Jenkins. 1970. Blocking the development of stimulus control. *Learning and Motivation 1*: 52–64.

Wagner, A. R. 1978. Expectancies and the priming of STM. In S. H. Hulse, H. Fowler, and W. K. Honig, eds., *Cognitive Processes in Animal Behavior*. Hillsdale, New Jersey: Lawrence Erlbaum Associates.

Weisman, R. G., and P. Dodd. 1979. The study of associations: Methodology and basic phenomena. In A. Dickinson and R. A. Boakes, eds., *Mechanisms of Learning and Motivation*. Hillsdale, New Jersey: Lawrence Erlbaum Associates.

13 BEHAVIORAL DYNAMICS OF THE PSYCHOMETRIC FUNCTION

Michael Terman

Psychophysical procedures restrict the observer's reports to varying extents. One extreme is the binary choice situation, in which the observer may say only "yes" or "no" upon presentation of a stimulus; another is the introspective approach, in which the domain of acceptable responses is free to vary widely. The more restrictive situations tend to yield data sets more amenable to experimental analysis (cf., Graham and Ratoosh, 1962). Yet regardless of procedure, psychophysicists have traditionally taken verbal reports to index sensations, and the relation of the observer's behavior to its consequences has only recently received attention paralleling that given the antecedents (cf., Green and Swets, 1966). Early research paradigms focused on specifying the stimulus of lowest intensity that could be detected ("absolute threshold") and the smallest stimulus change constituting a "just noticeable difference." Instructions to the observer were elaborate, implicating from a behaviorist's viewpoint a complex reinforcement history tapped by the experimenter but not under his or her explicit control. Feedback about the accuracy of the observer's judgments was not a feature of early psychophysical experimenta-

This research was supported by DHHS grants MH27442 and RR07143 and by NASA grant 22-011-074. I thank J. Terman for her collaboration and our students whose experiments are discussed—M. Green (louder and softer signals), G.D. Ruben (sequential dependencies), and S.R. Menich (circadian oscillations). P. Brandon's, J.A. Nevin's, and B. Scharf's comments are deeply appreciated.

tion: the observer reporting, "Yes, I heard it," was assumed to be under auditory stimulus control on that occasion.

In later work, "catch trials" were used as a check. Variability was assumed to be a basic characteristic of psychophysical judgments, so that positive and negative reports of the stimulus were averaged over many trials to achieve a reliable estimate of discriminability at each intensity. Even so, there were "good" and "poor" observers, and data from the latter would not make it into the literature. A poor observer might be under weak instructional control, suffer anomalous sensory function, or lack sufficient practice. For a good observer, when reports were averaged at each stimulus intensity, the percentage of "yes" reports proved generally to be a monotically increasing ogival function of intensity, whose slope, or mean, was considered to index the sensory threshold (Engen, 1971). The ubiquity of this curve shape across sensory modalities and procedural variations led to its characterization as the "psychometric function"—an objective, behavioral measure of the perception of minimal stimulus intensities or intensity differences. Animals and children, who could not follow verbal instructions, also might be expected to show psychometric functions, were it not for their (nonsensory) deficiency.

Some early tension between basic attitudes of psychophysicists and behaviorists delayed the development of a behavioral analysis of simple sensory phenomena. B.F. Skinner, for example, wrote to S.S. Stevens in 1935: "I do not agree ... that it is the sole business of psychology to test and measure the discriminatory capacities of organisms. That is your heritage from Wundt and Fechner. . . . What is happening in a discrimination, and what properties organisms actually do use in setting up classes . . . are far more important questions than what properties they could use or to what extent they could use them" (Skinner, 1979: 163). He did not doubt the data, but saw little behavioral interest in them. And for many years behavioral experimentation concentrated on the acquisition and maintenance of stimulus control, under carefully controlled conditions of reinforcement, using highly discriminable stimuli. Such a stimulus would not be "reported" by an organism without an explicit training history in which reinforcement was restricted to occasions when the stimulus was present. Effective training strategies were of great interest: The behavioral consequences were responsible for changing an arbitrary stimulus to a discriminative stimulus (S^D). Likewise, the lack of a consequent reinforcer changes stimuli into S^Δ—stimuli that do not occasion responding. Presumably, differential responding in a psychophysical test would be controlled by similar variables, but since the reinforcement history leading to effective instructional control was not in the experimenter's hands, the connection was not obvious.

Differential reinforcement procedures could be applied to make an "observer" out of a nonverbal organism, however. Hence, an animal psychophysics was born (cf., Stebbins, 1970), but it followed the development of reinforcement theory by nearly a generation. By establishing an S^D and gradually reducing its difference from S^Δ, an animal could produce a psychometric function with the same formal properties as that of a human observer. Comparative psychophysical investigations became possible, as well as investigations of physiological processes affecting psychophysical judgments. Behavioral methodology was conceived as a tool for extending psychophysical inquiry and not as a challenge to psychophysical theory. It was embraced by experimenters with primary interests in receptor function, perception, and decision theory. The psychometric function, for humans and other animals, was taken as a simple index of the discriminability of the experimenter-specified stimulus, because the probability of the reporting response changed as a monotonic function of stimulus intensity or intensity difference.

Concurrently, with the development of animal psychophysics, a new perspective on the variables controlling an observer's judgments arose from wartime studies of decisionmaking processes. This perspective was integrated into mainstream psychophysical thought under the rubric of "signal detection theory" (Green and Swets, 1966). The observer's report was elucidated as a joint function of stimulus intensity and a host of biasing variables, such as the probability of stimulus presentation and the payoffs associated with correct or incorrect responses (cf., Nevin, Chapter 1). In a paraphrase of the differential reinforcement principle, the observer's choice would be considered correct if he or she made a "hit" (signal judged present when actually present) or "correct rejection" (signal judged absent when actually absent). Complementary classes of errors were specified—"false alarms" (signal judged present when actually absent) and "misses" (signal judged absent when actually present).

The four detection outcomes covaried in orderly ways when positive and negative payoffs were manipulated for correct detections and errors, respectively. Given a stimulus presentation probability of

0.5 across trials, the percentage of correct detections proved to be an accurate index of stimulus discriminability only when biasing variables such as relative payoff were set so the two classes of error, false alarms and misses, were equally likely. If such variables favored yes over no reports regardless of the stimulus presented (as, for example, when payoff for a correct rejection was small in comparison to that for a hit), the percentage of correct detections would be depressed, yielding a spuriously low index of stimulus discriminability. By applying simple mathematical transforms suggested by signal detection theory, however, bias-free indexes of discriminability were derived that remained constant even when payoffs varied widely. The analysis suggested that some early psychophysical data may have confounded bias with discriminability in their treatment of the observer's reports. With "payoff" defined as "reinforcement," it became clear that behavioral considerations were integral to the interpretation of psychophysical data. But the traditional concept of a unitary variable remains. It is defined as "discriminability" and inferred from the psychometric function—now corrected for bias. For a modern approach to psychophysics that retains discriminability as a unitary variable, see McCarthy and Davison (Chapter 16).

The experiments to be discussed will examine aspects of the psychometric function that vary even when the stimuli and the rules for reinforcement are held constant. In the first case, discriminability is inferred from the latency of detection responses, suggesting that even when a report is incorrect, there is evidence for stimulus control. In the second, the psychometric function is shown to vary depending on the outcome of the previous trial in the testing sequence. In the third, discriminability oscillates on a circadian (near 24-hour) time base, when the observer is allowed to live without interruption in the testing environment. Taken together, the three experiments question the notion of a unitary concept of discriminability.

GENERAL METHODOLOGY

The experiments combine behavioral and physiological techniques to ask psychophysical questions, using the rat as an observer. Each reporting response has a well-defined outcome—a brief burst of reinforcing electrical brain stimulation for correct detections and a brief time out for errors. Before testing is begun, the animal receives a bipolar electrode implant in the posterior hypothalamic region, under surgical anesthesia. An electrode cap adheres to the skull surface and is attached to a flexible wire from an overhead commutator connected to a constant current, sine wave stimulator. The current amplitude is adjusted individually for each animal so that 0.5-second stimulations, pulsed by the programming apparatus, effectively reinforce the desired detection behavior. The stimulation does not interfere with the animal's weight regulation or health. Furthermore, unlike conventional food reinforcement, it does not lead to rapid satiation, so that it can be used effectively in thousands of detection trials within a single session. For a reliable and precise determination of the psychometric functions, the analyses require the accrual of large samples.

A self-paced procedure is used to initiate each detection trial. When the animal makes a set-up response, the stimulus is presented at a given probability across trials. Within a few seconds thereafter, the animal makes a detection response, considered as a "yes" or a "no" report. Reinforcement is delivered immediately for hits and correct rejections. After reinforcement or time out, the animal is free to initiate the next trial. Two procedures are used to measure the detection reports—(1) go/no-go (key or bar press = yes; no key or bar press = no); and (2) two choice (left bar press = yes; right bar press = no). Either procedure can successfully produce a psychometric function. Because the two-choice procedure has an explicit no-report of discernible duration, at least two benefits result. It formally equates the symmetrical response topographies of yes and no responses, as well as the temporal relationship between the reports and their consequences (reinforcement or time out). Such symmetries may serve to reduce the likelihood of developing biases toward one type of report at the expense of the other by eliminating hidden reinforcement contingencies. Lack of symmetry may in the extreme undermine the desired orderly relationship between stimulus intensity, or intensity difference, and response accuracy. Yet even with symmetrical response requirements and a stimulus presentation probability of 0.5, biases can develop (cf., Terman, 1970).

The go/no-go procedure directs the one explicit reporting response (yes) to a single location in the test chamber, which simplifies the analysis of response latencies. However, in such a case there may be a tendency to develop a no-bias, because the animal can receive the reinforcer for correct rejections simply by sitting still and not attending to the stimulus. Unbiased responding under go/no-go procedures relies upon a training history in which the yes report is established before correct rejections are reinforced (Green, Terman, and Terman, 1979). Formally, both two-choice and go/no-go procedures are variants of the yes–no paradigm of human psychophysics (Green and Swets, 1966), in that each trial presents a single stimulus value and the animal reports the presence or absence of the stimulus designated as the signal.

The psychometric function can be expressed in terms of a variety of discriminability indexes. One such index computes the percentage of correct reports at each stimulus intensity, or intensity difference, from the relative frequency of correct detections to total trials. This measure, however, is vulnerable to bias shifts: To the extent that the observer emits one type of report (yes or no) in preference to the other, without regard to stimulus value, the percentage of correct responses is depressed. When there is no such bias, the percentage of correct responses corresponds to the value of d'. This second index, d'—the sensitivity measure of signal detection theory—assumes normal distributions of sensory effect of equal variability for signal and noise (Green and Swets, 1966; see also Nevin, Chapter 1). Sensory effect is an intervening variable that reflects the perceived momentary value of the signal. The d' metric is unperturbed by variations in response bias and thus more fairly indexes discriminability, given that the assumptions of the theory are satisfied. This can be achieved by varying response bias experimentally (as by manipulations of the payoff matrix or stimulus probability), but such a validation of d' is practical only for experiments that concentrate on response bias analyses (e.g., Terman and Terman, 1972).

A third approach to quantifying the psychometric function is the use of nonparametric estimators of d', which compensate for variations in bias without assuming an unverified model of sensory effect in the calculations. One such measure, used in the present experiments, is the sensitivity index (SI) of Frey and Colliver (1973). Figure 13–1 illustrates the calculation strategy. The smooth curves, representing results that maintain a constant SI but vary in bias, are similar to the receiver operating characteristics of d', but the analytic transformations are based solely on the geometry of the unit square, with no assumptions about the underlying decision process. The SI scale is conveniently linear: Chance performance yields an SI of zero, and perfect discrimination yields an SI of 1.0. The psychometric

Figure 13−1. The unit square of signal detection theory, which correlates the relative frequency of hits (H) and false alarms (FA). Computation of the nonparametric sensitivity index is illustrated for a datum at SI = 0.67. Straight lines through the locus at (0.30, 0.93) originate from (0.0, 0.0) and (1.0, 1.0). The apex of the triangle formed on the base of the minor diagonal is bisected by a line extrapolated to the base. The linear distance from the major diagonal $(SI = 0)$ to the bisection point on the minor diagonal determines SI. The computation formula is:

$$SI = \frac{p(H) - p(FA)}{2[p(H) + p(FA)] - [p(H) - p(FA)]^2}$$

The data are for a human observer and were obtained in a variation of the experiment on sequential dependencies for trials following correct detections (●) and errors (o).

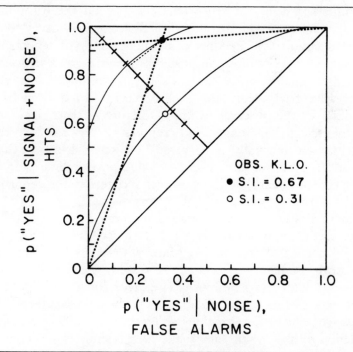

function (e.g., Figures 13-4 and 13-5) maps the stimulus values or differences into this range of SI values.

REPORT LATENCIES AND STIMULUS DISCRIMINABILITY

Yes-no data are often construed to reflect a simple binary decision process, with the observer either correct or incorrect on a given trial. Such an analysis treats a yes error, or false alarm, as a response formally equivalent to a correct yes, or hit; in both cases the signal is judged present. Indeed, signal detection theory (Green and Swets, 1966) schematizes the situation by drawing overlapping distributions of sensory effect for signal and noise, indicating that a given sensory effect obtained on one trial can come from either distribution, with differing probability, and that the observer's judgment is based on the momentary value of sensory effect, not on the stimulus itself, which can be expected to show much less variability under well-controlled conditions. Feedback on the accuracy of reports enables the observer to determine the probability that a given sensory effect arises from signal or noise sources and thus to make "best guesses" on successive trials. Until feedback is received on a given trial, it is impossible for the observer to know for sure whether signal or noise was presented. In this sense, all yes reports, correct and incorrect, are "quantitatively mutually replaceable" (Skinner, 1969) in that they are controlled by the same event—a value on the dimension of sensory effect that exceeds the observer's criterion for reporting the signal.

Studies of reaction time, a graded response measure, suggest that the interpretation of yes-no data as binary decisions obscures sources of stimulus control that differentiate yes reports made to signal or noise. Both human and animal data show that yes errors—false alarms—are made more hesitantly (i.e., with longer latency) than are correct yesses—hits. If so, at some level the observer must "know" or guess when he or she is making an error. Indeed, humans use lower confidence ratings when they make long latency errors (Emmerich, Gray, Watson, and Tanis, 1972), but their confidence is evidently not so low as to lead them to make the alternate, correct report. A problem with most such studies has been that the signal to be reported has been of greater physical intensity than its alternatives, and it is known that intensity per se can control the speed of responding even without differential reinforcement for correct and incorrect reports (e.g., Moody, 1969).

We examined the generality of such reaction time data by defining the stimulus to be reported as either the louder or the softer of the two 3-kiloHertz (kHz) sine tones. A trial set-up response resulted in a 0.5-second tone presentation, after which the rat had up to 4 seconds to report the presence of a signal. If the signal was not presented, the rat could make a correct rejection by withholding the reporting response for 4 seconds, at which time the same reinforcer was delivered as that which immediately followed hits. By varying the intensity difference between the tones designated as signal and noise through a 9-decibel range, psychometric functions were derived (Green, Terman, and Terman, 1979). With 100 versus 99 decibels (sound pressure level, SPL), discrimination performance was near chance level; with 100 versus 90 decibels, the performance typically exceeded 90 percent correct detections. The animal was first given the 100-decibel tone as signal; then, after reversal training, the softer tones (90, 93, 96, and 99 decibels in different sessions) were the signals. Over the two phases of the experiment, therefore, the yes report was appropriate for both louder and softer tones.

Latencies could be determined solely for either kind of yes report, correct and incorrect. No-reports, which are defined as the absence of a yes report within 4 seconds of trial initiation, could not be distributed into latency classes. Latencies were measured in 0.1-second class intervals, beginning with stimulus presentation and ending with the reporting response. The resulting distributions are displayed in cumulative format in Figure 13–2. Under all conditions, these measures increased as an ogival function of time. However, the median latency and the slope varied. Latencies were rarely less than 1 second long or greater than 2 seconds. False alarm distributions (labeled "noise") show latencies consistently exceeding those of hits (labeled "signal"), with the magnitude of displacement of the distributions proportional to intensity difference. At 10-decibel difference, the median false alarm latency was approximately 150–200 milliseconds longer than that of a hit; at 1-decibel difference, the two classes of report latency were nearly drawn together. As the discrimination became more difficult, average latency increased. When the two

Figure 13-2. Cumulative latency distributions for hits and false alarms across loud and soft signal conditions. Curves were fitted by eye. (Reprinted by permission of the *Journal of the Experimental Analysis of Behavior.*)

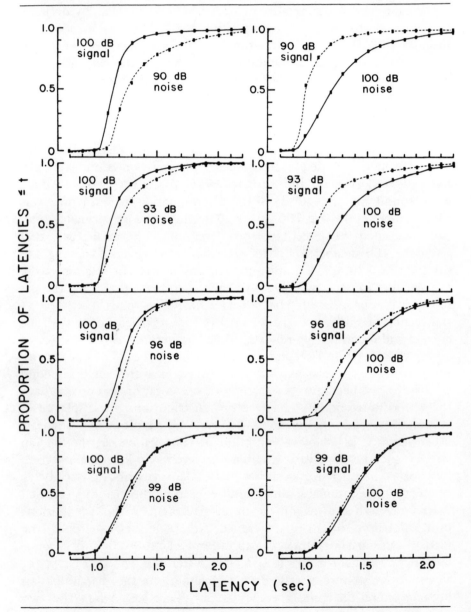

phases of testing are compared, it is clear that latencies were a function of intensity difference, not of the stimulus—louder or softer—designated as the signal.

Without any reference to the binary distribution of yes and no reports, there is evidence for discriminability between the tones based on the latency differentiation of hits and false alarms. The magnitude of the differentiation is approximately equivalent whether the signal is the louder or softer of the two tones, and the effect must be attributed to the differential reinforcement contingencies. Under a nondifferential reinforcement procedure, the distributions quickly converge. Therefore, correct and incorrect yes reports should not be considered to be quantitatively mutually replaceable. The observer must judge some variable other than momentary sensory effect in order to differentiate report latency. The controlling variable may be the distance measured along the dimension of sensory effect between momentary sensory effect and the observer's criterion for deciding between yes and no reports. Figure 13–3 surveys cases in which the observer exhibits varying criteria for signal and noise, along with estimates of "expected" sensory effects that fall on the yes side of criterion. Regardless of which tone—louder or softer—is designated as the signal, the expected sensory effects of noise fall closer to criterion than those of the signal. It has been suggested that report latency is an inverse function of the distance between momentary sensory effect and criterion (Gescheider et al., 1969). Thus, hit latencies would tend to be shorter than those of false alarms.

Direct manipulations of bias, which determine the position of the observer's criterion, would also be expected to affect report latencies (cf., Clopton, 1972): The more biased the observer, the further the criterion is displaced from the distributions of sensory effect and the shorter the resulting latencies will be. To the extent that the differentiation of hit and false alarm latencies produce evidence of discriminability, biasing factors—such as asymmetries in the payoff matrix—would interact. The simple distinction between discriminability and bias, developed in analyses of the binary distribution of yes and no reports, thus does not apply to analyses based on report latencies. Neither yes–no nor latency data should be characterized as "more sensitive" to stimulus differences, however. Although the false alarm latencies suggest that even some errors are under stimulus control, both yes–no and latency data are embedded in a

Figure 13–3. Theoretical normal distributions of sensory effect for signal (S) and noise (N), with means separated by one standard deviation unit. In the left-hand curves, signal intensity exceeds that of noise; in the right-hand curves, relative intensity is reversed. The position of the observer's criterion varies across the cases illustrated from an extreme yes bias to a moderate no bias. Shading is used to show the area of the curves to the yes side of the decision axis for two of the cases. For each criterion level, vertical arrows point to the expected magnitude of sensory effects leading to a yes report, given signal (E_S) or noise (E_N). These points were determined by halving the area of the curve to the yes side of the decision axis. In all cases, $E_N < E_S$, which relates to the proposition that report latency is an inverse function of the distance of sensory effect from criterion. Thus, hits tend to have latencies shorter than those of false alarms. As the yes bias becomes more extreme, the difference between E_S and E_N becomes proportionally smaller, thus accounting for reduced hit–false alarm latency differentiation. The relationship between E_S and E_N holds regardless of the relative intensity of signal and noise.

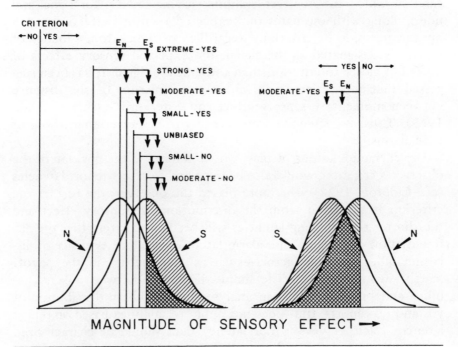

common sequence of test trials, and neither shows differentiation independently.

DETECTION FEEDBACK AND STIMULUS
DISCRIMINABILITY

Psychophysical reports are made in the context of a trial sequence. With signal probability set at 0.5, an unbiased observer will emit a series of detection responses that favors neither of the yes–no alternatives. Accuracy of reports will be proportional to stimulus intensity or intensity difference. Detection errors—false alarms and misses—will gain prominence for less discriminable stimuli, but even for highly discriminable stimuli, errors will not disappear entirely. Indeed, signal detection theory posits distributions of sensory effect for signal and noise that overlap indefinitely at the extremes and thus account for some legitimate confusability even among highly discriminable stimuli. Among the immediate antecedents of a detection response on a given trial, N, are (1) the outcome of trial $N-1$ and (2) the stimulus value on trial N. The following experiment suggests that both classes of antecedents control discriminative performance and that psychophysical reports are therefore not a simple function of the stimulus along the signal dimension under study.

The testing procedure is similar to the earlier experiment on report latency, with the rat trained to report the relative intensity of two 3-kHz sine tones presented randomly across successive trials. Upon initiating a trial and presenting the tone for 0.5 seconds, a 3-second report period follows in which the animal may either press the bar (yes) or withhold that response (no). False alarms and misses are followed by a time out of 0.5 seconds (equal to the duration of reinforcement), which is contiguous with a 5-second intertrial interval. A 100-decibel tone was the standard stimulus, and for each session an attenuated comparison tone was selected in mixed order. Data for trial N were sorted by computer into eight subsets, reflecting whether a hit, false alarm, correct rejection, or miss occurred on trial $N-1$ or $N-2$. In Figure 13-4, psychometric functions show the sensitivity on trial N for each subset. Figure 13-4A shows the contrast that results given a correct versus an incorrect report on the immediately preceding trial ($N-1$). Over intensity differences ranging

Figure 13-4. (A) Psychometric functions based on the data subsets for trials immediately preceded by each class of detection outcome. (B) Corresponding data preceded on trial $N-2$ by each class of detection outcome. (C) Cumulative latency distributions for hits and false alarms immediately preceded by correct detections and errors. Curves were fitted by eye. (D) Isobias functions based on the data subsets of trials immediately preceded by each class of detection outcome.

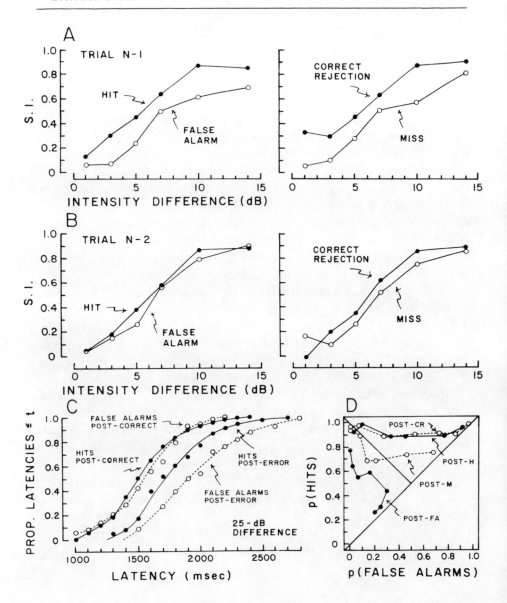

from 1 to 14 decibels, the performance showed an average decrement of 0.190 SI units (SD = 0.075), corresponding to a decrease of approximately 10 percent correct detections. The data subset for trial $N-2$ (Figure 13-4B) shows the psychometric functions nearly drawn together, given one trial of indeterminate outcome intervening between the anchor trial and the measured trial. In this case, the average decrement was only 0.074 SI units (SD = 0.055), corresponding to a decrease of approximately 3.7 percent correct detections. Thus, the influence of detection outcome over subsequent detection behavior reaches primarily to the immediately preceding trial.

As in the earlier experiment, distinct subclasses of yes reports were found in terms of latency. The cumulative latency distributions (Figure 13-4C) obtained across 4000 trials at 25-decibel difference show the differentiation of hit and false alarm latencies for trials immediately preceded by a correct detection or error. (Note that relatively few errors occurred at such a large stimulus difference.) All four distributions are characterized by smooth ogives, but their displacements along the abscissa reveal an underlying dynamic across trial types. Hit and false alarm latencies on postcorrect trials were nearly equal in their distribution, with medians close to 1500 milliseconds. Hit latencies on posterror trials showed an approximate 200 millisecond increase in median latency, to 1700 milliseconds. False alarm latencies on posterror trials showed an additional increment of 200 milliseconds above the corresponding hit latencies, to a median of approximately 1900 milliseconds. Therefore, hits and false alarms are quantitatively mutually replaceable response classes only on trials following reinforcement of a correct detection. False alarms can be considered "true" detection errors—that is, a simple function of signal value—only when couched in the immediately preceding history of an accurate detection. On trials following an error, both hits and false alarms show marked latency increments, and the latency differential between them is restricted to these occasions.

In light of the previous experiment on report latency, which found a latency differential for hits and false alarms pooled across the types of trial outcome, it might appear paradoxical to conclude that latency-based evidence for discriminability is actually restricted to trials that follow errors—that is, only when the observer's judgment has been disconfirmed. The solution to this problem is found in analysis of local fluctuations in the observer's bias. Figure 13-4D shows four isobias functions, extracted from the trial sequence on the basis of the outcome of trial $N-1$. On trials that immediately follow correct detections—hits or correct rejections—the isobias functions originate from a locus close to $(1.0, 0.0)$, reflecting nearly errorless performance at large stimulus intensity differences. These curves bow in slightly toward the minor diagonal as intensity difference is reduced to the 5-to-10-decibel range and then approach $(1.0, 1.0)$ at the smallest intensity differences. Such curves describe the performance of an observer with a strong yes bias for which the criterion is displaced on the dimension of sensory effect toward the left of both signal and noise distributions, as illustrated in Figure 13–3.

The isobias functions for trials that immediately follow errors— false alarms and misses—stand in sharp contrast to those that follow correct detections. On trials that follow false alarms, the animal shows a consistent, moderate no-bias. On trials that follow misses, the isobias function shows a small no-bias at intensity differences greater than 3 decibels and then crosses the minor diagonal, with a small yes bias at intensity differences of 1 and 3 decibels. Relative to the postcorrect functions, both posterror functions show less extreme biases, which tend toward no reports; the observer's criterion is thus closer on the dimension of sensory effect to the means of both signal and noise distributions. The criterion is seen to be in dynamic flux from trial to trial, with momentary values controlled by the outcome of trial $N-1$. Calculations of response bias indexes, or representations based upon data for all trials pooled across a test session, obscure such trends and therefore do not accurately represent the observer's decision process at any given moment.

According to the conceptual model of Gescheider et al. (1969), an observer's report latencies reflect measurement of the distance of momentary sensory effect from the criterion—the shorter the distance, the longer the latency. The present data suggest an elaboration of the model, with the observer construed to measure the distance between momentary sensory effect and momentary criterion. After emitting a correct detection, the observer's strong yes bias results in the shortest latencies obtained, with minimal hit–false alarm latency differentiation. In this case, the distances of momentary sensory effect from the criterion are proportionally more equal for signal and noise. In contrast, after emitting an error, the observer reduces bias, making a more "conservative" judgment. The distance of sensory effects from the criterion is shortened, and all latencies increase. The latency differentiation of hits and false alarms increases, since the difference in distance from criterion to signal and noise sensory effects is proportionally greater (see, e.g., the unbiased case in Figure 13-3). This analysis is congruent with the interpretation of long latency reports as showing lower confidence than short latency reports (cf., Emmerich et al., 1972). Confidence is understandably reduced on trials that follow errors.

If sequential dependencies underly the dynamics of the psychometric function, the posterror decrement in stimulus control and associated trends in latency should be seen across psychophysical experiments and should not be specific to the rat's judgments or the particular protocol for reinforcement.[a] To test for generality, we analyzed data for human observers under a similar paradigm. Using headphones, and seated at a response panel in an IAC sound-attenuating chamber, their task was to report the presence of a 300-Hz sine tone at 2 decibels SPL, which is only moderately discriminable against the background of noise in the audio system. A press on one telegraph key presented the tone on half of the trials, and a press on another served as the yes report. An instrument panel lamp flashed briefly after each correct detection, serving as positive feedback. In all other respects, the humans' and rats' tasks were identical. As shown in Figure 13-1, the results closely concurred. On trials following a correct detection, Observer K.L.O. showed an SI of 0.67 and a strong bias toward yes reports. On trials following an error, the SI declined to 0.31 (corresponding to a decrement of approximately 18 percent in correct detections), and the report latencies increased. Unlike the rat, however, the human observer showed differentially longer false alarm latencies on postcorrect as well as posterror trials, perhaps indicating greater precision in measuring distances of sensory effect from criterion while in the postcorrect, high bias state.

a. The human psychophysics literature contains several recent reports of sequential dependencies underlying choice patterns, some of which may relate to the posterror bias shifts and sensitivity decrements reported here. For absolute naming, Ward and Lockhead (1971) found the stimulus on trial $N-1$ correlated with the report on trial N even when the observer simply guessed a number and the only information was from feedback. When exteroceptive antecedent stimuli were available, the report on trial $N-1$ was also correlated with that on trial N. In an experiment on auditory intensity naming with feedback, Purks, Callahan, Braida, and Durlach (1980) showed sensitivity on trial N to be independent of the stimulus value on trial $N-1$, but there were sequential effects in response bias. Thus, they reasoned that feedback per se does not have the simple effect of improving accuracy by establishing the stimulus on trial $N-1$ as a standard from which to judge the stimulus on trial N.

CIRCADIAN OSCILLATION IN VISUAL LUMINANCE DETECTABILITY

Earlier reports (Rosenwasser, Raibert, Terman, and Terman, 1979; Terman and Raibert, 1974) showed that a rat living in a constant environment of dim illumination without day–night cues and trained to detect visual signals under a go/no-go procedure performed with accuracy levels that varied according to a circadian time cycle. Under such constant conditions, a wide variety of behavioral and physiological oscillations are known to exhibit "free-running" periodicity deviating from 24 hours in contrast to the precise 24-hour entrainment found under daily light–dark cycles. Such free-running periods increase in proportion to the intensity of ambient illumination in nocturnal species, and inverse proportionality is generally observed for diurnal species (Aschoff, 1960). For each circadian variable, a power spectral analysis can be applied to determine the peak phase of the oscillation, making it possible to estimate with precision the time of peak performance under control of the endogenous circadian "clock."

For the rat's visual detection behavior, we found that the circadian peak phase of accuracy precedes that of trial initiation rate by approximately 2 hours, suggesting that oscillating sensitivity to light is functionally distinguishable from other circadian variables. But given the go/no-go procedure and the unusual situation of continuous testing, large swings in report bias were sometimes found to covary with detection accuracy. Still, reliable oscillations in d' supported the conclusion that a signal of constant intensity is differentially discriminable as a function of circadian phase. The signal intensities we chose for long-term testing maintained performance in the midrange of report accuracy, so that the extremes of 50 or 100 percent correct detections were never reached.

In subsequent experimentation, we have given the animal signals throughout the detectability range and substituted a two-choice procedure that yields only small fluctuations in report bias uncorrelated with circadian phase. The animal lives in a chamber completely darkened except for the signals, with free access to food and water. Trials are initiated by breaking an infrared photobeam in an observation tunnel. On half of the trials, a monochromatic stimulus subtending a visual angle of approximately 3 degrees is flashed on a screen for

0.5 seconds. Two bars, symmetrically positioned on each side of the entrance to the tunnel, are available for making a yes or no report within 3 seconds of trial initiation. Given that a trial is initiated, the animal almost never misses the occasion to make a report. Signal intensity and wavelength are always held constant for more than two weeks of continuous testing, to provide steady-state performance samples that can be averaged across cycles. The averaging method requires that we determine the animal's free-running period by spectral analysis, thereby defining the length of a "subjective day" under the free-running condition. This value, divided by twenty-four, yields an estimate of one "circadian hour," which somewhat exceeds 1 hour of external clock time. The data are then pooled across corresponding circadian hours, and SI is calculated for successive 4-hour circadian time blocks within the cycle.

Figure 13–5A shows results for a 500-nanometer signal that was varied across a range of 6.6 log units relative intensity (with 0 log units set at 0.022 cd/m^2). The family of six curves was arranged on the common abscissa of circadian time by finding the value of α for each curve—the area exceeding the mean of the circadian oscillation—and anchoring the midpoint of α at 0 hours. The α midpoint serves as an "internal" phase reference for the free-running circadian variable in the absence of external timing cues, thereby allowing comparisons of phase interrelationships across samples of a given behavior or across concurrently measured classes of behavior. For example, circadian oscillations in trial initiation rate and food intake were found to phase lag that of luminance detectability by 1 to 3 hours. We have found similar phase relationships at a variety of test wavelengths.

Circadian oscillations in discriminability are apparent at all signal intensities except the highest, which supported nearly errorless performance across time (mean SI = 0.98). Thus, the behavioral oscillations were shown to depend upon stimulus luminance and not on some extraneous variable.[b] With increased attenuation from 0 log

---

b. Pursuing the logic of the detection feedback experiment discussed above, we examined samples of the visual discrimination data for bias shifts and sensitivity decrements on trials following errors at both circadian peak and trough phases. Neither bias nor sensitivity showed reliable sequential dependencies of this sort, perhaps as a result of the symmetry of choice response topographies or the different sensory modality. The circadian oscillation in discriminability thus cannot be attributed to a differential posterror decrement as a function of time of day.

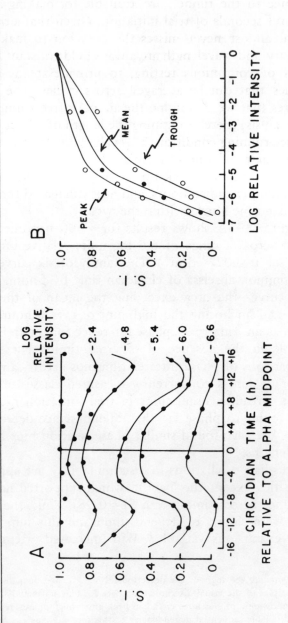

Figure 13–5. (A) *SI* cycles averaged across fifteen successive testing days in 4-hour blocks of circadian time. Independent samples obtained at each luminance level were phase anchored to the midpoint of α (see text). Curves were fitted by eye. (B) Psychometric functions derived from (A) for the circadian peak and trough phases, and the mean. Curves were fitted by eye.

units, the curves fall along the SI axis in monotonically decreasing order. The peak-to-trough amplitude of the circadian function is greatest in the midrange of intensities (at −5.4 log units), where SI is freest to vary in either direction. By comparison, the curves at −2.4 log units (with a mean SI corresponding to 93 percent correct detections) and at −6.6 log units (52.7 percent correct detections) show damping toward the extremes of the SI range. The five oscillating functions that extend from −2.4 to −6.6 log units line up coherently in phase: The circadian trough in discriminability occurs approximately 10 hours earlier than the α midpoint, and the peak occurs approximately 2 hours earlier. The wave form is thus asymmetrical across the circadian day, with a rise from trough to peak over 8 hours preceding the α midpoint and a more gradual fall over the next 16 hours. The oscillating functions show some overlap on the SI scale, indicating that the discriminability of a dimmer stimulus may exceed that of a brighter stimulus if samples are chosen from contrasting circadian phases.

In Figure 13–5B, three distinct psychometric functions are shown, based on the oscillating curves in Figure 13–5A. The function representing peak discriminability was derived by plotting the maximum of each oscillation curve across signal intensity. The function for the lowest circadian phase was derived independently from the minima. The function that represents mean SI over circadian time falls between these extremes. All three functions show the ogival form typical of such psychophysical methods (Engen, 1971) and span the range from near-chance performance, or minimal discriminability, to errorless performance. The slopes of the functions are nearly parallel within the range of rapid change (−4.8 to −6.6 log units), and as ogives, they converge on a common upper limit of 1 SI unit. The functions are differentiated at their origins, with a shift of approximately 1 log unit relative intensity between circadian peak and trough. Thus, it can be inferred that the rat's visual sensitivity undergoes a 1-log-unit shift every day and that psychometric functions based on brief test sessions, without reference to the observer's circadian phase, do not accurately represent the temporal dynamics of detection performance.

If the objective of an experiment is to specify the psychometric function that shows greatest sensitivity to a stimulus dimension, pushing the limits of the observer's behavioral resolving power, our data suggest that testing should be timed to coincide with the internally defined circadian peak phase. Under standard laboratory conditions, most animal observers are entrained to regular 24-hour light–dark cycles in the colony room and are transported to the operant chamber for discrete testing sessions. The situation is a complex one, since feeding schedules in the colony room or test chamber, and the mere act of daily physical transport and initiation of the session, may interact with the circadian pattern under light–dark entrainment (cf., Terman, forthcoming). Furthermore, individual animals show variation in peak circadian phase even with respect to a standard light–dark cycle, so there is no simple temporal anchoring reference point for the performance sample other than the individual's own oscillation phase. Under constant light, phase relationships across individuals will vary widely across the circadian day, even if they share common colony quarters. Under a 24-hour light–dark cycle, performance peaks tend to fall in the latter half of the 12-hour dark segment for the nocturnal rat, although some animals may peak even in the early hours of light (cf., Terman and Terman, 1975). If testing is performed during the light segment, as may often suit an experimenter's schedule, we may expect to find nonoptimal performance in both psychophysical and standard operant experiments. Relevant baseline measurements must still be made for various species. Diurnal species, such as the pigeon and monkey, are likely to show peak psychophysical performances phase displaced by approximately 180 degrees from the rat's.

CONCLUSIONS

Even after extensive training histories, steady-state detection performance shows dynamic fluctuation, both on the long-term circadian time base and within the short-term sequence of trial classes. Psychometric functions that pool data across these dimensions may be confounded by factors of oscillating sensitivity and the local pattern of detection feedback, thereby obscuring the relationship between the experimenter's stimulus dimension and the observer's reports. In this respect there is no unitary quantity, "discriminability," that fully characterizes the effect of a signal on the observing system. Stimulus control and response bias shift dynamically, and the various factors that influence the performance can be assessed by analyzing the psychometric function and its associated report latencies along each potential dimension of control.

REFERENCES

Aschoff, J. 1960. Exogenous and endogenous components in circadian rhythms. *Cold Spring Harbor Symposia in Quantitative Biology 25*: 11–27.

Clopton, B. 1972. Detection of increments in noise intensity by monkeys. *Journal of the Experimental Analysis of Behavior 17*: 437–481.

Emmerich, D.; J. Gray; C. Watson; and D. Tanis. 1972. Response latency, confidence and ROCs in auditory signal detection. *Perception and Psychophysics 11*: 65–72.

Engen, T. 1971. Psychophysics. I. Discrimination and Detection. In J.W. Kling and L.A. Riggs, eds., *Woodworth and Schlosberg's Experimental Psychology*, 3rd ed., pp. 11–46. New York: Holt, Rinehart and Winston.

Frey, P.W., and J.A. Colliver. 1973. Sensitivity and responsivity measures for discrimination learning. *Learning and Motivation 4*: 327–342.

Gescheider, G.; J. Wright; J. Weber; B. Kirchner; and E. Milligan. 1969. Reaction time as a function of occurrence of vibrotactile signals. *Perception and Psychophysics 5*: 18–20.

Graham, C.H., and P. Ratoosh. 1962. Notes on some interrelations of sensory psychology, perception, and behavior. In S. Koch, ed., *Psychology: A Study of a Science*, vol. 4, pp. 483–514. New York: McGraw-Hill.

Green, D.M., and J.A. Swets. 1966. *Signal Detection and Psychophysics*. New York: Wiley.

Green, M.; M. Terman; and J.S. Terman. 1979. Comparison of yes–no and latency measures of auditory intensity discrimination. *Journal of the Experimental Analysis of Behavior 32*: 363–372.

Moody, D. 1969. Equal brightness function for suprathreshold stimuli in the pigmented rat: A behavioral determination. *Vision Research 9*: 1381–1389.

Purks, S.R.; D.J. Callahan; L.D. Braida; and N.I. Durlach. 1980. Intensity perception. X. Effect of preceding stimulus on identification performance. *Journal of the Acoustical Society of America 67*: 634–637.

Rosenwasser, A.M.; M. Raibert; J.S. Terman; and M. Terman. 1979. Circadian rhythm of luminance detectability in the rat. *Physiology and Behavior 23*: 17–21.

Skinner, B.F. 1969. *Contingencies of Reinforcement: A Theoretical Analysis*. New York: Appleton–Century–Crofts.

_____. 1979. Letter to S.S. Stevens, 1935. Quoted in B.F. Skinner, *The Shaping of a Behaviorist*. New York: Knopf.

Stebbins, W.C., ed. 1970. *Animal Psychophysics: The Design and Conduct of Sensory Experiments*. New York: Appleton–Century–Crofts.

Terman, M. 1970. Discrimination of auditory intensities by rats. *Journal of the Experimental Analysis of Behavior 13*: 145–160.

344   EFFECTS OF RESPONDING AND REINFORCEMENT

_____ . Forthcoming. Behavioral analysis and circadian rhythms. In M.D. Zeiler, and P. Harzem, eds., *Biological Factors in Learning.* Chichester, England and New York: Wiley.

Terman, M., and M. Raibert. 1974. Circadian rhythm of luminance detectability in the rat: Operant–psychophysical analysis. Paper presented at meeting of the Psychonomic Society, Boston.

Terman, M., and J.S. Terman. 1972. Concurrent variation of response bias and sensitivity in an operant–psychophysical test. *Perception and Psychophysics 11:* 428–432.

_____ . 1975. Control of the rat's circadian self-stimulation rhythm by light–dark cycles. *Physiology and Behavior 14:* 781–789.

Ward, L.M., and G.R. Lockhead. 1971. Response system processes in absolute judgment. *Perception and Psychophysics 9:* 73–78.

14 THE ROLE OF DIFFERENTIAL RESPONDING IN MATCHING-TO-SAMPLE AND DELAYED MATCHING PERFORMANCE

*Leila R. Cohen, John Brady,
and Michael Lowry*

In a conditional discrimination, the stimulus associated with responses that are reinforced varies with some other aspect of the environment. One example that has been studied extensively is the matching-to-sample procedure, in which the correct choice from a set of comparison stimuli is determined by a sample stimulus. A response to the sample produces the comparison stimuli, from which the subject must choose one. In an identity task, the correct choice is the comparison that is most like the sample. In a nonidentity task, the relation between the sample and the correct comparison is arbitrary.

In all of the research from our laboratory, the samples and comparisons were either hues (orange and green) or line gratings (vertical and horizontal). For the identity tasks, both the samples and the comparisons were taken from the same stimulus dimension (hue-hue or line-line identity). For the nonidentity tasks, hue samples were arbitrarily paired with line comparisons (hue-line) or vice versa (line-hue). The subjects were White Carneaux pigeons.

We have reported two experiments that examined the effects of pretraining and maintenance of differential sample responses on the acquisition of the two identity and two nonidentity tasks just described (Cohen, Looney, Brady, and Aucella, 1976). In those studies,

This research was supported by NICHHD Grants HD 05124, HD 04147, and HD 07075.

we reported that differential sample schedule requirements (a differential reinforcement of low rate of 3 seconds [DRL 3 seconds] in the presence of one sample and a fixed ratio 16 [FR 16] in the presense of the other) produced rapid rates of acquisition that did not differ across tasks. Nondifferential sample requirements of either FR 16, DRL 3 seconds, or FR 1 in the presence of both samples were used with other naive pigeons to assess the effects of increased sample durations, exposure to the samples during pretraining with sample schedule requirements, and either schedule requirement per se. The rates of acquisition of all birds with differential sample schedule requirements were facilitated relative to all three of these control conditions.

While the rapid rate of acquisition was the same for all four tasks for the birds with differential sample schedule requirements, this was not the case when only a single peck (FR 1) was required in the presence of each sample. In fact, the rates were quite disparate for the four tasks. The order of difficulty for this nondifferential (FR 1) condition replicated that reported by Carter and Eckerman (1975)— hue-hue, hue-line, line-hue, and line-line, from least to most difficult. Those authors concluded that rates of acquisition of matching-to-sample tasks by pigeons can be accounted for by the rate at which the birds learn to discriminate between sample stimuli (successive discrimination) and between comparison stimuli (simultaneous discrimination). For example, since birds learn more slowly to discriminate between lines than between hues, the line-line task is acquired more slowly than the hue-hue task. The birds in our studies (Cohen et al., 1976) were pretrained with differential schedule requirements to discriminate between the two stimuli to be used as samples prior to the matching-to-sample training. If Carter and Eckerman's (1975) account is correct, then our birds acquired the four matching tasks at the same rate, because they could discriminate between the samples when they began matching training, and this discrimination was maintained with the continuation of the differential sample schedule requirements used in matching.

This chapter considers another possible account of these data— that choice performance in a matching-to-sample task with differential sample response requirements is controlled by the sample-specific performances generated by these requirements. For example, the choice of the orange comparison on an identity task may be controlled by the behavior performed in the presence of the orange sample (as specified by a DRL 3-second contingency), rather than by the orange sample directly. Likewise, the choice of the green comparison on this same task may be controlled by the behavior performed in the presence of the green sample (as specified by an FR 16 requirement), rather than by the green sample directly. Choice behavior on the line-hue task would be under the same control—namely, choose orange following DRL 3 second and green following FR 16. If this is the case, the four tasks (hue-hue, hue-line, line-hue, and line-line) are reduced to two (sample-specific behaviors—hue; sample-specific behaviors—line). These two conditional discriminations are then acquired at the same rates, since the simultaneous discrimination between comparisons is similar for hues and lines (Carter and Eckerman, 1975).

Other authors have shown that different values of fixed ratio schedules and different numbers of responses (Hobson, 1975; Pliskoff and Goldiamond, 1966; Rilling 1967, 1968; Rilling and McDiarmid, 1965) as well as differential reinforcement contingencies (Lattal, 1975) can control pigeons' choice behavior. The present studies extend the investigation of the control of pigeons' choice behavior to a situation in which either a visual stimulus or a behavioral stimulus could be prepotent. These studies also contribute to the analysis of discriminative effects of schedule-controlled performances, the central theme of this volume.

GENERAL METHOD

Our data come from a variety of experiments that share many methodological characteristics. We will first describe these and then go into the details of each of the four experiments.

Subjects

Experimentally naive adult White Carneaux hens obtained from Palmetto Pigeon Plant were maintained at 80 percent of their free-feeding weights throughout the experiments. They were housed in individual home cages with health grit and water continuously available under a 16 hour light–8 hour dark cycle.

Apparatus

The experimental chamber was a standard Lehigh Valley Electronics three-key pigeon chamber (Model #132–02), with the interior painted flat black. A minimum force of 0.25 N was required to operate each key. Three Grason-Stadler in-line display projectors (Pattern #E4580–153) transilluminated the response keys with vertical or horizontal lines or green or orange hues. A Spectra Brightness Spot Meter (Model #1505 UB) was used to calibrate the luminance of each of the four stimuli on each key. The luminance values were then equated for humans (± 0.06 log unit) across the three keys by adding neutral density filters to four of the stimuli. A ventilation fan and a white noise generator provided masking noise.

Experimental contingencies were programmed automatically by solid-state modules and a paper tape reader located in an adjacent room. Responses and interresponse times (IRTs) were recorded on counters and an Esterline-Angus event recorder.

Procedure

At the beginning of each experiment, birds were arbitrarily assigned to groups that were presented with either the hue-hue, hue-line, line-hue, or line-line tasks as the first matching-to-sample task. The birds were also assigned to different sample schedule pretraining and maintenance conditions. The differential condition was always DRL 3 seconds in the presence of one sample (either orange or vertical) and FR 16 in the presence of the other sample (either green or horizontal). Three nondifferential conditions were used—either DRL 3 seconds, FR 16, or FR 1 schedules were in effect in the presence of both samples (either orange and green or vertical and horizontal).

Magazine Training and Shaping

All pigeons were first trained to eat from the hopper with all keys dark and the houselight on. During the next session, subjects were trained to peck the center key (illuminated with one of the appropriate samples for each bird) by the method of successive approximations. Following the initial peck on the center key, a discrete trial procedure was arranged in which the response that met the schedule requirement (FR 2 for the differential birds in each group and FR 1 for the nondifferential birds) turned off the stimulus and produced 3-second access to grain. Each presentation of grain was followed by an intertrial interval (ITI), with the houselight on and all keys dark. Each of the two stimuli appropriate for a given bird was presented thirty times in a Gellerman (1933) series, with the FR schedule in effect for both stimuli. The ITI was increased from 3 to 10 seconds in 1-second steps. Following the shaping session, the birds in the differential and nondifferential conditions were exposed to three sessions with a discrete trial multiple schedule in effect on the center key.

Differential Pretraining

For the subjects in the differential condition, each pretraining session consisted of sixty trials, thirty with each stimulus, presented in a Gellerman series. The ITI was 10 seconds, and the reinforcer was 3-second access to grain. Only the center key was illuminated during trials, and pecks to any dark key had no scheduled consequence. A trial began with the onset of a stimulus on the center key, which remained on until the schedule requirement was met. On orange or vertical trials (depending on the stimulus task), a DRL requirement timed from the first response in the presence of the stimulus was scheduled. The DRL value was 3 seconds (DRL 3) for all three pretraining sessions. On green or horizontal trials, an FR requirement was scheduled. The FR value was increased from FR 4 during the first half of the first pretraining session to FR 8 for the second half. The value was FR 8 for the first half of the second pretraining session and then was increased to FR 16 for the remaining one and one-half sessions of pretraining.

Nondifferential Pretraining

For the subjects assigned to the nondifferential conditions, the three pretraining sessions were identical to those just described in all respects except one. For these subjects, the schedule requirements were the same in the presence of both samples. If the terminal requirements were DRL schedules, then the value was DRL 3 for all three pretraining sessions. If the terminal requirements were FR 1 schedules, then this value was also the same for all three pretraining sessions. If the terminal requirements were FR 16, then the FR value was increased from FR 4 to FR 16 in the same sequence that was used for the FR component in the differential condition.

Matching-to-Sample Training

During matching training, a trial began with the onset of one of the two sample stimuli on the center key. The schedules associated with the samples were the same as those used during the last session of pretraining. When the schedule requirement was met for center-key pecking, the comparison stimuli were presented on the side keys. When the side keys were illuminated (1) additional responses to the center key had no scheduled consequence; (2) a response to the incorrect comparison turned off the key lights and the houselight, leaving the bird in the darkened chamber for 3 seconds; (3) a response to the correct comparison turned off the key lights and produced 3-second access to grain. At the end of either blackout or grain presentation, a 10-second ITI ensued, with all keys dark, all responses ineffective, and the houselight on. Each eighty-trial session consisted of twenty random permutations of the four stimulus configurations; the correct comparison appeared equally often on each side key with each of the samples. Four different sequences of these permutations were rotated across sessions. Trials were arranged without respect to accuracy on the preceding trial (noncorrection). Daily experimental sessions were conducted whenever the birds were within 15 grams of their 80 percent free-feeding weights. All sessions utilized a simultaneous matching procedure in which the sample stimulus stayed on the center key until the bird pecked one of the comparisons, unless otherwise noted. Whenever an accuracy criterion is referred to, it consists of performance of at least 95 percent for three consecutive 80-trial sessions.

EXPERIMENT I

One way to assess control by the behavioral versus visual component of a sample is to present a transfer matching-to-sample task that can be performed accurately only if there is control by the behavioral samples. Specifically, pigeons were trained on the hue-line and line-hue (nonidentity) tasks with differential sample schedules in effect. A DRL 3-second requirement was in effect for both orange (on the hue-line task) and vertical (on the line-hue task) samples, and an FR 16 requirement for both green and horizontal samples, as shown in the top half of Table 14–1. The correct comparison choices were vertical following orange–DRL, horizontal following green–FR, orange following vertical–DRL, and green following horizontal–FR. When the birds reached criterion performance on these tasks, control by the behavioral sample was assessed by presenting the hue-hue and line-line identity tasks, with the same sample schedule requirements in effect. If, in the training tasks, the choice of orange was controlled by the DRL behavior and the choice of green was controlled by the

Table 14–1. Experiment 1.

	Training				Transfer		
Sample	Nonidentity Schedule	Correct Choice		Sample	Identity Schedule	Correct Choice	
	Differential				Differential		
Orange	DRL	Vertical		Orange	DRL	Orange	
Green	FR	Horizontal		Green	FR	Green	
Vertical	DRL	Orange		Vertical	DRL	Vertical	
Horizontal	FR	Green		Horizontal	FR	Horizontal	
	Nondifferential				Nondifferential		
Orange	DRL	FR	Vertical	Orange	DRL	FR	Orange
	or				or		
Green	DRL	FR	Horizontal	Green	DRL	FR	Green
Vertical	DRL	FR	Orange	Vertical	DRL	FR	Vertical
	or				or		
Horizontal	DRL	FR	Green	Horizontal	DRL	FR	Horizontal

Table 14-2. Results for Differential and Nondifferential Schedules.

Subject Number	Schedule Condition During Training and Testing	Order of Testing	Stimulus Condition During Testing	Percent Correct on Session 1
	Nondifferential Schedules during Tests			
501	DRL 3 sec/	1	Hue-hue	50
	DRL 3 sec	2	Line-line	50
5597	DRL 3 sec/	1	Hue-hue	50
	DRL 3 sec	2	Line-line	50
4987	FR 16/	1	Hue-hue	50
	FR 16	2	Line-line	50
5249	FR 16/	1	Line-line	65
	FR 16	2	Hue-hue	50
10287	FR 1/	1	Line-line	28
	FR 1	2	Hue-hue	55

FR behavior, then the birds could perform at high accuracy on the hue-hue task on the very first session. If, however, the choice of orange had been controlled by the vertical sample and the choice of green by the horizontal sample on the training tasks, it would be unlikely that the birds would perform with high accuracy on the first session of the hue-hue task. The same logic holds for the line-line transfer test.

Another way in which high accuracy might be obtained on the identity transfer tasks is if the birds choose the comparisons that are the same as the samples (i.e., true matching behavior) on the first session of an identity task. To assess this possibility, other birds were exposed to the same sequence of training (nonidentity) and transfer (identity) tasks with nondifferential sample schedules, either a DRL in the presence of both samples or an FR in the presence of both (see the bottom half of Table 14-1). These nondifferential subjects had exposure to both hues and both line orientations as samples and as comparisons prior to the first session on either identity task. Their

Table 14–2. continued

	Differential Schedules during Tests			
Subject Number	Schedule Condition During Training and Testing	Order of Testing	Stimulus Condition During Testing	Percent Correct on Session 1
4612	DRL 3 sec/	1	Line-line	95
	FR 16	2	Hue-hue	93
4377	DRL 3 sec/	1	Line-line	71
	FR 16	2	Hue-hue	60
9735	DRL 3 sec/	1	Line-line	77
	FR 16	2	Hue-hue	68
4023	DRL 3 sec/	1	Line-line	78
	FR 16	2	Hue-hue	75
4025	DRL 3 sec/	1	Line-line	77
	FR 16	2	Hue-hue	72
4026	DRL 3 sec/	1	Line-line	68
	FR 16	2	Hue-hue	80

high accuracy on the two nonidentity tasks demonstrated that they had learned the discriminations between the lines and the hues prior to the transfer tests.

Eleven subjects served in this experiment. Six had extensive histories with the two nonidentity tasks, with the differential sample schedules in effect as described above. Five had extensive histories with the two nonidentity tasks, with the nondifferential schedule requirements indicated next to each subject's number in Table 14-2, before being tested on the two identity tasks. All subjects had reached the accuracy criterion on the first training (nonidentity) task before being exposed to the other one and reached the same high accuracy criterion on the first transfer (identity) task before being exposed to the second one. The sample schedules during transfer tests were the same as those during training for each subject.

Table 14-2 presents the percent correct for the first session of transfer testing with each of the identity tasks (line-line and hue-hue) for each of the eleven subjects. For the five nondifferential subjects (left-hand columns) accuracies ranged from 28 percent (Subject 10287 on the line-line task), to 65 percent (Subject 5249, also on the line-line task), with seven of the ten values falling exactly at 50 percent (chance). First session accuracy levels for the six differential subjects (right-hand columns), on the other hand, ranged from 60 percent (Subject 4377 on the hue-hue task) to 95 percent (Subject 4612 on the line-line task), with the mean and modal values just above 75 percent correct. These performances should be viewed against the preceding sessions' accuracy levels of at least 95 percent correct for all eleven subjects. That is, it should be remembered that each subject reached the accuracy criterion on each of the training tasks (nonidentities) and each of the transfer tasks (identities) before proceeding to the next task or terminating the experiment.

These data indicate that no subject was able to perform at high accuracy levels on the first session of either identity task on the basis of exposure to the two nonidentity tasks unless differential sample response requirements were in effect on all tasks. That is, there was no evidence that the birds had a preference for the comparison stimulus that was the same as (matched) the sample stimulus.

The high first session accuracy levels for the birds with differential schedules show that comparison choice was controlled to some extent by the sample-specific behavior. The amount of control by the behavioral component of the sample varied across birds but was evident for all six subjects.

EXPERIMENT II

Further evidence of control by the behavioral component of the sample for subjects run with differential sample schedule requirements can be obtained by first exposing birds to the two identity tasks as the training procedures and then to the two nonidentity tasks as the testing procedures, as shown in Table 14-3. In the hue-hue and line-line tasks, the correct comparison choices were orange following orange-DRL, green following green-FR, vertical following vertical-DRL, and horizontal following horizontal-FR. When the hue-line transfer task is presented, high accuracy on the first session would be obtained if the birds had learned to choose vertical conditional on DRL behavior and horizontal conditional on FR behavior.

Table 14-3. Experiment II.

Training			Transfer		
Sample	Identity Schedule	Correct Choice	Sample	Nonidentity Schedule	Correct Choice
Differential			*Differential*		
Orange	DRL	Orange	Orange	DRL	Vertical
Green	FR	Green	Green	FR	Horizontal
Vertical	DRL	Vertical	Vertical	DRL	Orange
Horizontal	FR	Horizontal	Horizontal	FR	Green
Nondifferential			*Nondifferential*		
Orange	FR	Orange	Orange	FR	Vertical
Green	FR	Green	Green	FR	Horizontal
Vertical	FR	Vertical	Vertical	FR	Orange
Horizontal	FR	Horizontal	Horizontal	FR	Green

If, on the other hand, the visual sample controlled comparison choices during training tasks, there would be no basis for choosing vertical following orange and horizontal following green on the hue-line task. The same logic holds for the line-hue transfer task.

To further assess the control of comparison choices by the behavioral sample, two birds were prevented from emitting the differential behavior during the transfer tasks. For these birds, an FR 1 schedule was in effect in lieu of the differential sample schedules in the presence of both samples, as shown in the bottom half of Table 14-3. If the behavioral sample controlled comparison choice during training, the birds could not perform accurately on the transfer task without the behavioral samples present. Finally, to assess the possibility of some kind of savings or facilitative effect of maintaining the same sample schedule requirements during training and testing, one subject was exposed to all four tasks with the same nondifferential sample schedule requirements in effect.

Four birds served in this experiment. After exposure to the shaping and pretraining procedures described earlier, all four birds were exposed to the two identity tasks as training tasks. Three of the subjects (as indicated in the third column of Table 14-4) were trained on these two tasks with differential schedule requirements,

Table 14–4. Results for Experiment II.

Subject Number	Order of Training	Training Tasks (sample schedules)	Order of Testing	Transfer Tasks (sample schedules)	Session 1 Transfer Scores (percent)
9148	1	Hue-hue (DRL 3 sec/FR 16)	1	Hue-line (DRL 3 sec/FR 16)	97
	2	Line-line (DRL 3 sec/FR 16)	2	Line-hue (DRL 3 sec/FR 16)	90
5630	1	Line-line (DRL 3 sec/FR 16)	1	Line-hue (DRL 3 sec/FR 16)	80
	2	Hue-hue (DRL 3 sec/FR 16)	2	Hue-line (FR 1/FR 1)	56
1236	1	Line-line (DRL 3 sec/FR 16)	1	Line-hue (FR 1/FR 1)	53
	2	Hue-hue (DRL 3 sec/FR 16)	2	Hue-line (FR 1/FR 1)	54
98	1	Hue-hue (FR 1/FR 1)	1	Hue-line (FR 1/FR 1)	50
	2	Line-line (FR 1/FR 1)	2	Line-hue (FR 1/FR 1)	50

while the remaining bird was trained with a nondifferential (FR 1) requirement. In all cases, birds were exposed to each new task only after meeting the accuracy criterion on the preceding task. The birds were then exposed to the two nonidentity tasks as transfer tests, reaching the accuracy criterion on the first transfer task before being exposed to the second one.

The birds then differed with respect to the sample schedule requirements in effect during the test (nonidentity tasks), as indicated in Column 5 of Table 14-4. For one subject (Bird 9148), the same differential schedules used during training were maintained during testing on both nonidentity tasks. In both cases, accuracy levels were very high on the first session with each task (90 and 97 percent correct). A second subject (Bird 5630) was exposed to the first test (line-hue task) with the same differential sample schedule requirement and was at 80 percent correct for the first session on this task. In contrast, this subject showed an accuracy level of only 56 percent correct when presented with the hue-line task (the second transfer task) without the differential sample schedule requirements.

Finally, two of the birds were tested on both nonidentity tasks with nondifferential sample schedule requirements (FR 1); Subject 1236 had had training with differential sample schedule requirements on the two identity tasks, while Subject 98 had a nondifferential (FR 1) requirement in effect for all four tasks. As indicated in the sixth column of Table 14-4, in all five instances in which there were no differential sample schedule requirements on the tests, accuracy levels were at or near chance (50-56 percent correct). This was true whether the nondifferential schedule requirements on the tests were a change from training procedures (Birds 5630 and 1236) or not (Bird 98, with nondifferential sample schedule requirements on both training and testing tasks). These data further support the conclusion from Experiment I that the choice of a comparison stimulus on a matching-to-sample task with differential sample schedule requirements is controlled by the sample-specific performances generated by these schedules.

EXPERIMENT III

The data from the two preceding experiments indicate that for birds with differential sample schedule requirements, the sample may consist of two components—a visual component (a hue or a line orientation) and a behavioral component (behavior specific to the DRL 3-second or FR 16 requirement). The temporal relation between these sample stimulus components and the onset of the comparisons is different. On the simultaneous matching tasks used in Experiments I and II, the visual component of the sample remains on the center key, while the comparison stimuli are presented on the side keys. The behavioral component of the sample, however, is terminated at the onset of the comparisons—that is, the peck that meets the sample schedule requirement turns on the side keys, and no further pecks are required (or in fact emitted) to the center key. This termination of the behavioral component of the sample at the onset of the comparisons fits the definition of zero delay matching. Therefore, if the behavioral component of the sample is controlling comparison choice, the birds are already performing on a zero delay matching-to-sample task. Turning off the visual sample at the onset of the comparison stimuli should not disrupt accuracy. The change from simultaneous to zero delay matching might disrupt performance if comparison choice is controlled by the visual component of the sample, since the temporal relation between the visual sample and the onset of the comparisons would be changed.

Six of the fifteen birds that had served in Experiments I and II were used to assess the effect upon accuracy of a change from a simultaneous to a zero delay matching procedure. Three of the birds had already been exposed to all four stimulus tasks with the differential sample schedule requirements in effect while the other three birds had acquired all four tasks with nondifferential sample schedule requirements. Prior to the shift to the zero delay procedure, all six birds were exposed to eighty-trial sessions with the simultaneous matching-to-sample procedure, which included all four stimulus tasks in one session (twenty of each type), with the appropriate sample schedule requirement maintained for each subject. Now the hue-hue, line-line, hue-line, and line-hue tasks were randomized within a single session. The birds were run on this procedure until the accuracy criterion was again met.

After three consecutive sessions with 95 percent correct or better, each of the six birds was exposed to the zero delay procedure. In all other respects (for example, sample schedule requirements and the inclusion of all four stimulus tasks), the sessions were identical to the preceding ones. Table 14–5 shows (Columns 2 and 5) the sample

Table 14–5. Procedure and Results for Differential and Non-differential Sample Schedules in Experiment III.

Nondifferential Sample Schedules			Differential Sample Schedules		
Subject Number	Sample Schedule Conditions	Percent Correct on Session 1	Subject Number	Sample Schedule Conditions	Percent Correct on Session 1
501	DRL 3 sec/ DRL 3 sec	69	9148	DRL 3 sec/ FR 16	96
98	FR 1/ FR 1	68	5630	DRL 3 sec/ FR 16	92
10287	FR 1/ FR 1	77	1236	DRL 3 sec/ FR 16	97

schedule requirements for each bird and the accuracy on the first session with the zero delay procedure (Columns 3 and 6). All birds were performing at 95 percent correct or better on the preceding session with the simultaneous matching procedures; thus, the effect is quite clear. None of the subjects with differential sample schedule requirements was disrupted by the changed temporal relation between the visual sample and the onset of the comparisons (92–97 percent correct on Session 1). However, all the subjects with non-differential sample schedule requirements were substantially disrupted (68–77 percent correct on Session 1). These data support the conclusion that the choice of comparison stimuli for birds presented with a compound sample (containing both a visual and a behavioral component) will be controlled by the behavioral component.

EXPERIMENT IV

The observation by Cohen et al. (1976) that the rates of acquisition of four matching-to-sample tasks (hue-hue, hue-line, line-hue, and line-line) are the same when differential sample schedule requirements are used can be accounted for in terms of control by the behavioral component of the sample: The four tasks are reduced to two, where the samples in all tasks are the DRL 3-second and FR 16 schedules and their corresponding behavior patterns and the comparisons are hues or lines. The most rapid acquisition with nondifferential schedules occurs with a hue-hue matching task (Carter and Eckerman, 1975; Cohen et al., 1976). The still more rapid acquisition of hue-hue matching with differential sample response requirements suggests that the behavioral component is not only prepotent over the visual one, but also is in some sense a better sample for the pigeon. We proceeded to examine this possibility in the context of a delayed matching-to-sample task.

Nine additional naive birds served in this experiment. After exposure to the magazine training and shaping procedures, the birds were exposed to three sessions of the pretraining procedures—three birds each with differential, nondifferential FR 16, and nondifferential FR 1 requirements. Following pretraining, all birds were exposed to a zero delay, hue-line matching-to-sample task. This task was identical to the zero delay procedure described in Experiment III except that in this experiment, the entire session consisted of eighty hue-line trials. Each bird was run on this task until the accuracy criterion of at least 95 percent correct for three consecutive sessions was met. Following acquisition of zero delay matching, subjects were exposed to a delayed matching task. The procedure was the same except that the delay between sample offset and comparison onset was increased. The delay value began at 1 second and was increased by 1-second steps on the first session after the criterion was met or a minimum of five sessions was run at a delay value. The keys were dark and the houselight on during the delay.

Acquisition of the zero delay task was rapid for the differential subjects relative to the nondifferential birds. Introduction of delays resulted in a marked decrease in accuracy for the nondifferential birds but not for differential subjects. Figure 14–1 shows performance at some representative delay values for one subject (Bird 42) who had differential sample schedule requirements. This bird showed the least variable performance of all nine birds and has already been exposed to a delay value of 55 seconds without a drop of accuracy.

This highly accurate performance at long delays can be contrasted with data reported by Roberts and Grant (1976). After determining that sample presentation time was an important variable in pigeon's performance on a hue-hue delayed matching-to-sample task, they presented accuracy data for experienced birds on such a task with a 14-second sample presentation time at delays of 0, 20, 40, and 60 seconds. Accuracy levels were between 70 and 75 percent correct

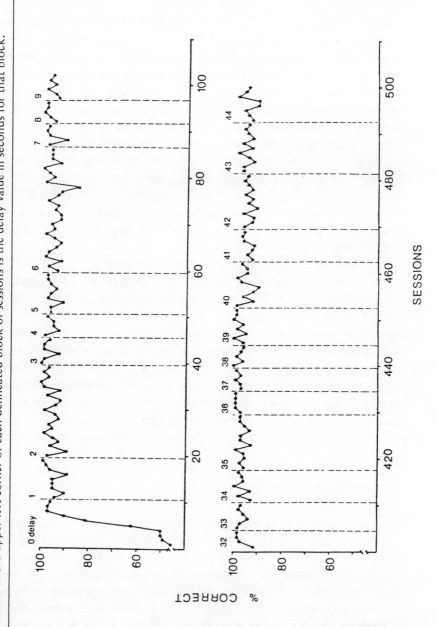

Figure 14–1. Delayed matching-to-sample performance for Bird 42. Each data point represents the percent correct from a single eighty-trial session on a hue line task with differential sample schedule requirements (DRL 3 seconds and FR 16). The number in the upper left corner of each delineated block of sessions is the delay value in seconds for that block.

at the three long delay values, while near 100 percent at the zero delay value.

Maki, Moe, and Bierley (1977) looked at the effects of various interference treatments on pigeons' performance on delayed matching-to-sample tasks with either stimuli (red and green), responses (FR1 and FR 20), or reinforcers (occurrences or nonoccurrences of food) as samples. They report common effects of the interference treatments and no dramatic differences between performance with the three types of samples. With conditions more favorable for delay performance than ours (that is, with a darkened chamber during the delay interval), the authors reported highly accurate performance for response samples at 7–9-second delay intervals. The data from our laboratory (Figure 14-1) indicate that, at least for one bird, compound (visual-behavioral) samples can yield remarkably accurate performance at much longer delays than have heretofore been reported for pigeons.

The most obvious explanation for this highly accurate conditional discrimination performance at such long delays would be mediation of the delay with differential behavior patterns, perhaps those performed during the samples (cf. Blough, 1959). We have observed and logged the performance of all birds during the first four sessions on each delay value, the last two criterion sessions, and other sessions when the birds appeared to be approaching criterion performance. Although there have been transient instances of apparently sample-specific delay behavior, this was the exception rather than the rule. Bird 42, who was very active during the delay periods, showed no patterns of behavior that were discriminable to us as sample specific.

CONCLUSIONS

That an organism's own response patterns can serve as discriminative stimuli for other behavior has been known for some time and is amply demonstrated in this volume. The studies reported here have attempted to assess the effectiveness of such stimuli in a context similar to that in which they most often occur—a context in which behavioral cues are only some of a number of environmental stimuli competing for control of the subject's behavior. We have found that, in pigeons, sample-specific performances will often overshadow visual stimuli with which they are correlated—that is, that a subject's own behavior can be prepotent over visual information in situations in which a choice is possible.

This finding may serve as a practical caution. Researchers have at times used differential response training as a way of facilitating differential control by visual or auditory stimuli. (This was in fact one of our original motives for the above studies.) Our results suggest that while such methods may produce accurate responding, they may in fact work contrary to the experimenter's purpose, discouraging rather than enhancing control by nonbehavioral stimuli.

On the other hand, the facilitation of delayed matching performance with differential sample schedules found in Experiment IV indicates that the presence of these schedules produces control superior to that exerted by visual stimuli alone. Experimenters whose goal is to generate the strongest possible differential control may find their task aided by the use of stimulus-specific response requirements.

REFERENCES

Blough, D.S. 1959. Delayed matching in the pigeon. *Journal of the Experimental Analysis of Behavior 2*: 151–160.

Carter, D.E., and D.A. Eckerman. 1975. Symbolic matching by pigeons: Rate of learning complex discriminations predicted from simple discriminations. *Science 187*: 662–664.

Cohen L.R.; T.A. Looney; J.H. Brady; and A.F. Aucella. 1976. Differential sample response schedules in the acquisition of conditional discriminations by pigeons. *Journal of the Experimental Analysis of Behavior 26*: 301–314.

Gellerman, L.W. 1933. Chance orders of alternating stimuli in visual discrimination experiments. *Journal of Genetic Psychology 42*: 206–208.

Lattal, K.A. 1975. Reinforcement contingencies as discriminative stimuli. *Journal of the Experimental Analysis of Behavior 23*: 241–246.

Hobson, S.L. 1975. Discriminability of fixed-ratio schedules for pigeons: Effects of absolute ratio size. *Journal of the Experimental Analysis of Behavior 23*: 25–35.

Maki, W.S., Jr.; J.C. Moe; and C.M. Bierley. 1977. Short-term memory for stimuli, responses, and reinforcers. *Journal of Experimental Psychology: Animal Behavior Processees 3*: 156–177.

Pliskoff, S.S., and I. Goldiamond. 1966. Some discriminative properties of fixed-ratio performance in the pigeon. *Journal of the Experimental Analysis of Behavior 9*: 1–9.

Rilling, M. 1967. Number of responses as a stimulus in fixed-interval and fixed-ratio schedules. *Journal of Comparative and Physiological Psychology 63*: 60–65.

_____. 1968. Effects of timeout on a discrimination between fixed-ratio schedules. *Journal of the Experimental Analysis of Behavior 11*: 129–132.

Rilling, M., and C. McDiarmid. 1965. Signal detection in fixed ratio schedules. *Science 148*: 526–527.

Roberts, W.A., and D.S. Grant. 1976. Studies of short-term memory in the pigeon using the delayed matching-to-sample procedure. In D.L. Medin, W.A. Roberts, and R.T. Davis, eds., *Processes of Animal Memory*. Hillsdale, New Jersey: Erlbaum.

15 LOCAL CONTRAST, LOCAL DIMENSIONAL EFFECTS, AND DIMENSIONAL CONTRAST

John C. Malone, Jr., and
David W. Rowe

A large part of Pavlov's (1927, 1955) research concerned the analysis of the formation of differentiations or the way in which discriminations among stimuli are formed and differential responding to them develops. His interpretation of a variety of data was expressed in the hypothetical fields of excitation and inhibition that he envisioned operating on the surface of the cortex. His physiology was not correct in detail, but the principles that governed his fields may yet be useful, despite the lack of attention they have received in this country (cf. Malone, 1975, 1976; Thompson, 1965).

In Pavlov's view, the course of discrimination learning reflected the action of several simultaneous processes, including irradiation and concentration of excitation and inhibition and positive and negative induction. However, he made it very clear that these processes were interdependent: One does not try to interpret one without consideration of others simultaneously acting.

Pavlovian irradiation is roughly analogous to what was later called stimulus generalization. Generalization has typically been regarded as an independent process, whether as a basic phenomenon (the "Pavlovian" version suggested by Spence 1936, or as a secondary effect

Research described here was supported by a Biomedical Sciences Support Grant to the University of Tennessee, Knoxville, and by NIMH Grants MH–24997 and MH–29774. We especially thank John M. Hinson for his contribution and J.E.R. Staddon and Norman Guttman for earlier guidance.

365

(Lashley and Wade, 1946). On the other hand, discrimination learning has frequently been treated as a different subject matter—that is, one studies stimulus generalization or discrimination learning. Generalization gradients have been studied after various types of discriminative pretraining (see the very thorough review by Rilling, 1977), but these are usually obtained in single session tests designed to reveal an "ideal gradient." Some research does not fit this description—for example, work with maintained generalization gradients by Blough (1969), Malone and Staddon (1973), and others does not treat generalization and discrimination as separate phenomena.

Local contrast during multiple schedule discrimination training appears to be directly analogous to the induction effects of Pavlov (Malone, 1976). In both cases, responding to a given stimulus may be strongly influenced by the immediately preceding stimulus, and details concerning the time course and direction (positive or negative) of the effects seem clearly parallel. As Pavlov believed induction and irradiation to be interdependent, the data below show that local contrast and generalization gradient form may be interdependent.

The theme of this volume, discriminative properties of reinforcement schedules, concerns aspects of reinforcement schedules that may influence behavior in addition to the direct influence of a particular schedule when it is in effect. For example, behavior at one time may be controlled discriminatively by properties of different schedules or by schedule performances present earlier. Local contrast represents an instance of such an effect in that response rate in a given component depends not only on the reinforcement schedule in that component, but also on the schedule and average response rate in a preceding component. This successive influence on performance during each component by its predecessor implies that overall performance (across all components) depends in part on the set of components appearing during a session.

The influence of local contrast may be quite large, producing effects on response rate that would be expected with alterations in reinforcement frequency or other familiar variables. A second and more recently discovered local interaction, the local dimensional effect, also exerts a substantial influence on overall responding. Local dimensional effects depend upon the positions of the discriminative stimuli along a continuum, as well as the response rates in their presence. In both cases, the influence of specific discriminative stimuli and their associated schedules of reinforcement is greatly modulated by the set of components (i.e., stimuli and reinforcement schedules) present during a session.

Our attention has focused on such phenomena accompanying discrimination training with multiple schedules and their influence on the form of maintained generalization gradients. To a degree, this parallels Pavlov's conviction that the phenomena of stimulus generalization and discrimination formation are best viewed as interdependent.

The first section below describes local contrast and attempts to clear up some misunderstandings concerning its characteristics and the conditions which produce it. The subsequent sections examine its influence on overall responding, particularly on certain features of generalization gradients which Blough (1975) has called dimensional contrast shoulders. The data below suggest that local contrast may not only accentuate these gradient forms, but that it may determine the form of such gradients in many cases.

LOCAL CONTRAST

Nevin and Shettleworth (1966) first adequately described local contrast, an effect that they called transient contrast, since it lasted only a few sessions under the conditions that prevailed in their study. In addition, the effects were transient during individual components, appearing most clearly at the onset of a component and diminishing with time in a component. That is, when a given component was preceded by a component in which reinforcement was more frequent, responding was initially depressed and increased through the component (negative local contrast). When the preceding component was associated with less frequent reinforcement, responding was initially elevated and decreased through the component (positive local contrast).

But local contrast need not be reflected solely in the pattern of responding, as is virtually always assumed (e.g., Arnett, 1973; Buck, Rothstein, and Williams, 1975; Rachlin, 1973; Schwartz, Hamilton, and Silberberg, 1975; Spealman, 1976). Differences in overall response rate during a component far more often reflect local contrast than is true of the pattern within a component. Local contrast depends upon the component that just preceded, but it does not necessarily appear most strongly at the onset of a component.

THE IMPORTANCE OF A BASELINE
FOR LOCAL CONTRAST

To evaluate the direction (positive or negative) and the magnitude of local contrast, it is essential that a baseline be available that allows an estimation of responding in the absence of local contrast. If one relies only on the pattern of responding, it is possible to interpret positive local contrast as a suppression of responding at the end of a component and negative local contrast as an enhancement of responding at the end of a component (e.g., Buck, Rothstein, and Williams, 1975). One possibility is to separate components by occasional time out periods, in view of the report by Mackintosh, Little, and Lord (1972) that 1-minute time outs eliminated local contrast. One could then compare responding in a component when preceded by another component with responding when a time out preceded the component. Unfortunately, time outs are apt to have independent effects on subsequent responding. An alternative baseline against which to assess local contrast was suggested by Jenkins (1970). The method is to simply include presentations of each component preceded by itself. This amounts to increasing the duration of the component and comparing responding during the first and second half. Using such a baseline, Malone and Staddon (1972) and Malone (1976) showed that local contrast is reliably seen in effects on overall response levels and may appear in the pattern of responding.

DETERMINANTS OF LOCAL CONTRAST

Malone and Staddon (1973) showed that local contrast appears among presentations of stimuli forming a maintained generalization gradient and that the direction and magnitude of the effects depends upon differences in average response rates in the interacting components. When average response rate in the preceding component was high, responding in a subsequent component was depressed (negative local contrast), and when average response rate in the preceding component was lower, subsequent responding was elevated (positive local contrast). Since this all occurred among components in which reinforcement conditions were identical (i.e., extinction), it is clear that different reinforcement conditions among components are not required.

It is tempting to interpret local contrast as a "rebound" effect, as Mackintosh (1974) did. According to this view, positive local contrast is a rebound (or a recovery) from an immediately preceding period of low response rate. If this were true, the direction (positive or negative) and perhaps the magnitude of local contrast would be inversely related to response rate in the immediately preceding component on specific occasions. Nevin and Shettleworth (1966) showed that this was not the case by showing negative local contrast in a VI component preceded by a component in which a differential reinforcement of other behavior (DRO) schedule maintained lower response rates while providing more frequent reinforcement. Thus, response rate in the preceding component was not a factor. Malone and Staddon (1973) examined positive local contrast during a VI component as a function of responding during specific instances of a preceding extinction component. Responding in the VI component was dependent upon average response rate (e.g., over a session or more) in the preceding component but was independent of the variations in response rate in the preceding component on particular occasions.

LOCAL CONTRAST AND DISCRIMINATION

Local contrast persisted over several months in Malone and Staddon's study, showing no signs of diminishing. But, as Nevin and Shettleworth (1966) reported, it is sometimes a transient effect that persists for only a few days. Pavlov (1927) found induction, an analogous effect, to be likewise transient under some conditions and persistent in other cases. In his view, induction characterized the formation of a differentiation, and thus would be expected to fade as the differentiation formed. Hence, the strength and persistence of induction, and perhaps local contrast, is apt to vary with the difficulty of the discrimination.

Malone (1976) traced the development of a simple discrimination in which 1-minute periods of a vertical (90-degree) line were accompanied by VI reinforcement and alternated with 30-second time out periods. Local contrast, appearing as a pattern of responding in 90 degrees, disappeared after a few sessions. When the time out was replaced with a 60-degree orientation presented in extinction, positive local contrast quickly reappeared in 90 degrees, evident in both overall response rate and in the pattern of responding. Negative local contrast appeared in 60 degrees. These effects vanished by days thirty-seven to thirty-nine of training but were reinstated with the addition of new stimuli presented in extinction.

FORMS OF LOCAL CONTRAST

The same component transitions may produce different effects under different circumstances, depending upon the number of sessions of training and the similarity of discriminative stimuli associated with components. Other factors, such as component duration and specific reinforcement schedules used, and other as yet unexamined factors may also influence the persistence of local contrast. The dependence of local contrast upon stage of training has concerned some researchers (e.g., Buck, Rothstein, and Williams, 1975), who point to the diversity of within component patterns and question the robustness of the effect.

Fortunately, this diversity is governed by a few simple rules suggested by Malone (1976) and derived from Pavlov (1927):

1. During the formation of a discrimination, defined as the gradual divergence of response rates in components associated with more and less frequent reinforcement, local contrast appears with or before the appearance of clear differential responding.

2. Positive local contrast may appear as elevated responding at the onset of a component and perhaps as elevated responding throughout the component. Similarly, negative local contrast appears as depressed responding that increases during a component or as depressed responding throughout. Local contrast of both types may be seen to be real increases and decreases in response rate by comparison with a baseline, such as responding during the second half of a double length presentation.

3. If the discriminative stimuli accompanying components are very dissimilar and/or few, local contrast may disappear rapidly and induction (in Skinner's sense) will appear (Malone, 1976). That

is, responding may be initially depressed in a VI component preceded by an extinction component and elevated in an extinction component preceded by a VI component.

4. If the discrimination is difficult, local contrast may persist over months, showing itself in the pattern of responding, in overall response rates, or in both.

5. A final rule applicable to local contrast, but not directly to Pavlovian induction, concerns the role of average response rates in individual components. The direction and the magnitude of local contrast depend upon average, but not momentary, response rates in each component. Thus, a component in which average response rate is higher than that in a subsequent component produces negative local contrast (suppressed responding) in the latter. This is true even on occasions when momentary response rate is zero in the preceding component (e.g., Malone and Staddon, 1973).

Thus, the few readily discriminable stimuli (e.g., red versus green key lights) and the small number of components used in most multiple schedule research may result in local contrast persisting for only a brief time. Subsequently, induction (in Skinner's sense) may be evident. Given different rates of discrimination formation by different subjects, one may therefore find what seem to be puzzling differences in the patterns of responding shown by different subjects. In all cases that we have seen (e.g., Buck, Rothstein, and Williams, 1975; Menlove, 1975; Williams, 1976), such differences in patterning may be attributed to the transition from positive local contrast to induction produced in an S+ during discrimination formation and (in the case of induction) after cessation of responding in S−. The absence of an appropriate baseline against which to assess these patterns as absolute increases or decreases in response rates prevents clear identification of local effects. The appreciation of the fact that local contrast, like Pavlovian induction, accompanies discrimination formation and follows the above rules, along with the use of a baseline for evaluation of the direction of the effects, would aid in the interpretation of such data.

Figure 15−1 provides a schematic illustration of the main characteristics of local contrast and those of the more recently discovered local dimensional effects. The upper panel shows the time course

Figure 15–1. Illustration of the main features of local contrast and of local dimensional effects. The upper panel shows the time course of local contrast during the formation of a simple discrimination, while the center panel shows effects during maintained local contrast. The lower panel illustrates local dimensional effects, which unlike local contrast, are stimulus specific. See text for details.

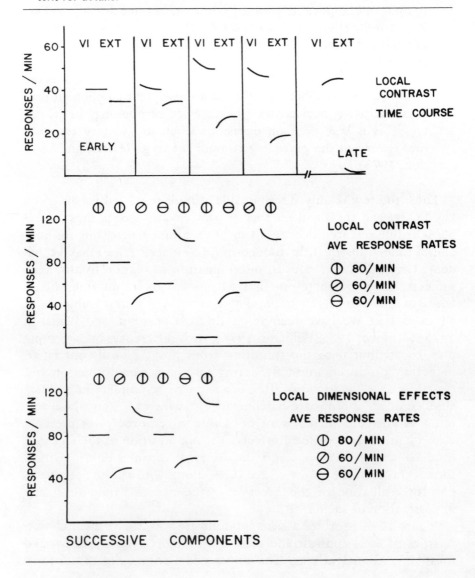

of local contrast, as it typically appears during training in which two stimuli, one associated with VI reinforcement and the other with extinction, alternate during experimental sessions (cf., Malone, 1976). Each segment of the panel represents performance in the two components during successive periods of training, ranging from early to late. Patterns of responding in VI and in Extinction (EXT) are typical of data averaged over a session or of patterns during an individual component. Since components alternate, responding during VI assumes an immediately prior presentation of EXT and vice versa.

The leftmost segment above shows nearly equal response rates in the two components, with no sign of positive or negative local contrast in the patterns of responding, followed (next segment) by positive and negative local contrast patterns, but still approximately equal overall response rates. The patterns of the leftmost segment may not appear, and local contrast may be evident by the time that there is any difference in response rates in the two components.

By the third segment, local contrast is very evident in the patterns of responding, and response rates in the two components have markedly diverged. Later (fourth segment), responding has decreased in EXT; while both positive and negative local contrast are still clear, they are less pronounced than in the preceding stage. Finally, late in training, responding in EXT nears zero, and local contrast has been replaced by induction, in Skinner's (1938) sense. Responding in the VI component is initially depressed, and that in EXT is initially slightly elevated.

The center panel shows local contrast under conditions in which it persists over weeks or months, as in Malone and Staddon's (1973) study. Here, we assume three components (though more may be present) associated with three line tilt stimuli, a vertical (90 degrees), a 45 degree, and a horizontal line, in which average response rates are eighty, sixty, and sixty per minute, respectively. Given that these average response rates are reasonably stable over sessions (i.e., steady-state performance), the direction and magnitude of local contrast is determined by average response rates in the interacting components.

Unlike the upper panel, this panel shows typical effects during a single session, as does the panel below, and the successive orientations at the top of the panel represent a real time sequence during a session. The sequence begins with two components associated with the vertical line, followed by the 45-degree component. Since average response rate in the 45-degree component is lower than in the vertical line component, negative local contrast appears during the former. The next component (horizontal line) is associated with the same average response rate as 45 degrees and thus is unaffected by the preceding component. A subsequent presentation of the vertical line shows a positive local contrast elevation, relative to responding when preceded by itself (second in the sequence).

As was pointed out in rule 5 above, local contrast depends upon average response rates, not response rates during the individual presentation of a component. The next component represents an instance of the vertical line component, in which average response rate is eighty per minute, where responding is abnormally low. Yet the effect on the subsequent component, horizontal line, is still negative local contrast, since it is the average, not the momentary response rate in the preceding component that determines the direction and the magnitude of the effect. Note also that the magnitude of negative local contrast in the horizontal line component is the same as that in the 45-degree component (presentation three) when each is preceded by the same component (vertical line) in which average response rate is higher.

The next component, 45 degrees, shows neither positive nor negative local contrast, since the preceding component is associated with the same average response rate (sixty per minute). Finally, positive local contrast appears during the vertical line component, and its magnitude is the same as when the preceding component was the horizontal line.

The bottom panel illustrates the characteristics of a different local effect, called local dimensional effects by Crawford, Steele, and Malone (1980). Like local contrast, these effects depend upon the immediately preceding component; unlike local contrast, local dimensional effects are affected by the similarity of the component stimuli along some dimension. Since the effects are local and sensitive to the position of component stimuli on some stimulus dimension, local dimensional effects seems the most descriptive label. These effects, which will be described in the data below, precede local contrast and fade once local contrast appears.

The sequence in the bottom panel shows the same three components used in the panel above, but with local dimensional effects occurring instead of local contrast. The sequence begins with the vertical line component preceding the 45-degree component. As in the panel above, this results in depressed responding during the latter and elevated responding during a subsequent vertical line component. Given the differences among average response rates in the components, these effects would be interpreted as negative and positive local contrast, respectively. The next component shows the return to the average response rate of eighty per minute in the vertical component preceded by itself.

However, the "local contrast" in this case is stimulus-specific, as is shown during the following component, the horizontal line. Responding during that component is suppressed, but to a lesser degree than was the case when the 45-degree line component was preceded by the vertical line component. That is, the degree of suppression depends not only on the average response rates in each component, but also upon the similarity of the stimuli accompanying the components. The degree of suppression is greater for more similar stimuli (vertical versus 45 degrees) than for less similar stimuli (vertical versus horizontal).

The following component (vertical line) shows a second stimulus-specific effect: The degree of elevation is greater when the preceding stimulus is more dissimilar. Response rate in the vertical line component is higher when the preceding component is accompanied by the horizontal line than it was when preceded by the 45-degree line component.

This rendition of local dimensional effects is somewhat tentative, but these are the characteristics that seem to appear in some of the data described below. We had originally called these effects "stimulus-specific local contrast," but the term local dimensional effects may better avoid confusion with local contrast as presently understood. In addition, it allows the inclusion of all local effects that are stimulus-specific, but that less closely resemble local contrast. For example, the local dimensional effects of Crawford, Steele, and Malone (1980) would be interpreted by few as resembling local contrast.

The data below derive from experiments with several stimuli forming a maintained generalization gradient and are interesting inasmuch as they show the effect of local contrast and local dimensional effects on overall response rates. Particular patterns of responding within components, though often used elsewhere to identify local contrast, were of little interest. The effects of these local influences on overall gradient form were of particular interest, since it may be that local effects play a part in determining certain gradient forms that have been the focus of some recent interest.

LOCAL EFFECTS AND GENERALIZATION GRADIENTS

The preceding section argued that local effects may be an important determinant of overall response rates, particularly in situations where a number of similar stimuli are presented in an irregular order and different stimuli are associated with different conditions of reinforcement. These conditions characterize maintained generalization procedures, which many have suggested may be far more useful than other procedures for assessing stimulus generalization (e.g., Blough, 1969). But it may be important to take local effects into account when interpreting the gradients of responding obtained with such procedures.

This caution may be especially relevant to the interpretation of gradient forms that Blough (e.g., 1975) has called dimensional contrast shoulders. Such gradients show minimum responding in S– values near an S+ or S+ set and maximum responding in S+ values near an S– or S– set. Such gradients have been reported by a number of researchers, using a variety of stimulus continua (Blough, 1975; Catania and Gill, 1964; Farthing, 1974; Malone, 1975; Reynolds, 1961). Several of these authors have taken their data as evidence against Spence's (1937) classic model for discrimination and generalization. Blough (1975) proposed an alternative model that was specifically designed to account for contrast shoulders; its virtues and shortcomings will be discussed elsewhere.

The possible relation between local effects and dimensional contrast is suggested by the data of both Catania and Gill (1964) and Farthing (1974), who carried on training long enough to see their contrast shoulders disappear. The former authors were able to restore them in a variety of ways, such as by changing the sequence of stimuli or by partially obscuring the stimuli, rendering them less discriminable. The disappearance of contrast shoulders under conditions in which local contrast would fade and the restoration of shoulders with methods that could be expected to restore local contrast suggests that contrast shoulders and local contrast may be importantly related. The data to follow show first how local effects in general influence overall response rates and then how such effects may anticipate and even determine overall patterns of responding.

LOCAL EFFECTS AND CONTRAST SHOULDERS

The first set of data derives from the work of John Hinson, who was working in our laboratory at that time (Hinson and Malone, 1980). Figure 15-2 shows maintained generalization gradients comprised of seven line orientation stimuli appearing during successive 30-second presentations. Pigeons' responding in the two extreme orientations— 0 degrees (horizontal) and 90 degrees (vertical)—was reinforced according to a VI 30-second schedule, while the remaining orientations (15, 30, 45, 60, and 75 degrees) appeared in extinction. Each session included 108 stimulus presentations arranged in eight blocks; each stimulus preceded itself and each other stimulus equally often within blocks.

The two panels of the figure show gradients averaged over five animals during two stages of training; these data are fully representative of the data for individual animals (Hinson and Malone, 1980). Each gradient shows the rate of response in each of the seven orientations when preceded by the orientation indicated. Thus, the leftmost gradient in both panels represents the gradient form when each orientation was preceded by 0 degrees.

The upper panel shows performance during sessions 17 to 19, shortly after clear gradients had appeared. The overall gradient was a W shape, with minimal responding in 30 and 60 degrees, as is the case for all gradients in the bottom panel. But it is apparent that local effects played an unexpected part in determining that overall form. When 45 degrees preceded each orientation, the gradient showed the classic U shape predicted by Spence's model, among others. But gradients produced when other stimuli preceded each stimulus showed local dimensional (stimulus-specific) effects, with higher response rates in more distant stimuli and lower response rates in more similar stimuli. It is clear how the combination of individual gradients (or of complementary pairs in particular) would produce an overall W form. It is also clear that local effects produced at least

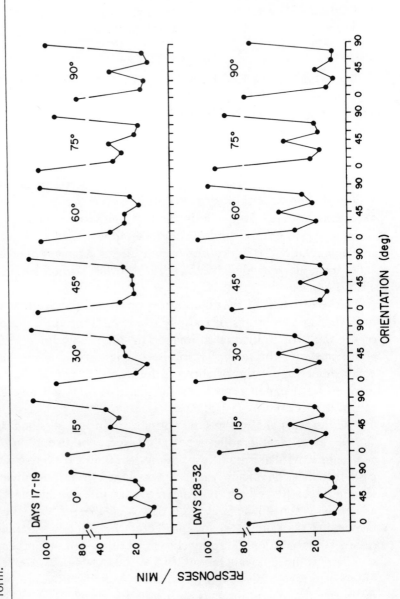

Figure 15–2. Maintained gradients during two stages of training in Hinson and Malone's (1980) experiment in which reinforcement was available only in the two extreme orientations (0° and 90°). Gradients were averaged over five animals but are fully representative of individual birds. In both upper and lower panels, gradients are shown as a function of the immediately preceding stimulus, thereby showing the influence of local dimensional effects and local contrast, respectively, on overall gradient form.

three quite different gradient forms—that produced by 0, 15, and 30 degrees; that produced by 45 degrees; or that by 60, 75, and 90 degrees.

These local dimensional effects faded by sessions 28 to 32 (bottom panel). By that time all gradients showed the W form characteristic of the overall gradient. One should note that there was still an effect produced by local contrast, but it was dependent only on average response rates. Thus, responding was lowest overall when the preceding stimulus was 0, 45, or 90 degrees, in which average response rates were highest, due to the suppressive effect of negative local contrast. When 30 or 60 degrees was the preceding stimulus, the overall gradients were elevated, due to positive local contrast produced in stimuli that followed them. Thus, the distribution of gradients shows an M shape, which mirrors the W form of the overall gradient.

Data for individual days and animals show the change in gradient form from the stimulus-specific forms of the upper panel to the more uniform shapes of the lower panel. They also suggest the possibility that local contrast modulated overall response rates to produce the final gradient form. Thus, the negative shoulder at 30 degrees appears the product of the stimulus-specific local effects produced by 0, 15, and 30 degrees, while 60, 75, and 90 degrees were responsible for the shoulder at 60 degrees. The net effect was a W–shaped gradient that remained with the fading of the stimulus-specific effects. Once the form of overall (average) responding was fixed, local contrast dependent only upon average response rates acted to maintain and accentuate that form.

Figure 15–3 shows the extremely close relationship between average response rates and local contrast during these sessions. For each bird, log responses per minute in all stimuli is plotted as a function of log response rate in the preceding stimulus. For example, the two rightmost points on each function represent log response rate averaged over all stimuli when the preceding stimuli were 0 and 90 degrees, those orientations appearing with VI reinforcement.

The lower right function represents the averaged performance of the five animals, and the regression line was calculated to fit those data. For the other birds, that best-fitting line (slope = −0.31) was simply fitted by inspection to the individual cases. The remarkably close fit of the average regression line to the individual cases shows that the relationship between average response rates and local con-

Figure 15–3. Log response rate in all stimuli as a function of log response rate in the preceding stimulus during sessions 28 through 32 of the Hinson experiment. This corresponds to the data in the lower panel of Figure 15–2. The regression line calculated for the group-averaged data (lower right) was adjusted vertically and fit by inspection to the data of each individual.

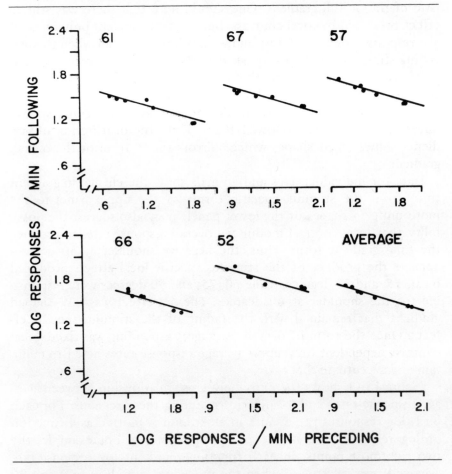

trast was extremely constant across birds. The vertical adjustment necessary to fit individual cases simply takes into account differences in overall response levels among subjects. The equation for the average regression line was $\log y = 2.01 - 0.31 \log x$ or $y = 102.33x^{-0.31}$.

A second experiment, carried out by David Rowe, was intended to show stimulus-specific local effects more clearly and to further assess their contribution to the form of the overall gradient. Pigeons again served as subjects, and the continuum of stimuli was the same as that in the study above. Initially, VI 1-minute reinforcement was available in all seven orientations. After fifty-eight sessions, conditions were changed so that the VI schedule was in force only during 0 (horizontal) and 15 degrees, while the remaining five orientations were correlated with extinction. Gradients quickly appeared during this condition, and negative contrast shoulders, with minimal responding in 30 and 45 degrees, were apparent in the data of each bird. Only two birds showed positive shoulders (maximum response rates in 15 degrees), and responding in the extinction orientations decreased rapidly (within fourteen sessions) to near zero. The unexpected rapid decrease in responding in the extinction components prevented an analysis of local effects that may have contributed to the contrast shoulders.

A second period of VI reinforcement in all stimuli followed by a repetition of VI in 0 and 15 degrees and extinction in the remaining stimuli led to even more rapid formation of gradients and diminution of responding in the extinction stimuli. Negative shoulders were again and more clearly apparent, with positive shoulders shown by the same two birds. Again, the rapidity of the process precluded any analysis of local effects.

We therefore learned that contrast shoulders are recoverable after an interpolated period of equal reinforcement in all stimuli and that the effect may appear more clearly the second time. But responding subsided so rapidly in the extinction stimuli that no sense or order could be made of the local effects that occurred; they were too fleeting.

To slow the formation of the gradients and thus allow a better assessment of local effects and their influence on the gradient, different VI schedules were put in force in the stimuli previously paired with VI and extinction during the subsequent condition. After eighteen sessions of VI 1 minute in all stimuli, VI 1 minute was present during 0 and 15 degrees, while a new VI 2-minute schedule was in force during the remaining orientations. We then examined the local effects that appeared as the gradients slowly formed over approximately sixty sessions. This analysis was (and still is) a formidable task; the main effects we have sorted out appear in Figures 15-4 and 15-5.

Figure 15-4 shows gradients for each animal averaged over five sessions during five stages of training. Unfilled circles show overall

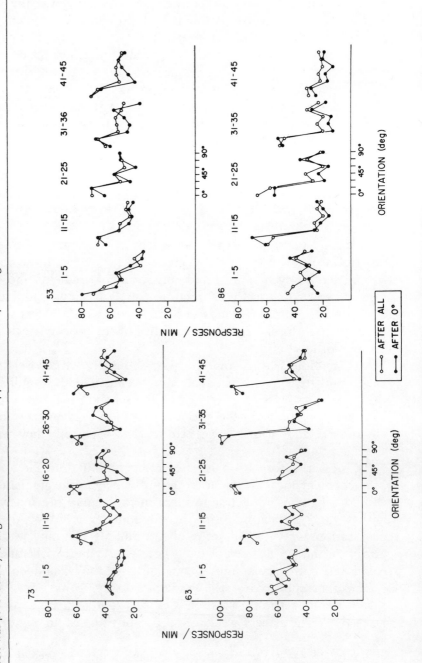

Figure 15–4. Maintained gradients for individual birds in Rowe's study shown as five-day averages during five stages of training. VI 1–minute reinforcement was available in 0 and 15 degrees, while a VI 2–minute schedule was in force for the remaining five orientations. Unfilled circles show overall averaged gradients; filled circles show gradients when each orientation was preceded by 0 degrees. Session numbers appear over each pair of gradients.

gradients during those periods, while filled circles show responding when each stimulus was preceded by 0 degrees, the extreme orientation paired with VI 1-minute reinforcement. Dimensional effects occurred after different amounts of training for different animals, and the average of five days was not always the best method of presentation. Nonetheless, Figure 15–4 shows an effect similar to that in Figure 15–2 and supports the interpretation given above for those data.

Consider Bird 73, which most clearly showed the effect. Contrast shoulders were apparent in the gradients calculated when zero preceded each orientation (filled circles) by sessions 11 to 15 and were clearest by sessions 16 to 20. Until that time, no sign of shoulders appeared in the overall gradients; response rates decreased from 30 to 90 degrees during sessions 11 to 15 and were roughly equal during sessions 16 to 20 in those stimuli correlated with VI 2-minute reinforcement. Thus, the 0-degree gradient clearly showed contrast shoulders, while the overall gradient showed no sign of them. By sessions 26 to 30, the overall gradient began to resemble the 0-degree gradient more closely, with decreased response rates in 30 and 45 degrees, those orientations adjacent to the VI 1-minute pair. By sessions 41 to 45 the gradients were nearly identical; the overall gradient had assumed the form predicted much earlier by the gradient produced by the local aftereffects of 0 degrees.

Similar effects appeared in the data for the other birds, though at different stages and with less clarity. Bird 53 showed positive shoulders in the 0-degree gradient by sessions 11 to 15 and a negative shoulder by sessions 31 to 36. A positive shoulder appeared in the overall gradient by that time, and only the suggestion of a negative shoulder appeared in the overall gradient during the last five sessions shown. Overall, effects were similar for all birds; negative shoulders appeared as minimal responding in VI 2-minute stimuli (i.e., 30, 45, and 60 degrees) earlier in the 0-degree gradient, and later the overall gradient tended to change form to more nearly resemble that gradient.

The later form of the gradient was most clearly anticipated by the 0-degree gradient, with lesser effects appearing with 15 degrees (the other orientation correlated with VI 1-minute reinforcement) as the preceding stimulus. In fact, as in Figure 15–2, quite different gradients resulted when local effects produced by each stimulus were considered. It will be recalled that gradients in the upper panel of

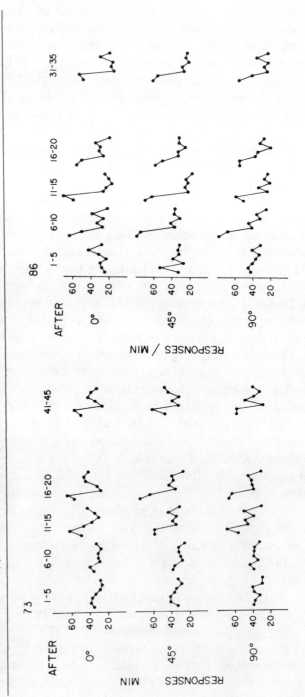

Figure 15-5. Data from the same period as those in Figure 15-4. For each bird, gradients are shown that resulted when the preceding stimulus was either 0, 45, or 90 degrees. Reinforcement was available on a VI 1-minute schedule in 0 and 15 degrees and on a VI 2-minute schedule in the remaining orientations. Contrast shoulders appeared frequently by the last sessions shown and appeared earlier in the gradients preceded by 0 degrees but not in those preceded by 45 degrees.

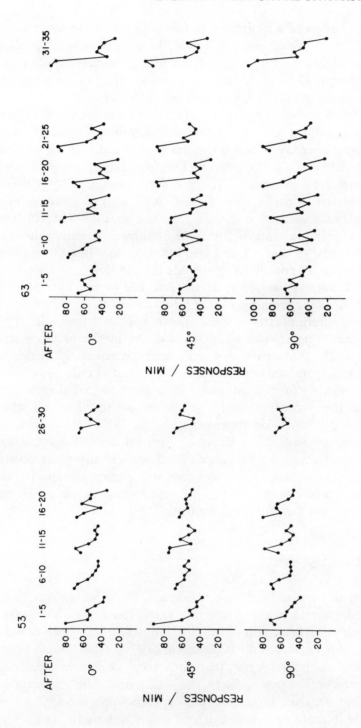

Figure 15-2 showed a symmetry of form, with complementary stimuli (e.g., 15 and 75 degrees) producing "local dimensional" gradients that were roughly mirror images. Gradients produced by 45 degrees showed a simple U form, however. A similar effect occurred here, at least concerning the effects produced by 45 degrees.

Figure 15-5 shows five-day averaged gradients for each bird over several periods of training. The figure shows gradients produced when the preceding orientation was 0 degrees (correlated with VI 1-minute reinforcement) or 45 or 90 degrees (two orientations correlated with VI 2-minute reinforcement). The gradients produced by 0 degrees showed negative contrast shoulders, though Bird 63 showed only a marginal effect and then only during the last sessions. The 90-degree gradients appear fairly steep (Bird 63) or showed negative shoulders (early for Birds 73 and 53 and late for Bird 86). But the gradients produced when all stimuli were preceded by 45 degrees showed little evidence of contrast shoulders at all (Bird 86) or not until the final sessions shown (the remaining three birds).

Gradients intermediate to those shown appeared when the effects of other preceding stimuli were assessed. As in the previous study (Figure 15-2), the extreme orientations (particularly 0 degrees) produced more and earlier evidence of contrast shoulders, with the effect diminishing to its least when 45 degrees preceded each stimulus. As in the preceding study, gradients produced by all stimuli approached the same (or approximately the same) form with continued training, aside from those of Bird 86 here. Thus, the local dimensional effects may be viewed as dependent upon the position of stimuli in the continuum, rather than solely upon the specific conditions of reinforcement or rate of responding prevailing in each stimulus, as is the case for local contrast.

DISCUSSION

These data show that local effects may greatly influence the form of maintained generalization gradients. The influence of local effects during generalization testing in extinction has already been noted by Donahoe, McCroskery, and Richardson (1970). The known properties of local contrast suggest that such local effects would tend to sharpen gradient slopes—as was the case—since the magnitude of positive and negative local contrast depends upon average response rates in the interacting stimuli (Malone and Staddon, 1973).

If, as appears the case, local dimensional effects are common, then the sequencing of stimuli could alter overall gradient shape considerably, as is evident in the upper panel of Figure 15–2. Contrast shoulders, which appear as the W shape of the overall gradient, were clearly the result of a combination of sequential effects produced by each component, no one of which produced such a gradient form. Later (bottom panel), local effects produced by each stimulus led to the same gradient form, that of the overall gradient.

The transition from the local dimensional forms of the upper panel to the stimulus-independent forms of the lower panel follows from what is known of local contrast. That is, local dimensional effects produced overall decreases in response rates in 30 and in 60 degrees (upper panel). Since the magnitude of local contrast depends upon average response rates in the interacting components (e.g., Malone, 1976), this would lead to greater negative local contrast in those stimuli, since more of the other stimuli were then associated with higher average response rates. Had 30 and 60 degrees been preceded only by 0, 15, and 30 degrees and by 90, 75, and 60 degrees, respectively, contrast shoulders may well have appeared earlier and been of greater magnitude. Similarly, a sequence in which 30 degrees was always preceded by 60, 75, and 90 degrees while 60 degrees was always preceded by 0, 15, and 30 degrees may have greatly diminished or eliminated the shoulders. A similar process may account for the data in Figure 15–4, where local effects produced by 0 degrees resulted in gradient forms that showed negative contrast shoulders early in training, with the overall gradients only later assuming that form.

Contrast shoulders would be predicted by the recent model for conditioning proposed by Rescorla and Wagner (1972), especially as it has been extended to cover stimulus generalization by Blough (1975) and Rescorla (1976). As was pointed out above, Blough's model was specifically designed to account for contrast shoulders. The model does not take local effects into account, but since it operates in a trial-by-trial fashion, sequential effects are derivable. Whether the sequential effects shown here are derivable is unknown at present. Unlike Blough's data, gradients here usually showed negative shoulders; Blough has not typically found negative shoulders. Indeed, his model is far more successful in simulating positive shoulders (see Blough, 1975).

We are confident of the existence of negative shoulders and of the close relationship between dimensional contrast shoulders and local effects. Contrast effects, both local and overall (i.e., behavioral contrast), are frequently viewed as side effects. Thus, during the formation of a discrimination, the conditions of reinforcement associated with different stimuli determine the "real" differences in responding, with sequential effects assumed to be dependent upon other factors. This view is exemplified in the additivity theory of contrast (e.g., Schwartz and Gamzu, 1977), which we have criticized sufficiently elsewhere (Hinson, Malone, McNally, and Rowe, 1978; Malone, 1976).

Data here certainly show that local effects may modulate overall responding in such a way as to anticipate final stable response rates. As shown elsewhere (Malone, 1976), local contrast may develop before clear differences in overall response rates appear. It is further possible that local effects may determine later overall response rates, thus producing dimensional contrast shoulders. One would think that this possibility could easily be tested, simply by separating stimulus presentations with time out periods long enough to eliminate local effects. If contrast shoulders appeared under such conditions, it would be obvious that local effects are not necessary to produce them. We have very recently found that contrast shoulders do occur in maintained gradients, even when 30-second time outs separate components. But we have also found that local effects were still present, transcending time out periods of that duration.

Whether local effects are necessary to produce contrast shoulders or whether they simply anticipate and accompany them is not of crucial importance. What is important is the fact that sequential effects are normally part and parcel of the discrimination process. Far from being capricious, they are governed by the rules listed earlier, and in the case of local contrast, they are remarkably regular, as shown in Figure 15-3. Most research has long concentrated on the outcomes of training procedures, particularly in the study of discrimination and generalization. We believe, with Pavlov, that the process involved is at least as worthy of study.

REFERENCES

Arnett, F.B. 1973. A local rate-of-response and interresponse-time analysis of behavioral contrast. *Journal of the Experimental Analysis of Behavior 20*: 489-498.

Blough, D.S. 1969. Generalization gradient shape and summation in steady-state tests. *Journal of the Experimental Analysis of Behavior 12*: 91–104.

_____. 1975. Steady-state data and a quantitative model of operant generalization and discrimination. *Journal of Experimental Psychology: Animal Behavior Processes 104*: 3–21.

Buck, S.; B. Rothstein; and B.A. Williams. 1975. A re-examination of local contrast in multiple schedules. *Journal of the Experimental Analysis of Behavior 24*: 291–301.

Catania, A.C., and C.A. Gill. 1964. Inhibition and behavioral contrast. *Psychonomic Science 1*: 257–258.

Crawford, L.L.; K.M. Steele; and J.C. Malone, Jr. 1980. Gradient form and sequential effects during generalization testing in extinction. *Animal Learning and Behavior 8*: 245–252.

Donahoe, J.W.; J.H. McCroskery; and W.K. Richardson. 1970. Effects of context on the postdiscrimination gradient of stimulus generalization. *Journal of Experimental Psychology 84*: 58–63.

Farthing, G.W. 1974. Behavioral contrast with multiple positive and negative stimuli on a continuum. *Journal of the Experimental Analysis of Behavior 22*: 419–425.

Hinson, J.M., and J.C. Malone, Jr. 1980. Local contrast and maintained generalization gradients. *Journal of the Experimental Analysis of Behavior 34*: 263–272.

Hinson, J.M.; J.C. Malone, Jr.; K.A. McNally; and D.W. Rowe. 1978. Effects of component length and of the transitions among components in multiple schedules. *Journal of the Experimental Analysis of Behavior 29*: 3–16.

Jenkins, H.M. 1970. Sequential organization in schedules of reinforcement. In W.N. Schoenfeld and J. Farmer, eds., *Theory of Reinforcement Schedules*. New York: Appleton–Century–Crofts.

Lashley, K.S., and M. Wade. 1946. The Pavlovian theory of generalization. *Psychological Review 53*: 72–87.

Mackintosh, N.J. 1974. *The Psychology of Animal Learning*. New York: Academic Press.

Mackintosh, N.J.; L. Little; and J. Lord. 1972. Some determinants of behavioral contrast in pigeons and rats. *Learning and Motivation 3*: 148–161.

Malone, J.C., Jr. 1975. Stimulus-specific contrast effects during operant discrimination learning. *Journal of the Experimental Analysis of Behavior 24*: 281–289.

_____. 1976. Local contrast and Pavlovian induction. *Journal of the Experimental Analysis of Behavior 26*: 425–440.

Malone, J.C., Jr., and J.E.R. Staddon. 1973. Contrast effects in maintained generalization gradients. *Journal of the Experimental Analysis of Behavior 19*: 167–179.

Menlove, R.L. 1975. Local patterns of responding maintained by concurrent and multiple schedules. *Journal of the Experimental Analysis of Behavior 23*: 309–337.

Nevin, J.A., and S.J. Shettleworth. 1966. An analysis of contrast effects in multiple schedules. *Journal of the Experimental Analysis of Behavior 9*: 305–315.

Pavlov, I.P. 1927. *Conditioned Reflexes*, translated by G.V. Anrep. London: Oxford University Press.

_____. 1955. *Selected Works*. Moscow: Foreign Languages Publishing House.

Rachlin, H. 1973. Contrast and matching. *Psychological Review 80*: 217–234.

Rescorla, R.A. 1976. Stimulus generalization: Some predictions from a model of Pavlovian conditioning. *Journal of Experimental Psychology: Animal Behavior Processes 2*: 88–96.

Rescorla, R.A., and A.R. Wagner. 1972. A theory of Pavlovian conditioning: Variations in the effectiveness of reinforcement and punishment. In A.H. Black and W.F. Prokasy, eds., *Classical Conditioning II: Current Research and Theory*. New York: Appleton–Century–Crofts.

Reynolds, G.S. 1961. Contrast, generalization, and the process of discrimination. *Journal of the Experimental Analysis of Behavior 4*: 289–294.

Rilling, M. 1977. Stimulus control and inhibitory processes. In W.K. Honig and J.E.R. Staddon, eds., *Handbook of Operant Behavior*. Englewood Cliffs, New Jersey: Prentice–Hall.

Schwartz, B., and E. Gamzu. 1977. Pavlovian control of operant behavior. In W.K. Honig and J.E.R. Staddon, eds., *Handbook of Operant Behavior*. Englewood Cliffs, New Jersey: Prentice–Hall.

Schwartz, B.; B. Hamilton; and A. Silberberg. 1975. Behavioral contrast in the pigeon: A study of the duration of key pecking maintained on multiple schedules of reinforcement. *Journal of the Experimental Analysis of Behavior 24*: 199–206.

Skinner, B.F. 1938. *The Behavior of Organisms*. New York: Appleton–Century–Crofts.

Spealman, R.D. 1976. Interactions in multiple schedules: The role of the stimulus–reinforcer contingency. *Journal of the Experimental Analysis of Behavior 26*: 79–93.

Spence, K.W. 1936. The nature of discrimination learning in animals. *Psychological Review 43*: 427–449.

_____. 1937. The differential response of animals to stimuli differing within a single dimension. *Psychological Review 44*: 430–444.

Thompson, R.F. 1965. The neural basis of stimulus generalization. In D.I. Mostofsky, ed., *Stimulus Generalization*. Stanford: Stanford University Press.

Williams, B.A. 1976. Behavioral contrast as a function of the temporal location of reinforcement. *Journal of the Experimental Analysis of Behavior 26*: 57–64.

VIII
A QUANTITATIVE INTEGRATION OF REINFORCEMENT AND DISCRIMINATION

16 MATCHING AND SIGNAL DETECTION

Dianne McCarthy and
Michael Davison

In the experimental analysis of behavior, as in much of the rest of psychology, the study of control by environmental stimuli and the study of control by reinforcement schedules have proceeded separately. Research on schedule control has, by and large, employed highly discriminable stimuli to signal different outcomes, and very little parametric variation of discriminative stimuli has been attempted. But failures to obtain expected schedule control relations have often been ascribed to failures of stimulus control (e.g., Baum, 1974). Likewise, parametric variation of schedules in work on stimulus control has been largely absent, although again, failures to obtain known stimulus control relations have been ascribed to problems in reinforcement control (e.g., Reynolds, 1963). In another sense, these areas have been growing apart. Schedule control research is now highly quantified (de Villiers, 1977), while stimulus control research is largely unquantified.

However, another area of psychology, signal detection theory (Peterson, Birdsall, and Fox, 1954; Tanner and Swets, 1954; van Meter and Middleton, 1954), has attempted, rather successfully,

The research reported in this chapter was supported entirely by the New Zealand University Grants Committee, to which organization we continue to be most grateful. Tony Nevin and Peter Jenkins provided constructive comments, and we thank them both. Our thanks also go to John Milkins and John Tull, who so ably look after our pigeons, and to the cooperative of masters and doctoral students who helped conduct these experiments.

the quantification of some stimulus effects. The signal detection approach has specified ways in which the discriminability of stimuli can be measured, and the measure is, under certain circumstances, independent of changes in behavior induced by outcomes, stimulus probabilities, and/or instructions. The effect of payoff—or reinforcement—on detection performance is measured by the signal detection term bias, or β, and this too is largely independent of discriminability. While the independence of these measures has sometimes been doubted (Wickelgren, 1968), this is neither the time nor the place to divert into detailed problems nor into the underlying theory of signal detection. The present chapter describes a program of research designed to develop a quantitative unified theory of reinforcement and stimulus control.

THE STANDARD SIGNAL DETECTION PROCEDURE

With minor variations, the signal detection procedure is a discrete trials procedure in which stimuli are presented to a subject trained to report which of two or more stimuli were presented. In general, correct responses (reporting S_1 when it was presented or S_2 when it was presented) are reinforced, with perhaps food or brain stimulation for animal subjects; or money, points, or feedback for humans. Sometimes payoffs for correct responses are given each time a correct response is emitted (continuous reinforcement, or FR 1), and sometimes it is given intermittently on variable interval (VI) or on probabilistic or variable ratio (VR) schedules. Usually, incorrect responses have no consequence or are punished in some way (e.g., time out with animals—Hume, 1974a, b; Hume and Irwin, 1974). The payoff matrix is a description of the arranged contingent events (reinforcers and punishers) for the various responses in the situation.

Figure 16-1 is a general stimulus response matrix showing, for example, the events in a yes–no signal detection task. Unlike the payoff matrix, W, X, Y, and Z refer to the numbers of events occurring in each cell. For example, with P denoting responses and R denoting reinforcers, P_w is the number of responses in cell W, and R_z is the number of reinforcements obtained in cell Z. S_1 and S_2 are two discriminative stimuli that may be related on the same physical dimension or that may be related by one having an additive property to the other (e.g., noise, signal plus noise) or that may be unrelated. P_1 and

Figure 16-1. Matrix of events in a standard yes-no signal detection procedure. W, X, Y, and Z refer to the numbers of events (responses emitted, reinforcements obtained) in each cell of the matrix.

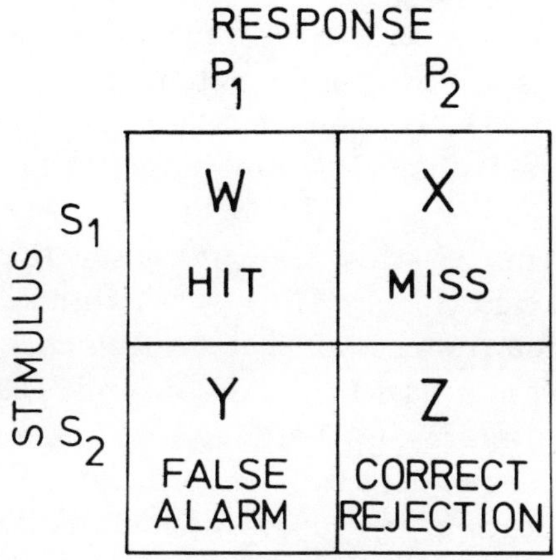

RESPONSE

	P_1	P_2
S_1	W HIT	X MISS
S_2	Y FALSE ALARM	Z CORRECT REJECTION

STIMULUS

P_2 are the two choice responses that may be emitted (perhaps yes and no or a left-key response and a right-key response). Throughout this chapter, we will assume that P_1 in the presence of S_1 and P_2 in the presence of S_2 are correct responses (hits and correct rejections) and that P_2 in S_1 and P_1 in S_2 are incorrect responses or errors (misses and false alarms).

The procedure can be viewed as rather like two multiple schedules (multiple VI EXT and multiple EXT VI) arranged simultaneously—a multiple concurrent schedule. A number of authors (e.g., Nevin, 1969; Stubbs, 1976) have commented on this procedural similarity and have suggested that, in principle, detection performance should be analyzable in terms of the matching of response ratios to reinforcement ratios (Baum, 1974; Herrnstein, 1970).

When two operants are concurrently made available to an animal, performance typically conforms to the generalized matching law (Baum, 1974), a quantitative specification of the relation between responses, P, and obtained reinforcements, R, on two (subscripts 1 and 2) concurrently available schedules of reinforcement. This relation may be expressed as:

$$\log \left(\frac{P_1}{P_2} \right) = a \log \left(\frac{R_1}{R_2} \right) + \log c \ . \qquad (16.1)$$

The parameter a is the sensitivity of the change in response ratios to changes in reinforcement ratios, and $\log c$ is a constant bias that the subject may show to one or other response alternative. If the value of a is less than or greater than unity, the subject is underestimating or overestimating reinforcement differences between the response alternatives. This is called "undermatching" or "overmatching," respectively (Baum, 1974). The matching law (Herrnstein, 1970) is a more constrained version of Equation (16.1), with $a = 1$, and $\log c = 0$.

Recently, three models have been proposed that integrate signal detection performance (Figure 16-1) with formulations describing the relation between responses and reinforcements in schedule control research (Equation [16.1]). Davison and Tustin (1978), and Nevin, Jenkins, Whittaker, and Yarensky (1977), for example, developed matching models of detection performance to describe behavior in the standard detection procedure in which only correct responses are reinforced. Interestingly, though these two models begin from different concepts, they both arrive at the same quantitative statement for the standard detection paradigm. This quantitative statement is similar to that derived from two other conceptual starting points—choice theory (Luce, 1959, 1963), and linear learning models (Bush, Luce, and Rose, 1964).

Davison and McCarthy (1980), and Nevin et al. (1977) extended the application of these models to procedures in which explicit reinforcement is introduced for incorrect responses, leading to a general model of choice behavior for both the standard (no error reinforcement) and the error reinforcement procedures. We now turn to a discussion of these models.

MATCHING MODELS FOR THE STANDARD SIGNAL DETECTION PROCEDURE

Davison and Tustin (1978)

These authors suggested that the generalized matching law (Baum, 1974) could be applied directly to the signal detection matrix (Figure 16-1). Davison and Tustin (1978) theorized that the ratio of reinforcers obtained for the two responses, $\log (R_w/R_z)$, would determine the response ratios in the presence of the two stimuli, $\log (P_w/P_x)$ and $\log (P_y/P_z)$, if the stimuli were indistinguishable. They further suggested that as the stimuli became more distinguishable, so performance in S_1 would become biased toward response 1 and performance in S_2 would become biased toward response 2. These biases are denoted $\log d$, and while they are correctly termed "stimulus biases," they are discriminability measures because they have the same function as discriminability measures like A' and d' in detection theory (Davison and Tustin, 1978). The reinforcement ratio for the two choices thus produces the bias (in the signal detection sense), and the discriminability of the two stimuli produces two further opposing biases (in the generalized matching law sense) in S_1 and S_2.

The basic equations for performance in S_1 and in S_2 are:

$$S_1: \quad \log \left(\frac{P_w}{P_x} \right) = a_{r_1} \log \left(\frac{R_w}{R_z} \right) + \log d + \log c \qquad (16.2)$$

$$S_2: \quad \log \left(\frac{P_y}{P_z} \right) = a_{r_2} \log \left(\frac{R_w}{R_z} \right) - \log d + \log c . \qquad (16.3)$$

Log c is inherent bias that is specifically associated with the two choice responses. Log d, discriminability, is by the nature of the matrix dissociated from the two responses and associated with the two stimuli. The parameter a_r is the sensitivity of response ratios to changes in reinforcement ratios.

As the sensitivity to reinforcement in S_1 equals the sensitivity to reinforcement in S_2 (i.e., $a_{r_1} = a_{r_2}$ —McCarthy and Davison 1979; 1980a, b), a stimulus function can be derived by subtracting Equation (16.3) from Equation (16.2):

$$\log \left(\frac{P_w}{P_x} \right) - \log \left(\frac{P_y}{P_z} \right) = 2 \log d \qquad (16.4)$$

where $\log d$ can be interpreted (Davison and Tustin, 1978) in the spirit of the concatination of the matching law (Baum and Rachlin, 1969) as equal to the ratio of stimulus values. Thus:

$$\log d = a_s \log \left(\frac{S_1}{S_2} \right) .$$

The stimulus function relates behavior to discriminative stimuli with reinforcement and inherent biases removed. With $\log d$ constant and reinforcement varied, Equation (16.4) is either identical to or equivalent to the standard signal detection isosensitivity equation depending on whether log or z transforms are used (Dusoir, 1975). However, this equation does not predict the exact data points, only the contour on which the data should fall. Equation (16.4) also acts as an isobias equation when the reinforcement ratio is kept constant and the stimuli are varied, and in this case, the position of the data point is predicted.

A bias function may be obtained by adding Equation (16.3) to Equation (16.2) to eliminate the effects of discriminability, log d,

$$\log \left(\frac{P_w}{P_x} \right) + \log \left(\frac{P_y}{P_z} \right) = 2 \, a_r \, \log \left(\frac{R_w}{R_z} \right) + 2 \log c \qquad (16.5)$$

This equation predicts behavior as a function of the reinforcements obtained for the two choice responses, taking inherent bias into account. It predicts isobias contours (but not data points) for the case in which the biasers on the right of the equation are constant and discriminability (log d) is varied as a parameter. With log d constant and reinforcements varied, however, it predicts isosensitivity contours and gives the exact location of data points.

Both the signal detection terms "isosensitivity" and "isobias" refer to Equations (16.4) and (16.5) only as they predict as a function of a parameter that does not occur within the equations. Equation (16.4) is indeed "isosensitivity," but only when the right-hand side of the equation is constant (hence "iso") and the bias parameter is varied. Equation (16.5) is "isobias," again, only when the equation equals a constant and discriminability is varied. We should point out, however, that the only direct prediction of behavior in S_1 and in S_2 comes from Equations (16.2) and (16.3). The stimulus and bias functions (Equations [16.4] and [16.5]) specify only the relations between these dependent variables. Their use is, of course, in specifying how estimates of discriminability and bias, which are independent of each other (McCarthy and Davison, 1980b), are to be measured:

$$\text{Discriminability} = \log d = \frac{1}{2} \left[\log \left(\frac{P_w}{P_x} \right) - \log \left(\frac{P_y}{P_z} \right) \right] \qquad (16.6)$$

$$\text{Bias} = a_r \log \left(\frac{R_w}{R_z} \right) + \log c = \frac{1}{2} \left[\log \left(\frac{P_w}{P_x} \right) + \log \left(\frac{P_y}{P_z} \right) \right] \qquad (16.7)$$

Nevin, Jenkins, Whittaker, and Yarensky (1977)

The model suggested by these authors is formally identical to the Davison–Tustin (1978) model except in one respect. Nevin et al. (1977) used the matching law (Herrnstein, 1970) rather than the generalized matching law (Baum, 1974), thus not allowing for under- or overmatching or for inherent bias. Nevin (Chapter 1), however, presents data that necessitate the inclusion of a parameter to account for nonunit reinforcement sensitivity.

The conceptual background to the Nevin et al. (1977) model is, however, very different. As Nevin outlines in Chapter 1, it is based on the generalization of the effects of reinforcement obtained for correct responses to error responses. In the matrix of Figure 16–1, reinforcements for response 1 in S_1 also affect, through generalization, response 1 emitted in the presence of S_2. The magnitude of the generalization depends on the discriminability of S_1 and S_2. If they are indiscriminable, the generalization is maximal. If they are perfectly discriminable, there is no generalization. The degree of discriminability is measured by a similarity parameter, η, which takes the values of 0 (perfect discrimination) through 1 (no discrimination). In Figure 16–1, the reinforcement obtained for P_1 in the presence of S_2 is thus ηR_w and for P_2 in the presence of S_1, ηR_z.

Formally, the model cast into logarithms is:

$$S_1: \quad \log\left(\frac{P_w}{P_x}\right) = \log\left(\frac{R_w}{R_z}\right) - \log \eta$$

$$S_2: \quad \log\left(\frac{P_y}{P_z}\right) = \log\left(\frac{R_w}{R_z}\right) + \log \eta$$

Since η falls between 0 and 1, $-\log \eta$ is positive and $+\log \eta$ is negative, giving the same formal model as suggested by Davison and Tustin (1978), but with unit reinforcement sensitivity and no inherent bias. Nevin et al. (1977) derived stimulus and bias functions similar to Equations (16.4) and (16.5) above (see Nevin, Chapter 1).

DATA SUPPORTING THE MATCHING MODELS

Davison and Tustin (1978) analyzed two sets of published data (Green and Swets, 1966; Stubbs, 1976) that supported their detection model. We now have considerably more data available that test the adequacy of the model in various ways.

McCarthy and Davison (1979) noted that neither matching model could easily handle the most common biasing operation used in signal detection research—variation of the probability of presenting each of the stimuli. However, they pointed out that, while stimulus presentation probability (SPP) did not change the payoff matrix (the arranged probabilities of reinforcement for the choice responses), SPP variation would systematically change the obtained numbers of reinforcements for the choice responses. Obtained, rather than arranged, reinforcement ratio is the critical variable in research on matching and, hence, in the signal detection matching models.

McCarthy and Davison (1979) carried out three experiments using the same pigeon subjects trained to detect differences in light intensity. The discriminative stimuli in these experiments were two intensities of white light displayed on the center key of a three-key pigeon chamber. S_1 was 33 cd/m^2, and S_2 was 7 cd/m^2. Following presentation of either S_1 or S_2 on the center key, a peck on the center key turned on the two side keys, which were illuminated red (left) and green (right). Correct responses were defined as a left-key peck following presentation of S_1 and a right-key peck following S_2 presentations.

In the first experiment, SPP was varied from 0.1 to 0.9 in steps of 0.2. Food reinforcement for correct choices was arranged on a single variable-ratio (VR) schedule, and unreinforced correct responses were followed by a 3-second magazine light. Errors were followed by a 3-second blackout. With such probabilistic scheduling, the obtained reinforcement ratio, log (R_w/R_z), will covary with the ratios of the frequencies of stimulus presentation and with the subject's performance. We therefore call this procedure an uncontrolled reinforcement ratio procedure (McCarthy and Davison, 1980a), and it is typical of most signal detection research. In the second experiment, reinforcement for correct left- and right-key responses was arranged on equal and nonindependent (Stubbs and Pliskoff, 1969; Stubbs, 1976) concurrent VI VI schedules, and SPP alone was varied. Finally, in the third experiment, SPP was held constant at 0.7, but the ratio of rein-forcements obtained for the choice responses was varied by changing the dependent concurrent VI VI schedules. We call these last two experimental procedures controlled reinforcement ratio procedures (McCarthy and Davison, 1980a) because the reinforcement ratio is set and cannot covary with either response ratios or SPP.

For the first and third experiments, in which reinforcement ratios either covaried with SPP or were directly varied, the data fitted nicely to Equations (16.2) and (16.3). In both these experiments, estimates of bias (Equation [16.7]) showed statistically significant trends across conditions. However, when SPP alone was varied with a controlled unit reinforcement ratio (Experiment 2), behavior failed to change with SPP, and no trends in bias were found. Estimates of discriminability (Equation [16.6]), as expected, showed no trends in any of the experiments and were not significantly different between the three experiments.

McCarthy and Davison (1979) concluded, therefore, that SPP is not a biaser per se and that its apparent biasing effects arise from changes in the obtained reinforcement ratio for the two choices. SPP clearly need not be shown as an independent variable in the matching models of signal detection performance.

Parametric variation of reinforcement schedules has received little consideration in signal detection research. For an adequate isosensitivity contour, an independent variable that controls—or biases—behavior is clearly needed, and these variables have been well specified by concurrent schedule research—for example, reinforce-ment rate, magnitude, immediacy, and quality (de Villiers, 1977) and also response requirements (Beautrais and Davison, 1977; Davi-son and Ferguson, 1978). Furthermore, because response bias is a function of the obtained reinforcement rate and not a function of stimulus presentation probability (McCarthy and Davison, 1979), a constant measure of response bias can only be reliably obtained from a procedure that controls the reinforcement ratio. In signal detec-tion theory, however, the common procedure is to arrange continu-ous (e.g., Hume and Irwin, 1974) or probabilistic (e.g., Elsmore, 1972; Hobson, 1975, 1978) reinforcement. As the number of rein-forcements obtained for the two choices can vary with the subject's behavior, this is an uncontrolled reinforcement ratio procedure that gives rise to exceedingly variable data on response bias (e.g., Hobson, 1975). Such varying biases can, however, be easily handled within

Figure 16–2. Log response ratios in both S_1 and S_2 as a function of the logarithm of the obtained reinforcement ratio at the two levels of difficulty. These plots correspond with Equations (16.2) and (16.3). The unfilled triangles and circles represent S_1 and S_2 performance, respectively, for the 5–second versus 30–second conditions. The filled triangles and circles represent S_1 and S_2 performance, respectively, for the 20–second versus 30–second conditions. The best-fitting straight line by the method of least squares is shown for each bird and for each stimulus at both discriminability levels. The slopes and intercepts are shown, for each bird, on each line. The data were summed over the last five sessions of each experimental condition. (*Source*: from McCarthy & Davison, 1980b.)

the matching models of signal detection. Because these models view bias as a function of the obtained reinforcement ratio, rather than from arranged payoff matrixes, they can specify true isobias contours. They suggest that the data usually presented as isobias contours do not arise from equal bias conditions. The data show, instead, alloiobias (varying sorts of, different, bias) contours (McCarthy and Davison, 1980a).

The Davison and Tustin (1978) model assumes that the behavioral effects of discriminability and bias are additive in logarithmic terms (Equations [16.2] and [16.3]), and hence, there is no interaction between these two variables. In a further experiment (McCarthy and Davison, 1980b), we tested empirically this assumption of independence by examining the biasing effects of reinforcement frequency for both an easy and a difficult discrimination. Pigeons were trained to detect differences in the duration of a white center key light under two levels of difficulty. At one level, one stimulus (S_1) was 5 seconds and S_2 was 30 seconds; at the other, S_1 was 20 seconds and S_2 was 30 seconds. The procedure was a standard signal detection yes–no design in which SPP was varied from 0.1 to 0.9 at both discriminability levels. On completion of the center-key stimulus, a peck on the center key darkened the center key light and turned on the two red side keys. Left-key pecks following S_1 presentations and right-key pecks following S_2 presentations were defined as "correct" and produced food reinforcement on a single VR schedule (an uncontrolled reinforcement ratio procedure). Unreinforced correct responses produced a 3-second magazine light, and errors (left following S_2, right following S_1) produced a 3-second blackout.

(Figure 16-2)

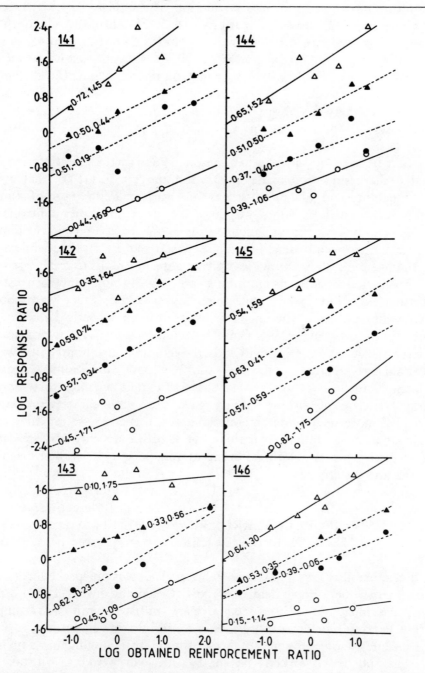

We found that sensitivity of behavior to changes in the obtained reinforcement ratio was not a function of the degree of difficulty. As Figure 16-2 shows, Equations (16.2) and (16.3) yielded the same positive slopes for both the easy and the hard discriminations. Thus, discriminability did not affect reinforcement sensitivity. Such parallelism also implies that discriminability is constant for all reinforcement bias values. We concluded, therefore, that there was no interaction between discriminability and bias and that these two measures are additive logarithmic quantities as proposed by Davison and Tustin (1978).

Finally, we (McCarthy and Davison, 1980a) have directly investigated the assumption made by Davison and Tustin (1978) that discriminability could be expressed as the logarithm of the ratio of stimulus values—that is, $\log d = a_s \log (S_1/S_2)$. Using both controlled and uncontrolled reinforcement ratios in our usual intermittent reinforcement procedures, S_2 was held constant at 30 seconds while S_1 was increased from 5 to 25 seconds in 5-second steps over successive experimental conditions. Stimulus variation did not affect bias estimates (Equation [16.7]), although, as expected, there was more variability in bias in the uncontrolled reinforcement ratio procedure. For both procedures, discriminability (Equation [16.6]) reliably decreased as S_1 was brought closer to S_2, but discriminability was curvilinearly related to the log ratio of stimulus durations. A more detailed analysis of these data showed that a stimulus difference interpretation of discriminability gave a more linear relation and yielded more reliable parameter estimates. However, we regard such a conclusion as tentative at this stage, and we are currently investigating its generality with different stimuli, varying both their magnitudes and differences.

REINFORCING ERRORS IN SIGNAL DETECTION PROCEDURES

Discriminability, as measured by signal detection procedures, is assumed to be independent of payoff (Green and Swets, 1966), and the matching models discussed above are consistent with this assumption if reinforcement sensitivities, a_r, and inherent biases, $\log c$, are the same in the presence of both stimuli. In a number of papers, Nevin and his coworkers (Nevin, 1970; Nevin, Jenkins, Whittaker, and Yarensky, 1977; Nevin, Olson, Mandell, and Yarensky, 1975) have shown that estimates of discriminability of constant stimuli decrease as errors (P_1 in S_2 or P_2 in S_1) are reinforced with increasing frequencies. (In this type of research, it is conventional to use the term "error" for responses in cells X and Y of Figure 16-1 even when they are reinforced.) From a behavioral point of view, we are just as interested in the effects of reinforcing errors as we are in the effects of reinforcing correct responses. If we can explain in a quantitative fashion how behavior changes as a function of stimuli and reinforcers for both situations, we also have the possibility of deriving a measure of discriminability that can be used in both situations. One such model was suggested by Nevin et al. (1977) and a second by Davison and McCarthy (1980).

MODELS FOR ERROR REINFORCEMENT PROCEDURES

Nevin et al. (1977)

The extension of the Nevin et al. model for the standard situation to the reinforcement for errors procedure is straightforward. The assumptions made for the standard situation—that reinforcement effects will generalize to the same response in the other stimulus in inverse proportion to the discriminability of the stimuli—was applied to all cells of the matrix shown in Figure 16-1. The reinforcement for responses in S_1 (P_1 in S_1) is now ($R_w + \eta R_y$); for P_1 in S_2, it is ($R_y + \eta R_w$); and so on. Without casting into logarithms this time, the model for performance in S_1 and in S_2 becomes:

$$S_1: \quad \frac{P_w}{P_x} = \frac{R_w + \eta R_y}{R_x + \eta R_z}$$

$$S_2: \quad \frac{P_y}{P_z} = \frac{R_y + \eta R_w}{R_z + \eta R_x}$$

Because the reinforcement terms on the right of these equations are different in S_1 and in S_2, they cannot be removed to give a reinforcement-free estimate of η or discriminability. The implication is that conventional point estimates of discriminability (obtained, for example, using Equation [16.6]) are affected by reinforcement, and the above equations correctly predict that as error reinforcement is increased, so discriminability measured in this way falls. On the other hand, point estimates of η obtained from the above two equations should not change as error reinforcement is varied.

Davison and McCarthy (1980)

Following the Davison and Tustin (1978) logic, Davison and McCarthy (1980) derived a model for the reinforcement for errors situation that is rather different from the Nevin et al. (1977) model. We make the same assumption as Davison and Tustin (1978) that overall allocation of choice responses to the two alternatives is determined by the reinforcements obtained for the two responses. In the reinforcement for errors procedure, however, this reinforcement ratio will comprise all reinforcers, and as in the Davison and Tustin model, behavior will follow this reinforcement ratio according to a certain sensitivity, a_r (Baum, 1974).

While we assume that discriminability, $\log d$ (the maximal ability of a subject to tell two stimuli apart), remains constant when errors are reinforced, the data reported by Nevin et al. (1975) indicated that conventionally measured discriminability shown by the subjects decreased when errors were reinforced. Thus, we make the additional assumption that the degree of discrimination that can be shown in the reinforcement for errors situation is a function of both the discriminability of the stimuli ($\log d$) and the degree of association between reinforcers and stimulus presentations. Discrimination, as distinct from discriminability, is thus given by:

$$\text{Discrimination} = \left(\frac{R_c - R_e}{R_c + R_e} \right) \cdot \log d$$

where R_c is the number of reinforcements obtained for correct responses ($R_w + R_z$ in Figure 16-1) and R_e is the number of reinforcements obtained for errors ($R_x + R_y$ in Figure 16-1). In other words, discrimination will be degraded by reinforcing errors.

Our full reinforcement for errors model is thus:

$$S_1: \quad \log \left(\frac{P_w}{P_x} \right) = a_{r_1} \log \left(\frac{R_w + R_y}{R_x + R_z} \right) + \left(\frac{R_c - R_e}{R_c + R_e} \right) \log d + \log c \quad (16.8)$$

$$S_2: \ \log\left(\frac{P_y}{P_z}\right) = a_{r_2} \log\left(\frac{R_w + R_y}{R_x + R_z}\right) - \left(\frac{R_c - R_e}{R_c + R_e}\right) \log d + \log c \ . \ (16.9)$$

When the association between reinforcement and stimulus presentations is 1 (i.e., only correct responses are reinforced), Equations (16.8) and (16.9) simplify to Equations (16.2) and (16.3) of the no error reinforcement model (Davison and Tustin, 1978). When the association is −1, only errors are reinforced, and the equations again simplify to the Davison–Tustin model. When, however, the association is 0, no discrimination between S_1 and S_2 is shown, and both response ratios are a function only of the obtained reinforcement ratio. Discriminability ($\log d$) cannot, therefore, be measured in the absence of the association of reinforcement and stimulus presentation.

Subtracting for the equivalent of a stimulus function gives:

$$\log\left(\frac{P_w}{P_x}\right) - \log\left(\frac{P_y}{P_z}\right) = 2\left(\frac{R_c - R_e}{R_c + R_e}\right) \log d \ , \qquad (16.10)$$

and adding for the equivalent of a bias function gives:

$$\log\left(\frac{P_w}{P_x}\right) + \log\left(\frac{P_y}{P_z}\right) = 2a_r \log\left(\frac{R_w + R_y}{R_x + R_z}\right) + 2 \log c \ . \quad (16.11)$$

Equation (16.10) shows correctly that discriminability estimates taken conventionally (Equation [16.6]) are only independent of payoff when no error reinforcement is obtained. More generally, then, the conventional discriminability measurement procedure assesses discrimination. It measures discriminability only when error reinforcement is absent.

REINFORCING ERRORS: DATA

The data from two major papers on the effects of reinforcing errors in a detection situation (Nevin et al., 1975, 1977) were kindly made available to us by the authors. Nevin et al. (1975) trained rats on a brightness detection task using an uncontrolled reinforcement ratio procedure in which reinforcements for correct responses and errors were scheduled probabilistically on two separate VR schedules, one for all correct responses and one for all errors. These data were fitted to Equations (16.8) and (16.9) combined by multiple linear regression to obtain two slope parameters (sensitivity to reinforcement, a_r, and discriminability, log d) and an intercept (inherent bias, log c). The results of this analysis are shown in Table 16–1, section A. All three rats showed reliable undermatching and small positive inherent biases, again demonstrating the necessity of including parameters to account for nonunit reinforcement sensitivity and inherent bias in behavioral models of detection performance. The discriminability measures and the other obtained parameters had small standard deviations, and the predictions made from these parameters accounted for a high percentage of the data variance.

A second analysis of the same type was carried out on the data reported by Nevin et al. (1977). In this experiment, pigeons discriminated between two durations of white key light. The scheduling procedure was different from that used by Nevin et al. (1975). Reinforcement probabilities in each of the four cells of the matrix in Figure 16–1 were determined by probability generators such that, on any trial, reinforcement was set up in only one cell. This reinforcement remained available, and no more became available until it was taken—a procedure that completely controls the obtained reinforcement ratio. Three levels of error reinforcement probabilities were arranged, including zero probability (the standard procedure). Twelve conditions were investigated, giving twenty-four data points for a combined fit to Equations (16.8) and (16.9). The results are shown in section B of Table 16–1. Again, all three subjects undermatched, though not reliably for Bird 58, and all parameters were estimated with small standard deviations. Bird 59 displayed a strong negative inherent bias, a result noted by Nevin et al. (1977) in their analysis of these data.

The data obtained by Nevin et al. (1977) were also analyzed in two other ways. Using their model, Nevin and his colleagues found that their measure of stimulus discriminability (η) showed apparently better discriminability when errors were reinforced than when they were not. This result seems quite counterintuitive. Hence, we analyzed their data separately for the standard (no error reinforcement) and the error reinforcement conditions. The results of this analysis (Table 16–1C and D) showed no evidence of consistent differences in estimated parameters between the two sets of conditions.

Table 16−1. Analysis of Data from Three Reinforcement for Errors Experiments According to Equations (16.8) and (16.9). *VAC* refers to the percentage of data variance accounted for by the predictions from the obtained parameters; and *N* the number of data points used in each analysis.

Subject	a_r (SD)	log d (SD)	log c (SD)	VAC	N
A. Nevin, Olson, Mandell, and Yarensky (1975)					
Rat D	0.82 (.06)	0.63 (.03)	0.09 (.03)	93	48
Rat E	0.92 (.03)	0.89 (.03)	0.19 (.02)	97	47
Rat F	0.56 (.07)	0.60 (.03)	0.07 (.02)	91	48
B. Nevin et al (1977): all data					
Bird 58	0.95 (.09)	0.48 (.06)	0.06 (.05)	89	24
Bird 59	0.89 (.08)	0.57 (.05)	-0.20 (.04)	94	24
Bird 60	0.86 (.09)	1.00 (.06)	0.10 (.04)	97	24
C. Nevin et al. (1977): no error reinforcement conditions					
Bird 58	0.83 (.21)	0.48 (.10)	0.02 (.10)	90	12
Bird 59	0.93 (.11)	0.53 (.06)	-0.20 (.06)	97	12
Bird 60	0.92 (.16)	0.99 (.08)	0.06 (.08)	98	12
D. Nevin et al. (1977): error reinforcement conditions					
Bird 58	1.08 (.12)	0.66 (.13)	0.08 (.06)	92	12
Bird 59	0.89 (.10)	0.83 (.11)	-0.23 (.05)	94	12
Bird 60	0.91 (.11)	0.79 (.11)	0.05 (.05)	93	12
E. Davison and McCarthy (1980a)					
Bird 121	1.39 (.20)	1.27 (.11)	0.13 (.09)	92	20
Bird 122	1.21 (.18)	1.30 (.15)	0.04 (.14)	89	18
Bird 123	1.13 (.07)	0.74 (.07)	-0.11 (.07)	98	12
Bird 124	1.24 (.10)	0.65 (.11)	-0.12 (.08)	93	18
Bird 125	1.69 (.29)	0.85 (.06)	0.11 (.06)	97	10
Bird 126	1.12 (.06)	1.01 (.11)	0.02 (.10)	94	12

In particular, measures of discriminability (log d) were not significantly different between the no error reinforcement and the error reinforcement conditions. The fits to these smaller sample were, of course, less good than those to the larger sample (compare section B with sections C and D).

If discriminability is the maximal ability of a subject to detect one stimulus relative to another, then any measure of discriminability should indeed remain constant. In this sense, then, the Davison–McCarthy (1980) model is preferable to the Nevin et al. (1977) formulation. However, since only small amounts of data are as yet available, a critical empirical test of the merits of these two models is not possible at the present time.

Nevin (1979) has pointed out to us that the phi coefficent (a nonparametric measure of association in 2 × 2 matrixes) could be used to modify log d instead of the stimulus reinforcement association measure used here. Our data analyses have shown that the phi coefficient is as good as our measure and may, in fact, explain performance better for some situations in which the reinforcements obtained are asymetrically distributed in the cells of the matrix (Figure 16–1).

In our own research on the effects of reinforcing errors in a signal detection paradigm (Davison and McCarthy, 1980), pigeons were trained to discriminate between two durations of a white center key light. Following presentations of a 5-second light, left-key pecks were defined as correct; and following presentation of a 10-second light, right-key pecks were defined as correct. All correct responses produced access to wheat with a probability of 0.7. The probability of food reinforcement for errors (left after 10-second light, right after 5-second light) was increased from 0 to 0.9, in steps of 0.1, in successive experimental conditions. Like Nevin et al. (1975), we used an uncontrolled reinforcement ratio procedure, as is common in most signal detection research. However, in the Nevin et al. (1975) study, the probability gates controlling correct and error reinforcements were tested on each trial, and reinforcements not taken were lost. In our study, on the other hand, the probability generator controlling food reinforcement for correct responses was interrogated only after each correct response had been emitted on either side key. Likewise, the probability generator controlling food reinforcement for errors was interrogated only after each incorrect response. Reinforcers not taken were saved, so that reinforcement could be available for both correct responses or errors on some trials. In addition, unlike Nevin et al. (1975, 1977), who arranged no outcomes on unreinforced trials, we followed unreinforced errors by a 3-second blackout, and unreinforced correct responses by 3-second magazine light illuminations.

The well-documented finding in this area of research (Nevin et al. 1975, 1977) is that, as error reinforcement probability is increased, so traditional measures of stimulus discriminability (e.g., Equation [16.6]) fall. One such measure, A' (Grier, 1971) is shown in Figure 16-3 as a function of the arranged probability of error reinforcement. The value of A' for these birds remained high as the probability of error reinforcement was increased to moderate levels, but fell thereafter to levels close to chance (0.5). In our procedure, if few errors are emitted, few error reinforcements will be obtained, although the obtained probability (per error response) of error reinforcement will be as arranged. Figure 16-3, therefore, also shows the relative number of reinforcements obtained for correct responses, which can be seen to covary with the value of A'. Clearly, it is the obtained frequency of error reinforcement, rather than the arranged probability of error reinforcement, that affects discriminability.

Because near-exclusive choice responding developed in the final stages of this experiment (when error reinforcement probabilities were high), the data are a stringent test of our error reinforcement model. The analysis of the data according to Equations (16.8) and (16.9) is shown in Table 16-1, section E. The parameters were again estimated with small standard deviations (an exception being the reinforcement sensitivity shown by Bird 125), and a good percentage of the data variance was accounted for. It is interesting to note that all birds showed overmatching.

The analysis of these three sets of data on reinforcing errors in signal detection paradigms, covering both controlled and uncontrolled reinforcement ratio procedures and two different species of subject, show that the Davison–McCarthy (1980) model fits the data very well. Estimates of stimulus discriminability and reinforcement sensitivity from the error reinforcement conditions seem at least as good as those from the standard no error reinforcement conditions (Table 16-1 C and D). Point estimates of discriminability from the error reinforcement situation (Equation [16.10]) are thus for the first time available. Apart from the benefits of such a general measure of discriminability, our model is more importantly a predictor of choice behavior in both the standard and the error reinforcement signal detection procedures.

Figure 16–3. Discriminability, measured by A', as a function of the arranged probability of reinforcement for errors. The probability of reinforcement for correct responses was 0.7. Also shown is the obtained relative frequency of reinforcement for correct responses (reinforcements for correct responses divided by total reinforcements).

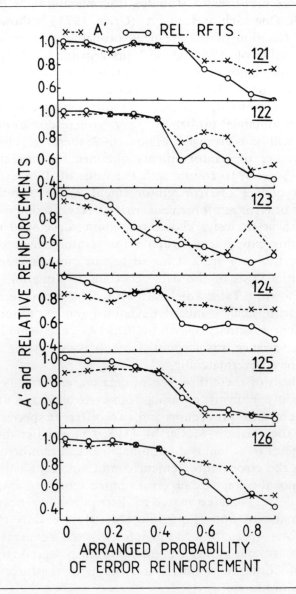

STIMULUS MEASURES FROM SCHEDULE
CONTROL DATA

In schedule control research, we see a great need for quantification of free operant stimulus effects. Measures of both discrimination and discriminability in complex free operant procedures are of considerable importance in the study of behavior. A direct approach to this issue is now possible with the generalization of our behavioral model of signal detection performance to the equivalent free operant paradigm.

Multiple concurrent schedules (Pliskoff, Shull, and Gollub, 1968), for example, have the same matrix of events as a reinforcement for errors detection procedure, with the exception that the former arrangement is a free operant procedure, while the latter uses discrete trials. Davison and McCarthy (1980) analyzed two sets of multiple concurrent schedule data (Lobb and Davison, 1977; Nevin, Mandell, and Whittaker, 1978) from which stimulus discriminability measures had not previously been obtained. Our analysis yielded precise parameter estimates and reliable undermatching. In addition, we showed time allocation data (e.g., White, 1978) to be a useful way of obtaining stimulus discriminability measures in multiple schedules. These reanalyses of schedule control data suggest that the present behavioral models may be useful in giving a more complete understanding of behavior in a wide range of situations.

At the present time, however, no data are available with which to compare values of stimulus discriminability between free operant procedures and signal detection tasks. An experiment currently in progress in our laboratory is designed to provide such data. The birds were trained in three procedures. The first was a standard signal detection design in which the birds produced either two bright or two dull key lights for 3 seconds and then reported which stimulus had been presented. In the second procedure, the two bright or two dull stimuli were randomly presented on a trial, and the birds were required to peck the left key if one pair was presented and the right key if the other pair was presented. As in the first procedure, all correct responses were reinforced, making the second procedure a multiple (concurrent FR 1 EXT) (concurrent EXT FR 1) schedule.

The third procedure was the same as the second except that VI 60-second schedules, rather than FR 1 schedules, were used and, as in the second procedure, the trial ended with reinforcement. The third procedure was thus multiple (concurrent VI 60 EXT) (concurrent EXT VI 60). In each procedure, the stimulus presentation probability was varied over five values. Initial results showed that stimulus discriminability was significantly lower in the signal detection procedure than in the multiple concurrent schedule procedures. The implication is that the yes–no detection procedure does not provide optimal measures of discriminability, and further conditions are now arranged to test whether the critical difference is the fact that, as in the multiple concurrent schedules, the stimuli are present when the choice is made.

The reanalyses of the data from Lobb and Davison (1977) and from Nevin, Mandell, and Whittaker (1978) and the initial results reported above suggest that we may be able to understand quantitatively discriminative stimulus effects in schedule control experiments. The initial part of our chapter has been concerned with understanding reinforcement effects in studies of signal detection. The caveat is that, for generality, experiments focusing on one of the controlling variables (reinforcement or stimulus) should take adequate care to control the other (stimulus or reinforcement) variable. In our reanalyses of Lobb and Davison (1977), our obtained measures of discriminability cannot be pure measures of stimulus discriminability, since more than one reinforcement was delivered in each component and equal numbers of components were given in strict alternation. Thus, both reinforcement rate and sequential information were additionally available to, and either could have increased or could have overshadowed, stimulus control. The common ground between signal detection procedures, stimulus control procedures, and schedule control experiments is the random component, multiple concurrent schedule with components terminating in reinforcement (Procedure three, above). It is, we believe, in this particular design that the matching models of signal detection performance will complete the unification of schedule and stimulus control.

REFERENCES

Baum, W.M. 1974. On two types of deviation from the matching law: Bias and undermatching. *Journal of the Experimental Analysis of Behavior 22*: 231-242.

Baum, W.M., and H.C. Rachlin. 1969. Choice as time allocation. *Journal of the Experimental Analysis of Behavior 12*: 861-874.

Beautrias, P.G., and M.C. Davison. 1977. Response and time allocation in concurrent second-order schedules. *Journal of the Experimental Analysis of Behavior 25*: 61-69.

Bush, R.R.; R.D. Luce; and R.M. Rose. 1964. Learning models for psychophysics. In R.C. Atkinson, ed., *Studies in Mathematical Psychology*. Stanford: Stanford University Press.

Davison, M.C., and A. Ferguson. 1978. The effects of different component response requirements in multiple and concurrent schedules. *Journal of the Experimental Analysis of Behavior 29*: 283-295.

Davison, M., and D. McCarthy. 1980. Reinforcement for errors in a signal-detection procedure. *Journal of the Experimental Analysis of Behavior 34*: 35-47.

Davison, M.C., and R.D. Tustin. 1978. The relation between the generalized matching law and signal-detection theory. *Journal of the Experimental Analysis of Behavior 29*: 331-336.

De Villiers, P.A. 1977. Choice in concurrent schedules and a quantitative formulation of the law of effect. In W.K. Honig and J.E.R. Staddon, eds., *Handbook of Operant Behavior*. Englewood Cliffs, New Jersey: Prentice-Hall.

Dusoir, A.E. 1975. Treatment of bias in detection and recognition models: A review. *Perception and Psychophysics 17*: 167-178.

Elsmore, T.F. 1972. Duration discrimination: Effects of probability of stimulus presentation. *Journal of the Experimental Analysis of Behavior 18*: 465-469.

Green, D.M., and J.A. Swets. 1966. *Signal Detection Theory and Psychophysics*. New York: Wiley.

Grier, J.B. 1971. Nonparametric indices for sensitivity and bias: Computing formulas. *Psychological Bulletin 75*: 424-429.

Herrnstein, R.J. 1970. On the law of effect. *Journal of the Experimental Analysis of Behavior 13*: 243-266.

Hobson, S.L. 1975. Discriminability of fixed-ratio schedules for pigeons: Effects of absolute ratio size. *Journal of the Experimental Analysis of Behavior 23*: 25-35.

_____. 1978. Discriminability of fixed-ratio schedules for pigeons: Effects of payoff values. *Journal of the Experimental Analysis of Behavior 30*: 69-81.

Hume, A.L. 1974a. Auditory detection and optimal response biases. *Perception and Psychophysics 15*: 425–433.

_____. 1974b. Optimal response biases and the slope of ROC curves as a function of signal intensity, signal probability and relative payoff. *Perception and Psychophysics 16*: 377–384.

Hume, A.L., and R.J. Irwin. 1974. Bias functions and operating characteristics of rats discriminating auditory stimuli. *Journal of the Experimental Analysis of Behavior 21*: 285–295.

Lobb, B., and M.C. Davison. 1977. Multiple and concurrent schedule performance: Independence from concurrent and successive schedule contexts. *Journal of the Experimental Analysis of Behavior 28*: 27–39.

Luce, R.D. 1959. *Individual Choice Behavior.* New York: Wiley.

_____. 1963. Detection and recognition. In R.D. Luce, R.R. Bush, and E. Galanter, *Handbook of Mathematical Psychology*, vol. 1, New York: Wiley.

McCarthy, D., and M. Davison. 1979. Signal probability, reinforcement and signal detection. *Journal of the Experimental Analysis of Behavior 32*: 373–386.

_____. 1980a. On the discriminability of stimulus duration. *Journal of the Experimental Analysis of Behavior 33*: 187–211.

_____. 1980b. Independence of sensitivity to relative reinforcement rate and discriminability in signal detection. *Journal of the Experimental Analysis of Behavior 34*: 273–284.

Nevin, J.A. 1969. Signal-detection theory and operant behavior: A review of D.M. Green and J.A. Swets' "Signal-detection theory and psychophysics." *Journal of the Experimental Analysis of Behavior 12*: 475–480.

_____. 1970. On differential stimulation and differential reinforcement. In W.C. Stebbins, ed., *Animal Psychophysics.* New York: Appleton–Century–Crofts.

_____. 1979. Personal communication.

Nevin, J.A.; P. Jenkins; S. Whittaker; and P. Yarensky. 1977. Signal detection, differential reinforcement and matching. Paper presented at the meeting of the Psychonomic Society, Washington, D.C., November.

Nevin, J.A.; C. Mandell; and S. Whittaker. 1978. Contrast and induction in multiple schedules of discrete trial concurrent reinforcement. *Journal of the Experimental Analysis of Behavior 30*: 53–61.

Nevin, J.A.; K. Olson; C. Mandell; and P. Yarensky. 1975. Differential reinforcement and signal detection. *Journal of the Experimental Analysis of Behavior 24*: 355–367.

Peterson, W.W.; T.G. Birdsall; and W.C. Fox. 1954. The theory of signal detectability. *Transactions of the IREE Professional Group on Information Theory*, pp. 171–212.

Pliskoff, S.S.; R.L. Shull; and L.R. Gollub. 1968. The relation between response rates and reinforcement rates in a multiple schedule. *Journal of the Experimental Analysis of Behavior 11*: 271–284.

Reynolds, G.S. 1963. Some limitations on behavioral contrast and induction during successive discrimination. *Journal of the Experimental Analysis of Behavior 6*: 131–139.

Stubbs, D.A. 1976. Response bias and the discrimination of stimulus duration. *Journal of the Experimental Analysis of Behavior 25*: 243–250.

Stubbs, D.A., and S.S. Pliskoff. 1969. Concurrent responding with fixed relative rate of reinforcement. *Journal of the Experimental Analysis of Behavior 12*: 887–895.

Tanner, W.P., and J.A. Swets. 1954. A decision-making theory of visual detection. *Psychological Review 61*: 401–409.

Van Meter, D., and D. Middleton. 1954. Modern statistical approaches to reception in communication theory. *Transactions of the IREE Professional Group on Information Theory*.

White, K.G. 1978. Behavioral contrast as differential time allocation. *Journal of the Experimental Analysis of Behavior 29*: 151–160.

Wickelgren, W.A. 1968. Unidimensional strength theory and component analysis of noise in absolute and comparative judgements. *Journal of Mathematical Psychology 5*: 102–122.

AFTERWORD

John A. Nevin and
Michael L. Commons

The psychophysical approach to the analysis of stimuli lets us identify the effective dimensions of stimuli and determine the metric on each of those dimensions. Much of the research within this volume falls within the psychophysical domain, thereby helping us understand the effective dimensions of reinforcement schedules in discrimination situations. These dimensions and their metrics should be helpful in studying the effect of reinforcement schedules on responding per se.

A substantial portion of the work described in this volume either uses the signal detection paradigm explicitly or uses ideas and analytic methods derived from detection research. Several variations on the signal detection theme are represented. One is the use of detection methods to derive bias-free indexes of sensitivity to schedule variables, where the latter are treated exactly like the physical stimuli of modern psychophysics. The chapters by Commons, Killeen, Lattal, and Mandell exemplify this approach. Mandell and Commons, using rather different reinforcement-scheduling methods, demonstrate and analyze sensitivity to reinforcement rate, while Killeen and Lattal demonstrate sensitivity to the contingency between responses and their consequences.

A second variation is the exploration of interrelations between sensory discrimination and reinforcement, as exemplified by Terman

419

and by McCarthy and Davison. Terman's work demonstrates molecular sequential dependencies between trial outcomes and the level of discrimination, while McCarthy and Davison show how discrimination at a molar level is independent of reinforcer allocation to one or the other choice response but depends systematically on the extent to which reinforcers are correlated with the stimuli.

A third variation attempts to model discrimination of particular stimulus dimensions in schedules, in order to understand how organisms may process or represent these dimensions. The theoretical signal detection concept of the ideal observer enters here: How does an organism treat its observations so as to conform to some more general process? Commons' chapter explores the pigeon's conformity to a time-weighted sum of events model of the discrimination of reinforcement and nonreinforcement where matching emerges as the general process, while Gibbon's chapter deals with implications of various models for the scaling and discrimination of time where Weber's Law emerges as the general process. Both exemplify the complexities that are likely to be encountered as analyses of schedule discriminations become more refined.

A fourth variation involves attempts to model behavior in the signal detection paradigm as a topic of interest in its own right. The chapters by Nevin and by McCarthy and Davison provide closely related approaches to signal detection performance in relation to reinforcement. Development of their models may lead to a general understanding of behavior in choice situations with confusable stimuli and uncertain outcomes—perhaps a laboratory version of the perplexities of daily life.

A fifth theme involves procedural variations away from the conventional discrete trial signal detection procedure that permits psychophysical interpretation. For example, Stubbs and Dreyfus report a procedure that is intermediate between free operant interval schedules and discrete trial choices based on temporal cues and treat the data in relation to signal detection concepts of detectability and bias. Brandon provides a related analysis of free operant counting behavior, while Hobson and Newman derive more traditional measures of sensitivity from the variability of counting behavior and relate them to the count required for reinforcement.

Other themes represented in this volume cut across procedural concerns. For example, discriminations based on response-produced cues of the sort studied by Brandon and by Hobson and Newman figure importantly in Cohen, Brady, and Lowry's studies of matching-to-sample performance. When the sample is a compound of visual and response rate elements, response-produced cues may be especially salient. This result is relevant to some differences between stimulus functions in classical conditioning, where responses are not required, and in operant conditioning, where cues derived from the required response may overshadow environmental stimuli. At a more molar level, Malone and Rowe demonstrate that the average rate of responding in the presence of one stimulus determines the average rate in a following stimulus, even though rate of responding does not enter into the definition of the contingency in the following stimulus. This sort of sequential dependency on responding in free operant discrimination has a parallel in Terman's work on the signal detection situation where performance (and its outcome) on one trial determine performance on the following trial.

Another major theme relates to the control of responding by the rate of reinforcement. In addition to Commons' and Mandell's demonstrations of discrimination of reinforcement rate in detection procedures, Innis analyzes how the rate of change in reinforcement rate can affect behavior in cyclic interval schedules. Her data suggest, perhaps surprisingly, that the rate of change of the rate of reinforcement must be fairly gradual if it is to control subsequent behavior effectively. This result suggests a mechanism of temporal integration that includes more than the immediately preceding reinforcer. Both Mandell's and Commons' discrimination data support this suggestion. Commons' analysis suggests temporal weighting of each component of the sum, dependent upon a background rate of reinforcement—an integration mechanism that merits exploration in related settings. Rilling and Howard's method for the analysis of memory is very promising in this respect. Their work shows clearly that reinforcers are especially memorable events, overshadowing relatively neutral environmental stimuli. Their method permits the direct exploration of the decay of stimulus control by prior reinforcers and may help to identify the time span over which integration takes place.

A still more complex integration is suggested by Baum's research on the response–reinforcer correlation. In his situation, reinforcement rate is not sufficient to cue the appropriate performance; the subject must also be sensitive to the feedback function describing the correlation between its rate of responding and the resulting rate of reinforcement. That is, a combination of response-based and reinforcement-based cues and the relation between them appear to be necessary. It is possible to recast Baum's results in terms of delay of reinforcement: There will be a shorter average delay between responses and reinforcers when the correlation is positive than when it is negative in his procedure. Killeen and Lattal, in slightly different ways, show that pigeons are exquisitely sensitive to whether events are correlated with their behavior in discrete trials and discuss their results in relation to discrimination of the delay of reinforcement. It remains to be seen whether Baum's molar results can be explained in relation to more molecular temporal aspects of response–reinforcer dependencies.

In summary, the research described in this volume leaves one impressed with both the richness and the orderliness of the control of behavior by environmental stimuli and reinforcers. Behavior at one time may depend on the earlier occurrence of reinforcers or particular rates of reinforcement, preceding numbers or rates of responses, temporal intervals separating events, response–reinforcer delays, and response–reinforcer correlations, depending on how these dimensions enter into subsequent contingencies. The fact that each of these dimensions can function discriminatively does not, of course, mean that it must always do so; as with conventional physical stimuli, the determination of controlling dimensions is an empirical matter. But surely a knowledge of how organisms discriminate aspects of reinforcement schedules is essential to a complete understanding of their operant behavior.

NAME INDEX

Andersen, J.J. *84*
Appel, J.B. 117, *131*
Arnett, F.B. 367, *388*
Aschoff, J. 338, *343*
Aucella, A.F. 345, *363*
Autor, S.M. 32, *49*
Avin, E. *50*

Baum, W.M. xxii, xxv, *xxvi*, 4, 17, *26*, *27*, 95, 104, 105, *107*, *111*, 115, 117, *133*, 152, *155*, 202, 204, 205, 209, 211, 212, 214, 215, 217, 218, 219, *221*, 247–256, 247, 248, *255*, *256*, 279, 393, 395, 396, 399, 406, *415*
Beautrais, P.G. 401, *415*
Bedarf, E.W. 95, *111*
Bem, D.J. 105, *107*
Berryman, R. 95, *108*, 119, *132*, 227, 233, 234, 235, *243*
Bierley, C.M. 119, *132*, 304, *318*, 362, *363*
Bindra, D. 93, *107*, *110*
Birdsall, T.G. 393, *416*
Bitgood, S.C. 158, *189*, 197, 199, 216, 216 (foot), *223*
Bitterman, M.E. 94, *107*
Blough, D.S. xxii, *xxvi*, 194, 221, *221*, 238, 239, *243*, 362, *363*, 366, 367, 376, 385, *389*

Blough, P.M. 194, 221, *221*
Boakes, R.A. 94, 104, *107*, 315, *318*
Boren, J.J. 249, *255*
Boyer, S.S. 115, 117, 122, 126, *132*
Brady, J. 345–364, 345, *363*
Braida, L.D. 337 (foot), *343*
Brandon, P.K. xxv, 94, 196, 209, *221*, 225–244, 234, 235, 237, *243*, 248
Bfandon, S.E. 94, *107*
Breland, K. 94, *107*
Breland, M. 94, *107*
Brown, J.S. 130, *131*
Brown(e?), M.P. 130, *133*
Bryan, A.J. 117, 127, *132*
Buck, S. 367, 368, 370, 371, *389*
Bullock, D.H. xxii, *xxvi*, 248, 249, *256*
Bunge, M. 90, *108*
Bush, R.R. 12, *26*, 396, *415*

Callahan, D.J. 337 (foot), *343*
Campbell, D.T. 90, *108*
Carter, D.E. 346, 347, 360, *363*
Catania, A.C. 95, *108*, 113, *132*, 137, *154*, 157, 166, *189*, 197, 199, 200, 201, 202, 204, 215, 216, 218, *221*, 281, *285*, 292, *318*, 376, *389*
Chase, S. xxii, *xxvii*, *50*
Church, R.M. 138, 139, *154*, *155*, 157, 158, 160, 164 (foot), 167, 168,

175, *189*, 196, 199, 215, 216, 216
(foot), 220, *222*
Clark, R.L. 281, *285*
Clopton, B. 331, *343*
Cohen, L.R. xxvi, 345–364, 345, 346,
359, 360, *363*
Cole, B.K. 54, *84, 133*
Colliver, J.A. 98, *108*, 326, *343*
Commons, M.L. xvii–xix, xxv, 24, 33,
44, 46, *49*, 51–85, 52, 54, 59, 65,
67, 77, 80, 81, 83, *84*, 103, *108*,
119, *132*, 248, *256*, 279, *285*
Cook, T.D. 90, *108*
Crawford, L.L. 374, 375, *389*
Cumming, W.W. 44, *50*, 54, *84*, 119,
132, 197, 199, 220, *223*
Cunningham, C.L. 94, *111*

D'Amato, M.R. 54, *84*
Damm, V. 119, 126, *132*
Davis, H. 93, *108*
Davison, M.C. xxvi, 12, 15, 17, 18, 19,
24, 25, *26, 27*, 32, *49*, 103, *108*,
324, 393–417, 396, 397, 398, 399,
400, 401, 402, 403, 404, 406, 407,
409, 410, 411, 413, 414, *415, 416*
DeCasper, A.J. 157, *189*, 197, 199,
200, 216, 216 (foot) *222*
de Charms, R. 105, *108*
Delehanty, D.L. 306, *319*
Deluty, M.Z. 93, *108*, 157, 158, 160,
167, 168, 175, *189*, 196, 199, 215,
216, *222*
de Villiers, P. xxii, *xxvi*, 11, *26*, 139,
154, 248, *256*, 393, 401, *415*
Dews, P.B. 138, *154*
Dickinson, A. 315, *318*
Dodd, P. 292, 295, *319*
Donahoe, J.W. 384, *389*
Dreyfus, L.R. 137–156, 158, 199, 248
Ducheny, J.R. 52, 77, 83, *84*
Dufort, R.H. xxiii, *xxvi*
Duncan, B. 32, *50*
Duncan, T. 238, 239, *244*
Durlach, N.I. 337 (foot), *343*
Dusoir, A.E. 398, *415*

Eckerman, D.A. 346, 347, 360, *363*
Eiserer, L.A. 93, *108*
Eisler, H. 166, *189*
Elsmore, T.F. 196, *222*, 401, *415*
Emmerich, D. 328, 337, *343*
Engen, T. 198, *222*, 322, 341, *343*

Fantino, E. 32, *50*
Farthing, G.W. 376, *389*
Ferguson, A. 401, *415*
Ferster, C.B. 131, *132*, 138, *154*, 193,
222, 248, *256*, 257, 281, *285*
Fetterman, G. 200, *222*
Fink, C.D. 119, 126, *132*
Fitzner, R. 277, *285*
Fleshler, M. 251, *256*
Foree, D.D. 314, *318*
Fowler, H. 290, *318*
Fox, W.C. 393, *416*
Frey, P.W. 98, *108*, 326, *343*

Galanter, E. 7, *26*
Gamzu, E. 388, *390*
Garcia, J. 94, *108*
Gellerman, L.W. 349, *363*
Gerding, J.D. 195, *223*
Gescheider, G. 331, 336, *343*
Getty, D.J. 157, *189* 196, 199, 216,
220, *222*
Gibbon, J. xxv, 95, 101, *108*, 137,
138, 139, *155*, 157–189, 158, 160,
164, 164 (foot), 168, 172, 174,
181, 182, 183, 188, *189*, 197 (foot),
200, 215, *222*
Gilbert, R.M. xxii, *xxvii*
Gill, C.A. 376, *389*
Goldiamond, I. 33, *50*, 119, *133*, 198,
215, *223*, 347, *363*
Gollub, L.R. 11, 21, *27*, 413, *416*
Goodall, G. 294, *318*
Goodkin, F. 94, *108*
Gould, S.J. 107, *108*
Graham, C.H. 321, *393*
Grant, D.S. 54, *84*, 307, 316, *319*,
360, *364*
Gray, J. 328, *343*
Green, D.M. 10, 12, 14, 15, 17, *26*,
36, *50*, 97, *108*, 124, *132*, 151, *155*,
193, *222*, 321, 323, 326, 328, *343*,
400, 403, *415*
Green, K.F. 94, *108*
Green, M. 238, 239, *243*, 326, 329,
343
Grice, G.R. 92, *108*
Grier, J.B. 124, *132*, 230, *243*, 411,
415
Gruber, H.E. 119, 126, *132*
Guevrekian, L. 194, 196, 197, 199,
200, 205, 212, 217, 218 (foot),
219, *223*

Guilford, J.P. 147, 150, *155*
Guttman, N. xxiii, *xxvi*

Hall, G. 92, *110*, 294, *318*
Halliday, M.S. 104, *107*
Hamilton, B. 367, *390*
Hanson, S.J. 93, 95, 104, *109*
Harlow, H.F. xxiii, *xxvii*
Harzem, P. 200, *222*, 258, *285*
Hawkes, L. 138, *155*
Hearst, E. 44, *50*, 54, *84*, 93, *108*, 130, *133*
Heinemann, E.G. xxii, *xxvii*, 33, 47, *50*
Hemmes, N.S. 198, *222*
Herrnstein, R.J. xxii, *xxvii*, 11, *26*, 32, *50*, 82, *84*, 395, 396, 399, *415*
Hinson, J.M. 377, 378, 380, 388, *389*
Hirvonen, M. *84*
Hiss, R.H. 117, *131*
Hobson, S.L. xxv, 33, *50*, 103, *108*, 193–224, 194, 196, 198, 200, 201, 202, 211, 214, 218, *222*, 225, 226, 228, *244*, 248, 347, *363*, 401, *415*
Hoffman, H.S. 251, *256*
Honig, W.K. 258, *285*, 290, 307, 316, *318*
Howard, R.C. 289–319, 294, 300, 303, *318, 319*
Hull, C. 89, *109*
Hulse, S.H. 290, *318*
Hume, A.L. 394, 401, *416*
Hume, D. 90, 91, 92, *109*
Hursh, S.R. 32, *50*
Hurwitz, H.M.B. 93, *108*

Innis, N.K. xxvi, 257–286, 258, 259, 261, 265, 267, 271, 273, 275, 281, 282, 283, *285*
Irwin, R.J. 394, 401, *416*

Jacobs, W.J. 314, *318*
Jenkins, H.M. 91, 93, *108, 109*, 138, *155*, 301, *319*, 368, *389*
Jenkins, P. *27*, 396, 399, 403, *416*
Joffe, J.M. 103, *109*
Johnson, C. 294, 300, *319*
Johnson, D.M. 194, 196, *223*

Kahneman, D. 91, 105, *109*
Kalat, J.W. 94, *109*
Kamil, A.C. 51, *84*
Kamin, L.J. 93, 95, *109*

Keller, F. 227, 233, 234, 235, *243*
Keller, J.V. 282, *285*
Kelley, H.H. 105, *109*
Kello, J.E. 258, *285*
Kendall, S.B. 93, *109*
Killeen, P.R. xxv, 32, *50* 89–112, 93, 94, 95, 99, 104, *109*, 117, 121, 126, 128, *132*, 138, 153, *155*, 248
Kimble, G.A. xxiii, *xxvi*, 93, *109*
Kinchla, J. 196, *222*
Kirchner, B. *343*
Krane, R.V. 106, *109*
Krupa, M.P. *84*
Kuch, D.D. 158, *189*, 197, 199, 215, 216, 216 (foot), *222, 223*

La Joie, J. 93, *110*
Lamb, M. *84*
Lang, J. *133*
Lashley, K.S. 366, *389*
Laties, V.G. 196, 197 (foot), 209, 211, *222*, 281, *285*
Latranyi, M. 194, 201, *223*, 234, 235, *244*
Lattal, K.A. xxv, 93, 95, 103, *109, 111*, 113–133, 115, 117, 118, 119, 120, 121, 122, 123, 125, 126, 127, 128, 129, *132*, 194, 248, 249, *256*, 347, *363*
LeBuffe, P.A. 195, *223*
LeFevre, F.F. 195, 196, 197, 197 (foot), 201, 207, 219, *222*
Lerner, N.D. 157, *189*, 196, 199, 216, 220, *222*
Lett, B.T. 93, *110*
Libby, M.E. 164 (foot) *189*
Limpo, A.J. 4, *27*
Lindstrom, F. 51, *84*
Little, L. 368, *389*
Lobb, B. 413, 414, *416*
Lockhead, G.R. 337 (foot), *344*
Lolordo, V.M. 314, *318*
Looney, T.A. 345, *363*
Lord, J. 368, *389*
Loughead, T.E. 198, *223*
Lowe, C.F. 200, *222*
Lowry, M. 345–364
Luce, R.D. 12, *26*, 396, *415, 416*

Mackie, J.L. 90, *110*
Mackintosh, N.J. xxii, *xxvii*, 294, *318*, 368, 369, *389*
Maier, S.F. 95, *110*, 130, *133*

Maki, N.S. 119, *132*, 304, *318*, 362, *363*

Malone, J.C. xxvi, 365–390, 365, 366, 368, 369, 370, 371, 373, 374, 375, 376, 377, 378, 384, 385, 388, *389*

Malott, R.W. 197, 199, 200, *223*

Mandell, C. xxv, 18, 20, 23, 24, *26, 27*, 31–50, 82, *110*, 139, *155*, 248, 403, 409, 413, 414, *416*

Mankoff, R. *133*

Martello, M. 294, *318*

McCarthy, D. xxvi, 12, 15, *26, 27*, 103, 324, 393–417, 396, 397, 398, 400, 401, 402, 403, 404, 406, 409, 410, 411, 413, *416*

McCroskery, J.H. 384, *389*

McCullough, T.A. 195, *223*

McDiarmid, C.G. 33, *50* 119, *133*, 194, 195, 196, 198, 199, 215, *223*, 225, 227, *244*, 289, 290, *318*, 347, *364*

McGowan, B.D. 94, *108*

McNally, K.A. 388, *389*

Mechner, F. 194, 196, 197, 198, 199, 200, 201, 202, 205, 211, 212, 215, 217, 218, 218 (foot), 219, *225*, 226, 233, 234, 235, *244*

Menlove, R.L. 371, *390*

Michotte, A. 105, *110*

Middleton, D. 393, *417*

Miles, R.C. 95, *112*

Mill, J.S. 90, *110*

Miller, N.E. 92, *110*

Milligan, E. *343*

Mintz, D.E. 195, *223*

Moe, J.C. 119, *132*, 304, *318* 362, *363*

Moody, D.B. 238, 242, *244*, 329, *343*

Moore, B.R. 93, *110*

Morse, W.H. xxii, *xxvii*, 138, *155*, 194, *223*

Mosteller, F. 67, *84*

Mulick, J.A. 103, *109*

Narens, L. 82, *84*

Neuringer, A.J. 103, *110*, 153, *155*

Nevin, J.A. xxi–xxvii, xxii, xxv, *xxvii*, 3–27, 4, 8, 9, 11, 14, 18, 19, 21, 22, *26, 27*, 53, 59, 98, 103, *110*, 124, *132*, 139, 151; 152, *155*, 193, 200, *225*, 247, *256*, 311, 315, *318*, 323, 326, 367, 369, *390*, 395, 396, 399,

403, 404, 406, 407, 408, 409, 410, 411, 413, 414, *416*

Newly, W. 93, *109*

Newman, F. 193–224, 226, 248

Nisbett, R.E. 91, 105, *110*

Notterman, J.M. 195, *223*

Olson, K. *27, 110*, 403, 409, *416*

Osborne, S.R. 93, 95, 103, 104, *109, 110*

Patnaik, P.B. 184, *189*

Paul, S.M. 279, *285*

Pavlov, I.P. 293, *318*, 365, 369, 370, *390*

Pearce, J.M. 92, *110*

Peden, B.J. 130, *133*

Perin, C.T. 92, *110*

Perkins, C.C. 92, *110*

Peters, J. 51, *84*

Peterson, W.W. 393, *416*

Piaget, J. 91, *111*

Platt, J.R. 137, 138, *155*, 158, 160, 167, *189*, 194, 196, 197, 198, 199, 211, 216, 216 (foot), *223*

Pliskoff, S.S. 11, 21, 22, 23, *27*, 33, *50*, 119, *133*, 198, 215, *223*, 347, *363*, 400, 413, *416, 417*

Pohl, J. *84*

Poli, M. 104, *107*

Poresky, R.H. 118, *133*

Powers, R.B. 279, *286*

Purks, S.R. 337 (foot), *343*

Rachlin, H. xxii, *xxvii*, 99, 104, *111*, 115, 117, *133*, 152, *155*, 247, 248, *256* 367, *390, 415*

Raibert, M. 338, *343, 344*

Ratoosh, P. 321, *343*

Rawson, R.A. 103, *109*

Reid, H.M. 306, *319*

Reid, R.L. xxii, *xxvii*

Renner, K.E. 92, *111*

Rescorla, R.A. 92, 94, 104, *111*, 385, *390*

Revusky, S. 93, 95, 106, *111*

Reynolds, G.S. 4, *27*, 281, *285*, 290, 292, *318* 276, *390*, 393, *417*

Reynolds, M.D. 281, *285*

Richardson, W.K. 198, *223*, 384, *389*

Rilling, M. xxii, xxvi, *xxvii*, 33, *50*, 119, *133*, 194, 195, 196, 198, 199,

201, 215, 221, *223* 225, 227, *244*,
289–319, 289, 293, 294, 300, *318,
319*, 347, *364*, 366, *390*
Roberts, S. 138, *155*
Roberts, W.A. 54, *84*, 307, 316, *319*,
360, *364*
Rose, R.M. 12, *26*, 396, *415*
Rosenwasser, A.M. 338, *343*
Rothstein, B. 367, 368, 370, 371, *389*
Rowe, D.W. 365–390, 382, 388, *389*
Rozin, P. 94, *109*

Schneider, B.A. 138, 153, *155*, 257,
258, 259, 261, 281, *286*
Schoenfeld, W.N. 44, *50*, 54, *84*, 117,
133
Schwartz, B. 367, 388, *390*
Seligman, M.E.P. 95, *110*, 130, *133*
Senkowski, P.C. 194, 196, 198, 211,
223
Shettleworth, S.J. 367, 369, *390*
Shimp, C.P. xxii, *xxvii*, 138, *155*, 303,
305, *319*
Shull, R.L. 11, 21, *27*, 279, *286*, 413,
416
Sidman, M. 249, *255*
Silberberg, A. 119, *133*, 367, *390*
Simmelhag, V.L. 93, 95, *112*, 257,
279, *286*
Simon, H.A. 90, *111*
Sizemore, O.J. 93, 95, *111*
Skinner, B.F. xvii, xxi, *xxvii*, 92, 93,
95, *111*, 113, 119, 131, *132, 133*,
138, *154, 155*, 193, *222*, 248, *256*,
257, 281, *285*, 322, 328, *343*, 373,
390
Skucy, J.C. 104, *111*
Smith, W.C. xxii, *xxvi*, 248, 249, *256*
Sosa, E. 90, *111*
Speakman, R.D. 367, *390*
Spear, N.E. 290, *319*
Spence, K.W. 365, 376, *390*
Spencer, P.T. 200, *222*
Staddon, J.E.R. xxii, *xxvii*, 92, 93,
95, *111, 112*, 138, 153, *155*, 197,
199, 220, *224*, 257, 258, 259, 261,
265, 267, 268, 271, 273, 275, 279,
281, 282, 283, 284, *285, 286*, 294,
303, 305, 307, 314, *319*, 366, 368,
369, 371, 373, 384, *389*
Stebbins, W.C. 323, *343*
Steele, K.M. 374, 375, *389*

Stubbs, D.A. xxv, 15, 17, *27*, 119,
133, 137–156, 138, 139, 140, 143,
150, 151, *156*, 157, 158, 167, 170,
189, 194, 196, 197, 199, 200, 202,
215, 216, 216 (foot) *224*, 248, *256*,
306, *319*, 395, 400, *417*
Sullivan, M.A. *50*
Sutherland, N.S. xxii, *xxvii*
Swets, J.A. 10, 12, 14, 15, 17, *26, 27*,
36, *50*, 97, *108*, 124, *132, 133*, 151,
155, 193, *222*, 226, *244*, 321, 323,
326, 328, *343*, 393, 400, 403, *415,
417*

Tallon, R.R. 279, *285*
Tanis, D. 328, *343*
Tanner, W.P. 393, *417*
Terman, J.S. 238, 239, *243*, 326, 329,
338, 342, *343, 344*
Terman, M. xxvi, 238, 239, *243*, 321–
344, 325, 326, 329, 338, 342, *343,
344*
Terrace, H.S. xxii, *xxvii*
Testa, T.J. 94, *112*
Thompson, A.A. *84*
Thompson, R.F. 365, *390*
Thompson, R.L. 95, *108*
Tukey, J.W. 67, *84*
Tustin, R.D. 12, 17, 18, 19, 24, 25,
26, 103, *108*, 396, 397, 399, 400,
402, 406, 407, *415*
Tversky, A. 91, 105, *109*

Uhl, C.N. 104, *112*

Van Meter, D. 393, *417*
Vautin, H.M. 306, *319*
Von Saal, W. 301, *319*
Von Wright, G.H. 106, *112*

Wade, M. 366, *389*
Wagman, M. 227, 233, 234, 235, *243*
Wagner, A.R. 92, 106, *109, 111*, 307,
319, 385, *390*
Wallace, W.A. 90, *112*
Ward, L.M. 337 (foot) *344*
Ward, W.C. 91, *109*
Watson, C. 328, *343*
Watson, J.B. 92, *112*
Weber, J. *343*
Weisman, R.G. 292, 295, *319*

Weiss, B. 281, *285*
Weissman, A. 54, *84*
Welker, R.L. 95, *112*
Wheatley, K.L. 95, *112*
White, K.G. 413, *417*
Whittaker, S. 15, *27*, 396, 399, 403, 413, 414, *416*
Wickelgren, W.A. 53, 73, 74, *84*, 394, *417*
Williams, B.A. 51, *84*, 95, 106, *112*, 367, 368, 370, 371, *389, 390*

Wilson, T.D. 91, 105, *110*
Wolfe, J.B. 92, *112*
Wright, J. *343*

Yager, D. 238, 239, *244*
Yarensky, P. *27, 110*, 396, 399, 403, 409, *416*

Zeiler, M.D. xxii, *xxvii*, 113, 114, 117, *133*, 153, *156*, 157, *189*, 197, 199, 200, 216, 216 (foot) *222*, 250, *256*

SUBJECT INDEX

A', 124, 129, 231, 233, 236–237
  definition of, 230
Accuracy in choice behavior, 350,
  353–362
Acquisition, 345–347, 359–360
Actual substimulus density, 67–69
Additivity theory, 388
"Adjunctive" behavior, 95, 106
Allocation of behavior, 93, 278–281
Alloiobias contours, 402
Arousal, 93, 95, 104
Associative value, 306–317
Autoshaping, 294–296
Average reinforcement rate, 81

B'', 124, 231, 233
  definition of, 230
β (beta), 394
Backward conditioning, 295–297
Baseline frequency of incentives,
  104
Baselines in local contrast research,
  368, 370, 371
Base rate theories, 53
Behavior during interreinforcement
  intervals, 278–281
Behavioral component of compound
  samples, 354–363. See also
  sample–specific performances

Behavioral contrast, 388
Bias, 54, 59–63, 98–99, 103, 106,
  131, 151, 342, 394, 408
  in choice performance, 124, 126,
  128, 140
  and circadian oscillations, 338
  definition of, 229
  and discriminability, 323–324, 326,
  397–399, 400–403
  in estimation of run lengths, 225,
  229–231, 233–243
  and latency, 331, 335–336
  and point of subjective equality, 150
  and stimuli, 17–19, 238, 397
Biomodality, 207–209, 218
Binomial model, 62
Biological relevance of stimuli,
  303–304
Bisection function, 168–171, 182
  definition of, 168
Blocking, 300–301
"Bursting," xxii, 207, 209, 218
  definition of, 199

Causal inference, 89, 91–92, 95, 97,
  105–106
Causality, 90
  threshold of, 126–128
Chained reinforcement schedules, 52

"Chains of causality," 92
Choice certainty, 238
Choice points, 228, 237, 240
Choice performance, 36–44, 119–130, 141, 346–347, 354–359, 362–363, 396–411, 420
Choice procedure, 58–59, 194, 199, 321, 395
Circadian hour, 339
Circadian oscillation, 338–341
  definition of, 338
Classical conditioning, 4–5, 315–316, 421
Cognitive processes, 316
Collateral dimensions, variability in, 215–219
Comparison stimuli, 345–347, 350, 354, 358–359
Component duration and local contrast, 370
Compound sample, 358–359, 362
Compound stimuli and overshadowing, 291, 293–303, 313–314, 317
Concurrent chained schedules, 31–32
Concurrent peak–pause schedule, 115, 122, 124–129
Concurrent schedules, 11, 127, 153, 395, 401, 413–414
Conditional discrimination, 316–317, 345–347, 362
  definition of, 316–317
Conditional probabilities, 229, 232–233, 238, 243
  definition of, 226
Conditional stimulus, 293, 303–304, 309–311, 315–316
Conditional reinforcement, 92–93, 106, 119
Confidence ratings, 328, 337
Conjunctive schedules, 250–252
Conjunctive FR/FT schedule, 279–281
Constant conjunction, 90, 94–95
Contingencies, definition of, 113–114
Continuous binomial model, 59, 62, 75
Contrast shoulders. See Dimensional contrast shoulders
Contribution of events, 73, 77, 82–83
Controlled reinforcement ratio procedures, 401, 403, 411

Correlations, response–reinforcer, 249–255, 420–422
Counting schedule, response-terminated
  definition of, 194, 226–228
  effect of upper limit on, 227, 235, 237, 243
  and signal detection theory, 228–243, 420
Counting schedule, stimulus-terminated, 194, 228
Criterion, 10, 104, 172–174
  latency and, 331, 336–337
  multiple decision criteria, 238
  and payoff matrix, 101–103, 151
Cues, 420–421
  behavioral, 362
  molecular, 248, 249, 250, 255
Critical events, 70
Cyclic interval schedule, 258–285, 421
Cycle length, 53–56, 58–64, 67–74, 81–82

d', 10, 36, 54, 59–62, 75, 82, 124, 129, 326–328, 338
Davison–Tustin model, 17–18, 103, 396–398, 402
Decay function, 74, 77, 421
Decision points, 228, 237, 240
Decision rule, 10, 67, 75
  definition of, 58
Decrement in control, 77
Delays, discriminability of, 100–103
Delay duration, effect on discriminability of, 128
Delay of reinforcement
  as controlling discrimination, 254–255
  effect on conditioning, 92–94, 95, 103–104, 106, 254, 422
Density of reinforcement, 32–33, 44–47, 51–85
  as defining characteristic of molar analysis, 57
  discrimination of, 44–47
  scaling of, 51–85
Differential behavior patterns, 355, 362
Differential reinforcement, 225, 323, 331, 368–369

Differential reinforcement of low rate
(DRL) schedules, 119–124, 128,
137, 154, 346–359 *passim*
Differential reinforcement of other
behavior (DRO) schedules,
114–115, 117, 120–122, 126,
128, 131, 369
in conjunctive schedules,, 250–255
Differential responding and local
contrast, 365, 370
Differential sample schedule requirements, 345–363 *passim*
Differentiation, 365–366, 369–370
definition of, 365
Dimensional contrast shoulders, 367,
376–389
Discrete trial procedure, 349, 394,
413, 420
Discriminability of stimuli, 23–24,
122–131, 322–325, 329–331,
394–414
and bias, 323–324, 397–399,
401–402
and bisection function, 168
and circadian oscillations, 339–342
and signal detection theory,
394–414
unitary concept of, 324, 342
Discrimination, 114–117, 338–342,
388
of correlations, 249–255, 420
differentiation of, 365–366
models of process of, 167–168,
406–407, 413–414
at molar level, 248, 254
of rates of reinforcement, 248–250,
419, 421
See also Temporal discrimination
Discrimination indexes, 251, 289
definition of, 297, 326–328
See also d', SI
Discrimination learning and local
contrast, 365–367, 370, 388
Discrimination reversal procedure,
xxiii
Discriminative stimulus
autoshaping sequences as, 296
biological relevance of, 303–304
for nonreinforcement, 300–303,
314, 317
number of responses as, 290

order of events as, 292
as reinforcing stimulus, xxii, 3–6,
17–18, 24–26
response patterns as, 325–326,
362–363
response–reinforcer relations as,
117–131
See also Compound stimuli and overshadowing; Food as a discriminative stimulus; Stimulus control
Dissimiliarity, 177
Duration discrimination, 139,
167–168
Duration of schedule sample, 36–39,
53

Effective value of reinforcers, 51
Encode–decode symmetry problem,
160–162, 165, 182
Endogenous clock, 281, 338
"Energizing effect," 242
Error reinforcement, 403–414
Evolutionary pressures, 91, 105, 107
Excitation, 365
Excitatory conditioning, 315–316
Expectancy ratio formulation,
174–175
Extinction, xxii–xxiii, 104, 248–249,
373, 384
definition of, xxi
discriminative effects of reinforcers
during, xxii–xxiii
effects of, xxii
and incitement, 104
in mixed schedules, 248–249

Feedback function, 99, 421
definition of, 4
Fixed Consecutive Number, 226
Fixed-interval scallop, 257, 294
Fixed-interval schedules, xxiii, xxiv,
32, 115, 127
behavior in, 257–258, 278–281
compared to VI schedules, 47–49
discriminable properties of, 32–36
temporal control in, 257–258, 261,
271–275, 278–281
and temporal discrimination, 137,
138, 140–154, 163–164
temporal tracking in, 271–275,
278–281

Fixed-interval timing schedules, 204–209, 211, 217–219
  counting in, 201, 204–205, 221
  definition of, 199–201
  See also Timing schedules
Fixed-ratio counting schedules
  definition of, 202
  as discriminative stimuli, 194, 198, 200–207, 209–220
  timing in, 201, 207, 221
  See also Counting schedules
Fixed-ratio schedules, xxiii, 200, 248
  and choice performance, 346–360 passim
  definition of, 193
  as discriminative stimuli, 119, 193–198, 227–228
  in matching-to-sample procedures, 346, 348
Fixed-time schedules, xxiv, 275
Food as a discriminative stimulus, 291, 293–303, 313–317
Forgetting, 52–54, 70–72, 73–74, 77, 83, 303
Forward conditioning, 295, 296
Free-operant avoidance procedures, 137, 249
Free-operant choice procedures, 139–140, 146, 151, 154, 199, 413–414

Generalization and stimulus control, xxii
Generalized matching law, 395–398
Generalization of reinforcement effects, 399, 404
Generalization testing, 33, 35, 47–49
Geometric mean of time values as subjective "middle," 158, 167, 174, 177, 179

Hues, 345–347, 351–357, 359–360
Hysteresis, 252

Ideal observer performance, 52, 75, 83, 420
Identity tasks, 346–348, 351–354, 357
  definition of, 345
Index responses, 157–159, 160, 164
Indirect variables, 113, 120, 121

Induction, Pavlovian, 365, 366, 369, 371
Induction, Skinnerian, 370, 371
Inhibition, 365
Instructional theory of memory, 307, 316–317
Interference treatments, 362
Interim activities, 257–258, 276, 278–281
Intermittent reinforcement, xxiii–xxiv
  and associative value, 311–315, 317
Interreinforcer interval
  averaging of, 32, 47
  behavior during, 278–281
  discrimination of, 38–44, 46–47, 248, 254–255
  effect on discrimination, 53
  and pausing. See Postreinforcement pause
  See also interval duration
Interresponse time schedule, 199, 220
Interstimulus interval functions, 93
Intertrial interval, 349
Interval durations, interreinforcer, temporal control by, 258–261, 267–277, 279–285
  sequences of, 261–269, 278
Interval schedules, xxiii–xxiv
"Interventionist" theory of causality, 106
Inverse probability transformation, 63
Irradiation, 365–366
Isobias curves, 8–10, 336
  and matching law, 12–18, 398, 402
Isoreinforcement curves, 19–26
Isosensitivity curves, 7–10, 59–63, 123
  and isoreinforcement curves, 19, 23, 24
  matching law and, 12–18, 398, 401

Latency, response
  confidence ratings and, 328, 337
  and discriminability, 328–331, 335, 342
  index, 160
  as stimulus intensity, 238–243
Likelihood ratio, 171–175, 183–186
  definition of, 171–174
Line gratings, 345–347, 351–357, 359–360

Local contrast, 366–379, 384–388
  definition of, 366
Local dimensional effects, 366–367,
  371, 374–388
  definition of, 366–367
Locus of control, 97
Log timing system, 157–158,
  165–167, 172, 174, 177–182,
  186, 188

Macro level of analysis, 56, 59–63, 80
Maintained generalization gradients,
  366–368, 375–388
Matching law and model, 65–67, 75,
  77–80, 83
  and signal detection theory, 11–19,
  103, 395–414, 420
Matching-to-sample procedure, 119,
  122, 126–28, 227–228, 316,
  348–350, 357, 359–362, 421
  definition of, 345–346
Matching-to-sample procedure,
  delayed, 128–129, 360–363
Memory, 291, 303, 305, 307, 315
  Definition of, 290
  models of, 307, 316–317, 421
  See also Retention; Trace stimulus
  control
Memory trace, 307, 316
Method of Ascending Limits, 227
Method of differences, 90
Micro level of analysis, 58–59, 72–74,
  77–83
Mixed schedules, 118, 120, 281
  definition of, 248
  and discrimination of correlations,
  248–255
Modified T schedule, 54
Molar analysis, xxv, 57, 58, 63–70,
  77–81, 83
  compared to molecular analysis, 3,
  247–250, 254
  definition of, 3–5, 247
  of discrimination of correlations,
  254–255, 420
  as unifying stimuli and reinforcers,
  5–6
Molecular analysis, xxiii, 3, 58, 59,
  70–72, 78–80, 82, 83
  compared with molar analysis, 3,
  247–250, 254–255

definition of, 3, 247
  of VI schedules, 36–44
Multiple schedules, 21–23, 117–118,
  395, 413–414
  local contrast in, 366, 367, 371

"Neutral" stimulus, 4
Noise, 89, 97, 100–101
  in response terminated counting
  schedules, 229, 230, 238
  See also Sensory effect
Nondifferential sample requirements,
  346–360 passim
Nonidentity tasks, 346–348,
  351–354, 357
  definition of, 345
Nonreinforcement, discriminative
  stimuli for, 300–304, 314, 317
Number of responses as discriminative
  stimulus, 290

Operant behavior, definition of, xxi
Operant conditioning, definition of,
  4–5
Operant discrimination as stimulus
  control, xxii
Overcounting, 229–230, 233, 235,
  237, 242, 243
Overmatching, 396, 411
Overshadowing, 291–296, 303,
  313–314, 316, 317, 362–363

$p(L)$, 54, 59–63. See also Bias
Partial reset procedure, 206. See also
  FI timing schedule
Payoffs, 52, 65, 77, 80, 89, 101–103,
  106, 394
  as biasing variables, 99, 103,
  323–324, 326, 331
  matrix of, 151–152, 323–324, 326,
  394, 400
  as part of contingency, 89
Peak performance, 338, 341–342
Perceived density, 51–85 passim
  definition of, 63
Percentage response rule, 165
Percentile procedure, 160
Point of subjective equality, 146–147,
  150
Poisson timing system, 172, 174,
  178–181, 184–185, 187

Postreinforcement pause, 44, 257
  and interreinforcer interval dura-
    tions, 258–261, 267–285
Power law, 162–165, 167, 174, 182
Preference situation, 77, 83
Probability functions, 140, 143–147,
    150–153, 229
Programmed reinforcement rate, 65
Progressive interval schedules,
    258–271, 273–275, 277–284
  types of, 265–268
Psychometric functions, 35–36, 150,
    323–326, 329–335, 337, 341–342
  definition of, 322
  discrimination and, 323–324, 342
  and real time, 157, 167, 170
Psychophysical procedures, 333,
    419–422
  development of, 321–324
  and reinforcement schedules as stim-
    uli, 33, 193–195, 289–290
  and response oriented experiments,
    227
  and temporal discrimination,
    137–141, 146–154, 292

Random interval schedule, 56, 141
Rate averaging models, 69
Rate of acquisition, 36, 346–347,
    359–360
Rate of incitement, 104
Rate of reinforcement
  and bias and sensitivity, 151
  as discriminative stimuli, 31–49,
    248–249, 254–255
  effect on discrimination, 249–250,
    252
  and response rate, 247
Rating, ROCs from, 238–239
Ratio comparitor, 158
Ratio counting schedules. See Fixed-
    ratio counting schedules
Ratio discrimination, 195, 197, 212
  definition of, 195
Ratio schedules
  definition of, xxiii–xxiv
  discriminability of, 220
  and feedback function, 4
  psychophysical properties of, 195
Reaction time, 328–329

Receiver operating characteristic
    (ROC), 7–9, 59, 98–99, 104,
    326–328
  of counting behaviors, 229–233,
    235–243
  definition of, 7–9
  of FR schedules, 198
  of ratio and timing schedules, 200
Rehearsal theory of memory, 307
Reinforcement, probability of
  as control, 46–47, 56
  and response strength, 311
Reinforcement schedules
  as discriminative stimuli, xxiv,
    32–49, 113–131, 289–290,
    419–422
  effect of schedule size on.
    See Schedule size; W–ber fractions
  and stimulus control, 5–6, 289–291
  See also Signal detection paradigm
    and theory
Reinforcement schedules, differentiat-
    ing effects of, 113–117, 119, 130,
    225
Reinforcement schedules, discrimina-
    tive effects of, 113–131
  during extinction, xxii–xxiii
  research on, xxv–xxvi
Reinforcement schedules, dynamic
    effects of, 113–131 passim, 225
Reinforcer, electrical brain stimulation
    as, 324–325
Reinforcers, generality of, 314
Reinforcers as inciting behavior, 93
Reinforcing stimulus
  definition of, xxi, 3–4
  and discriminative stimulus, xxii,
    3–6
Relative-time-weighted-sum theory,
    53
Relative timing process, 139
Relative value of reinforcers, 98–99
Response chaining, 93, 281
Response-dependent reinforcement,
    114–115, 117–118, 131, 248–249
Response-independent reinforcement,
    114–115, 117–118, 131, 248–249
Response number as discriminative
    stimulus, 290
Response patterns and local contrast,
    367–368, 370–373, 377

Response rate and rate data, 117, 121, 141, 146, 152–153, 238–239, 247
and local contrast, 366–388
Response-reinforcer relations, 114–131. *See also* Correlations, response-reinforcer
Response rules, 171. *See also* Likelihood ratio; Similarity rule
Response sequence, 228, 237–238
Response-stimulus asynchrony, 102
Response strength, 77, 311, 315
Response differentiation of run length. *See* Counting schedules
Response differentiation of temporal aspects of responding. *See* Timing schedules
Retention
associative value and, 292, 306–317
and biological relevance, 303–304
determinants of, 291–292
of various stimuli, 303–305, 316, 317
test, definition of, 293
See also Memory; Trace stimulus control
Retention of food as a discriminative stimulus, 294–305, 313–314, 316–317
Run length
in FR counting schedules, 194, 201–219
in response-terminated counting schedules, 229–243
See also Sensitivity to run length differences
Run time, 200, 205–207, 209, 211

Sample durations, effect on acquisition of, 346
Sample presentation time, 360–362
Sample-specific performances, 346–347, 351–363
Sample stimuli, 345, 346, 354
Scalar theory of temporal control, 220
Scalar timing system, 172, 174, 178–182, 185–188
Scaling, 51–85, 137, 420
Schedule control, 5–9, 19–23, 393–394, 413–414. *See also* Signal detection paradigm and theory

Schedule performance, 138–139
Schedule size, effect of, 199–200, 216, 218, 220
Schedule value, 31–32, 33, 35, 47–49, 193
Sensitivity, 18, 58–62, 75, 82, 131, 150–151
and choice performance, 124
and circadian oscillations, 338–342
as contingency specific, 216–217
to duration discriminations, 140, 182
indexes, 326–328, 419
and ratio discrimination, 198, 220
Sensitivity index (SI), 324–326, 337, 339–341
Sensitivity to reinforcement, 24–25, 397, 399, 402–406, 411, 419
Sensitivity to run length differences, 194, 225–227, 230–236, 242, 243
definition of, 229
Sensory effect, 326–328, 331, 333, 336–337
definition of, 326
Sensory phenomena and behaviorism, 322
Sequence generalization test, 293, 314
Sequential effects, 385–388, 421
Signal detection paradigm and theory, 11–26, 54, 104, 106, 124, 171, 323–324, 328, 333, 394–397
and causal relations, 89–90. 97–98
definition of, 7–9
and the matching law, 11–19, 103, 395–414, 420
models from, 10–18, 326, 419–422
and reinforcement schedules, 151–152, 193–194, 198, 227–243, 289–290, 419–420
as unifying schedule and stimulus control, 7–11, 393–394, 413–414
See also A'; B''; Bias; d'; $p(L)$; Sensitivity
Sign-tracking, 93–95
Similarity of stimuli and local effects, 374–384
Similarity rules, 175–182, 187–188
definition of, 171–172
Simple counter model. *See* Poisson timing system
Simultaneous discrimination, 346, 347

Simultaneous matching-to-sample procedure, 350, 358–359
Spatial contiguity and causality, 90, 94
Steady-state performance, xxiv, 4
Stimulus change, subjective evaluation of, 96, 106
Stimulus control, 226, 328, 337
  in compound stimuli, 293–303, 316, 317
  definition of, 290
  research in, xxii, xxv, 322–323, 342, 393
  unified with schedule control, 5–6, 114, 117–131, 289–290, 393–394, 413–414
  See also Discriminative stimulus; Retention; Signal detection paradigm and theory; Trace stimulus control
Stimulus description, levels of, 56–58, 80–83
Stimulus generalization, 238, 365–367, 376. See also Maintained generalization gradients
Stimulus generalization test, 293
Stimulus intensity, 238–243, 321–324
Stimulus presentation probability (SPP), 323–324, 326, 400–401, 414
Subjective time scale
  as power function of real time, 157, 159, 160, 162
  as logarithmic, 157–158, 165–167, 171, 172
  See also Log timing system; Poisson timing system; Response rules; Scalar timing system
Successive discrimination, 346
Summative trace decay theory, 53
Superstition, 90, 95–96, 103, 106–107

T schedules, 54, 74
Temporal asynchrony, 104
Temporal control, 261, 294, 314
  by interreinforcer interval duration, 257–261, 267–285
Temporal differentiation procedures, 157–159, 199, 202, 215, 218

Temporal discrimination, 103, 137–154, 194, 198–199, 215. See also Duration discrimination
Temporal estimation data, 157, 158, 160, 182
Temporal memory system, 160–162
Temporal pattern of reinforcers, 52, 257, 285
Temporal precedence and causality, 90, 92
Temporal properties of schedule, 126–129, 257–261, 267–285, 358–359, 422
Temporal tracking, 259, 267–285
  determinants of, 282, 284
Terminal-link reinforcement schedules, 32
Terminal response, 257, 276
Terminating response, 226–228, 279
Threshold, percentage, 162–166
Threshold, ratio, 198
Threshold, sensory, 321–322
Time allocation data, 413
Time as a stimulus dimension, 198–200
Time-averaging models, 69
Time base, 53
Time discrimination, 157–158, 167–168
Time outs, effect on discrimination of, 291, 368–370, 388
Time window, 53, 162. See also Threshold, percentage
Timing schedules, 195, 198–200
  compared to counting schedules, 200–201, 215–217, 219–220
  definition of, 194
  See also FI timing schedules
Topographical features and choice performance, 44
Trace stimulus control, 129, 290–317
  and associative value, 311–315
  and biological relevance, 303–304
  of food, 303–304, 314
  See also Memory; Retention
Trace strength theory of memory, 307, 316
Transfer matching-to-sample task, 351–357
Transient contrast. See local contrast
Trial procedures
  and circadian phases, 341–342

go/no-go, 325–326, 338
self-paced, 325
two-choice, 325–326, 338
yes–no, 333
See also yes–no paradigm

Uncertainty and latency, 244
Unconditional discrimination, 292,
    316–317
Unconditional stimulus (US),
    303–304, 315–316
Uncontrolled reinforcement ratio
    procedure, 400, 403, 407–408,
    411
Undercounting, 229–230, 235, 242,
    243
Undermatching, 18, 396, 408, 413

Variable interval schedules, xxiii, 32,
    56, 118, 400–401, 413–414
discriminative properties of, 32–33
and local contrast, 369, 371–373,
    377, 381–383

and micro level of analysis, 83
in mixed schedules, 249
molecular analysis of, 36–44
as preferred over FI, 47–49
See also Interval schedules
Variable ratio schedules, xxiii, 118,
    400, 401. See also Ratio schedules
Variable time schedules, xxiv, 118,
    127–128, 250–252, 255

Weber fractions, 152, 198, 200,
    221–221
definition of, 147–150
Weber's law, 158, 167–171, 174,
    180–181, 185–188, 213, 215, 420

Yes–no paradigm, 7, 328, 394, 414

Zero-delay matching-to-sample
    procedure, 122–123, 128,
    358–362

ABOUT THE EDITORS

Michael Lamport Commons was born October, 1939, in Hollywood, California. He did his undergraduate work at the University of California at Berkeley, and then at Los Angeles, where in 1965 he obtained a B.A. in Mathematics and Psychology. In 1967 he received his M.A., and in 1973 his Ph.D, from Columbia University in Psychology. Before coming to Harvard University in 1977 he taught and did research at Northern Michigan University. His research is on the perception of utility and how it develops in infrahumans and humans studied across the lifespan, and includes the subareas of perceived causality and perceived value.

John A. Nevin received his B.E. in Mechanical Engineering from Yale University in 1954 and his Ph.D. in Psychology from Columbia University in 1963. He taught at Swarthmore College from 1963 until 1968, and at Columbia University from 1968 until 1972. He has been teaching at the University of New Hampshire since 1972. He has served as the Editor of the *Journal of the Experimental Analysis of Behavior* since 1979. His research interests includes schedules of reinforcement, stimulus control, conditioned reinforcement, and animal psychophysics.

LIST OF CONTRIBUTORS

William M. Baum, University of New Hampshire
John Brady, Northeastern University
Paul K. Brandon, Mankato University
Leila R. Cohen, Northeastern University
Michael L. Commons, Harvard University
Michael Davison, University of Auckland, New Zealand
Leon R. Dreyfus, University of Maine at Orono
John Gibbon, New York State Psychiatric Institute
    and Columbia University
Sally L. Hobson, Adelphi University
R.C. Howard, Michigan State University
Nancy K. Innis, University of Western Ontario
Peter R. Killeen, Arizona State University
Kennon A. Lattal, West Virginia University
Michael Lowry, Northeastern University
John C. Malone, University of Tennessee, Knoxville
Charlotte Mandell, University of Lowell
Dianne McCarthy, University of Auckland, New Zealand
John A. Nevin, University of New Hampshire
Frederic Newman, Adelphi University
Mark Rilling, Michigan State University
David W. Rowe, University of Tennessee, Knoxville
D. Alan Stubbs, University of Maine at Orono
Michael Terman, Northeastern University